Disciples *P*$_{at}$*rayer*

**The Spirituality
of the
Christian Church
(Disciples of Christ)**

Disciples at Prayer

The Spirituality
of the
Christian Church
(Disciples of Christ)

William O. Paulsell

Foreword
Peter M. Morgan

Chalice  **Press**
St. Louis, Missouri

in partnership with
Disciples of Christ Historical Society
Nashville, Tennessee

Biblical quotations, unless otherwise noted, are from the *New Revised Standard Version Bible*, copyright 1989, Division of Christian Education of the National Council of the Churches of Christ in the USA. Used by permission.

Cover design: Bob Watkins
Art Director: Michael Domínguez

10 9 8 7 6 5 4 3 2 1   95 96 97 98 99

Library of Congress Cataloging–in–Publication Data
(pending)

Printed in the United States of America

Contents

Foreword

Spirituality is in the air today. That vaguely defined term floats and adheres to a variety of human experiences: the meeting of small groups in mission-driven businesses, the family-values rhetoric of politicians, the chanting of the practitioners of New Age religion, the euphoria of joggers talking about running their favorite course. "Spirituality" even floats into church on Sunday.

William O. Paulsell has given us a timely book. Many in fellowship with the church and some outside the fellowship are asking what the church has to teach about spirituality. That question brings an opportunity, a "teaching moment," to give clarity and depth to the spiritual life of prayer offered by the church when it is in conversation with scripture and history. *Disciples at Prayer* introduces the Stone-Campbell Movement to its own spirituality through their journals of the nineteenth century. The Disciples of Christ's introduction to its prayer tradition continues as Paulsell reports from the journals of the twentieth century.

William Paulsell is a scholar/pastor. He is pastor of North Christian Church (Disciples of Christ) in Columbus, Indiana. In previous ministries he served Lexington (KY) Theological Seminary as dean and then president. Earlier, he was professor of religion at Atlantic Christian (now Barton) College. For thirty-five years, he has actively pursued his scholarly passion of medieval spiritual theology. You can't be long in the presence of Bill Paulsell without hearing of Bernard of Clairvaux or of the life of the

Cistercians. He served the larger church through his articles in ecumenical journals, lectures at Disciples' colleges and universities, and by leading spiritual retreats in the regions of the Disciples of Christ. Broad appreciation for his gentle influence has caused many to affectionately think of him as the spiritual director of the Disciples of Christ.

He brings his gifts as a historian and spiritual leader and offers them to his own church in this book. He is a disciplined historian. He is slow to bring his own views or style to the writing. By and large, the reader hears our leaders of prayer speak their own words. Occasionally Paulsell the historian helps the reader notice what may be overlooked. Alexander Campbell, for example, is very critical of a mystical approach to religion. Yet Paulsell points to occasions when he describes prayer by using language that is compatible with the mystical tradition. Toward the end of the book, he does give us his own comments on the development of prayer in this church across its history. He also knows the limits of his work. He reports only from journals. He encourages broader research by publishing the beginnings of a list of books on prayer by Disciples.

This book will be useful to pastors and teachers in this time when questions are being asked about spirituality in the popular culture. It is also a promising doorway to those who wish to use it in personal spiritual reading. When selected short segments are read slowly, prayerfully, it can be *lectio divina*. *Disciples at Prayer* is also classroom friendly. Words of past Disciples' leaders spoken by the voices of today's Disciples become enriching resources as students explore and work out their own devotional practices.

Today the ill-defined term "spirituality" floats in the air and adheres to many human experiences. Long after the vague use of the term has been blown beyond popular usage by the winds of new fads, *Disciples at Prayer* will still be picked up, read, and prayed over by those in the Stone-Campbell Movement who thirst for a refreshing life of prayer. They will be guided by Disciples prayer pilgrims of two hundred years who escort us to the source.

Peter M. Morgan

Preface

William O. Paulsell was selected in 1994 as The Forrest H. Kirkpatrick Lecturer. He was asked to give this lecture at the Disciples of Christ Historical Society dinner during the Pittsburgh General Assembly is 1995. Because of his deep concern for spirituality, his writings and teachings, Paulsell was asked to prepare a lecture exploring spirituality in the life of the Christian Church (Disciples of Christ).

Work began and it soon became evident to Paulsell that there was far more material than he had realized and his research was providing more information than could possibly be condensed into a forty-five minute lecture. The decision was made to use the material in the preparation of a book on the same theme. His work continued.

Again the amount of material from which to do research and about which to write confronted Paulsell. He chose to limit his writing to the subjects included in this volume. He then took his Kirkpatrick lecture from the material in the book.

As pastor of the North Christian Church, Columbus, Indiana, his efforts were recognized by Mrs. Clementine Miller Tangeman and thus a grant was made from The Christian Foundation to assist in the publication of the book. We are indeed grateful to Mrs. Tangeman for the grant.

We are also grateful to Dr. Forrest H. Kirkpatrick and the Forrest H. Kirkpatrick Fund for Lecture and Research at the Historical Society for providing the lecture that instigated this research. An annual lecture and

Historian's Seminar, held each spring in Nashville, and both underwritten by the Kirkpatrick Fund.

We are equally grateful to William O. Paulsell for his undertaking this research and writing. It has brought together the information on the concern and the understanding of spirituality in the life of the Disciples of Christ.

James M. Seale

Introduction

When James Seale, the President of the Disciples of Christ Historical Society, asked me to write a book on Disciple spirituality, I was hesitant to accept the assignment. Although I have been a Disciple since early childhood and have great love for our tradition, I felt that it was a topic on which I was poorly informed. I studied Disciples history in seminary and wrote a doctoral dissertation on a small part of our history. However, I really knew nothing about our heritage of spirituality.

During my academic career I focused on the history of Christian spirituality, but primarily in the medieval period. I studied with great interest the Christian monastic tradition, the classical spiritual writings, and the tradition of Christian mysticism. I was deeply impressed with Augustine, Bernard of Clairvaux and the Cistercians, Francis, Teresa of Avila, John of the Cross and others. Who had the Disciples ever produced of similar stature?

We Disciples are an activist lot. We feel a calling to make the world better, we want our faith to have some life- and society-changing impact. We tend not to be a contemplative people. If anyone suggests to us a spiritual discipline, we immediately want to ask, "What good will it do?"

Frankly, when I began this study I did not expect to find anything of the depth of what I found in the spirituality of the Middle Ages. In fact, when I told friends and colleagues that I was doing research in Disciple spirituality, they often said, "You haven't found much, have you?"

To my surprise I have found a great deal, far more

than I expected. We have a rich heritage; it's just that no one knows much about it. Ronald Osborn made that same point in his Griggs lecture at First Christian Church in Tulsa in 1995.

The study of Disciple spirituality could be a lifetime project for a scholar. There is much to be studied: our worship styles, our hymnody, our various understandings of the Lord's Supper and baptism, church prayer groups. One could work through the many service books, books of prayers for elders, and devotional material that we have produced in great abundance.

Since moving from thirty years in higher education to a local church pastorate in 1992, I found that my time for such research was severely restricted, and often nonexistent. Making use of one day off a week was simply not enough for the thorough study that this task demands, especially since the needs of the church often meant that some weeks there would not be a day off. It became obvious that I would have to restrict the focus of this project. How could I find a representative sample of Disciple thought on spirituality that I could study and write about in a reasonable period of time?

My decision was to study some of our periodical literature. It has often been said that Disciples never had bishops, they had editors. I decided to see what we were trying to teach our membership through some of the periodicals that our people have read. I haven't used all of them. Time just did not permit. One could also do a good study of Sunday school materials to see what they taught about spirituality.

My decision was to work through the *Millennial Harbinger*, edited by Alexander Campbell, the *Christian Messenger* of Barton W. Stone, and the journals that were distributed through local churches as well as by individual subscriptions: *The Christian-Evangelist*, *The Christian*, and *The Disciple*. I made an arbitrary decision to stop the research at the end of 1990 volume of *The Disciple*.

This book is not an institutional history of the Disciples. For that the reader can turn to *Journey in Faith* by William Tucker and Lester McAllister, *Joined in Discipleship* by Mark Toulouse, *Cane Ridge in Context*, edited by Anthony Dunnavant, and a host of other good accounts of our history. Such books will provide a historical context into which the information in this book can be set.

Spirituality is a loosely used word among us these days. Different people mean different things by it. My definition is that spirituality refers to the ways we know and experience God. What kinds of things do we do to create an openness to God's presence? How do we experience God in our lives, our worship, our personal devotion?

During my years teaching at what is now Barton College and serving on the staff at Lexington Theological Seminary I was frequently invited to lead spiritual life retreats for ministers, local churches, and other groups. I shared much of what I had learned in my study of medieval spirituality, not realizing what our Disciple heritage had to offer. Writing this book has made me aware of the richness of our spiritual heritage, and I hope our people will learn more about it.

There is much work to be done. This little book should be seen only as a beginning. I hope it will stimulate other scholars to continue this study and explore some of the material I have left alone.

I must express my appreciation to the marvelous congregation of North Christian Church in Columbus, Indiana. Those good folks have been encouraging and supportive when I have asked for occasional time off to get a jump start on a new chapter. They probably got tired of hearing me talk about the project, but never complained.

I also want to thank the staff of the library at Christian Theological Seminary. They have all been most gracious and hospitable in allowing me to work there.

Finally, I want to thank Mrs. Clementine Miller Tangeman, a thoughtful, gracious, and generous Disciple, for making a grant from The Christian Foundation to the Historical Society for the publication of this book.

William O. Paulsell
North Christian Church
Columbus, Indiana

1

The Spirituality of Alexander Campbell

Those who have any awareness of church history at all know that the Christian Church (Disciples of Christ) has its roots in the ministry of Alexander Campbell. For many years we were often referred to as "Campbellites." That word was not always used as a compliment, since Campbell was often controversial. Nevertheless, Disciples who have respect for history look to Campbell as a source of our tradition.

It may be that we have moved well beyond Campbell today. Some of his views on biblical scholarship were ahead of his time; others seem outdated now. There are ideas in Campbell's thought that many Disciples would reject today, yet his influence lives on in Disciple churches in a variety of ways. This chapter will attempt to note some of those influences in the area of spirituality.

One of the foundations of Campbell's religious philosophy was the idea that faith is belief in testimony. He believed that the evidence of the gospel in the apostolic witness was compelling, and that was the reason to believe. Hence, he was skeptical of a faith based on any kind of "religious experience."

In the very first issue of his well-known periodical, *The Millennial Harbinger*, published from 1830 until 1870, Campbell wrote, "All who believe and preach Christ should be able to give a reason for the hope which they entertain by adducing the evidences of the gospel—not by telling their experience, which will never convince anybody but an enthusiast."[1] The best reason for faith, he said, "is a well authenticated testimony, or confirmed evidence."[2]

Campbell was hostile to religious mysticism, and blamed many of the church's problems on its advocates. In a particularly polemical passage he wrote, "The preachers of the modern gospel of mystic influences exhibit more rancorous spirits, more pride, insolence, and covetousness—in one word, more of the spirit of this world, than any other class of preachers with which I am acquainted. Some of the most uncivilized, impolite, barbarous, and persecuting spirits of my acquaintance, are those disclaimers upon mystic operations."[3] He expressed his clear opposition to any approach to religion based on something other than "the persuasion that the Gospel is true."[4]

A number of modern-day Disciples have rediscovered the Christian monastic tradition. Some ministers and laypeople both have begun to make retreats in monasteries and have been impressed by the spiritual disciplines of that tradition.

Campbell, however, would have had none of it. In an 1832 article on "Christian Character," Campbell condemned the whole monastic enterprise. "The anchorite deserts the race to which he belongs, and seeks for perfection in the neglect of all social duties," he wrote. "The whole sisterhood of vestal nuns, the whole brotherhood of cloistered monks [are] leagued against nature, reason, and society, outlaws to God's government, rebels against social order, and contemners of their own race." It is those who live ordinary lives, he believed, who best reflect the Gospel. Offering what today would be called "family values," Campbell said, "The purest women that ever lived were wives and mothers; and the most holy and renowned men of every age were husbands and fathers."[5]

Christian character, Campbell believed, consisted in fulfilling our duties in our particular station in life, whether parent, sibling, spouse, master, or servant. "Thus in handling the hoe, the mattock, and the spade; in driving the loom, the plough, or the harrow; in making a hat, a coat, or a shoe, as the Lord commanded these things to be done, a person adorns the doctrine of God our Saviour."[6]

Nevertheless, for all of his hostility to mystical religion, Campbell did write a good bit about the importance of communion with God. "Man was made for communion with God," Campbell said, "but he lost it in Adam the first. In Adam the second he is restored to that communion."[7] However, Campbell insisted that while we are in our mortal bodies, that communion takes place only by the Holy Spirit through Jesus Christ.

"Without communion with God there is nothing gained by faith or hope, by promises or commands, by professions, confessions, or institutions," Campbell wrote in an article that he titled, "Prayer, or Communion with God." "This is the sanctum sanctorum, the holy of holies, the inmost temple of religion." He defined communion with God as "the reciprocation of the common sentiment and common feelings." It is an experience that language cannot describe, it is "two sentimental spirits in conversation with each other, two spirits in kindred thought and kindred interests pouring into each other the overflowings of congenial views, feelings, desires."[8]

This communion with God, however, was not something mystical for Campbell. God has spoken to humanity, he said, through angels, patriarchs, prophets, Christ, and the apostles. God speaks to us now in the written word and we speak to God through our prayers. However, our prayers are heard only if we listen to God. "If we hear him not, he hears us not," Campbell said.

But, if we have listened to God we can "lift our voice to him. We utter our adorations, confessions, thanksgivings, petitions, and our unconditional submission to the will, authority, wisdom and goodness, mercy and love of him, 'who is, and was, and evermore shall be.' Thus our spirits ascend to the heavens and commune with God."

Without this communion with God—"these constant aspirations, ejaculations, and soarings to the throne of mercy and favor"—we are unfit for heaven. Without this, Campbell believed, talk about sound doctrine, ordinances, institutions, and related matters lacks life and power.[9] For him, communion with God involved reading scripture and prayer.

In writing about the spiritual influences that work upon us, Campbell noted that there are those who say that everything depends upon the word of God alone. This, he said, produces "a cold, lifeless, rationalism and formality." Then there is the approach that depends upon the Spirit alone. This, in Campbell's judgment, produces "a wild, irrepressible enthusiasm; and, in other cases, a dark, melancholy despondency."

Also, he said, there is a compound system in which Spirit quickens the soul and makes it spiritually alive, but without generating any morality. Then the Word brings about conversion later.

Campbell took a different approach. He began with the assumption that in our Fall, we lost our union with God, our original righteousness, and our original holiness. We forfeited life and became subject to the physical evils of the world. We are, therefore, doomed to destruction. However, God has devised a remedial system that comes from the "free, sovereign, and unmerited favor of God," and restores us to the kind of life enjoyed before the Fall of Adam. This "scheme of almighty love" makes possible a more intimate union with God than was enjoyed in the Garden of Eden, a union "enduring as eternity—as indestructible as the divine essence." This gift bestows on us "everlasting righteousness, a perfect holiness, and an enduring blessedness in the presence of God forever and ever."[10]

How do we know that we are pardoned for our sins? For Campbell, it was not an emotional experience that convinces us. He complained about people who thought their sins were forgiven because of a particular feeling that they had. "Ask such what they know concerning the pardon of their sins, and they generally refer to that idea, feeling, or impression as proof that they were pardoned. Their feelings were the premises, and their pardon is the conclusion."[11]

For the ancient converts to Christianity, however, their assurance of the forgiveness of sin was "the testimony of God." Campbell concluded, "On testimony true and faith, the ancients built; on inference the moderns rely."[12] The earliest Christians had the same reason to believe that their sins were forgiven that they had that Jesus was the Messiah, namely "the testimony of God confirmed." Early Christians, he said firmly, "acted upon testimony only." Obedience to God's commands confirmed the truth of the testimony. "Ask one of these converts if his sins were pardoned," Campbell said, and the person would answer "Yes." In response to the question of how one could be sure, an individual would answer, "I was immersed in obedience to a divine command for the remission of my sins."[13]

In 1849, nineteen years later, Campbell was still advocating that same position. All of the ideas we have of the material world are the result of sensation and reflection. Campbell was reflecting the influence of the British empiricist, John Locke, whose thought he had studied before coming to America, in making that kind of a statement.[14]

Our supernatural knowledge, or knowledge of God, he said, comes by faith and faith itself comes from hearing the word of God spoken. He described the process: "The intellectual and moral arrangement is therefore—1. The word spoken; 2. hearing; 3. believing; 4. feeling; 5. doing. Such is the constitution of the human mind."

Christian faith, then, is "a persuasion that God is true; that the gospel is divine; that God is love; that Christ's death is the sinner's life. It is trust in God. It is a reliance upon his truth, his faithfulness, his power." It is not, Campbell insisted, "merely a cold assent to truth, but a cordial, joyful consent to it and reception of it." Still, he was firm in his belief that faith was dependent on testimony. "No testimony, no faith."[15]

The hearing that produces faith is of a unique kind. The gospel is heard with the outward ear, the ear that hears only sounds. But, according to Campbell, God has given us an inward ear that recognizes sense. Faith, then, is impossible without language and without the knowledge and understanding of language. This fact led Campbell to make several fundamental points.

First, he said, "I repudiate [the] whole theory of mystic influence and metaphysical regeneration as a vision of visions, a dream of dreams, at war with philosophy, with the philosophy of the mind, with the Bible, with reason, with common sense, and with all Christian experience."

Second, he said no living person has ever had a single conception of Christianity, "or one spiritual thought, feeling, or emotion, where the Bible, or some tradition from it, has not been before him." Without the Bible, Campbell believed, "there is not one single spiritual idea or action."

Third, no one who has been illuminated, converted, or sanctified by the Holy Spirit can have a single idea that is not already found in the Bible. "In conversion and sanctification," he said, "the Spirit of God operates only through the Word of Truth," the Bible.

Fourth, the method that the Holy Spirit uses in addressing unconverted people is "signs addressed to the sense, and words to the understanding and affections." The Spirit, he said, used "rational means; therefore, we argue, such means were necessary, and are still." This leads to the fifth point, that the Holy Spirit operates "only by and through the Word, spoken or written; and neither physically nor metaphysically.

Sixth, Campbell believed that the gift of tongues at the first Pentecost meant that language is essential. We cannot arrive at the knowledge of God, he said, by the mere contemplation of nature. People cannot come to the knowledge of God by reason alone. He quoted Paul's words to the Corinthians, "The world by wisdom knew not God." It is by faith, not reason alone, that we know God. Remember that for Campbell, faith was the belief in testimony.

Seventh, Campbell said that God would use light [illumination], knowledge, and the gospel to convert people. He affirmed that he could not conceive of a religion "without knowledge, without faith, with an apprehension, an intelligent, as well as a cordial reception of the gospel of Christ." This led him to a very controversial conclusion: "I repudiate, therefore, with my whole heart, the notion of infant, idiot and pagan regeneration—this speculative conversion without light, knowledge, faith, hope or love. It is no advocate of Christ; it is no comforter of the soul, on the hypothesis of infant, and pagan, and idiot regeneration."

Finally, Campbell said that the Holy Spirit and the word of God are not separated and distinct kinds of power, "but both acting conjointly and simultaneously in the work of sanctification and salvation." Therefore, one who resists the word of God, the Bible, resists the Holy Spirit. The Holy Spirit always operates through the Word. Hence, said Campbell, "faith comes by hearing, and hearing by the Word of God."[16]

Campbell wrote many articles in the *Millennial Harbinger* on prayer, often writing series of articles on the subject. In 1838 he wrote, "No person can live and walk with God, nor enjoy that communion with the Father and the Son...unless we continue instant in supplications and prayers and thanksgivings night and day." Confessing that prayer was "rather out of fashion," Campbell insisted that "it is just as needful now as ever." People still must do battle with the world, the flesh, and the devil, all of which are opposing our religious development. Hence, there is a need for a "constant praying in the spirit, which creates a relish for communion with God in the closet and the society of kindred spirits."

One may, in fact *should,* pray silently, "in the spirit." This, believed Campbell, "is not only practicable in the midst of all the business of life, but it is the only way in which the apostolic exhortation of 'praying without ceasing' can be obeyed." The spiritual disciplines of meditation, self-examination, communing with the heart, and Bible study create within us desires that "will cause our spirits to breathe towards the skies and to pour themselves out in prayer and praise to God."[17]

Much later, in 1854, Campbell wrote about prayer in a series of articles he titled, "Elementary Views." Prayer, he said, "is but the Christian's breath. Without it, he cannot live or be happy a single day." He called prayer a "divinely chartered right, privilege, and honor of every one who, through this all glorious Mediator, comes to God."[18]

Prayer has many uses. Campbell noted that Jesus taught us to pray for food, raiment, health for ourselves and for others, but that we should not expect that the laws of nature will be changed so the prayers can be answered. God will answer our prayers "in subordination to these established arrangements." We pray in faith when we ask for things that God has promised.

Campbell noted that "to pray for humility is the shortest and safest means to be humble. To pray for sincerity, goodness, benevolence, love, etc. is the best means to possess them. God will hear the prayer of the righteous for his ears are open to their cry."[19]

However, in responding to an article by a certain T.H., Campbell rejected the idea that the only legitimate prayer is one for "a holy state of mind." Campbell reminds us that Jesus taught us to pray for daily bread, which no state of mind, by itself, can provide. Abraham and Hannah prayed for sons and the Lord gave them. Jesus himself said, "What things soever you desire, believe that you will receive them, and you shall have them." In this particular article, Campbell said that God taught us to pray so that we would ask for things.[20]

Campbell believed that the physical and moral laws of the universe operate with regularity. However, they do not operate apart from God's superintendence. God has various agents, such as angels, to be used in answering our prayers. "For special purpose he has special agents; for general purpose he has general laws."[21]

However, there is one major exception to God's intervention. Since the apostolic age, Campbell believed, "no new revelation, not a single new idea has, in answer to prayer, been communicated to any man since the apostolic age passed away." No matter how earnestly we pray, we will not receive any new ideas that are contrary to the ancient gospel.[22]

One of Campbell's rules for interpreting scripture was that the Bible is understandable on its own. We do not need any miraculous intervention of the Holy Spirit for us to interpret it correctly. "The Bible is addressed to our reason and understanding and moral feelings," he wrote, "and consequently we are to interpret it in such a way as we do any other book that is addressed to the faculties."[23]

Campbell was aware that many people tend to misuse prayer. In one of his early articles[24] on prayer he called prayer "one of the most interesting, solemn, and exalted exercises which falls to the lot of mortal man." Its practice can be secret or it can be public. Secret, or private, prayer provides less temptation to depart from the real purposes of prayer, for in secret we do not worry about what others think of our prayers. Campbell said, "There is no school under the heavens in which the art of prayer can be so easily acquired as in the closet, in the fields, or forest, where no human ear can hear, and where no human eye can see us. Besides, no prayers have so much influence upon ourselves as those which are offered up in secret to God."

Private prayer, when it comes from the heart, is characterized by "propriety in our terms and a pathos in our expressions which easily distinguish them from all the language of art and the studied forms of speech." Prayers that are barren in language and have a dry, frigid, and stiff style indicate that the person is "a great stranger to secret communion with God."

Public prayer, however, is subject to all sorts of abuse and misuse, and Campbell cataloged the major offenses. He complained that many public prayers were designed more for human ears than for God. "There is so much of the studied and set phrase of ordinary and artificial composition in our addresses to the throne of the universe, that there is more apparent concern in the speaker to please the ears of his auditors, than to worship and adore the Majesty of the Universe."

Campbell criticized those who pray only for the sake of praying. He called such prayers "insipid and irksome things and might as well be dispensed with altogether." Campbell believed that when you prayed, you ought to have something specific in mind. Praying evening and morning just for the sake of one's conscience is "as useless to others as counting beads by the hour, or the hebdomadal repetition of "Pater noster" to a person who knows not the meaning of a single word." When we pray, we should have "some special consideration which at the time induces us to the exercise." If we pray for some afflicted person, we should focus on that and omit anything unrelated. If two or three people should gather together to pray for some purpose, "that should be the whole and exclusive burden of the prayer." If we would focus on these things, said Campbell, "there would be no danger of falling into that unmeaning monotony of expression and insipid uniformity of matter and manner, so irrational and unscriptural."

A second complaint concerned those who used public prayer to promote their particular doctrinal positions. Campbell objected to prayers that included lines such as, "God, we thank thee that we do not hold this or that; and that we believe this."

Third, Campbell was irritated by "a verbose redundancy in the use of epithets and phrases which swell the period without increasing the sentiment or exalting the devotional of the soul." This included pompous addresses to God in which the speaker literally exhausts a vocabulary "to astound the audience and display his elocution." Such a person is seeking personal glory and often confounds the audience. Campbell concluded that "plain and unaffected language, which does no more than give scope to the feelings of the heart, is the proper language of public prayer."

A fourth complaint was rapidity of pronunciation. Whenever we address God, in public or private, "great deliberation becomes us," Campbell said. In public prayer, the speaker should make every effort to unite the congregation with him or her. "Hence, the necessity of giving sufficient time to the company to apprehend the full force and meaning of every word and sentence." Campbell reported that he had heard many prayers where he found it impossible to keep up or unite with the speaker. "The whole prayer appeared like the sound of a mighty rushing wind!"

Fifth, Campbell criticized those who spoke at random, that is, those who began a sentence before they knew what they were going to ask. "The apparent indecision of the speaker led us to suppose that he knew not what to ask while the words were still falling from his lips." It was better to pause a few minutes before a petition than to attempt one at random. As a general principle, Campbell said that public speakers ought to cease to speak when they have nothing to say, and criticized those who "continue to speak a long time after they are done."

Campbell did write in a positive way about the spiritual disciplines. He stressed the importance of prayers of confession. "Confessions are to be made of all our sins of which we are conscious, and remission asked in the name of the High Priest of our profession." We should also not forget that there are sins of which we may not be conscious that also need to be forgiven by God. However, he did not believe that the same sins should be repeatedly confessed, for that indicated an unbelief of where we stand with Christ.[25]

He also spoke a good word for fasting. It was a frequent practice among the "primitive disciples," although we should remember that Jesus taught us in the Sermon on the Mount how to demean ourselves when we fast. Fasting, he said, "contributes much to the sanctification of Christians to deny even their natural and necessary appetites occasionally, that they may glorify God with their bodies and spirits which are God's, to be more spiritually minded and more consecrated to the Lord."[26]

Styles of praying were different in the mid-nineteenth century. In an 1858 *Millennial Harbinger* article, Campbell expressed his shock at seeing people sitting while they prayed. He wondered if they were actually skeptics or unbelievers! He described seeing people sitting at the act of prayer as a "heart-chilling and a soul-paralyzing spectacle."

Standing for prayer is, he insisted, "a Divinely sanctioned attitude. Sitting in devotion or worship is never acceptable to God, unless in such cases God may have made standing impossible, as in the case of the lame, the maimed, and the paralytic." We should glorify God with our bodies as well as with our souls and spirits, Campbell believed.[27]

In an 1843 article in which he discussed his new hymnbook, Campbell said that Christians can demonstrate their piety by the songs they sing and the prayers and thanksgivings they offer. "Indeed, the sacred song and the social prayer are but the express image and living form of the pious emotions, religious taste, spiritual discernment, and the holy affections of those who unite in them."[28]

One of the more controversial elements in Campbell's beliefs about prayer was his conviction that God does not hear the prayers of people without faith. In an 1830 article he doubted an account of a German professor who prayed to a God he did not believe in and was converted.[29] We have already noted an 1849 article in which he doubted "infant, pagan, and idiot conversion."

As late as 1851 Campbell was still advocating this idea. "No one can enjoy Christian experience until he is a Christian," he wrote. To call anything prior to conversion a "Christian experience" is wrong. "No one can have the evangelical experience of a Christian before faith and baptism." Part of this was a reaction against Baptist churches that required some account of Christian experience before baptism. This would be impossible in Campbell's thought.[30]

This leads to the whole question of religious experience, a term that left Campbell very uncomfortable. In 1830 he wrote a series of articles on "Christian Experience." He called that term a "hackneyed phrase," and felt that it was "misleading the religious community and imperceptibly substituting an artificial and inoperative religion for the pure and undefiled religion of the gospel." In part, he was reacting to the accusation that he taught a "head religion" and disliked any approach "which captivated the heart, moved the affection, purified the soul, and reformed behavior." On the contrary, he thought that a religion that emphasized experience did not fill "the conscience with peace, the heart with love, the affections with love, the soul with hope, and the life of good works." Any religion that does not do this, he said, "is not worthy of an untimely fig." But to call anything Christian experience "before a person obeys the gospel; or, in other words, before he submits to the government of Jesus Christ, appears to me absurd."

To feel like Christians, Campbell insisted, we must first become Christians. "We must come to Christ, and take his yoke upon us, before we can find rest and peace to our souls. Neither can we conceive how a person can feel like a Christian who does not act like one." Faith, Campbell believed, must be professed, possessed, and obeyed before we can enjoy its fruits.[31]

Just as the laws of nature change the seasons, and animals and plants reproduce themselves according to unchangeable principles, so the moral laws are just as firm and unchanging. Moral laws, said Campbell, are as unchangeable as the laws of nature. "There are means, or there are channels," he said, "through which, and through which alone, God's favor can flow into the human heart." One of these laws is that God resists the proud, but gives the blessings of grace to the lowly. "Hence it is that the humble, and the humble alone, can experience the joys and the seasons of refreshment from the presence of the Lord." To experience what Enoch, Elijah, Paul, Elizabeth, or Mary experienced, "we must walk with God and be blameless observers of all God's commands and ordinances, as were they." When we have been pardoned, justified, and sanctified by the name of Jesus, "the quickening, animating rays of the Sun of Righteousness, shine into our hearts; we feel their heat and power; they impart life and comfort." All Christian experience, then, is dependent upon a change of state in our lives.[32]

Campbell was not totally opposed to religious experience. He was opposed to it in a generic sense. Authentic religious experience for the Christian can come only after conversion and baptism.

It is impossible to overestimate the importance of the Bible for Campbell. People of strong Christian character, he believed, spend much time reading the Bible. That is what produces genuine experience. He concluded, "If every unfeigned Christian under heaven were to tell his Christian experience, and to give utterance full, and express the feelings of his heart, he would say, 'O how I love thy Word! It is my study all the day. It is more precious to me than rubies—it is sweeter to my soul than honey and the honeycomb.'[33]

Emotion was not absent in Campbell's piety, regardless of how much he criticized it. The Spirit of God, he said, generates in the soul tastes, relishes, desires, longings, sighs, and groans. Those who are led by the Spirit enjoy life and peace.[34]

The gospel, for Campbell, when taken seriously, enlarges our conception of God, causes Christ to live within us, and elevates us to communion with the Father and his Son Jesus. Unfortunately, he never explains very clearly exactly how this is experienced. He may not be favorably inclined toward mystical religion, but when he talks about Christ living within us and communion with the Father, he is certainly using some of the language of the Christian mystical tradition.

No doubt the emotional excesses of frontier religion repulsed him. Many Disciple churches today are notable for their lack of emotion. But he did have a sense of religious experience and believed that the faithful Christian would know the mercy of God and the presence of the Holy Spirit. As a rationalist, influenced by John Locke and British empiricism, he kept his religious expression on an intellectual level. But as we read his writings we have the sense that he was more than a cold rationalist, that the emotions do play some role in our religious development.

NOTES

[1]*MH*, 1830:13.
[2]*MH*, 1830:14.
[3]*MH*, 1830:23.
[4]*MH*, 1830:28.
[5]*MH*, 1832:463.
[6]*MH*, 1832:462-464.
[7]*MH*, 1834:586.
[8]*MH*, 1832:123.
[9]*MH*, 1832:123-124.
[10]*MH* 1849:362-363.
[11]*MH*, 1830:498.
[12]*MH*, 1930:499.
[13]*MH*, 1830:500.
[14]See Tucker and McAllister, *Journey in Faith* (St. Louis: Bethany Press, 1975), p. 98.
[15]*MH*, 1849:367.
[16]*MH*, 1849:361-372; 421-432.
[17]*MH*, 1838:290-292.
[18]*MH*, 1854:550, 552.
[19]*MH*, 1831:471-474.
[20]*MH*, 1851:534-535.
[21]*MH*, 1833:187.
[22]*MH*, 1833:188.
[23]*MH*, 1832:69-70.
[24]*MH*, 1831:497-503.
[25]*MH*, 1832:64.
[26]*MH*, 1831:188-189.
[27]*MH*, 1858:39-40.
[28]*MH*, 1843:131.
[29]*MH*, 1830:497.
[30]*MH*, 1851:374.
[31]*MH*, 1830:259-260.
[32]*MH*, 1830:359-361.
[33]*MH*, 1830:424.
[34]*MH*, 1833:7.

2

The Spirituality of
Robert Richardson

Robert Richardson, while devoted to Alexander Campbell, had a somewhat different style of spirituality, as his writings in the *Millennial Harbinger* reveal. He wrote a number of articles, including a series called "Communings in the Sanctuary," on spirituality issues. Because of the popularity of the *Millennial Harbinger*, Campbell had called Richardson to come to Bethany and help him with editorial duties. Richardson, originally an Episcopalian, had been a physician in Ohio, was one of the first faculty members at Campbell's newly founded Bethany College, and later became Campbell's biographer.

Richardson's writing was characterized by long, involved sentences and arguments that moved from point to point with logical clarity. For example, in 1849 he published an article on "Spiritual Life," in which he traced biological development from the vegetative and animal stages through the intellectual and moral, to the spiritual level.

There are many people, he said, who have intellectual ability without any moral discernment, and some who have achieved both the intellectual and moral stages of development who have no spirituality. Animal, or sensual enjoyment, he said, is "but the happiness of the chattering idiot," but intellectual pleasures are "the lofty and sublime delight which enrapt the soul."

However, the moral life is even better. The moral life, he said, "unseals the deep-welling fountains of feeling and pours upon the soul a flood of sensibilities and affections as novel as they are delightful." However, the "moral frame" is a fragile thing. "The slightest cause disturbs its healthful action; the most trifling circumstance mars its harmony, and the least touch inflexes a stain upon its purity." As exalted as it is, the moral life is inferior to the spiritual life. The spiritual life involves "communion with its Creator." Using the language of Christian mysticism, Richardson said, "It is here that the finite merges with the infinite, that the human blends itself with the divine nature, and that the feeble rills of moral life mingle their waters with the boundless ocean of being and blessedness." All other forms of life, such as intellectual and moral, are just the "scaffolding" of the spiritual life. Richardson urged the Christian to "cherish that spiritual union to God through which he enjoys this purest, loftiest, and most blissful life!"[1]

In an article on the "Spirituality of the Gospel," published in 1850, Richardson complained that many people saw Christianity as nothing more than a system of morality. Such folks believe that faith, penance, forgiveness, the Holy Spirit, and the word of God are there just to make us moral. They think the gospel has fulfilled its purpose "if men are rendered quiet and well-behaved members of civilized society."

Richardson called this "the great error" of Protestant Christianity. Historically, morality became a more prominent theme in the faith than spirituality and has continued to be the real test of Christian fellowship. If "the decent restraint of the grosser passions" is achieved, Christianity is seen as a success.

The sin of Adam and Eve, he said, was not "excessive indulgence of the animal appetite." The real sin was that they failed the test of their love and fealty to God. So the real purpose of the gospel is "to reunite man to God in holy spiritual fellowship," to achieve "the spiritual renovation of the soul."

Christian morality, for Richardson, was not just "an outward conformity to the proprieties of civilized society." Rather, "it is a fixed principle of action emanating from self-renouncing love." He described true morality as "an inward purity which pervades the secret thoughts, a holy charm which subdues the wayward feelings, an ever-active energy, which controls the action of every faculty of human nature." He insisted that "unless an individual attain to the spirituality of the Gospel, it is impossible to practice full its morality." Practical virtue is but "a cold and meagre philosophy" compared with what results from "a true connexion with the spiritual system."

Richardson concluded this article by saying that "No part of Christianity can be duly comprehended without spiritual discernment, and no one of its commandments can be acceptably obeyed without spiritual relation to God." The medium of spiritual communication is faith.

The world would be far different, he believed, if everyone would seek "habitual intercourse of the soul with God." One who enjoys "habitual fellowship with God," he said, "is the residence of the Divine Spirit," and has reached "the blissful purpose of the Gospel."[2]

Richardson, however, was no nature mystic. He condemned a "religion of fancy" that worships the beauty of the earth. Such a religion, impressed with the splendors of nature, would seek to find the source of it "and become lost beyond earth's limits, in outer darkness and perpetual winter." Such a religion is characterized by "that intolerant bigotry which persecutes in matters of faith." It infuses people with "the lust of power and coolly calculates the profits of oppression." It has no consideration for the rights of conscience or the pleadings of the heart. It is simply "the speculation of opinionists" and is concerned only with "the cold abstractions of a perverted reason." That seems like a pretty harsh judgment for a man like Richardson to make.

For him, however, true religion had to involve the cross of Jesus. Before this "the magnificence of earth is vanity, and the power of intellect but pride. And oh! how much they have to unlearn, who have been taught in these schools of error, before they can realize that God's grace is glory; that His foolishness is wiser than men, and His weakness, superior strength!"

It is the Christian Gospel that "shines forever the true lamp of wisdom; here is continually provided the bread of life; here ascends the most acceptable incense; and, behind the veil of outward symbols, we are admitted to bow before the spiritual mercy seat, overshadowed by the wings of cherubim and the radiant glory of the divine presence."

Richardson was no cold rationalist. He insisted that reason "must be subjected to the mysteries of revelation.

17

The mysteries of faith are more sublime than those of reason."[3]

If these are to be the pursuits of the Christian, how are we to free ourselves for our attachments to the world? We cannot do it by simply willing or desiring it. What frees us from being enslaved by the world is our devotion to the gospel. "If the light of the glorious gospel of Christ hath shone upon us...then shall we be drawn by irresistible attractions, and strengthened more and more by added grace to ascend above the world, and to approach the bright source of being and blessedness. It is by dwelling upon the glorious image of our Redeemer...that we shall be filled with light and life and love, and become participants of that glory upon which we gaze."[4]

Those words could just have easily come from a medieval mystic. Such language was found in another "Communings in the Sanctuary" piece where he wrote, "That truth which came from heaven, and thither re-ascends, shall bear to the bosom of the Infinite, those who have been purified by its love."[5] Ascetical tendencies are seen in admonitions to "redeem a few sweet hours from the evil days of earth's corroding cares." Richardson complained that the Christian is often "lulled by the treacherous cup of earthly pleasure. How important, then,...to watch and pray lest the sleep of the soul should steal upon them and steep their spiritual sensibilities in lethal oblivion."[6]

Finally, Richardson believed strongly in the power of prayer and wrote an article by that title in the *Millennial Harbinger* in 1850. Without prayer, he said, "there can be no spiritual life; no fellowship with God, no hope of heaven."

He was concerned that prayer has been disconnected from faith, and seemed to be one with Alexander Campbell in the idea that prayer without faith is ineffectual. "It is the prayer of faith that saves," he wrote. It is the effectual fervent prayer of a righteous man that avails; and it is when we ask in accordance with the will of God that we are alone authorized to expect an answer to our petitions."[7]

NOTES

[1]*MH*, 1849:163-167.
[2]*MH*, 1850:314-320.
[3]*MH*, 1848:8-10.
[4]*MH*, 1849:50-51.
[5]*MH*, 1849:205.
[6]*MH*, 1849:644-645.
[7]*MH*, 1850:211-213.

3

The Spirituality of Barton W. Stone

Barton Stone, pastor of the Cane Ridge, Kentucky, Church and publisher of the *Christian Messenger* (1826-1845), had an approach to spirituality somewhat different from that of Alexander Campbell. He too came out of the Presbyterian tradition and had a strong sense of human sinfulness. He believed that people are fundamentally "alienated from God, and prone to evil." However, we all possess "rational faculties, capable of knowing and enjoying God."

How can we know this invisible God? For Stone, we know God by faith in the testimony given in God's word. "Then we have evidence that God is always present with us," Stone said, reflecting the same approach Campbell used. He described God as One who is "infinitely holy, hates every sin, searches the hearts and tries to reign in the children of men, gracious and merciful, unchangeable," and "what he has spoken once, he speaks always."

For Stone, true religion is that which causes the soul, "to pant after God, rejoice in his love, follow holiness, resist the devil, overcome temptations, fight against all sin, joy in tribulations [and] cheerfully endure persecutions in the name of Christ." Nothing, Stone said, can satisfy us but God. He quoted an old catechism with approval, "The chief end of man is to glorify God and enjoy him forever."[1]

In an article titled "Faith and Feeling," Stone described faith as much more than just intellectual assent to a truth. True faith, he said, is "believing with the heart—the whole heart." Any faith that does not affect the heart is not a true faith. Authentic faith, he believed, always produces repentance and reformation. If it does not draw us away from lust and the desires for the "wealth, honors and pleasure of the world," it is not true faith. True faith, he believed, is characterized by a praying spirit. Anyone who does not pray is still in his or her sins. Finally, truth faith is that through which people receive the Holy Spirit. Anyone who has not received the Holy Spirit "is yet in unbelief."[2]

How did Stone define prayer? Throughout his periodical, *The Christian Messenger*, he gave various definitions. In an 1827 article, he defined prayer as "the offering up of our desires to God for things agreeable to his will." The habit of prayer, he believed, produces an habitual sense of God's presence and an awareness of our dependence on God. This, Stone believed, is the foundation for a holy life. There is good reason to hope for the direct and immediate action of God upon our minds in answer to prayer. So, for Stone, prayer is a means of forming a holy character. It is, he felt, the means by which the grace of God is received, the way we enjoy communion with the Father and the Son."[3] Nine years later, in 1836, he offered the exact same definition of prayer as the offering of our desires to God.[4]

In a lengthy 1834 article by Stone called "On Prayer," he said that "prayer in all ages has been the delightful exercise of the pious." He called it our "highest privilege." It is the way we converse with God and receive the promises of grace.

In this article he dealt with a major issue that concerns many Christians: why should we pray when God already knows our wants? Stone called this objection to prayer "ingenious but sophistical." He agreed that God does not become more benevolent or kindly toward us because of our prayers. However, God has made it a duty for us to pray for those very things God has in store for us. Prayer teaches us our dependence upon God and generates within us a spirit of gratitude for all we have received from God.

One of the primary objections to prayer, Stone noted, is the belief that God created the world to operate on the basis of certain natural and moral laws. There are those who would say that God has left nature to be governed by fixed laws. Likewise, there is a moral law that, if obeyed brings blessings and if disobeyed brings misery. If, indeed, we are governed by immutable laws, there would be no point in prayer.

However, Stone noted that since the beginning of Christianity, the saints have prayed and their experience is that their prayers have been answered. We simply cannot pray in the belief that we are left only to obtain what we can by the laws already given.

The gospel is made up of promises, and faith in these promises engenders hope. By that hope we draw near to God in prayer, and through prayer God gives us the promised blessings. To those who ask, God gives the Holy Spirit and by that Spirit we are "made alive, sanctified, and comforted."

Some say that the value of prayer is only to be found in the person praying or those who hear the person, that it is useless to pray for someone beyond the sound of the voice of the one praying. Stone called this "a secret blow at the life of Christianity."

There are those who hesitate to pray for sinners, those who do not believe, assuming that God will not operate in an unbeliever. But Stone said, "It is our duty to pray for sinners, believing sinners." The example is Jesus. On the cross he prayed for forgiveness for those who killed him. In the Gospel of John, Jesus prayed for the world that all people might believe.

We cannot tell God how to answer our prayers, nor can we ask how God can or will answer them. If we pray according to God's word and promise, God will answer. Heaven and earth would pass away before the promises of God would fail. "Let us therefore come boldly to the throne of grace," Stone said. "Let us draw near with a true heart, in full assurance of faith." Prayer is so vitally important. Stone concluded his article by saying, "If more time were spent in prayer and less in public speaking, when we assemble together, happier effects would be felt and seen among us."[5]

There were other questions. One, from a Dr. J. P. Andrews of Cincinnati, asked whether a sinner has the right to pray before immersion. We have already noted that Alexander Campbell did not believe one could pray to God before faith and baptism. Stone, however, disagreed. He noted that Saul of Tarsus, Cornelius, the Publican, Lydia, the Syrophenician woman and many others prayed before they were immersed, and their prayers were heard and accepted.[6] In fact, said Stone, it is the duty of sinners, of those not saved, to pray. He cited Isaiah 55:6–7,

> "Seek the LORD while he may be found,
>   call upon him while he is near,
> let the wicked forsake their way,
>   and the unrighteous their thoughts;
> let them return to the LORD,
>   that he may have mercy on them,
> and to our God, for he will abundantly pardon."

Another question by Dr. Andrews asked if there was a New Testament authorization for inviting mourners to come forward and pray with the congregation. Stone replied that he knew of no scriptural warrant for the practice. However, there was no scriptural warrant for many things that were done in worship and that did not necessarily make them illegitimate. The practice of mourners praying with the congregation was not, in his judgment, contrary to the spirit of the gospel. Stone said, "I am commanded to pray for all men, the mourners not excepted. And where can be the evil in inviting such to come and unite with me in prayer."

This led to a brief excursus in which Stone complained about those who required an apostolic precept for everything. He complained about such rigid people. "In them," he said, "I discover generally an unenviable temper—a leanness and barrenness of soul—no tender compassion for brethren in error—no yearnings of soul for the unconverted—no fervent prayer for their salvation. Such cold hearted professors may dream for reformation—yet such must themselves reform or else sin or greatly injure the good cause they espoused. What is reformation in the letter of truth without the spirit of it—the spirit of love, power, or of a sound mind?"[7]

For whom is the Christian to pray, Stone asked in an 1836 article. He gave two answers. First, we are to pray for each other. The apostles, he noted, always told the churches to which they wrote that they prayed for them without ceasing and, at the same time, asked for the prayers of the church. Second, we should pray for sinners that they may receive salvation. "It is to our selfish interest that they be saved, for then we will be able to lead a quiet and peaceable life and not be persecuted with malice and hatred."[8]

We associate the name Barton W. Stone with the famous Cane Ridge Revival in the summer of 1801. The emotional excesses of that event are well documented. What was Stone's attitude toward revivals? However he may have felt about the Cane Ridge event, his views on revivals by 1834 were decidedly moderate, if not negative.

Stone was concerned that the emotions aroused during revivals were often short-lived. He wrote in the *Christian Messenger*, "We have seen many things called revivals—great revivals. We have seen congregations greatly excited—many crying aloud for mercy, and many praising God for delivering grace. We have seen this taste of things continue but a short time, and then disappear for years. We have seen many of these converts soon dwindle, sicken and die, and become more hardened against the fear of God than they were before—many of them becoming infidels." Some, he noted, remained in the churches, but for the wrong reasons. Finally, a few took their faith seriously and were "truly pious and accepted of God."

There were some good results that came out of revivals, Stone believed, but there were also negatives. The greatest evil was those who made a public profession of faith, but then fell from it. Such folks, said Stone, "are of all people in the most pitiable situation, seldom do they ever after embrace religion." Their example discouraged others and created a prejudice against religion.

Stone was particularly concerned about the sporadic nature of revivals. They came and went, once every few years. While some reasoned that God pours out the Holy Spirit at certain seasons, Stone thought that idea represented a dangerous tendency. It said that the means of salvation are not always of the same efficacy. God, as Stone understood it, wanted to save people every day, not just at revival time. Whenever in our hearts we believe and obey the gospel, "God gives us his holy, quickening spirit; he gives us salvation and eternal life."[9]

Finally, a word about praying to be filled with the Holy Spirit. This, for Stone, was essential. We possess the Holy Spirit according to our faith and obedience. Our condition would be miserable, Stone believed, if we did not have the promise of the Spirit and the authority to ask for it. Those who have the Holy Spirit are characterized by love, joy, peace, long-suffering, gentleness, goodness, fidelity, meekness, and temperance. "O Christians," Stone admonished, "believe and pray to be filled with the Spirit, that we may be quickened in the ways of God, and shine forth as lights in the world."[10]

NOTES

[1] *The Biography of Eld. Barton Warren Stone, Written by Himself with Additions and Reflections.* Cincinnati: J. A. and U. P. James, 1847, pp. 192, 204, 235.

[2] *CM*, 1835:271-273.

[3] *CM*, 1827:235-237.

[4] *CM*, 1836:55.

[5] *CM*, 1834:202-204.

[6] *CM*, 1833:86.

[7] *CM*, 1833:86-87.

[8] *CM*, 1836:57.

[9] *CM*, 1834:210-212.

[10] *CM*, 1836:129-121.

4

The Christian-Evangelist

The Christian-Evangelist was the oldest continuously published journal among the Disciples. It was originally founded as the *Gospel Echo* in Carrollton, Illinois, by Elijah Craig in 1863. In 1868 John C. Reynolds bought the journal and moved it to McComb, Illinois. In 1869 J. H. Garrison became co-editor, beginning an association that would last until his death in 1931. In 1872 the journal became known as the *Gospel Echo and Christian*. By now it was located in Quincy, Illinois, and had changed from a weekly to a monthly. Garrison had full financial responsibility, and in 1874 the operation was moved to St. Louis. In 1882 he merged his journal with *The Evangelist*, a periodical that dated back to 1850, and the new *Christian-Evangelist* appeared on October 5, 1882.

What did Garrison and his successors attempt to teach Disciples about prayer through the pages of *The Christian-Evangelist*? While the journal ran prayers, devotionals, and articles on prayer, much of the teaching was done through editorials. Although we have to number them as infrequent, they were strong statements.[1]

Through 1911, Garrison wrote occasional editorials on prayer and later dealt with the subject as Editor Emeritus in his "Editor's Easy Chair" column.

This chapter will attempt to present what *The Christian Evangelist* tried to teach about prayer by looking, first, at editorials, and second, at articles by Disciple leaders. While many of the editorials were unsigned, we can assume that they were either written by or had the approval of the editors. During J. H. Garrison's editorship, there were at least seven major editorials on prayer.

Editorials

In 1887 there was a piece called "Prayer as Key to Success." The success referred to was that hoped for success of carrying out the work of Christ in the world. Such an effort would require "Christ's spiritual presence and potential aid." Prayer, said the writer, is what opens the door for Christ's entrance "and so is the key to success." Prayer "is what unites us with Christ."

The essential condition of prayer is a spirit of submission that asks that not our will, but the will of God be done. This is a spirit that recognizes the limitations of human strength and wisdom and puts things into the hands of God.

God does not bless "prayerless efforts" because that would generate too much pride in people over their accomplishments. The editorialist noted that many preachers had a sense that their sermons had failed because they had neglected prayer. The "nice phrases, beautiful illustrations and convincing logic were powerless because [the] heart was not on fire with love of God and love to man." The preacher "had not spoken with the conviction and power which comes from communion with God in prayer."

Steady communion with God produces a "strong, robust, Christian life." The call was for a habit of prayer that did not wait for stated hours or seasons of prayer, but one that can turn to God naturally in thankfulness or petition "in the crowded thoroughfare, amid the cares of home, following the plow, or toiling in the workshop."[2]

In 1903 prayer was referred to in an editorial as "Man's Highest Privilege," exceeding "earthly glory, wealth, or enjoyments of life." It was called "a priceless privilege." Prayer, this piece said, has several benefits for us.

First, it reveals to us the real nature of our souls. If we do not pray regularly, we really do not know our own moral condition. When we are face to face with God alone, self-deceptions disappear and we sense our own spiritual poverty and need for God.

Prayer, according to this editorial, "brings us into the atmosphere of God." It lifts us above the routine of earthly life and puts us in communion with God. But it also puts us in a right relationship with others, for we "dare not carry malice and enmity and an unforgiving spirit into the presence of God" while asking for God's mercy toward our own imperfections.

Prayer is a subject that must not be neglected in the pulpit because it touches daily life at so many points. It is essential to those who are "carrying burdens, fighting battles, struggling against temptations, and seeking to save others as well as themselves."[3]

In 1911 *The Christian-Evangelist* ran an editorial that defined prayer in a variety of ways.

> It is faith laying hold on God's promises. It is love coming into the holy intimacy of communion. It is weakness leaning on omnipotence. It is the heart's trysting time with God. It is the breath of heaven breathing through the life of man. It is the believer's outstretched hand and uplifted vision seeking all the fullness of God. It is the open door by which the individual or the church may pass from weakness to strength and from struggle to everlasting victory.[4]

The editors were much interested in the philosophical issues surrounding prayer. For example, in 1901 there was an editorial on the efficacy of praying for rain.

The Governor of Missouri had issued a proclamation asking people to pray for rain. This raised the question we have already encountered, but which keeps coming up again and again, of whether in a world that operates on the basis of natural law prayer can actually change anything.

The Christian, said the writer, probably J. H. Garrison, believes in a personal God who is behind all natural laws and, indeed, is the source of such laws. However, science has not yet discovered all of the laws and conditions that govern weather. "Who is wise enough to say that none of these forces or conditions are of such a nature as to be modified by spiritual force?" the editorialist asked. The human body is governed by natural laws, yet it is clear that mental attitudes may affect it.

The editorial suggested that "we look at the doctrine of divine immanence square in the face." If we believe that God is present in the natural world and human history, "the idea of prayer for rain loses its apparent absurdity." Is it not fully possible that God, hearing the cries of people for needed rain, might make use of a higher law to fulfill their need? "Why may not prayer itself be that higher spiritual force which, through the will of God, may affect the needed change?" The argument concluded, "There is too much in this wide realm that we do not know for anyone to be dogmatic as to the uselessness of prayer."

This piece did provide an out, however, in case there was no rain in response to prayer. The withholding of rain may teach people about their dependence on God. "Unbroken prosperity, it would seem, is not good for any of us." There is value in adversity if it should humble us and cause us to turn to God. The final prayer is always, "Not my will, but thine be done."[5]

Four years later, another editorial on the same theme appeared titled "Prayer and Modern Thought." It raised the question, "Is there anything in the results of modern scientific and philosophical thought to discredit prayer?" The answer in the mind of the editor was, of course, no. "There is nothing in any generally accepted view of science or philosophy that is contrary to Christ's teaching concerning prayer."

The primary argument was that "as long as we recognize a personal God who is the source of all law, there is a rational basis for prayer." By following moral law, people can make themselves better. Likewise, it is reasonable to assume that prayer is based on spiritual laws. God is not a prisoner in a divinely created universe. Rather, God is free to minister to the needs of people.

Describing evolution as "God's way of doing things," and referring to God as "the great Evolver," the piece affirmed a personal God who has plans for every created thing. Prayer may well be one of the means that God has created for our spiritual development. The discovery of electricity suggests that there are unseen and spiritual forces at work in the universe. Nothing that modern science has discovered should discourage us from prayer.[6]

There were other, less profound editorials on prayer during Garrison's tenure. For example, in 1887 there was a piece that argued against the rote saying of prayers. It referred to people who say their prayers before going to bed every night, yet the practice seems to have no influence on their conduct. Others believe that they must say their prayers morning and evening without fail, yet their lives are unchanged. We are warned, "Do not rest in forms, nor think for a moment that the simple saying of prayers is praying."

However, the editor was not ready to discount totally the habit of prayer. "Without such habit, spiritual communion, spiritual growth, spiritual life are scarcely possible." But the only prayer of value is that which brings us into subjection to the will of God and helps us do it. "Saying prayers is a poor substitute for a life of obedience," the writer concluded.[7]

In 1908 Garrison ran an editorial on the importance of silence in our spiritual development. Silence is essential to close communion with God. Silent prayer is necessary to overcome the problem of being "too much in the busy struggle of commerce, too much under the influence of ostentatious parade." True devotion requires "reverential silence and speechless awe." The complaint was that "prayer is too greatly estimated by the words that are used rather than by the spirit which inspires words." Prayer, which does not always need words, "ought to be the very spiritual breath which every Christian breathes."[8]

By 1913 the name of A. S. Smithers was appearing on *The Christian-Evangelist* masthead as Managing Editor. He, too, ran editorials on various prayer issues. One of his first was a reflection on many people's complaint that they have no time for prayer. Such people, he said, do not know how much they need the "illumination and courage and strength that come from communion with God."

Smithers noted that some of the great people of prayer are often the busiest. No one would dispute that Martin Luther, leader of the Protestant reformation, was constantly busy. Yet he gave hours each day to prayer. John Wesley was constantly on the move, leading an effort for spiritual renewal in England. But even on his busiest days he found time for prayer. Our own Alexander Campbell was an editor, publisher, preacher, and college president, but he insisted on time for prayer. "No Christian," said the editorial, "has ever achieved greatly in the things of the kingdom who was not a man of prayer." We should recognize that we cannot afford not to take time for prayer.

The writer suggested a schedule for daily prayer. Morning prayer is a time to ask for God's help in all the trials and temptations the day will present. At noon we should seek the guidance and help of the Spirit. Evening prayer is a time to pray for forgiveness of the sins and failures of the day. Finally, before going to sleep we should commit ourselves to the God who does not slumber or sleep.[9]

In 1913 Smithers ran a more general editorial about prayer that expressed the view that prayer is a way of knowing God. Prayer is a way "to feel His presence." It is our "highest exercise" and a means of "communion with God." In prayer we are able to meet and talk with God face to face. Prayer, this piece stated, "lifts man above mere animalism and places him in the ranks of those spiritual intelligences that are transfigured by the vision of God." Prayer is the supreme form of education, for it makes possible the realization of the presence of God. But it goes even farther than that. "Prayer connects man's life with God and makes him a partaker of the divine nature," is an expression of Eastern Orthodox Christianity and not often found among Disciples and most Protestants. The "great results" in life, the editorial concluded, usually come from "quiet seasons of secret prayer."[10]

Two years later, under Smithers' editorship, an editorial was published on "Churches at Worship." It affirmed that "the supreme need in our churches is personal piety on the part of our membership." The Disciples have long emphasized their particular religious position and have been committed to some fundamental first principles of Christianity. Now, however, "we need a new emphasis on spiritual culture." That will be developed and enhanced by "prayerful imitation" of the thought, purpose, and life of Jesus.[11]

With regard to the Disciple position, it is to be expected that there would be an admonition to pray for the unity of the church. "If we are to have Christian union," said a 1914 editorial, "we must, above all, pray for it." Jesus prayed that his followers might be one that the world might believe.

The editorial praised the work of the Federal Council of Churches. There was praise for a new spirit of cooperation between churches that would not have happened a century earlier. Churches are working together in "opposing the liquor traffic, the divorce evil, and the white slave plague; and in pleading for clean politics, good citizenship, and international peace and good will." Such cooperation generates an irenic spirit and is a major step toward the unity for which Jesus prayed.

But, said the writer, "it is futile to talk about union unless we pray for it." We need to pray that all Christians will receive the truth, be of the same mind, and say the same thing. "If this prayer were offered in every pulpit in Christendom, and at every family altar, and in every closet of devotion, it would do much to hasten the coming of the time when there shall be one flock even as there is one Shepherd."[12]

On a related subject, Smithers published a piece responding to a Presbyterian call for a year of intercessory prayer for the "speedy evangelization of the world." The editorial affirmed the "power of such intercession and called for other editors to do the same. It urged pastors to cultivate a "holy fellowship with God" in their own hearts and challenge their congregations to do the same. A revival of prayer, it was insisted, would fill churches pews with "happy, hopeful, effective workers for Christ and his church.[13]

There were a couple of interesting negative editorials on spirituality. One, called "Religious Inconsistencies," was about Carthusian monks who supported themselves by the manufacture and sale of "intoxicating liquors." Carthusians are known for their rigorous asceticism and lives of prayer, but this particular writer could not understand how they could engage in a business that alienates people from Christ. It was simply one of those "peculiar religious inconsistencies for which there is no reasonable explanation."[14]

Another complained about poor preparation for public prayer. It said that prayer is one of the most important parts of a worship service, yet most ministers did very little preparation for it. There are ministers who are excellent preachers, yet whose prayers "are pathetically lacking in power either to edify the congregation or to voice the spiritual yearnings of the people sharing in worship."

Most pastors, the editorial complained, hope for the inspiration of the moment. They "launch on a sea of words... swept by the waves of emotion and driven by the winds of fancy words and know not in which direction to steer for the harbor of the Amen." On the ship of Prayer the pilot has lost control.

If the minister is to spend time in careful preparation, let it be on the prayers more than the sermon. If the minister is to write out what is to be said, let it be of the words "with which the minister shall appear before the great High Priest on our behalf." The editorial concluded, "We plead for more prayerful preparation for public prayers on the part of all our preachers."[15]

In 1916 Frederick D. Kershner was editing *The Christian-Evangelist*. He published an editorial that would have made Alexander Campbell very uncomfortable, yet one which many of today's Disciples might appreciate. The title was "Our Greatest Weakness," and that weakness was "our neglect of the mystical note in religion." Such neglect has not been the fault of the Disciple plea, but "an imperfect apprehension of the plea." The New Testament, said Kershner, "was filled with the spirit of mysticism," and prayer was "one of the great essentials of all its work." The Disciples, Kershner believed, have never denied the reality of the spiritual side of Christian faith, but on the other hand, they have never emphasized it. Our focus has been more on the logical and intellectual side of faith, leading us to forget that "the heart has a place in our faith as well as the head."

Mysticism, as Kershner defined it, is "the consciousness of the direct reality of the spiritual world. It is the assurance of the reality of God as a living, conscious Presence." It is an essential element in Christianity. Without it, we have morals and ethics, but not Christian religion. Disciple tradition and Wesleyan spirituality would have been an ideal combination. "The mystical presence is as necessary as the logic of the philosopher," and Kershner believed that the Restoration plea provided the best ground for the synthesis.

He admitted that we were put off by the extremes of Wesleyan mysticism as seen in such things as the mourner's bench, and as a result fell into a "coldly mechanical intellectualism." We talked about a logical "plan of salvation," not recognizing that salvation is more than a plan. If we had logical appeal and a mystical approach, our evangelism might have had more spiritual and emotional power. "We simply threw away an element of supreme value when we neglected it."

Kershner called for a revival of "Apostolic spirituality." In his judgement, we do not pray enough. Our theory about the New Testament church might be correct, but we will lack its power if there is "no abiding consciousness of the presence of God in our midst." God cannot be just an intellectual concept; God is a living reality.[16]

In the last issue of 1917 there was an editorial on the problem of unanswered prayers. Admittedly, many Christians had various levels of doubt caused by the fact that very earnest prayers appear not to have been answered. Brooding on the problem could lead to the "dark bleak way of unbelief."

However, Christians must realize that any prayer which includes, "Thy will be done, not mine," is always answered. Sometimes God withholds what we ask for and responds in another way. There are times when "No" is a real answer. Beyond this, however, we must wait. We are blinded by impatience, not realizing that our prayers may be answered in the years to come, for praying lays up treasurers in heaven.[17]

B. A. Abbot was the editor in 1918. This was at the end of World War I and several of the editorials on prayer were related to that event. For example, his first major editorial on prayer was titled "Prayer and Patriotism." This would be a highly controversial subject today.

Abbott urged that there not be a divorce between patriotism and religion. Winning the war is no guarantee that freedom and idealism will prevail unless what we do is based on the righteousness of God. Patriotism that is based on "an intense attachment to one's own nation" does not generate any desire for fair play or justice, and that is the very root of war. Leaders who believe in God, that God is involved in human affairs, and who seek God's help in prayer "Make the greatest lights in their own country and impress upon mankind the truth by which all nations may do well and by which the weak will be safe even in the presence of the strong."

Citing Woodrow Wilson's statements that we fought the war for no selfish ends, Abbott insisted that prayer will "purify and make sincere our patriotism because it will deliver us from selfishness." Prayer, he believed, cultivates moral and spiritual insight so that we are able to tell the false from the true.

Beyond that, prayer "puts us in the attitude of letting God's power flow into our souls." This editorial expressed no interest in the philosophical questions about prayer discussed by earlier editors. People who pray, he said, know that their prayers are answered. "When a nation is in the right, it is on God's side and it harnesses itself to divine omnipotence."

However, prayer coupled with patriotism also helps us discover defects in ourselves. It is self-revealing because it forces us to be frank with ourselves and our nation. True nationalism, the editorial said, must be based on God's will. German nationalism, said Abbott, had been "entirely selfish" and led people into atheism and, hence, into war. But patriotism based on prayer seeks to give everybody their rights.[18]

Six months later Abbott ran another editorial on the same issue. In this piece he raised an important question. The Germans prayed as well as the Allies. Did God not hear the prayers of the Germans? Obviously, God could not give success to both sides in the war. Abbott's answer is, "if two children contest for a thing, the father gives it to the one who is in the right." In light of the outcome of the war, the answer seemed simple: the Germans were wrong and the Allies were right.[19]

The problematic side of prayer seemed to occupy most of the editorial writing on the subject during Abbott's tenure. In 1918 he ran a piece called "Is There Any Reason Why God Should Answer Our Prayers?" The statement was made that before we complain about whether our prayers are answered, we need to make sure we have really prayed. Prayer is not simply expressing a desire in a casual way with our eyes closed. "Real prayer comes of the great deep, and it is of the heart, will and mind, and sometimes it costs blood, like Gethsemane." Prayer is "no easy, light thing."

Then the editorial asked, "Do we always recognize the answer when it comes?" Paul, for example, prayed to have his thorn in the side removed. It wasn't, but he was given the grace to do his ministry and be glad in spite of it.

A related problem was that we often ask for trivial things when we should focus on major issues. We should pray for loaves, not crumbs. The editorial concluded, "When our prayers are so small, so trivial, and often so selfish, is there any reason why they should be answered?"[20]

J. H. Garrison, now Editor Emeritus, devoted one of his "Editor's Easy Chair" columns to a concern about groups in the church leaving the Disciple brotherhood at the recent national Convention. Part of the problem, Garrison believed, was a lack of "such increasing and prevailing prayer, personal and intercessory, as will bring us into complete union with God." There will never be a united Christendom unless there is union with Christ and the Father. What makes us one with Christ is not selfish praying, but "praying that involves the complete surrender of our wills to his will."

Although there has been an increase in prayer at the Conventions, too many people neglect the early morning hour of prayer. "Why not have an hour for prayer in the midst of business sessions," Garrison asked. Serious prayer at the coming St. Louis Convention, he said, could make that "an epochal event in our history," one that would help the church overcome many obstacles.[21]

In 1927 Abbott published an editorial calling for more extemporaneous prayer in Disciple churches. It quoted from a British paper about the decline of extemporaneous prayer in the Free Churches. "This sounds the note of an evil that may befall any of our churches," the editorial warned.

Written and memorized prayers were not without value, the editorial stated, "but one must have his own experience with God and leave the place for the bubbling up of new fresh words of worship when we come into the presence of God." Real prayer arises spontaneously and uses its own form of speech.

The piece concluded with an eloquent definition of prayer: "To pray is to touch hands with the Infinite; to reach far out into the eternities; to be the subject of transcendent experience; to feel the force of the miraculous life, and the cleansing, refreshing, strengthening, comforting touch of the living God upon the heart."[22]

A 1931 Abbott editorial responded to a complaint by a pastor that congregations don't pray enough. The editorial stated that a church that does not pray is impotent and defeated, but a church that really prays is irresistible. "Prayer energizes with spiritual health and power every fiber of the being and fills men with courage, inspires them to good works, to love, to firmness of faith in God and makes the pulpit blaze and echo with spiritual eloquence, appeal, and proclamation."[23]

There were some positive editorials, however, during Abbott's tenure. In 1926 a piece appeared called "When Walter Scott Prayed." Scott could not understand the meaning of the passage that says we must be born of water and spirit. He reported that he prayed, and the meaning was made clear to him. It was what the editorial called a "mystical passage in which matter and spirit seemed to blend." Scott's experience excited him with so much enthusiasm that he wrote his book *The Messiahship.*

The lesson here is that prayer can help us understand and interpret scripture. The Bible is "too profound, too fine, too intricate, too brilliant and wonderful to be understood without prayer." This, of course, was an approach different from Alexander Campbell, who said we need no miracles to understand the Bible. It is self-interpreting.

The editorial concluded by noting that many people think Walter Scott actually gave the Disciples their theology. His theology of conversion, then, came from "a flash of light that came to him in answer to prayer."[24]

"Prayer and the Silence of God" appeared in 1927. It admitted that many people have been frustrated by praying and having a response of silence.

There are some positive values, however, in God's silence. For one thing, it teaches us patience and forces us to reach out to others. The editorial insisted, however, that "God's silence is often temporary." We will eventually know and see God, and many of our prayers will be answered in heaven. We are encouraged to wait and lay up for ourselves treasures in heaven by prayer.[25]

One of the points on which Disciples obviously have a great variety of opinions is the purpose of prayer. Do we pray to know God or do we pray to ask for things we want? A 1933 editorial in *The Christian-Evangelist* saw the notion of praying to establish communion with God as "a strange statement." Prayer is communion with God, but it is also more. It is "petition for definite objects." Christ asked for specific things when he prayed, and the Lord's Prayer contains very definite "askings." The piece concluded, "If we ask directly and live straight we shall accomplish things worth while."[26]

Articles

During the twentieth century, the pages of *The Christian-Evangelist* carried articles on prayer by some of the most outstanding leaders of the Disciples: Archibald McLean, Edgar Dewitt Jones, J. H. Garrison, George Earl Owen, Edward Scribner Ames, Leslie R. Smith, Frederick D. Kershner, and Robert Burns.

They reveal much about what our leadership tried to teach the brotherhood, as it was known in those days, on the subject.

In 1910 Archibald McLean, who became a leader in Disciples mission work and believed strongly in cooperation with other denominations on the field, published an article on the transfiguration of Jesus. His theme was that prayer affects our physical appearance. Moses, after spending forty days with God on Mount Sinai, had to wear a veil because the experience caused his face to shine with a glory that was too bright for people's eyes. As was the case for Jesus when he was transfigured before his disciples, so for us "prayer imparts a new and strange beauty to the countenance, a beauty beyond that which comes from any other source, a beauty that never was on sea or land."[27]

Peter Ainslie, the pioneering ecumenical leader among the Disciples and pastor of Christian Temple in Baltimore, wrote an article called "Prayer—Just Prayer," in 1911. No one, he said, can live without prayer. "It is among the first in the fundamental principles of Christianity." He called doubts about prayer "the shame of this age," and said that the greatest need of the church is "the spirit of prayer." Christians must go into the inner chamber before going out into the world. Until we pray for the rule of Christ in our lives, we cannot pray for the rule of God over others.

Prayers of petition, Ainslie insisted, are outside of the will of God when they are for "purely personal desires." People are weak in service because they are weak in prayer. "The secret of strength is found in the recognition of the companionship of Jesus Christ," and that is attained through prayer. "The one test of prayer," wrote Ainslie, "is our relationship with God."[28]

Edgar Dewitt Jones, who later became the famous pastor of Central-Woodward Christian Church in Detroit, expressed some unusual ideas on praying the Lord's Prayer. He raised a question about whether the disciples prayed it "as a form or ritual, or did they simply fashion their own prayers after this model in a general way?" Growing in the spiritual life, he believed, meant growing in prayer. People's ideas about prayer change as they grow older, and they outgrow the prayers of their childhoods.

Jones said that as we outgrow "Now I lay me down to sleep," so we should also outgrow the rote saying of the Lord's Prayer and develop "an expression of our own, framed independently, and growing out of our personal needs and experience." We can pray the content of the Lord's Prayer in our own words and style. He concluded that "until one gets this far along in his prayer life, it can scarcely be said he has really learned to pray."[29]

Thirty years later Jones wrote another article, "The Ladder of Prayer." He described growth in prayer in terms of ascending the rungs of a ladder.

The first rung is just "saying a prayer." The next step up, the second rung, is "praying a prayer." Here one passes from just rote repetition to real communion with God. The third rung is praying for oneself. It is a petitionary, self-centered prayer. The fourth step on the ladder is prayer for others. This is a nobler form of prayer that deepens and widens. Finally, the top rung of the ladder is "praying in the Spirit." This, Jones said, is the acme of prayer. Here the Spirit of God and the human spirit "meet and merge in triumphant trust."[30]

In 1913 *The Christian-Evangelist* published a symposium on "The Place of Prayer in the Life of the Church." Three local pastors contributed. H. D. Smith, of First Christian Church in Hopkinsville, Kentucky, complained that "we are so prayerless!" We neglect prayer meetings, family prayer, and private prayer, for the sake of the pursuits of commerce. But, he said, there is great profit in prayer. God answers our prayers in accord with the divine wisdom, not our own folly. Furthermore, prayer makes us aware of God's presence and engenders gratitude and humility. "Prayer," Smith said, "through making God seem near and real, transfigures our losses as being occasions of the divine comforting, and our gains as being gifts of the divine bounty."

A. D. Harmon, pastor of First Christian Church in Lincoln, Nebraska, claimed that the two biggest needs of the church were great attendance and a richer worship life. Worship, he said, is absent if there is no spirit of prayer present. When there is a strong awareness of God, however, "people breathe forth a mist which the preacher returns in floods, and all go forth conscious that they have been sitting together in heavenly places."

Harmon urged that the church stop using "the devices of public entertainments" in worship and feed people's souls. The way through the problems of attendance, worship, and soul-winning "must be traveled on the knees."

Finally, the symposium was concluded by M. L. Pontius, a minister in Peoria, Illinois, who contributed a piece on "How to Kill the Prayer Meeting." His concerns were such things as using old-fashioned methods in the meeting, "having the long-winded deacon lead the meeting," having the minister lead a discussion for which no preparation has been made, trying to accomplish too many things other than prayer, and using topics arranged by a committee outside the local church.[31]

While such admonitions were entertaining and clever, J. H. Garrison brought *The Christian-Evangelist* discussion back to a deeper level. In 1916 he published a piece called "Alone with God," in which he reaffirmed the importance of a mystical approach to religion. He saw value in solitude and in silent, wordless prayer. "To be alone with God in the highest sense is to be at one with God," he wrote. "Prayer is at its best when it is spoken or breathed into the ear of God alone."

When we are alone with God, Garrison believed, we do not always need words or speech. "What blessed mysticism this is," he said, when our yearnings cannot find words, but are understood "by the Searcher of hearts." Those who are bored with solitude do not understand that "God dwells in secret places and that they may enter into communion with him, and make their lonely hour a trysting time with the Most High." For those practical types who think prayer is a waste of time and Christians should be out doing good deeds in the world, Garrison reminded that Jesus felt it necessary to spend much time in communion with God. The Christian must engage in serious social action, but the "wisdom, strength, patience and grace necessary for such service" can only be found in communion with God.

Many people neglect prayer because their conception of God is too transcendent. They think of God as being remote and far away. The nearness of God is not a matter of space, Garrison said, but a matter of our "moral attitude." He affirmed that God is "immediately accessible to all who spiritually apprehend him." He concluded, "The very fact of our tender relationship to God, as our Father, should make it a delight to be in his presence."[32]

In 1919 *The Christian-Evangelist* published a series of six articles by W. F. Richardson on "Prayer and the New Life." In these articles Richardson addressed the life, culture, dynamic, chemistry, altruism, and projection of prayer.

The religious life, he said, is "essentially a life of prayer." It lies at the heart of religion. We are, he believed, "incurably religious." The practice of prayer is built on the faith that God will grant "the better thing" when we pray, even if our prayer is not answered as he thought it should be.[33]

The prayer life needs constant cultivation, such as excluding those influences that distract us from the voice of God. Many prayers failed, Richardson said, "because the doors that open into the world are left open."

Richardson outlined the traditional elements in prayer: praise, thanksgiving, confession, petition, and intercession.[34]

His phrase, "the dynamic of prayer," refers to the power of prayer. To have power, prayer must be real, not formal. It must be offered in complete submission to God's will, for "when we wish what God wishes we cannot be denied."

Real prayer is costly. Richardson listed some examples of people who had made sacrifices because of their encounters with God, such as the missionaries William Carey and David Livingston. He added, "It will cost the rich man his gold, the scholar his learning, and everyone his life." Prayer has remarkable power. It "releases mighty human spiritual energies and unites the power of divine and human dynamos for the common task."[35]

The chemistry of prayer is such that it brings power to the human soul. It moves us from weakness to strength and transforms the soul "into the divine likeness." Like Moses descending Mount Sinai, Stephen during his stoning, and Jesus during his transfiguration, prayer changes us. "Prayer," Richardson wrote, makes "the bitter become sweet, the heavy burden light, and even the thorny road to bloom with roses so fragrant as to make one forget the pain of plucking them."[36]

The life of prayer, as Richardson understood it, becomes a life of unselfish service. This is what he meant by the "altruism of prayer." It is prayer that gives us the power to serve others, and none of us can give adequate service to others until we have prayed for them.

Richardson had a deep sense of the mystery of prayer and faith. Like Paul seeing in a glass darkly, we can know only partially the depths of the finite love of Christ. It is like an ocean. We "may sail upon its bosom, fish in its waters, divine a little way into its depths but fathomless waves defy their sounding, and never can all its mystery be explained to them."[37]

Finally, Richardson addressed the "projection" of prayer. Prayer, he said, "presses in every direction." It not only ascends to God, but it goes outward across the earth.

The prayers of John Wesley, for example, "spread like a holy contagion through the British empire," and gave life to a church deadened by formalism. A praying church has effects on the church abroad. Nothing encourages a missionary as the knowledge that he or she is supported by prayers from home.

Richardson concluded his series by saying, "Wherever you go, whatever your daily task, see to it that the holy fire of prayer is always burning upon the altar of your heart."[38]

George Earl Owen, who became one of our major Disciple leaders in the 1950s and 1960s, had an article in *The Christian-Evangelist* in 1934 called "The Lost Reality of Prayer." Prayer, he said, is the source of the spirit of the Christian. The church's power and influence depend upon the devotional life of its members. He complained that Disciple religious life had become superficial. "Our personal experiences with God have been banal," he wrote, "because we have lost the reality of prayer."

He defined prayer as "practicing the presence of God." Our petitions are not prayer if there is no awareness of God's presence. "The essence of religion is contact with God," he said. "If there is no contact with God, if we have no sense of God, we have no religion."

Owen offered some suggestions for renewing our life of prayer. First, he suggested that we be natural and use a friendly conversational tone in our prayers, "without wax or gloss." Second, we should be original and avoid "old stereotyped prayer." We must reach out to God in our own way. Third, our prayers should be specific, not just generalities. Fourth, our prayers should be thankful and joyous. Fifth, while public prayer has its place, we should also practice private prayer. In solitary prayer "we can lose the consciousness of others...and find God consciousness." Finally, Owen called us to be imaginative. We need to imagine God present and think of Jesus standing by our side with his hand on our shoulder.[39]

The next year appeared "The Art of Public Prayer: The Confession of a Pastor." The author, we are told, wrote anonymously to avoid offending his elders. He complained about benedictions given by elders that ranged "from Dan to Beersheba," yet really went nowhere. Prayers at the communion table "may take the turn of a weather report, a review of the political situation, a sermonette on the changing morals of the times, and whatever else may come into the elder's mind."

Several suggestions were offered to elders. First, if offering a prayer at the table, "no subject should be introduced that will take the mind off the Supper and the great event which it commemorates." The prayer should include three basic elements: thanksgiving for Christ, a prayer for recognition of the presence of Christ, and "a blessing upon the emblems."

The benediction should be a simple blessing of dismissal, nothing more. "A long prayer at that time spoils a good sermon; it adds no saving grace to a bad one."[40]

Edward Scribner Ames was a name long associated with the Disciples Divinity House at the University of Chicago. The House was a major source of liberalism among the Disciples and produced a number of important denominational leaders. Ames, contrary to others we have noted, said that a "clear and convincing idea of God" is not required for authentic prayer. A child does not understand what it is to be a parent, yet that does not hinder it from unburdening its heart to father or mother.

Prayer, Ames said, is "an experience of rising to the level of the divine mind so far as possible." The divine mind is an impartial mind, and prayer may help us look at ourselves impartially. "Entering into the mind of God, in order to view the perplexity or bafflement we feel, may so illuminate and clarify our thought as to provide insight and the attainment of a plan of action and the will or courage to carry it through."

Prayer, for Ames, has three moods. One is dependence: "Thy kingdom come." A second is acceptance: "Thy will be done." The third is active participation: "Forgive us our trespasses as we forgive those who trespass against us." The implication of that for Ames is that God does not do things for us unless we do something ourselves. Jesus, he believed, taught us "to take responsibility for the great concerns of life and religion."[41]

Leslie R. Smith, who would have a distinguished ministry at Central Christian Church in Lexington, Kentucky, and served as a President of the International Convention, wrote on "Prayer: A Resource for Difficult Times" in 1944.

Prayer, he said, should "combine unselfishness with intelligence." To think that God has spared our life when others who prayed just as earnestly died only leads to egotism and confusion. God's sustaining power is present for us no matter what our condition of life. Intelligent and unselfish prayer will lead us to a deeper religious experience.

Prayer, Smith believed, must be a continuing experience for us, not just a single act. It is the development of a devotional spirit over a period of time that leads to a consciousness of God's presence. Furthermore, prayer is not done to change God's mind. "Prayer should change us into thinking like God instead of getting God to think as we do." The most important value of prayer is that it "makes us a channel for God's power to express itself in life."

Prayer, for Smith, provides strength for our daily tasks. In the spirit of prayer our work is no longer drudgery. "There is no limit to one's strength to meet the daily tasks if such task is met in the spirit of prayer."[42]

Long after his editorship had ended, Frederick D. Kershner wrote a regular column called "Think on These Things." Two of these, in the mid-1940s, were devoted to the subject of prayer. We have already seen that he had a deep appreciation for the mystical tradition in Christianity.

However, he did not see prayer as a substitute for intelligent action. Jesus, he noted, prayed "a great deal" but "never attempted to make his devotions a substitute for industry." It would be a good thing, he said, if everyone would pray for an end to industrial disputes in America, but added, "we are not sure that this procedure alone will completely discharge our responsibilities in the present situation."

A year later, however, he complained in another column that there is no evidence now that prayer is a factor in the average home. Private prayer, he noted, was confined to "devout circles" and the "mystically minded." This, he said, is why the time is "so distraught, so ill at ease, so filled with phobias, and forebodings."[43]

Robert Burns, pastor of Peachtree Christian Church in Atlanta for many years, wrote on "Why I Believe in Prayer," in 1954. He listed a number of reasons. First, he believed in prayer because it meant so much to Christ. Second, because "the finest, the best of our race believed in and practiced prayer." Third, he was impressed by the prayer experiences of many friends. Fourth, he believed in it because of what it had meant to him personally. He concluded, "I pray because I must. At every single turning point in my life, I can look back and see where prayer has helped me."[44]

NOTES

[1]See Lester G. McAllister and William E. Tucker, *Journey in Faith* (St. Louis: Bethany Press, 1975), pp. 219-222.

[2]*CE*, 1887:355.

[3]*CE*, 1903:389-390.

[4]*CE*, 1911:114.

[5]*CE*, 1901:933.

[6]*CE*, 1905:137.

[7]*CE*, 1887:243.

[8]*CE*, 1908:1220-1221.

[9]*CE*, 1913:52.

[10]*CE*, 1913:1697.

[11]*CE*, 1915:423.

[12]*CE*, 1914:619.

[13]*CE*, 1913:1436.

[14]*CE*, 1913:53.

[15]*CE*, 1915:422.

[16]*CE*, 1916:419.

[17]*CE*, 1917:1400.

[18]*CE*, 1918:507-508.

[19]*CE*, 1918:1348.

[20]*CE*, 1918:1052.

[21]*CE*, 1918:1053.

[22]*CE*, 1927:718.

[23]*CE*, 1931:1262.

[24]*CE*, 1926:1123.

[25]*CE*, 1927:1103.

[26]*CE*, 1933:1238.

[27]*CE*, 1910:1691.

[28]*CE*, 1911:109.

[29]*CE*, 1911:292.

[30]*CE*, 1941:261.

[31]*CE*, 1913:1348-1349.

[32]*CE*, 1916, 423.

[33]*CE*, 1919:1167.

[34]*CE*, 1919:1191.

[35]*CE*, 1919:1216-1217.

[36]*CE*, 1919:1248-1249.

[37]*CE*, 1919:1271-1272.

[38]*CE*, 1919:1296-1297.

[39]*CE*, 1934:383.

[40]*CE*, 1935:121.

[41]*CE*, 1937:460.

[42]*CE*, 1944:1076-1077.

[43]*CE*, 1947:253.

[44]*CE*, 1954:77,87.

5

The Christian

In 1960, *The Christian-Evangelist* changed its name to *The Christian*. One of the most important articles from the point of view of spirituality that was published early in the new journal was "A Ministry of Redemption," by Frank C. Mabee. In the article Mabee complained that many Christian education programs did not produce a significant level of religious depth in people. He believed that educational programs based on "environment and correct methods" have failed. The mission of the church, he insisted, is the "redemptive reconciliation of man to God," where people can become "new creatures in Jesus Christ." That is what the teaching mission of the church should be trying to accomplish.

Unfortunately, Mabee said, many ministers have been preoccupied with gimmicks, gadgets, and methods "that would equal the best that Madison Avenue can do." What have we achieved, he asked, if, after attending church school for years "a person has the same hatreds, prejudices, fears, and sense of meaninglessness to their life" they have always had? What kind of teaching job has the church done, for example, "if our young people can go to twelve years of church school and in six weeks have their faith shattered by new discoveries at college?"

Mabee concluded, "If we are not bringing persons, whatever their age, into a new relationship that restores their awareness of the meaning of life then we had better review what it is we are doing."[1]

Tommie Bouchard made the same affirmation. The mission of the church, he wrote, is to lead "every man, woman and child before the throne of God." The church, "because of its very nature, (is) charged with the responsibility to bring all nations under the rule of God."[2]

Finding God

Several articles in *The Christian* raised the question about how that is to be done. Three articles, for example, were titled, "How on Earth Do I Know God?" "How Can I Make God Real?" and "How Can Anyone Find God These Days?" Good questions.

Hayden Stewart, the author of the first of these, said that the first answer to the question of how we know God is to search. We all need help in knowing God, but "in the end each one of us must do his own searching." Such a search demands our whole being and will continue throughout life. We are assured, however, that we will find God afresh as long as we live out our days as searchers. "Our experience of God," he wrote, "can only be a result of your own seeking him with all your heart."

It helps the process to know other people who are also searching. Knowing another's experience can make us more hungry for the goal of our own seeking and can stimulate a deepened commitment to the search.

The search for God is never completed and the "excitement and rewards" of our search do not stop. "To the accumulating joys and wonders of our relationship with God there is no end."

Second, Stewart said that we must respect our doubts, "for in your doubts you come to know him better." If we never doubted our childhood concepts of God, how could we ever come to a more mature understanding of God? "By never doubting my unknowing," he said, "I condemn myself to remain in my unknowing."

Third, a strong commitment is essential. By that he meant a total yielding of the self to God. The surrender of the self helps us understand that new life belongs more to God than to the self.[3]

Norman Mohn answered the question of "How Can I Make God Real?" by suggesting that reading the Bible is the first way we have of knowing that God exists. Second, we grow close to God by our actions and by "looking for opportunities to serve God's great purpose." Third, when we engage in some form of creativity, such as painting, composing music, writing poetry, sewing, or growing things, we share in God's creative activity and thus grow closer. Finally, when we have consecrated our lives to God to a high degree we become one with God.[4]

In the 1960s and 70s there was a great deal of discussion about the absence of God. A few theologians had ventured that God was dead and hence not experienced anymore. John Thompson suggested that "we may have created a world that obscures him." If prayer seems a dry experience, Thompson suggested, it may be because we are praying for anything except God's truth and love. It could even be that our search for God is too frantic, and God is waiting for a time of stillness in our lives in order to break through to us.

The task of Disciples, Thompson believed, was not to prove that God was active in the first century; the task is to affirm God's presence in the twentieth century. Our understanding of God must be a growing experience. Every generation must take another look at the understanding of God it has inherited. Many adults still have the conception of God they developed as children in Sunday school and have never critically examined it.

Some of the theological movements that upset us, Thompson wrote in 1972, may "sweep some of the cobwebs out of our minds in order that our image of the Eternal One may have life and meaning for this day." God does not need our defense; the problem may be the insecurity of our own belief. What we need to do is "stretch our minds to know God in the fullness of his glory."[5]

Don McEvoy insisted that before anything else the Christian must have "a vital experience with God revealed in Christ." When people seek to make a Christian witness without first "waiting in the presence of the Living Christ" the message becomes "artificial and sterile."

When we have known God face-to-face we are transformed people. "Greed changes to generosity. Bigotry is replaced by understanding. Pettiness is replaced by magnanimity. Self-concern becomes neighbor-love." When this happens, said McEvoy, "ordinary persons like ourselves will be endowed with an extraordinary spirit."[6]

How is Christ present with us now? How does he live with us? Otto Kretzmann attempted to answer this question in a 1961 article. Obviously, we cannot see or touch Christ physically. However, "he has his own way of being with us in the world." We know him through his words and his sacraments. Through them the Emmaus experience is repeated today.

"Our living Savior abides with us," Kretzmann affirmed. When Christ draws near to us our eyes are opened. "This," he said, "has always been the blessed experience of the believing heart." When we are aware of the presence of Christ, "we can forget the huge, invisible load of care and sin, the tolerable burden of the remembered years, and all the cares and sorrows which make life so dark for the men and women who walk the way of the world without him."[7]

The Christian-Evangelist, The Christian, and *The Disciple* all ran devotional pieces, usually on the inside of the front cover. Many of these tended to be pretty superficial and reflective of a popular piety that lacked real spiritual depth. Hence, they have not been used in this study. There was one, however, by Beulah G. Squires, titled "The Voice of God," that was unusually good. It appeared in 1963 and, rather than talk about discovering God's presence through prayer and an interior focus, Squires described God's presence in human events. The voice of God, she said, "speaks loudly through the disorder of the world." She affirmed that

God speaks in the pitious cry of hungry children,
in the wail of the homeless.
God speaks in the sobs of the disillusioned—
his voice echoes through the streets
in the hoarse shouts of the illiterate.
God's voice is in the drumbeat of the revolutionist—
it is in the cry of the downtrodden.
God's voice is in the poignant cry of the hurt—
it is in the clamor of the crowd for justice.
God's voice is in the heartbreak of the bereaved—
the lonely, the neglected and the despairing.

God's voice, she said, is "a seeking, searching voice." It "dissolves platitudes, it crumbles walls of prejudice, it sears disunity and annihilates armaments. Its overtones are social justice, equity, honor, law and righteousness." That is a powerful statement, reminding us of liberation theology and the spirituality of other social justice activists.

Spiritual Disciplines

The Christian published a number of articles on various spiritual disciplines, especially prayer. They ranged from an article on "Dial-a-Prayer"[9] to a "A Housewife's Prayer" written by a man,[10] to "The Meaning of Prayer for Modern Man."

Peter H. Hampton of the Psychological Services Division of the University of Akron wrote an interesting article on teaching children how to pray. He said that children are ready to pray as soon as they can talk and "accept the idea of praying quite readily." The first experiences of prayer should be at bedtime. Later, mealtimes and other occasions can be added.

For a child, prayer should be a way of conversing with God through Christ. A child's prayer should be personalized. That is, it must relate to experiences that are already good for the child. The child should be taught to refer to persons he or she loves and to express thanks for things held dear.

Hampton outlined the subjects of prayer for different age groups. For example, children up to eight years of age usually pray for particular things they want. We should teach them to give thanks to God for things such as the stars in heaven and the food we eat. They also tend to ask for special privileges and for help in doing things they think they cannot do by themselves.

Preadolescents, ages nine to fourteen, find prayer a means of "asking God for help in doing right and avoiding wrong and help in getting what they want." It is also a way of "getting rid of frustrations and anxieties,...a chance to talk out difficulties with God."

Through all of these stages, said Hampton, "we as teachers must strive to help children know God through

Jesus Christ. Prayer for children must become more than asking God for things; it must become a way that they give of themselves to Jesus Christ.[11]

Frank Johnson Pippin claimed that of all human needs, the need for prayer is the greatest. He noted that prayer "takes time and tears and a strange courage." The importance of prayer is that it introduces us to the reality of a personal God.

Pippin had some curious comments about prayer. He insisted that "prayer saves us time. It gives us a genius for sensing Christian opportunity." Later he said, "Prayer takes the brown taste out of our souls." A prayer whispered to God "gathers force on the upward way and ends in the ears of God with the sound of a great Amen!" The most important benefits of prayer, for Pippen, were the forgiveness of sin and the peace that prayer brings.[12]

A professor at Bethany College, Jack Sibley, explained in a 1969 article that prayer reflects our conception of God. When people think that their prayer can change the will of God and prayers are not answered as they wish, "they end up destroying both their religious faith and their conception of God." A view of prayer as some kind of magic is detrimental to faith. Jesus' prayer, "Not my will, but yours be done," may be the only prayer we can legitimately pray.

Prayer, Sibley wrote, is not a matter of our changing God, but of God changing us. At its best, prayer "works creatively to change the human personality." It is effective only when it moves individuals and groups to seek the highest and holiest in life.[13]

Intercessory prayer is probably the most widely used form of prayer. David Sassoon called it "the noblest form which prayer takes," and urged its practice without apology. "I have discovered that prayer is the secret of power in every life under the sun," he wrote.

Intercessory prayer has an effect on us. We cannot hold ill will or animosity toward people if we keep praying for them. While we may not change others, the act of prayer may change us. Intercessory prayer is "the best arbitrator of all differences among human beings, the best promoter of true friendships and the best cure for envy and jealousy."

Prayer for others changes our disposition and energizes our wills. It troubles our consciences and moves our wills to action. When we pray for another, Sassoon said, we are not just asking God to take an interest in those for whom we pray. "We are simply rendering proof to God of our interest in them, are submitting that interest to him for purification and are thus making ourselves sensitive to his guidance and receptive to his power." Prayer, Sassoon concluded, "is love raised to its greatest power.[14]

Articles on other spiritual disciplines also appeared in the pages of *The Christian*. For example, Thomas Slavens, the librarian at Drake Divinity School, encouraged going on retreats. He noted that before selecting the twelve apostles, Jesus went out into the hills to seek fellowship with God and growth in understanding.

When away from home on a retreat people grow in love for one another and for God. A retreat is a time when we may listen for God and hear that "still small voice." But to hear it, we have to cultivate our ability to listen. A retreat provides a good setting for that cultivation.[15]

Jasper Timbs encouraged self-examination as a spiritual discipline. Such an inner look brings our thoughts, standards, and beliefs under the judgment of God. Exposing our life to God in this way has many benefits. Timbs listed the removal of illusions of self-importance, becoming more God centered, growth in grace, and the keeping of faith alive as benefits of self-examination. He concluded, "Take no shelter behind the adequacy of your own virtues without submitting them to God in self-examination.

The use of a spiritual director to help us grow in our relationship with God was advocated by Harold Edwards, a pastor in El Paso, Texas. This has not been a traditional Disciples practice, but one in which interest has grown in recent years. Edwards pointed out what many have experienced, that people are led to the gospel and the acceptance of Christ, but then left there without much further guidance.

There is an assumption that as we pray, study, and work, we will grow in our faith. However, we are not often given good guidance in how we must pray, study, and work. There is a need for people who have experienced "the deeper realities of faith" to help the rest of us on the way. Christians who have lived in the contemplative tradition have usually had spiritual directors, but those of us living out in the world have lacked that kind of guidance. Edwards concluded, "Let's explore the practice of spiritual direction and restore it to the life of the church."[16]

Harold Roberts pushed for the "Cultivation of the Devotional Life," in a 1969 article in *The Christian*. He complained that we do not pray enough, that we lack a sense of reference, and that we worship poorly. We live in a world that is so noisy we cannot hear God. Consequently, we fail to commune with God. We are frustrated at our ability to know God and want to pray with Job, "Oh, that I knew where I might find him!" Hence, the emptiness of life.

It does not have to be like this, Roberts said. We can worship better. We can "sense the mystical presence of God and hear the divine voice." We can know the love and companionship of God. Such things, however, require discipline. "They are the reward of a loving quest of spiritual values. They come when we take time to be holy." There is still, he insisted, "a serious call to the devout and holy life." Communion with God is an adventure that makes it possible "to walk in the traffic of the world's life, there to heal and serve in the name of our Lord."[17]

For Cecil K. Thomas, a Professor of Biblical Theology at Phillips Graduate Seminary, the problem is that we have lost the sense of the presence of the Holy Spirit. The early church, he said, "was radiant with the activity of the Spirit within it."

Disciples are often nervous about talk of the Holy Spirit. Thomas noted that there is a fear of reviving the "confusing gifts of the Spirit in the Corinthian Church." However, that does not necessarily follow. God often works in ways we do not expect, beyond the limits we tend to set. The Spirit might embarrass our plans. "But it is certain that the Spirit of God dwelling in us will seek to change us."

An awareness of the Spirit's presence may generate sanctification, another term that makes Disciples uncomfortable. Thomas defined it as "continuing growth into the likeness of Christ." We need to recapture the idea of sanctification in order to find a new depth of Christian living.[18]

Editor and Columnist

There were a number of regular contributors to *The Christian*, editors and columnists, who wrote about spirituality issues from time to time. Howard Short had left his position as a popular professor of church history at Lexington Theological Seminary to become editor of *The Christian*. Several of his regular editorials focused on prayer.

In a 1968 piece, he wrote that "prayer is a difficult phenomenon for many people to understand." It assumes the existence of a personal God who can be contacted by us. Short said that we are not always sure what we are doing when we pray. The "ask and you shall receive" teaching of Jesus, he believed, was overemphasized in Christian piety to the point that people become very self-centered in prayer. Consequently, we neglect our own role in the answering of our prayers.[19]

An editorial on observing World Communion Sunday remarked that the Disciples "have made their highest witness to the oneness of the Church at the Lord's Table." He noted that Disciples have not always agreed on the meaning of the Lord's Supper, and that young ministers tended to think that the older generation of ministers did not give enough attention to the deeper meaning of the observance.

However, apart from that, Short affirmed that Disciples did tend to think that the Table was a place where God was encountered. "We have created an atmosphere where individuals have felt that God said something to them direct. They have communed and have felt good effects from the experience."[20]

This notion of an encounter with the Divine also appeared in an editorial on Easter. Short's theme was that Jesus is "eternally contemporary." The risen Christ is a presence that can be known in human experience. People, said Short, "have been awakening to the sense of his presence all through the centuries." He cited John Wesley as an example of one who was not successful in his ministry "until his heart was strangely warmed by the presence of Christ in an Aldersgate meeting." Christ is a living presence for all of us.[21]

God has been revealed in history and that revelation is not just in the past but constant, Short affirmed in an editorial titled "Access to Mystery." While some people think that God is shrouded in such mystery that only a few can really comprehend, Short insisted that every person can know God. All of us can know God through reason and experience. "Used wisely, and with due consideration to the history we have at hand, they make the mystery meaningful." We do not have to contemplate God in abstractions, Short said. Jesus lived in history. "He has a concrete history about which to reason."[22]

Charles Kemp was a distinguished professor of pastoral care and counseling at Brite Divinity School. He was a popular teacher and a strong influence on several generations of Disciple ministers. He wrote a regular column in *The Christian* that appeared under several different general headings, but each one had its own title. In general, the pieces dealt with pastoral care matters. He had a strong interest in spirituality, knew the classics in the field, and had obviously studied the lives of many of the saints. In several of his columns in 1969 he recommended studying St. Francis, the prayers in the Episcopal *Book of Common Prayer*,[23] Robert Louis Stevenson, Ignatius Loyola,[24] Augustine, the prayers of the Gelasian Sacramentary, and Walter Russell Bowie.[25] He wrote with appreciation of the mystics "who depended primarily on periods of silence and meditation and the inner voice."[26] Some of his columns were repetitious, but those who read them regularly would have learned much about prayer and the spiritual life at a level far above that of the usual popular devotional writing.

A number of his columns dealt with the issue of religious experience, a topic not particularly common to rational oriented Disciples. In one on "Varieties of Religious Experience," Kemp noted that people have different approaches to religious experience. However, he listed five common elements. First, people who have deep religious experience are sincere. "Without sincerity there can be no great religious experience." Second, all had a deep personal need. The needs may have been different: meaning, forgiveness, guidance, strength, but there was some fundamental need that led to religious experience. Third, people who had had religious experiences usually gave themselves in service to others. Fourth, all had faith in something beyond themselves. Their theologies might be different, but they had a sense of being dependent on God. Finally, Kemp noted that they had an element of adventure in their religion. "Their religion was not proved by argument but by experience." This was a long way from Campbell's definition of faith as belief in testimony.[27]

Kemp understood that we have different levels of religious experience. For example, attending church may be a vital enriching experience for some people, while for others it is a habit with little meaning. Church membership can be life-changing for some; for others it is just a matter of belonging to another community organization. He asked, "How sincere and persistent have I been in my attempts to understand spiritual realities, to live by faith and learn to live a life guided by prayer and characterized by dedication and commitment?"

He admitted that we cannot live on the mountaintop all the time. Even the great saints, Kemp noted, had their periods of dryness, doubt, and uncertainty, "yet they also had moments of awareness, periods of spiritual insight." The keys, he believed, are sincerity of desire, persistence of effort, and the courage of commitment.[28]

One of the key factors in the spiritual life, for Kemp, was continuing growth. "Spiritual growth is the primary demand of all Christians," he wrote. "In fact, it should never cease." The lives of the great spiritual leaders in Christian history reveal that they never stopped growing "in their consciousness of God, in their life of prayer and worship."

Spiritual growth, Kemp believed, depends in good part upon our growing knowledge of spiritual truth: the meaning of life, the Scriptures, the value of prayer. We need to study the lives of those Christians who have something to teach us about spiritual growth. Yet the most important thing is to dedicate ourselves to lives of prayer and worship. We can read and study about prayer, but most of all we need to pray. We must find the time and we must be persistent in order to grow in prayer. Furthermore, we must practice the whole range of prayer: praise, adoration, confession, gratitude, intercession, and commitment.

Spiritual growth, for Kemp, also involved service. Self-forgetful giving of ourselves to others stimulates spiritual growth. "God is discovered by those who give themselves to the causes which he is concerned about."

Growing spiritually, as Kemp understood it, is not a painless process. Struggle, disappointment, and pain are all part of the process. Such experiences can make us cynical. Others, however, discover that in the midst of them God is present, "a very present help in time of trouble." Their issues are resolved, not always by finding answers, but by experiencing forgiveness and power.[29] The key is persistence of effort. "No one ever drifted off into a real spiritual experience. It comes after much searching and persistence of effort."[30]

Many of Kemp's columns in *The Christian* dealt with the specific issue of prayer. In a 1960 column, he listed a number of suggestions about prayer. For example, he recommended reading good books on prayer as well as some of the classics of the devotional life, those that have "stood the test of centuries." The primary source book, however, is the Bible, particularly the Psalms and the life of Jesus. Beyond that, he suggested studying the lives of people of prayer, not just preachers and theologians, but also scientists, philosophers, physicians, and statesmen.

Ultimately, however, Kemp believed that if we want to learn to pray, we must actually pray. He listed a number of realities that we must face: prayer requires time, effort, and persistence; we must follow some method of plan, we must be sincere, it must be accompanied by honest thought and effort, and it must be done in an attitude of faith. "Such prayer is the heart of religion."[31]

As a therapist, Kemp would be expected to write a column on "The Healing Power of Prayer." He began the piece, "For generations, prayer has been one of the great healing forces in life." In the article, however, he referred to many kinds of healing. Prayer has healed a lack of faith, it has healed a lack of insight and direction, it has healed guilt, it has made people aware of things for which they should be grateful, and it has healed self-centeredness by turning our attention away from ourselves and toward others. Prayer can relieve anxiety, save us from littleness, and provide quiet reassurance. It has helped people of prayer through dry periods to times of deeper faith.[32]

Kemp did not deny "The Problem of Prayer," the title of one of his columns. Many of the saints, he noted, discovered that it took years to attain the high levels of prayer we associate with them. Too many people, said Kemp, "want to start with results and not go through the struggle that produces them."

He reminded us again that reading about the prayer experiences of others is a helpful thing to do, but it is not a substitute for prayer itself. However, he did suggest reading the actual prayers of other people as a stimulus for our own prayer. But ultimately, prayer depends upon our attitudes of sincerity, humility, receptivity, and trust. With those attitudes we can pray and "use hardly any words at all."[33]

NOTES

[1] *Christian*, 1961:740-741.
[2] *C*, 1962:1508-1509.
[3] *C*, 1962:1413-1414.
[4] *C*, 1964:324-325.
[5] *C*, 1972:324-325.
[6] *C*, 1960:357.
[7] *C*, 1961:6,24.
[8] *C*, 1963:790.
[9] *C*, 1960:882.
[10] *C*, 1960:925.
[11] *C*, 1962:1317-1318.
[12] *C*, 1964:463.
[13] *C*, 1969:740.
[14] *C*, 1970:200.
[15] *C*, 1960:1096.
[16] *C*, 1965:10.
[17] *C*, 1969:72.
[18] *C*, 1961:1189-1190.
[19] *C*, 1968:40.
[20] *C*, 1961:1255.
[21] *C*, 1961:423.
[22] *C*, 1960:615.
[23] *C*, 1969:975.
[24] *C*, 1969:1039.
[25] *C*, 1969:1134.
[26] *C*, 1971:1565.
[27] *C*, 1961:650.
[28] *C*, 1963:131.
[29] *C*, 1962:494.
[30] *C*, 1971:174.
[31] *C*, 1960:498.
[32] *C*, 1969:911.
[33] *C*, 1972:1003.

6

The Disciple

The Christian-Evangelist, which had become *The Christian*, became *The Disciple* in 1974. At first a bi-weekly, economic necessity eventually caused it to become a monthly. There was unbroken continuity with its predecessor, and many of the same features continued.

One of these was Charles Kemp's columns. Some of these contained ideas previously expressed in *The Christian*, but the persistence of the spirituality theme continued. For example, Dr. Kemp discussed "Growth in the Practice of Prayer," and made several suggestions. First, reading about prayer is helpful, but should never become a substitute for prayer. Second, reading and meditating on the prayers that others have written has value in creating a mood for prayer and stimulating us to pray. We can find good models to use in patterning our own prayer. Third, and this was something not mentioned earlier, we need to develop a program of prayer.

Each person, Kemp believed, should discover those methods of prayer with which he or she would be most comfortable. We can pray kneeling, walking, or lying down. We can pray in the morning or the evening or both. We can pray out loud or silently. We can write our prayers or pray spontaneously. Different personalities will prefer different styles. We can pray in a church, in nature, or in our own private rooms. The main thing is that a place of prayer should be free from interruptions and distractions.

There are some common elements in all styles of prayer, Kemp believed. People of prayer pray "regularly, persistently and sincerely." They have disciplined themselves to pray whether they feel like it or not, and persisted "even when they were tired, confused by doubt, or discouraged.

The methods we use, said Kemp, must be open to change as our understanding and experience with prayer grow and change. What is helpful one year may not be in another year. The constant is an attitude of sincerity and commitment.

Finally, whatever way of prayer we use must include the entire range of prayer: thanksgiving, confession, intercession, petition, and commitment.[1]

A few months later he focused on the issue, "Growth in Worship." He listed a number of ways to do it. They included such items as preparing ourselves in both mind and spirit. He noted that "those who find public worship meaningful are usually the ones who find private worship meaningful." He suggested using the quiet moments in a worship service for prayer and meditation, such as before the service begins or during the serving of communion. We all need time to be still and meditate on the reality that God is with us. Finally, Kemp urged regular worship attendance. "The benefits of worship are usually achieved over a period of time. The values derived from worship are cumulative in their influence."[2]

On a related matter, Kemp had a column on finding the time to pray. He admitted that with all the demands of job, family, community, and church, this is a real problem for many people. He suggested that we honestly evaluate our own schedules and see if we are making the best use of the time we have. Is everything we do really so worthwhile as to crowd out time for prayer? Even in the midst of busy lives, we can express thanks for the good things in our lives, confess to God our mistakes, and pray for others. "God hears the prayer of intercession just as well when we are busy as when we are at worship." There are many times during the day when we can offer silent petitions for guidance when we have to make decisions and meet responsibilities. The important point is that regular prayer, however we work it into our daily lives, "reminds us that we are always in God's presence and can communicate directly to his Spirit."[3]

Kemp once illustrated the value of prayer in building personal faith by telling the story of an agnostic woman who was challenged by an Episcopal priest to pray for five minutes a day for thirty days. She was to do this in solitude and muster as much faith as she could that God would be revealed to her.

She agreed to try, but for a while nothing happened. Her husband ridiculed the idea. But at the end of the thirty days something happened. "She had the feeling of God's presence, a new sense of direction."

Kemp saw four values in the woman's effort. First, she sought help. Second, she learned about prayer by praying. Third, she persevered in spite of discouragement. Fourth, this act of prayer diverted attention from herself and her personal problems to something beyond herself. The story reinforced Kemp's constant admonition in his columns to be persistent in prayer.[4]

In the area of spiritual disciplines, Kemp lamented the fact that Protestantism has no sacrament of penance. There is something deep within us, he believed, that makes us want to atone for our guilt in some way. The Roman Catholic tradition had the practice of penance. Many people have self-imposed a penance on themselves. Sometimes this takes the form of giving money to churches or agencies, many of which Kemp believed would be in serious financial trouble of if no one ever felt any guilt!

He reminded us that penance is not a matter of buying the forgiveness of sins. We receive that through repentance and faith and God's grace. "Penance," he said, "is a means whereby we take the wrong we may have done and make it both creative and redemptive."[5]

Finally, Kemp reminded pastors that they are supposed to be persons of prayer. "The pastor has many responsibilities," he wrote, "but he or she should, first of all, be a person of prayer." Beyond those occasions of public prayer and prayer with individuals should be the solitary times when a pastor prays. Included in those prayers should be intercessions for the people in his or her congregation.[6]

Another regular columnist in *The Disciple* was Rev. C. Roy Stauffer, the Senior Minister of Lindenwood Christian Church in Memphis. His piece, "Since You Asked," appeared at the end of each issue and was a response to questions sent to him. One person asked, "Just how important is it for the Christian to pray every day? Is it necessary?"

Stauffer's answer was a ringing affirmative. Prayer, he believed, is fundamental to our faith, the basic source of power for Christianity. "Prayer is the soul of religion," he wrote, "the language of the Christian community, and the heart of the Christian life. Without it we have nothing."

For Stauffer, the depth of our faith is directly related to the depth and constancy of our prayer lives. He described prayer as "mystical." We don't understand it, but experience teaches us that it does work. "More things that could happen don't happen because people don't pray," he concluded. Stauffer noted that there is "a hungering and thirsting for a new spirituality. But," he said, "it will never come without the power of prayer."[7]

One issue Stauffer wrestled with was prompted by a reader's question, "Since the Scriptures tell us that God already knows what we need before we ask, why pray?" His answer was basically that prayer opens us to God. God does not use force in coming into our lives, but comes into our hearts and lives when we open the way.[8]

In recent years there has been a change in the language of prayer. Newer translations of the Bible that no long use "thees" and "thous" have had some influence in removing those terms from prayers and substituting the more familiar "you" in addressing God.

Professor Keith Watkins, who recently retired from years of teaching worship at Christian Theological Seminary, has written about that subject. In an article in *The Christian* he had urged the use of contemporary language in prayer in public worship. He called for change "from the archaic to the contemporary." We need a kind of craftsmanship in composing prayers that we have not needed before. "This means," he said, "that people need to write prayers, at least for use in the study even if public prayer continues to be extemporaneous."[9]

In *The Disciple*, Professor Watkins focused on the question of inclusive language in prayer. He urged avoiding the use of gender related language in referring to God, and provided a number of examples.

For instance, in using ascriptions of sovereignty, Watkins noted that terms such as "king, lord, master" are no longer used in our political experience. A more gender neutral term like "ruler" would be preferable.

Ascriptions of creativity, such as "creator" and "maker," tend to be more gender neutral. However, there are additional possibilities that express more fully the work of God, such as "sustainer, source, fountain, fashioner." In trying to characterize God's beneficence, we might use terms such as "redeemer, savior, guardian, healer," which have no gender reference.

One of the most controversial language issues in prayer is the use of "Father." It was a term often used in reference to God. Is it an appropriate term to use in a day when we are trying to see beyond the limitations of gender? Watkins thinks that we use the term frequently, not because we have experiences of God as Father, but because we do not give enough thought to our prayers.

There are some, said Watkins, who want all masculine terminology stricken from prayer. Others are willing to keep Father if a corresponding Mother-language is developed to broaden our understanding of God. The other option is to develop language that transcends the male/female division. The challenge is "to develop a richer and truer set of metaphors and figures with which to speak of God."[10]

Joseph B. Fitch was a local church pastor who had a keen interest in early Disciple history. He wrote several articles for both *The Christian,* and *The Disciple* about the founding fathers of the denomination. In an article in *The Christian*, he wrote that although Alexander Campbell and other early leaders were opposed to what they thought was "a false mysticism," they did believe in prayer. Walter Scott felt a need for the "morning hour" and felt that devotional practice should begin when young.

For a long time, however, Fitch said, our leaders did not teach much about prayer. In recent years that has changed, and the emergence of popular Spiritual Life Conferences has filled a need felt by many people. Fitch called for local churches to study the life of prayer. Unfortunately, Fitch said, many of our pastors have not had enough experience with prayer to lead such a study successfully.[11]

For *The Disciple*, Fitch wrote an article called "Our Praying Forefathers," in which he focused on Alexander Campbell's development in the area of prayer. He listed some of Campbell's idiosyncrasies on prayer. For example, Campbell believed it was shocking that some people sat while in prayer, he attacked "commodious" houses of worship, he believed that sinners could not pray, he opposed the mourner's bench, he was against "praying societies," and said that "spiritual influences" had no relationship to salvation. Fitch noted that Campbell modified some of this thinking on prayer later in life under the influence of Robert Richardson, Walter Scott, and Barton Stone. Campbell did believe, said Fitch, that prayer could be used to understand the Scriptures, "though never at the expense of reason."[12]

Royal Humbert, for many years a professor at Eureka College, had a more devastating article on Campbell in *The Disciple*. He believed that in reacting to the abuses of mysticism, Campbell overreacted. His view of God as creator and lawgiver made God seem remote from human experience. This kind of theology left no room for any immediate sense of God's presence in one's life and no element of sacred mystery. Humbert himself spoke a good word for mystical Christianity. "In contemplation," he wrote, "we come to the awareness of the ineffable reality of what is beyond experience." Early Disciple leaders wanted to purify corruptions in faith, but "it is the task of our generation to fill the spiritual vacuum left by that purification process."[13]

There was a wide variety of general articles in *The Disciple* about prayer. They ranged from admonitions by Robert Bray and Heber H. Pitman[14] to use the Lord's Prayer as a model prayer, to news reports about Easter Prayer Vigils.[15]

Bonnie Bowman Thurston, a professor of New Testament at Wheeling Jesuit College and, for a time, President of the Thomas Merton Society, had a fine article on the importance of praying in solitude and silence. Solitude is important because it forces us to confront our own nothing-ness. Noise, she said, is "the most dangerous spiritual pollutant in our society." We want sound around us and we make sound because we are spiritually lonely. Unfortu-nately, that cuts us off from what can ultimately overcome our loneliness.

Thurston offered some practical suggestions for daily prayer. One is to set aside a time and place for solitary prayer. Another was to use short prayers throughout the day. She did not oppose praying with other Christians and felt that could be a source of strength, but the emphasis in this article was on the importance of solitude. Finally, she suggested taking advantage of retreats and other events where prayer is discussed and taught.[16]

Robert Gaylord, minister of Cascade Christian Church in Grand Rapids, Michigan, did a little survey of what people are asking their pastors. He reported that the top two were, "Why do people suffer, experience pain, and die at an early age?" and "Does God truly answer prayer?"[17]

Kenneth A. McCullough noted that sometimes chil-dren die when whole communities have prayed for them, when their parents are faithful Christians, and the chil-dren themselves are incapable of doubt. Prayer is misdi-rected, he said, if it is used to try to manipulate God. McCullough said that sometimes his prayers in such cases are more of "an unarticulate groan" than requests for God to change the natural order of creation. "So, I pray, not for miraculous healing, but for strength, courage, hope, caring presence and community to help see me and others through whatever comes." The important point is that we do not have to go through our suffering alone.[18]

Dale Patrick wrote about facing the reality of our an-ger with God in prayer. There is no reason why we should accept suffering passively and without protest. Expressing our anger to God is an important part of prayer. Patrick said, "I have detected a new receptivity among Christians to Job's angry prayer. For the first time in Christian his-tory, the outcry of the psalmist, the bitter complaining of Jeremiah and the outrageous blasphemies of Job appear justified to many believers."

Why should we deny our anger when we or someone we love has suffered unjustly? Why should we not face our doubts and fears in prayer? Using the story of Job as an illustration, Patrick called for honest prayer. The danger of self-pity is always there, but as long as our protest is part of our dialogue with God, we have a check on our self-righteousness.[19]

One of the concerns people have had in recent years is whether seminaries are doing enough to foster the spiritual development of ministerial students. In a 1977 article, William Paulsell asked, "Are We Teaching Ministers to Pray?" He noted that seminaries have had problems with teaching subjects like prayer because it is difficult to deal with them academically. However, students can study the classical literature in the field, and that can be part of an academic program.[20]

Harold Lunger, a professor at Brite Divinity School, and Alberta Lunger responded to Paulsell's piece by describing what his seminary at Texas Christian University was doing about the matter. A course in "Spiritual Resources and Disciplines" was being offered. The purpose of the course was "to help participants in their spiritual development, so that they may have inner resources for their own ministries and become equipped to lead others into a more vital spiritual life." In the class, students would explore a variety of traditions and styles of spirituality.[21]

Alberta Lunger influenced many people through retreats and other events that she led. Kathleen Joy Morgan wrote an article about Mrs. Lunger in 1976, expressing appreciation for her leadership in the area of spirituality. She told how Mrs. Lunger committed herself to ninety days of morning quiet time in which she went through "a thorough inner housecleaning." She found peace in her life and freedom from mood shifts that had once been a problem for her. Mrs. Lunger said that if you really want a regular quiet time you must ask God for it and then accept the discipline of meeting God there.

As her spiritual life developed, Alberta Lunger developed her "Seven L's." They were:

1. Love God with all the heart, soul, and mind.
2. Look into the face of Jesus. Every day, look at a picture of Jesus and also look at him in the gospel stories of his life.

3. Loosen every attachment to things, people, our wants and desires, and our defiant self-reliant ego.
4. Learn from His word. Read the Bible, primarily the Gospels, small portions at a time.
5. Listen in silence for his voice within.
6. Lift others to God in intercession, in loving identification with them in their need.
7. Live our faith, moment by moment, as we go forth from the quiet time.[22]

There were a variety of miscellaneous articles about prayer that appeared in *The Disciple* from time to time. Henry F. Henrichs, the editor of *Sunshine* magazine and founder of a press that published inspirational literature, said that it is the ten minutes after prayer that matters, ten minutes of waiting for God. So often we pray, and before God can give an answer, "we are up and away!" The psalmist said, "Be still and know that I am God." Henrichs said, "Be still after prayer and hear God."[23]

Keeping a journal as a way of fostering a strong prayer life was advocated by Gary Prichard, formerly the pastor of Irving Park Christian Church in Chicago and later in the word processing business. A journal, he said, becomes a record of our spiritual growth. "Months later," he wrote, "you will see how God has responded to your prayers. You will see our petitions and intercessions of yesterday become thanksgivings in the days that follow."

He described prayer as "simply conversation with God." For Prichard, it could be:

Asking for help.
A request in behalf of someone else.
Simply saying "Thank you" or "I'm sorry."
A time of quiet adoration and listening.
Sharing your hopes and dreams with God.

Prichard developed journal worksheets that could be ordered from him. A sample worksheet was shown in *The Disciple*, and included the following headings, under which a person was to write about the topic.

Being Present to God—Events of My Day
Admitting My Mistakes
My Concerns for the World
My Concerns for Others

> Offering and Dedicating My Life
> This was the Great Day of _____.
> Looking Ahead and Asking God's Help
> My Hopes
> My Plans
> Help Requested

Prichard insisted that we should not feel enslaved to a particular structure for prayer. His suggestions were just for getting started. There might be time when no stimulus was needed. A journal, however, provides a basic discipline for prayer.[24]

Ralph Palmer, at one time on the staff of the United Christian Missionary Society and later Chair of the Division of Science and Math at Jarvis Christian College, had a thoughtful article on answers to prayer. He noted that "most of us have difficulty in recognizing and accepting God's answer to prayer these days."

People who tell us that God has spoken directly to them tend to be suspect, Palmer said. We hear too many stories of people doing terrible things, like murder, because God told them to do it. It is difficult, sometimes, to tell the difference between an authentic claim to religious experience and mental illness.

Palmer affirmed that God does answer prayer, but it may be with a "Yes," a "No," a "Maybe," or even by causing us to wait for a time. God opens and closes doors for us and often gives us a choice of possibilities, any of which may have good outcomes.

It is hard to accept a "No" answer, but we forget that "only God can see the whole picture." However, that may be the fulfillment of the prayer, "Thy will be done."[25]

Concern about the decline of Disciple membership was expressed by James T. Grooms, an Ohio pastor. He praised the denomination for developing new curriculum, restructuring itself, and the new reconciliation effort. However, he believed that now we needed something deeper, the restructuring of our spiritual lives. This should be an effort no less massive than the Restructure itself. He called for the putting together of a panel on the inner life "to study the mystical relationship between God and man, develop the disciplines of devotion and meditation which enable Christians to experience the real presence of God, distribute the rich treasury of classical and contemporary helps at a reasonable price, and foster Christian experience through making available such materials for home libraries."[26]

There were occasional references to popular forms of Eastern spirituality. For example, William A. Longman, a Peoria, Illinois, pastor, noted the popularity of transcendental meditation, which many were using as a relaxation technique. Longman felt that it was actually a religion and should be seen as such. Its weakness, he felt, was that it did not emphasize a power beyond as well as within, which is God. Life is more than just living calmly. However, the idea of meditating on one word as suggested by a fourteenth century classic, *The Cloud of Unknowing*, did have some appeal.

"I challenge you," offered Longman, "to try sitting quietly in a comfortable, relaxed position for ten or twenty minutes, without saying or thinking a word save "God." It may well be a whole new experience in this noisy world! You, too, can live with steadfastness and serenity, not being anxious about tomorrow, letting God guide you today."[27]

NOTES

[1]*D*, July 21, 1974:14.
[2]*D*, October 27, 1974:24.
[3]*D*, February 19, 1978:19.
[4]*D*, April 17, 1977:14.
[5]*D*, April 20, 1975:18.
[6]*D*, February 15, 1976:29.
[7]*D*, February, 1984:50.
[8]*D*, August, 1987:66.
[9]*C*, January 7, 1968:7.
[10]*D*, July 1, 1979:7-9.
[11]*C*, September 25, 1960:1224-1225.
[12]*D*, January 17, 1982:12-14.
[13]*D*, January 4, 1976:12-14.
[14]*D*, October 5, 1975:38 and January 16, 1977:19.
[15]*D*, May 21, 1978:21.
[16]*D*, January, 1985:15-16.
[17]*D*, January, 1986:11-13.
[18]*D*, January, 1984:16-17.
[19]*D*, July 15, 1979:35.
[20]*D*, February 6, 1977:9-10.
[21]*D*, February 20, 1977:13-14.
[22]*D*, July 18, 1976:37-38.
[23]*D*, March 21, 1982:8-9.
[24]*D*, April, 1988:26-29.
[25]*D*, November, 1987:32-34.
[26]*D*, March 31, 1974:10-11.
[27]*D*, January 2, 1987:2-4.

Conclusion

Disciple spirituality has come a long way since the early nineteenth century. There have been so many approaches to the matter that we actually should speak of Disciple spiritualities.

Alexander Campbell was suspicious of any claim to religious experience, and believed that all that was needed for the Christian was belief in the testimony of the New Testament. When he spoke of communion with God, he did not have in mind the mystical sense. Rather, it was a matter of God speaking to us through scripture and our speaking to God through prayer. Any kind of spiritual experience would only reflect what is already in the Bible.

Probably the most controversial element in his thought was the belief that God does not hear the prayers of people who have no faith. There can be no Christian experience prior to conversion.

Robert Richardson emphasized the importance of communion with God. For him, Christianity was not just morality. Rather its purpose was to unite us with God. He used phrases such as "the intercourse of the soul with God," and "habitual fellowship with God," and he believed that "reason must be subjected to the mysteries of revelation."

Barton Stone agreed with Campbell that we know God by having faith in the scriptural testimony. However, he did believe in prayer before baptism. He saw prayer as the foundation of holy living. It produced an habitual sense of God's presence and an awareness of our dependence on God. He was less rigid than Campbell in that he did not believe that there had to be a biblical warrant for everything done in worship.

In the early years of *The Christian-Evangelist* there was much emphasis on praying for the evangelization of the world. J. H. Garrison had real appreciation for modern science. In facing the question of whether God, whom he called the great Evolver, would violate natural law to answer a prayer, Garrison said there is much about natural law we do not know. Perhaps it is possible for nature to be modified by spiritual forces. He compared electricity with the unseen spiritual forces in the universe.

Frederick D. Kershner was one of the first to call boldly for a mystical element in religion. He believed that the New Testament was filled with mysticism. J. H. Garrison had a similar appreciation, and Edward Scribner Ames wrote of prayer as "rising to the level of the Divine Mind."

In *The Christian* there were a number of articles emphasizing the need for Christians to continue searching and to face their own doubts. John Thompson wrote of the importance of growing in our knowledge of God, an idea echoed by Charles Kemp. Kemp himself attempted to teach his readers about the Christian mystical tradition and the great spiritual classics. Now we are seeing references to the value of having a spiritual director and going on retreats.

The Disciple opens up some new themes: the use of modern and inclusive language in prayer, the values of nonverbal prayer, and the need to be honest when we are angry with God. The language of Christian mysticism continues to appear.

Yes, the Disciples do have a strong tradition of spirituality. It is clearly worthy of study. It is too bad that it is not more widely known. Kershner, Kemp, Ames, Garrison, and many others have all contributed to it in profound ways.

Who can say where we will go in the future in our spirituality? We have certainly moved from a rather narrow biblicism to an appreciation of what the whole Christian tradition has to teach us. We have become truly ecumenical as we have drawn from the experience of the whole church. When Disciples make retreats at Catholic monasteries, study Orthodox spirituality, see what they can learn from the Wesleyan tradition, adopt some Episcopal liturgical elements, and are willing to dialogue with anyone who has something useful to teach about spirituality, we have been true to our ecumenical heritage. We have said that Christian unity is our polar star, and that star has led us to explore traditions that would have made our founding father shudder.

So, it may be that we have accomplished more ecumenically than we have realized. We have found unity, not at the institutional level, but at the level of spirituality, and that is a development of enormous importance.

Appendix:
Books by Disciples on Prayer

While this book has focused on periodical literature published by Disciples, it is important to know that Disciples have produced many books on prayer and spirituality. It is impossible to list, much less find, them all, but here is a sampling of a number of our important efforts.

Reference has already been made to Robert Richardson's columns in the *Millennial Harbinger* titled "Communings in the Sanctuary." In 1872 a volume of "Communings" was published. The chapters covered both public and private worship and made reference to communion with the unseen, fellowship with God, arrangements favorable to devotion, penitence, the mysteries of the gospel, and other related matters. Richardson affirmed that establishing and maintaining communion with God is "the great end of religion."

J. H. Garrison, a former editor of *The Christian-Evangelist*, published a book in 1891 called *Alone with God*. It was designed as a series of meditations with forms of prayer for private devotion, family worship, and other occasions. Approximately half of the book contains instruction on prayer and half consists of prayers composed by Garrison himself on a wide variety of topics.

In a 1896 book, *The Heavenward Way*, designed for new converts, Garrison said, "If there be no desire to pray, no conscious need of prayer, one may well doubt the genuineness of his conversion. The hunger of the new-born child is not more natural than the hunger of the new-born soul for God, and the absence of any such desire may well alarm any one as to his spiritual condition" (p. 35).

Herbert L. Willett, long associated with the Disciples Divinity House at the University of Chicago, and Charles Clayton Morrison, once an editor of *The Christian Century*, put together *The Daily Altar*, a book of prayers for each day of the year. For each day there is a theme statement, a brief scripture passage, and a prayer.

Two books by Kirby Page deserve mention. Page, best known for his work with the YMCA, was a social activist with a deep spirituality. He published *Religious Resources for Personal Living and Social Action* in 1939. The first quarter of the book contains a discussion of his philosophy about various matters such as peace and social reform. It also has chapters on seeking companionship in prayer and action and on worshiping God in silence, beauty, and harmony.

The major part of the book consists of fourteen weeks of daily readings. Each reading is about four pages in length. There are several prose readings, some poetry, and prayers for each day selected from the writings of people such as Harry Emerson Fosdick, Rufus Jones, William Cullen Bryant, Evelyn Underhill, the Gelasian Prayer Book, Christina Rosetti, Ralph Waldo Emerson, Julian of Norwich, Reinhold Niebuhr, and many others. It reveals an astonishing familiarity with a broad range of literature.

In 1941, Page produced *Living Prayerfully*, designed to stimulate the practice of the presence of God and the following of Jesus' way of life. It, too, contained a variety of prayers and readings, grouped around the subjects of awe and adoration, praise and thanksgiving, contrition and confession, aspiration and commitment, petition and intercession, communion and fellowship, and social action.

In 1952 he also published a little booklet called "How to Pray." His social concerns come through strongly. For example, he suggested, "Spend time before God in thinking about the distance toward the Third World War the nations have already traveled, and contemplate the speed at which they are now moving toward the brink of the cataclysm. Try to think God's thoughts about the race of armaments" (p. 24). The booklet ends with, "Praying can become the most important thing you do, because it can fill you with creative power and radiant joy" (p. 29).

Peter Ainslie, one of the early ecumenical leaders of the Disciples and for many years pastor of Christian Temple in Baltimore, wrote a brief little book, *God and Me* (1908). He regarded it as a "Brief Manual of the Principles that Make for a Closer Relationship of the Believer with God." He wrote, "To be on speaking terms with God is my greatest privilege. Just to pray is the sweetest condition of human life." The book begins with a Morning Prayer, covers a variety of topics about our relationship with God, and concludes with an Evening Prayer.

The Disciples published a number of small pamphlets on prayer by some of the major leaders of the church. For example, The Committee on War Services of the Disciples of Christ put out one on "Training the Devotional Life" by G. Edwin Osborn, for many years a professor at Phillips Graduate Seminary. Osborn stated, "The lifting up of your soul to God in personal devotion is one of the most important things you can ever do." He discussed the problem of finding time for prayer, suggested "Helpful Ways of Praying," and provided ideas for using the Bible in prayer. He defined prayer as "quietly waiting in the silence with God, 'practicing His Presence,' communing with Him, entering into spiritual fellowship with His purpose, exchanging thoughts and desires with Him."

The Christian Board of Publication's Bethany Tracts series included "God Answers Prayer" by A. W. Fortune, dean of The College of the Bible and later senior minister of Central Christian Church in Lexington, Kentucky. The answering of prayer by God, he said, cannot be scientifically proven; it is a matter of faith. But he affirmed, "Prayer not only enables us to make use of the power that we have, but it gives us additional power. It puts us in touch with the great God upon whom we are dependent."

A. Dale Fiers, for many years president of the United Christian Missionary Society and the first general minister and president of the restructured Disciples, wrote a little booklet, "Lord, Teach Us to Pray," published by the Department of Christian Women's Fellowship of the UCMS in 1960. Fiers suggested that we study the power of prayer in Jesus' life, then get to know some of the great saints who revealed the power of prayer in their lives, and finally, learn about prayer from people "near at hand who have demonstrated the mastery of spiritual power through prayer." The next step, then, is to discover the power of prayer within ourselves and how this relates to our Christian lives. He offered some suggestions on praying prayers of praise and thanksgiving, petition, and intercession.

George Earle Owen published a little book on *The Nature of Prayer* in which he illustrated prayer by using poetry, much of which had appeared earlier in Disciples periodicals.

A number of publications on prayer were related to our foreign mission efforts. The old Foreign Christian Missionary Society published "Intercessory Prayer" by Archibald McLean. McLean complained that "intercessory prayer is neglected by the Church at the present time." He did affirm, however, that "If prayer is to be definite and fervent and in faith, it must be intelligent." We must know about the things for which we wish to pray. The thrust of this pamphlet was the need to pray for those on the mission field.

In 1929 the UCMS published "Come Ye Apart, A Year of Missionary Devotions for the Individual," edited by Mayme Jackson Scott. She and her husband had been missionaries in India. C. Manly Morton, a missionary in the Caribbean area and South America and the first male graduate of Atlantic Christian College, wrote *Adventures in Prayer*, published in 1966. He described a series of crises in his missionary career that led to a deepening of his own prayer life. He affirmed, "What we say in prayer has very little importance—it is what is uppermost in our hearts that really matters to God." He said that the purpose of prayer is not to change God, but to change us, "to get ourselves in a condition so that we are able to receive that which God wants to give us."

The Christian Women's Fellowship Department of the UCMS published a little booklet, "A Manual for Prayer Groups" in 1955. It was written by Harold Freer and Francis B. Hall and suggested that an active prayer group can revitalize a whole congregation. The booklet provided suggestions for organizing a group, the kind of discipline the group should expect of its members, how to integrate new members, and what to do when the group gets too large or stagnates.

Several more recent books have expanded on that subject. In 1974 Charles F. Kemp, whose columns have already been cited, published *Prayer-Based Growth Groups*. He, too, discussed methods and procedures for developing groups. He understood such a group to be "a small group of people who are seeking to attain growth in their understanding of religion and in religious experiences which should result in growth in personal awareness and self-fulfillment."

After describing the organization of groups, he provided a number of classical prayers with commentaries on them. The prayers reveal Kemp's broad knowledge of the classical tradition of Christian spirituality.

Robert Boyte, pastor of First Christian Church in Decatur, Georgia, and his daughter Kelly Boyte Peters, pastor of First Christian Church in Henry, Illinois, wrote *Spiritual Growth in the Congregation* (1988). They recognize that many people are seeking something deeper in their church life these days. Many are searching for some kind of experience with God. Each chapter of the book gives a guideline for developing spiritual growth in a congregation. For example, a congregation should develop programs for prayer and study as well as for social justice. People need to become more comfortable with "lesser-known" images of God. There is a need to guard against "spiritual elitism." At the end of the book there are specific programmatic suggestions.

Disciples have published a large amount of daily devotional material. For many years we have been publishing *The Secret Place*, a daily devotional guide modeled after the Methodist *Upper Room*. Today the Christian Board of Publication provides devotional books to be used on a daily basis during Advent and Lent.

In 1943, *Every Day a Prayer* by Margueritte Harmon Bro, a former missionary, appeared. It contained a scripture passage, a brief meditation, and a prayer for each day of the year. In 1952 the Bethany Press published *Forty Days with Jesus* by M. E. Willcockson, which consisted of a scripture, a meditation, and a prayer for each day of Lent. More recently Katherine Kinnamon, chaplain at

Midway College, and Michael Kinnamon, Dean of Lexington Theological Seminary, published a book of daily prayer titled *Every Day We Will Bless You*. The book has a helpful chapter on the importance of daily prayer, the history of that practice in the church, and recommendations for a pattern of daily prayer. There follows a four-week cycle of materials. For each day there is an opening prayer, a psalm, a scripture reading, and suggestions for intercessions. Three themes cycle through the days: reconciliation with the church, reconciliation with neighbor, and reconciliation with God. The emphasis for each Sunday is the Lord's Supper. The book concludes with a variety of materials that may be used to enhance daily prayer.

Leslie Smith, senior minister of Central Christian Church in Lexington, Kentucky, wrote *Four Keys to Prayer,* which he dedicated to the eight prayer groups in his congregation. The book contains four sermons he preached as part of the church's School of Prayer program. Their topics were listening, meditating, receiving, and giving. Each sermon is preceded by a brief devotional for each day of the week.

Mabel A. Niedermeyer's book, *Some Time Every Day*, published by the Bethany Press in 1948, contains devotional material for boys and girls in the Junior Department of a local church. Each devotional is one-and-a-half to two pages in length and contains a meditation, often in story form, and a prayer.

In 1970, the Disciples Divinity House of the University of Chicago published *Prayers and Meditations* by Edward Scribner Ames. The book is divided into two roughly equal parts, the first part containing prayers Ames had written, and the second part containing meditations he had used in a variety of circumstances. Ames was one who felt that the Disciples had neglected their liberal heritage, and his meditations reflect that outlook.

Disciples have written many books on prayer. Lloyd V. Channels, a Michigan pastor, wrote *The Layman Learns to Pray*. He described prayer as conversation with God, and his book discusses the content of prayer, how God speaks to us, and attempts to answer some questions people often have about prayer. For him, the fruits of prayer included a better understanding of God and ourselves, an increase in our sense of kinship with others and a better understanding of the world, the fulfilling of God's purpose for us, the bringing of God's help, and the maintenance of good health and peace of mind.

John W. Harms' *Prayer in the Market Place* deals with the issue of offering prayers on secular occasions such as the opening of conventions, commencement exercises, NAACP mass meetings, political gatherings, and other similar occasions. After an introduction, the book contains prayers that have been used at such events.

G. Curtis Jones, a Disciples pastor, wrote *Patterns of Prayer*, published by Bethany Press in 1964. For this book he collected many definitions and understandings of prayer from others. He had good suggestions for prayers by pastors and included a number of prayers on various topics.

Please Lead Us in Prayer (1980) was written by Norman L. Cullumber for those who are called on to pray, often at the last minute. It contains suggestions for prayers at various occasions such as at the time of death, at the beginnings of meetings, for anniversaries, and other occasions. It also gives good instructions for invocations, pastoral prayers, and offertory and communion prayers. A number of sample prayers are included in this valuable book.

A good basic book on beginning to pray is Nancy Cook's *Prayer Primer*, published by Net Press in Lubbock, Texas. It is designed for both individuals and groups. After some introductory material on the basics of prayer, five exercises are presented based on the themes of getting to know God, being thankful, forgiveness, guidance, and asking.

William Paulsell's *Taste and See: A Personal Guide to the Spiritual Life* and *Rules for Prayer* draw on the classical Christian spiritual tradition for suggestions about deepening one's prayer life.

Living Inside Out by Jan Linn, a professor at Lexington Theological Seminary, explores how to pray the Serenity Prayer. This prayer, attributed to American theologian Reinhold Niebuhr, is familiar to many and begins, "God give us the grace to accept with serenity things that cannot be changed; courage to change the things that should be changed; and the wisdom to distinguish the one from the other." Professor Linn looks at this prayer in depth and discusses the many possibilities for personal prayer based on it. He has chapters that explore the meanings of the key words in this prayer.

Bonnie Bowman Thurston, a Disciple New Testament scholar, has a book on *Spiritual Life in the Early Church* (1993). Specifically, it is a study of the spirituality and prayer of Acts and Ephesians.

We have many collections of prayers. Toyozo W. Nakarai, for many years a professor of Old Testament at Christian Theological Seminary, published two editions of *An Elder's Public Prayers.*

Our Christian Board of Publication has produced a number of books of prayers for elders. In 1925 a collection edited by B. A. Abbott, a former *Christian-Evangelist* editor, was produced under the title *At the Master's Table*. It contained poems, meditations, and prayers for use at communion services. The book went through twelve printings, the latest in 1955.

Thomas Toler wrote *The Elder at the Lord's Table*, published in 1954, which would go through thirteen printings until 1977. After presenting a brief history of the Lord' Supper, Toler discussed the qualifications of elders. The third section of the book contains communion prayers by a variety of people.

Merrill Cadwell wrote a little book on *The Work of the Elders in the Christian Church (Disciples of Christ)* which has a chapter on prayers at the table. Russell Harrison edited two small volumes, *Brief Prayers for Bread and Cup* and *More Brief Prayers for Bread and Cup* (1986) which contain pairs of prayers for bread and cup. A year later Michael Dixon's *Bread of Blessing, Cup of Hope* presented prayers for bread and cup for each Sunday of the liturgical year.

Jane McAvoy, a professor of religion at Hiram College, edited *Table Talk: Resources for the Communion Meal*. The meditations and prayers, drawn from many sources, are organized around the seasons of the Christian year.

Over the years Disciples produced a number of service books and books about worship. One of the standard volumes used by many ministers was *Christian Worship—A Service Book*, edited by G. Edwin Osborn and published by

Christian Board in 1953. It contained a wealth of information about designing worship services, weddings, funerals, baptisms, receiving new members, blessing children, and ordaining and installing ministers and church officers. The majority of the book was made up of scripture selections and prayers, many composed by Osborn himself.

In 1987 CBP Press published *Thankful Praise: A Resource for Christian Worship*. It was edited by Keith Watkins of Christian Theological Seminary with assistance from Ronald and Linda McKiernan-Allen, Katherine and Michael Kinnamon, and Peter Morgan. It, too, contains a wealth of resources. Designed to encourage the renewal of worship, the book begins with an introductory chapter, then presents a Sunday service and a commentary on it. The rest of the book contains liturgical material: responsive readings and litanies, invitations to communion, prayers for various parts of the service, and the earlier version of the *Common Lectionary*. Resources are provided for the major seasons of the Christian year: Advent and Christmas, Epiphany, Lent, Easter, and Pentecost.

Finally, one of the most popular and inspirational recent books is Mae Yoho Ward's *The Seeking Heart*. The book is a prayer journal, covering her retirement years from 1977 until her death in 1983. The entries are in the form of letters to God. Ward was a missionary in South America and later on the staff of the UCMS. The entries reveal a thankful life that has grown in its awareness of God. The last entry begins, "I'm still on a pilgrimage," a statement that is true of every authentic Christian.

Index

Revisionary Interventions into the Americanist Canon

New Americanists   *A Series Edited by Donald E. Pease*

REVISIONARY INTERVENTIONS

Donald E. Pease, Editor

INTO THE AMERICANIST CANON

DUKE UNIVERSITY PRESS   Durham and London 1994

Library of Congress Cataloging-in-Publication Data

appear on the last printed page of this book.

The text of this book originally was published

without the present preface or index as

Vol. 17, No. 1 of *boundary 2*.

Contents

Preface

Revisionary Interventions into the Americanist Canon had a complex genealogy. The book initially appeared as a special issue, the first of the *boundary 2* volumes published at Duke University Press, and as a rejoinder to Frederick Crews's excoriating critique in the *New York Review of Books* of a group of books (including two of my own) by younger Americanists in violation of what Crews understood to be the presuppositions constituting the field of American studies. Because the purpose of gathering together these essays was to bring into existence an alternative to the field of American studies—one able to include matters that Crews had eliminated—I had intended the volume to be the founding text for a New Americanists book series. After its publication, however, I became aware of the volume's limitations as the inaugural event for an emergent field of new American studies. The *boundary 2* volume had provided a forum for the return of sociopolitical questions, counter-national discourses, and minoritarian perspectives to American studies, but it also threatened to renew preconstituted categories and master narratives of an earlier American studies. To call attention to the need for a global rather than national analytic framework for this emergent field, I have placed this text in the New Americanist series after *Cultures of United States Imperialism*, a collection of essays I coedited with Amy Kaplan that is interdisciplinary in scope and international in its perspective. This placement indicates the inevitably retrospective standpoint of any founding gesture in a series that aspires to advance the understanding of the formation of local and oppositional identities positioned across multiple coordinates of race, class, ethnicity, and gender as well as across locales and nationalities.

Because the *boundary 2* collective has enabled my renewed understanding of the revisionism inherent in every founding act, I extend my gratitude to its entire editorial collective. I am particularly indebted to Paul Bové, its present editor, and Meg Sachse, its managing editor, for seeing this volume into print as a *boundary 2* volume, and to Reynolds Smith for his enthusiastic and loyal support for the New Americanists series.

New Americanists: Revisionist Interventions into the Canon

Donald E. Pease

The term "New Americanists" derives from the lengthy review article entitled "Whose American Renaissance?" Frederick Crews contributed to the twenty-fifth anniversary issue of the *New York Review of Books* (October 27, 1988). Crews uses the term in ways homologous with other neologisms—new historicism, neo-Marxism, poststructuralism—devised to mark shifts in the organizing principles and self-understanding of a field. Crews's "New Americanists" deploy these and other revisionist practices to intervene in the restructuring of American Studies. In keeping with this usage, Crews applies the term to the authors of close to thirty essays in two volumes of collected essays, as well as five recent books by single authors.[1]

1. *The American Renaissance Reconsidered: Selected Papers from the English Institute, 1982–1983*, ed. Walter Benn Michaels and Donald E. Pease (Baltimore: Johns Hopkins University Press, 1985); Russell S. Reising, *The Unusable Past: Theory and the Study of American Literature* (New York: Methuen, 1986); *Ideology and Classic American Literature*, ed. Sacvan Bercovitch and Myra Jehlen (Cambridge: Cambridge University Press, 1986); Donald E. Pease, *Visionary Compacts: American Renaissance Writings in Cultural Context* (Madison: University of Wisconsin Press, 1987); Jane Tompkins, *Sensational Designs: The Cultural Work of American Fiction, 1790–1860* (New York: Oxford

As the title of the essay indicates, he uses F. O. Matthiessen's *American Renaissance* as the established mastertext in American Studies against which to assess the New Americanists' work. Although he will complicate his reasons later in the article, Crews rationalizes his associating of these disparate critics within an inclusive designation in the following passage:

> But to New Americanists (and to many others) this [attention to ca-nonical mastertexts] is all sheer ideology, false consciousness that calls for the exposure of its historical determinants. . . . This ques-tioning of absolutes is now being conducted in all branches of lit-erary study; it reflects an irresistible trend in the academy toward the spurning of unified schemes and hierarchies of every kind. What gives the New Americanist critique a special emotional force, how-ever, is its connection both to our historic national shames—slavery, "Indian removal," aggressive expansion, imperialism, and so forth —and to current struggles for equal social opportunity. When a New Americanist shows, for example, that a canonical work such as *Huckleberry Finn* indulges in the stereotypical "objectifying" of blacks, Native Americans, women or others, a double effect results. First, the canon begins to look less sacrosanct and is thus readied for expansion to include works by long-dead representatives of those same groups. Second, their contemporary descendants are offered a reason for entering into an academic dialogue that had previously slighted them. In short the New Americanist program aims at alter-ing the literary departments' social makeup as well as their dominant style of criticism.[2]

The animus informing this lengthy quotation can be reduced to a single complaint: the New Americanists have returned ideology to a field previously organized by an end to ideology consensus. But this reduction does not begin to do justice to the density of register and tone in the pas-sage. Among the many remarkable features at work here and elsewhere in the article is the complex stance Crews adopts in relation to the New Americanists. He writes from the dual vantage point of a specialist in a field

University Press, 1985); David S. Reynolds, *Beneath the American Renaissance: The Subversive Imagination in the Age of Emerson and Melville* (New York: Alfred A. Knopf, 1988); Philip Fisher, *Hard Facts: Setting and Form in the American Novel* (New York: Oxford University Press, 1985).
2. Frederick Crews, "Whose American Renaissance?" *New York Review of Books* 35, no. 16 (October 27, 1988): 68–69.

about to undergo a drastic change in its orientation, yet one whose previous experiences within the field enable him to recognize the shortcomings in the new orientation as more or less familiar mistakes. Throughout the review article, Crews negotiates this dual stance into a series of assertions which shift the balance of power on display back and forth between the good faith practices of the old Americanists and the power politics of the new. By way of such shifts in register, Crews can at once acknowledge the fact that a change is taking place in the field, but can also refuse, until the review's conclusion, to concede its value either for or within that field. In place of this concession, Crews re-situates the rise of the New Americanists within otherwise unrelated contexts. Following this displacement, the New Americanists' rise to power can be said to take place not within the field of American Studies, but within the more inclusive debate between traditionalists and relativists throughout the academy, an academy turned by the sixties activists into a place more hospitable to their politics. Having shifted the field for their emergence, Crews can designate the New Americanists' critique of the ideology at work in the formation and practice of American Studies as an expedient response to a change in the mood of academic politics. Following from this reductive characterization, the New Americanists' critique of "slavery, 'Indian removal,' aggressive expansion, imperialism, and so forth" reasonably seems to Crews indistinguishable from the demands of academic special interest groups.

Crews's remarks here are valuable for the urgent need he displays at once to displace and dismiss. In attending more fully to the threat he experiences in the New Americanists, we can discover what Crews believes to be at stake in this change within American Studies and can develop the terms of discovery necessary to introduce a volume of New Americanists. Crews, as the author of *Sins of the Fathers*, his benchmark study of Nathaniel Hawthorne (a canonical figure in the field of American Studies), had previously internalized the norms, working assumptions, and self-understanding of the field. While tacitly held, these assumptions work the way other self-evident principles do, that is, they remain exempt from critical scrutiny. As the unquestioned basis for practices within the field of American Studies, these assumptions constitute what might be called a disciplinary unconscious: an Americanist cannot at once act upon these assumptions and be conscious of them. Or rather, an Americanist cannot describe them as uncritically held assumptions without disaffiliating himself from the field of American Studies. And, the New Americanists, in consciously delineating the literary standards presupposed in Crews's book on Hawthorne as the results of an ideological state apparatus complicit with aggressive expansionism, patronage politics, and slavery, break faith with the constitutive principles of Crews's field. For by associating literary artifacts with the "historic national shames" of American politics, the New Americanists do not write from *within* the field but from a someplace else, a someplace Crews, depending on his argumentative mood, locates as the field of academic politics, the sixties' counterculture, or the affirmative action office. Yet, in Crews's difficulty in finding a specific place in the academy for the New Americanists, what matters is not so much the itinerary of their displacements but Crews's need to displace them. Certainly the movement from the overly generalized realm of a pervasive academic debate, through the *realpolitik* of sixties radicalism, and to the overly particularized space of the affirmative action office consistently associates Crews's inability to place the New Americanists within a specific academic field with the unavailability of legitimate academic places for them. Still, his need derives from the New Americanists' having questioned the most self-evident (hence least available to critical scrutiny) of beliefs Americanists hold—that American literary imagination transcends the realm of political ideology.

When offering a summary account of the New Americanists' critique, Crews carefully recounts their claim that an American literary imagination was in fact an ideological construct that developed out of the consensus politics of liberal anti-communism of the postwar era. Having accurately formulated their critique of the liberal consensus, however, Crews recovers his site within the liberal consensus by denying their account any effect on his practice. As if he had only mechanically repeated their words, rather than understood their meaning, Crews, throughout the remainder of the review, responds to the ideological critique of the New Americanists with remarks revealing the tacit assumptions of the liberal consensus. He recovers those assumptions in the following passage:

> Perhaps the key shaper of "Americanness" criticism was the Lionel Trilling of *The Liberal Imagination* (1948) [sic] who helped to replace Vernon Parrington's sociological conception of American literature with an explicitly cultural one. For Parrington American history was a record of successive emancipations from aristocratic and sectarian European roots and American literature in all its variety reflected that record of linear democratic progress. It followed for Parrington, that we should cultivate all those elements of our heterogeneous literary tradition that manifest that record. But a culture, Trilling wrote in re-

buke of Parrington, "is not a flow . . . ; the form of its existence is struggle . . . it is nothing if not a dialectic. And in any culture there are likely to be certain artists who contain a large part of the dialectic within themselves, their meaning and power lying in their contradictions; they contain within themselves, it may be said, the very essence of the culture. The real America is to be sought in those relatively few books produced by "dialectically" capacious minds.[3]

This lengthy quotation constitutes an eventful moment in Crews's argument. Crews turns to Trilling on Parrington after his paraphrase of the New Americanists' critique. In turning to Trilling, rather than to Matthiessen, as the key figure responsible for the shaping of "Americanness," Crews tacitly draws upon a distinction Trilling made in his 1946 review article— separating an ideological from a literary conception of American literature— to do more or less the same work. To do this work, Crews needs to recover from Trilling's essay a working assumption about the difference between American literature and ideology, an assumption that will enable him to find in the New Americanists' work ideological shortcomings more or less homologous to those Trilling found in Parrington's. More importantly for the distinction crucial to his argument, Crews must recover this difference as a *tacit* assumption, a principle self-evident enough to be above suspicion as ideology.

But whereas Crews needs to recover this assumption tacitly to establish a secure critical perspective on the academic politics of the New Americanists, Trilling, writing in the late 1940s, needed to discriminate between American literature and Stalinist ideology threatening to his idea of America. This shift becomes clearly discernible in the concluding clause from *The Liberal Imagination*, a clause Crews pointedly leaves out of his quotation. Trilling's entire concluding clause should read, "they [true American artists] contain within themselves, it may be said, the very essence of the culture *and the sign of this is they do not submit to serve the ends of any one ideological group or tendency*" (my emphasis).[4] That Crews feels free to leave out of his paraphrase Trilling's qualifiers underscores the difference between a critic who accepts "the end of ideology" hypothesis as a self-evident principle and a critic who worked hard to end specific ideological

3. Crews, "Whose American Renaissance?" pp. 70–71. *The Liberal Imagination* first appeared in 1950; see footnote 4.
4. Lionel Trilling, *The Liberal Imagination: Essays on Literature and Society* (New York: Viking, 1950), p. 9.

6

encroachments on literature in his time. For at the time Trilling wrote *The Liberal Imagination*, many of his contemporary critics had recovered their prewar concerns with the relationship between politics and literature.

Pre-eminent among those who recovered after the war their engagement with political questions was F. O. Matthiessen. If we pressure the analogy Crews adduces between the New Americanist and the Parrington line, F. O. Matthiessen, the founder of American Studies, emerges as a 1948 New Americanist. And while Crews cites Trilling's condemnation of Parrington, he pointedly fails to mention Trilling's criticism of Matthiessen. But in 1946, Trilling found the author of *American Renaissance* a greater threat to his idea of American than Parrington, who published *Main Currents in American Literature* in 1927–30 and whose views, by 1946, were considered dated.[5]

Trilling's essay, tendentiously entitled "Reality in America" and reprinted in *The Liberal Imagination*, itself originally appeared as two separate review articles.[6] The Matthiessen critique appeared in the April 1946 issue of *Nation*. Trilling's review took the form of a response to Matthiessen's favorable review of Theodore Dreiser's work. Dreiser had decided to join the Communist Party in August 1945, and Trilling believed the indulgence with which Matthiessen and other progressive liberals addressed his work implicitly approved of Dreiser's doctrine. In turning to Matthiessen's review of Dreiser, by way of an analysis of Parrington's shortcomings, Trilling intended to identify Matthiessen's progressive liberalism with Parrington's antiquated vision of America. Parrington, in Trilling's usage of him, identified liberal progressivism with communism and the liberal imagination with liberal anti-communism. Since Matthiessen, in his preface to *American Renaissance*, had already definitively analyzed the shortcomings in Parrington's *Main Currents in American Literature*, Trilling's citation of Parrington was strategic. He intended to split off rhetorically the Liberal Progressive in Matthiessen by reminding Matthiessen of what he had had to say about the Progressives in 1941.

5. In *Professing Literature: An Institutional History* (Chicago: University of Chicago Press, 1987), Gerald Graff emphasizes Parrington's importance for American Studies in terms of the "link between the academic study of American literature and the progressive social outlook" (235). Graff also underscores Trilling's need to attack Parrington's influence in the academy by recharacterizing him as an ideologue with dated politics rather than (as did other academics) a powerful opponent of the genteel tradition; see pp. 214–20.
6. The first review, entitled "Parrington, Mr. Smith and Reality," first appeared in *Partisan Review* 7 (1940):24–40; the second appeared as "Dreiser and the Liberal Mind" in *The Nation* (April 20, 1946):466–72.

Like the Parrington of 1928, the Progressives, Trilling argues, elevated the work of crude social realists (like Theodore Dreiser) above that of refined artists (like Henry James) and valued proletarian concerns with social change over aesthetic preoccupation with form. After distinguishing Parrington's Progressivist reduction of artistic forms to the level of social forces, by extolling Henry James's capacious internalization of the entire social dialectic within his literary imagination, Trilling, in his review, identifies the ability to craft such a synthesis as the achievement of the liberal imagination. He then turns to the recent work of Matthiessen, whose magisterial study of American classics previously discriminated what partakes of the reality of America from what does not. "Nor can Mr. Matthiessen," Trilling writes in an effort to secure this discrimination within the work of the founder of American Studies, "be thought of as a follower of Parrington—indeed in the preface to *American Renaissance* he has framed one of the sharpest and most cogent criticisms of Parrington's method." [7] And having conflated Dreiser and Parrington into versions of the same misrecognition of ideology as literature that Matthiessen had himself earlier underscored, Trilling criticizes Matthiessen for making the same mistake. "Yet Mr. Matthiessen, writing in the *New York Times Book Review* about Dreiser's posthumous novel *The Bulwark*, accepts the liberal cliche that opposes crude experience to mind and establishes Dreiser's value." [8]

In his review, Trilling redirects the target of Matthiessen's earlier critique of ideology and finds the enemy *within* the consciousness of the author of *American Renaissance*. Having exiled what is un-American in the mind of the founder of American Studies into the ideological realm of a liberal cliche, Trilling turns *The Liberal Imagination* rather than *American Renaissance* into the field-defining work for American Studies. This redefinition of the basis of the field elevates the liberal imagination (and the liberal anticommunist consensus) into the field's equivalent of a reality principle. As Trilling demonstrates, when properly exercised the liberal imagination can enable every Americanist to do for himself what Trilling's essay does for Matthiessen, that is, produce an internal division that splits the capacious literary consciousness of dialectical processes off from any public world.

Trilling's splitting off of the literary imagination from any public world constitutes the ideological work, what might be called the field-defining *action*, of Trilling's review article. Following this split, the readiness within the reader/writer of American literature to actualize the relationship be-

7. Trilling, *The Nation*, p. 468. See also Trilling, *The Liberal Imagination*, p. 15.
8. Trilling, *The Nation*, p. 468. See also Trilling, *The Liberal Imagination*, p. 15.

tween a literary idea and a political question itself undergoes a critical transformation. And when *re-experienced* from within this liberal imagination,
the willingness *not* to realize the relation between the literary idea and the
public realm produces for the reader/writer what Trilling calls, after Keats,
a negative capability. This ability, best exemplified in James's writing, both
negates a reader/writer's need to realize literary ideas in the public realm
and enables her experience of the *separation* between what is and what is
not literary. The experience of this separation, by which literary possibilities
can be realized as determinate actions or as particular referents, in turn
results in the internalization of that dialectical contradiction (the yes and
no) Trilling earlier defined as the agency of American cultural history. When
exercising his liberal imagination, an otherwise politically engaged liberal
subject can experience the disconnection between what commits him and
the place where commitment can be realized. Thus, Trilling's liberal imagination produces two disconnected realms—the cultural and the public. And
in diverting their attention from the "limited" world of politics (preoccupied
by the larger and permanent dialectical contradiction that sets, for Trilling, the United States' freedom against the Soviets' totalitarianism) to the
densely nuanced, complexly differentiated realm of high modernist culture,
American readers/writers experience a surrogate fulfillment of their deepest drives and an ersatz wholeness for their authentic selves. By promising
wholeness for selves partitized within the public world and an infinity of private locations for the fulfillment of drives left unrealized in the public realm,
the cultural sphere's attraction increases, according to Trilling, in direct proportion to the needs for such compensatory gratifications produced within
the public realm.

As this brief account should make clear, once he has constructed
himself within the autonomous cultural realm defined by Trilling's liberal
imagination, a liberal subject has difficulty identifying with any alternate
self-construction. Crews exemplifies this difficulty when he paraphrases the
New Americanists' critique of the liberal imagination, but then denies that
critique any effectiveness within his review. When the New Americanists
criticize the liberal imagination as an ideological contruction, they articulate
the critical difference between themselves and their predecessors in American Studies. For the New Americanists, the liberal imagination discloses
itself as ideological when it produces an *imaginary separation* between the
cultural and the public sphere. This imaginary separation enables liberal
subjects to experience the otherwise threatening cultural contradictions released by the cold war consensus as the negative capability of a whole
self. Crews, when confronted with the New Americanists' critique of the

liberal imagination and his own critical persona constructed out of it, turns to Lionel Trilling's essay to repeat the spell Trilling cast upon the ideology critique of his own day.

Throughout the remainder of his 1988 review, Crews repeats the terms Trilling provided in 1946 for both critical blame ("reductionism," "partisan myopia," "sermonizing," "eagerness for moral certainties about the relationship between the books and their politics") and critical praise ("irresoluteness," "irony," "concentrated suggestiveness derived from the fusing and decontextualizing of many rhetorial strategies"). When deployed as his means of assessing the New Americanists, these terms of critical praise and blame reconstitute Frederick Crews's critical subjectivity within the realm of The Liberal Imagination. To give the liberal imagination effective placement in his review of the New Americanists, Crews finds a precise replica of it in Lawrence Buell's account of Uncle Tom's Cabin in New England Literary Culture. Crews quotes Buell approvingly: for Buell, the literary imagination at work in Uncle Tom's Cabin has "the status of an autonomous rhetorical and thematic force." Moreover, Crews continues his citation of Buell, this imagination would cease to be comprehensible as an effective social force if it were "unmasked" as a merely ideological effect.[9] What Crews misrecognizes by way of this citation and elsewhere in the review is the simple fact that Trilling used The Liberal Imagination as a history-shaping force in an ideological struggle, after the manner in which Stowe used Uncle Tom's Cabin. One of the strong and enduring historical results of Trilling's ideological usage was the appearance of an autonomous culture sphere; another result, the construction of an American Studies movement for which the end of ideology consensus became the dominant ideology. In recognizing the autonomy of the liberal imagination, but from within the displaced form of Buell's account of Uncle Tom's Cabin, a novel Trilling explicitly identified with ideological propaganda rather than literature, Crews comes as close as he ever gets to acknowledging the ideological agenda within the liberal imagination.

A Crisis in the Field Imaginary of American Studies

Earlier I suggested one other place in his review where Crews misreads the ideology of his own critical attitude. When he fails to quote Trill-

---

9. Crews, "Whose American Renaissance?" p. 75. The passage he quotes from Buell appears in New England Literary Culture: From Revolution through Renaissance (Cambridge: Cambridge University Press, 1986), p. 19.

ing's critique of Matthiessen in "Reality in America," Crews silently uses *The Liberal Imagination* to displace *American Renaissance* as the master-text with which to discriminate among New Americanists. Crews's displacement of Matthiessen's master-text with Trilling's follows his paraphrase of several New Americanists—most notably Jonathan Arac in "Authorizing an American Renaissance" [10]—who call explicit attention to the residual ideology in *American Renaissance*. After having quoted the lines cited earlier from Trilling's *The Liberal Imagination*, Crews differentiates *his American Renaissance* from the New Americanists' by correcting their accounts of Matthiessen's politics: "Other accounts, however, reveal that from the Thirties onward Matthiessen was precisely a fellow-traveller—that is, someone who abstained from Party membership while generally hewing to positions set forth by the Kremlin. And insofar as his suicide registered political as well as personal despair, the disillusioning shock of Soviet *Realpolitik* in Eastern Europe had as much to do with it as McCarthyism." [11] Following this correction, Crews is able to do in 1988 for his review article's *American Renaissance* what Trilling had done in 1946 for his review article's—associate Matthiessen's politics with totalitarian ideology and read it out of the master-text for American Studies.

After separating his American Renaissance from the New Americanists', Crews presumes, in a review article entitled "Whose American Renaissance?" (1988), to reclaim legal proprietary rights over his field. But instead of exercising the proprietary liberties of *The Liberal Imagination* (1950) and banishing the New Americanists from his American Renaissance, Crews concludes the review with a staggering acknowledgment:

> The truth is that for any works written before the last seventy years or so, the most influential academics get to decide who's in and who's out. And the New Americanists themselves seem destined to become the next establishment in their field. They will be right about the most important books and the most fruitful ways of studying them

10. In "F. O. Matthiessen: Authorizing an American Renaissance" in *The American Renaissance Reconsidered*, Arac also draws cogent attention to Trilling's cold war politics: "Lionel Trilling devoted his career to portraying American [progressive] 'liberal' culture as so Stalinized as to make impossible any live or complex literary response. Such claims depend upon ignoring Matthiessen, as Trilling did, or considering his politics as unrelated to his critical accomplishments, as Irving Howe has done" (p. 98).

11. Crews, "Whose American Renaissance?" p. 74.

because as they always know in their leaner days, those who hold the power are right by definition.[12]

I have already suggested the value of Crews's review of the New Americanists lies in the precarious stance Crews has to adopt. The New Americanists' working with a set of assumptions about the relationship between literature and the public world quite different from his own produces a self-division within Crews, separating his critical subject representative of *The Liberal Imagination* from his reviewer's critical representations of the New Americanists. Crews comes to terms with this self-division by constructing and then policing an institutional boundary line that distinguishes true laborers within the field of American Studies from ideologists, activists, and academic special interest groups represented by New Americanists. While he remains a subject constructed out of *The Liberal Imagination*, Crews cannot recognize New Americanists as members of his field. At the startling conclusion of the review, however, he recognizes the New Americanists as the "next establishment in *their* field" (my emphasis). But without anywhere else in the review having proposed terms supportive of this recognition, his conclusion seems written by someone of another mind about the New Americanists than Frederick Crews. Instead of taking final possession of Crews's *American Renaissance*, that final paragraph seems a contextually dispossessed literary property, but one developed within a text-milieu separable from the one articulated in the remainder of the review.

In articulating these concluding sentences in terms he elsewhere discredits, Crews, at the conclusion of the review, makes clear the ideological crisis New Americanists effect for his field. And my preceding sentences, as they reconstruct "Crews" in terms held self-evident by New Americanists, deconstitute the "Crews" of *The Liberal Imagination*. In bringing Crews's earlier constructions together with this reconstruction, my analysis articulates what might be called a crisis in the field-Imaginary of American Studies.

By the term field-Imaginary I mean to designate a location for the disciplinary unconscious mentioned earlier. Here abides the field's fundamental syntax—its tacit assumptions, convictions, primal words, and the charged relations binding them together. A field specialist depends upon this field-Imaginary for the construction of her primal identity within the field.

12. Crews, "Whose American Renaissance?" p. 81.

Once constructed out of this syntax, the primal identity can neither reflect upon its terms nor subject them to critical scrutiny. The syntactic elements of the field-Imaginary subsist instead as self-evident principles.

Throughout my discussion of Crews's review, I have treated *The Liberal Imagination* as the location of Crews's field-Imaginary. A partial list of the titles of master-texts within the field of American Studies will enable me to describe its field-Imaginary as if it represented a primal scene: F. O. Matthiessen's *American Renaissance* (1941); Henry Nash Smith's *Virgin Land* (1950); R. W. B. Lewis's *The American Adam* (1955); Richard Chase's *The American Novel and Its Tradition* (1957); Harry Levin's *The Power of Blackness: Hawthorne, Poe, Melville* (1958); Leslie Fiedler's *Love and Death in the American Novel* (1960); Marcus Bewley's *The Eccentric Design* (1963); Leo Marx's *The Machine in the Garden* (1965); Richard Poirier's *A World Elsewhere* (1966); Quentin Anderson's *The Imperial Self* (1971); Sacvan Bercovitch's *American Jeremiad* (1973).

While these master-texts in American Studies provide slightly different meta-narratives with which Americanists define their practices, all of these titles presuppose a realm of pure possibility (*Virgin Land, A World Elsewhere*) where a whole self (*American Adam, The Imperial Self*) can internalize the major contradictions at work in American history (*The Machine in the Garden, The Power of Blackness*) in a language and in a set of actions and relations confirmative of the difference between a particular cultural location and the rest of the world (*Love and Death in the American Novel, The Eccentric Design, The American Novel and Its Tradition, American Jeremiad, American Renaissance*).

I described earlier this autonomous place apart from a culture as the construction of *The Liberal Imagination*, but as this list of titles should indicate, *The Liberal Imagination* works with pre-oedipal wishes, narcissistic drives, and primal words to produce a compelling primal scene. Here the urge for absolute union with cultural goods becomes wholly indistinguishable from identification with instinctual drives. In this realm, intensities take the place of referentials and negations possess no language with which to be distinguished from affirmations.

Like the primal scene within an individual's psyche, the scenario organizing the field-Imaginary of American Studies depends upon the *separation* it enables *from* potentially traumatic material. The binding power of materials from this primal scene becomes visible in Crews's review at those moments when the New Americanists either criticize this separation as an ideological construction or propose a relation between the separated realms. Whenever New Americanists question the separation of the cultural from the public realm, they undermine the (imaginary) relation between Crews's primal identity as a specialist in American Studies and the field's primal scene.

Crews explicitly negotiates the difficulties resulting from this crisis in the field-Imaginary and tacitly present in his review in his discussion of his former colleague Henry Nash Smith's essay in a volume of essays by New Americanists. In this essay Smith, the author of *Virgin Land* (1950), does for that founding text what Crews never does in his review; he reconsiders the text in terms of a New Americanist critique. Whereas Smith did not intend his designation of the nineteenth-century West as "virgin land" to be ideological, Richard Slotkin, in *The Fatal Environment* (1985), finds, this designation to be, in both its conception and deployment, an ideological cover-up for Indian removal, frontier violence, government theft, land devastation, class cruelty, racial brutality, and misogyny. In reconsidering, Smith acknowledges some truth to these claims, but then wisely remarks that at the time he was working on *Virgin Land* (1947–50), the critical self-consciousness with which Slotkin scrutinized its ideology was simply not available: "This cluster of concepts, which I would call an American ideology, is constantly present in *Virgin Land* but, so to speak, off stage, only occasionally given explicit recognition."[13] Crews, however, never cites the substance of Smith's remark, nor does he comment on what was crucially at stake for the field of American Studies in Smith's change of mind. In place of such commentary, Crews questions the motives of the editors of *Ideology and Classic American Literature*, who included Smith's posthumous essay as "a kind of trophy." Crews then goes on to concern himself with the "liberal attitude" displayed in Smith's change of mind. Smith, Crews writes, "acceded to Slotkin's implied [sic] critique of his work, confessing that he had been blind to the way such catchwords as 'free land' and 'frontier initiative' had been used to rationalize atrocities."[14]

In this passage, Crews misrecognizes the New Americanists' threat to *his* field in the displaced form of Henry Nash Smith's (posthumously published) response to Richard Slotkin's defacement of *Virgin Land*. In *The Fatal Environment*, Slotkin constructs an alternate primal scene within which New Americanists construct themselves and define their objects.

13. Henry Nash Smith, "Symbol and Idea in Virgin Land," in *Ideology and Classic American Literature*, p. 23.
14. Crews, "Whose American Renaissance?" p. 74.

This alternate radically threatens the identity Crews constructed out of *Virgin Land* (and the other founding texts in his field-Imaginary). To restore that identity, Crews, in this passage, uses Smith's placement within an alien text-milieu to conduct a rescue mission for the corpse of one of the founding fathers of the field's primal scene.

By invoking this image of a rescue mission for a founding father's corpse, I intend to reactivate Crews's language deployed in *The Sins of the Fathers* and to propose a location for Crews's concluding review paragraph. Throughout his study of Hawthorne, Crews depends upon a psychoanalytic understanding of the guilt accrued to Hawthorne by his ancestors' misdeeds in New England's witch-haunted glades. Crews, following Levin's *Power of Blackness*, argues that Hawthorne's narratives obsessively return to the primal scene of ancestral guilt to reconstruct the psyche in its terms. In *The Fatal Environment*, Slotkin constructs an alternate primal scene out of what might be called the political unconscious of the *Virgin Land* and of *The Power of Blackness*. Slotkin's book proposes this scene (and his meta-narrative about it) as an alternate context within which Americanists can construct their critical personae, canonical objects, and disciplinary practices.

In *Virgin Land*, Smith idealized the American West as that permanent place in nature where Americans could separate from their pasts and recover the forever inviolable status of a new beginning. Smith wrote *The Virgin Land* in the postwar years when returning veterans needed a place in which to recover from the traumas of a war fought over conflicting ideologies. As a romance-fulfillment of a wished-for America of endlessly renewable possibilities, possibilities which could be readily transported abroad in the Americanization of Western European nations, a *Virgin Land* eliminated ideological considerations about this place as un-American. But writing in the post-Vietnam era, Slotkin rereads *Virgin Land* in terms that recall American imperialism—its generalized domination of nature and native cultures. As an anti-romance of America's origins, Slotkin's *Fatal Environment* finds in Smith's *Virgin Land* a paradigmatic context for the naturalization of racist and sexist stereotypes. As the primal scene of America's endlessly recoverable origin, *Virgin Land*, Slotkin argues, is predicated upon the denial of the difference between "virgin land" and every other place in the culture. After underscoring the violence in this denial, Slotkin associates the originary violence he finds in the denail of difference of America's primal self-image with the violence of America's western settlers directed against native peoples. More significantly, Slotkin's work, *The Fatal Environment*, thereby re-establishes the relationship between the cultural and political spheres Smith's *Virgin Land* denies.

In order to recover the separation of these spheres, Crews performs his characteristic act of denegation. He ignores the political content of Slotkin's ideological critique of *Virgin Land* and attends instead to Smith's placement of that founding text within *The Fatal Environment*. In rescuing the body of Smith's text from that alien context, Crews contrasts the "characteristically magnanimous style" of "the late Henry Nash Smith's classic (and classically liberal [sic]) *Virgin Land*" with the "catch-words" of the "macabre" Slotkin thesis.[15] In other words, he frees Smith's founding text from an alien New Americanist context through the exercise of negative capability—he negates the specificity of Slotkin's thesis, then reduces the terms of Slotkin's critique to "catch-words" like "macabre" obsession. Following his impoverishment of Slotkin's critique, Crews repossesses Smith's revisionist account in *Virgin Land* by reading the work as an example of "magnanimous style." For by identifying with Smith's style, in place of what he considers Slotkin's impoverished politics, Crews effectively separates that style from *The Fatal Environment*'s politics and then reconstructs for Smith a fresh start in *Virgin Land*.

By removing Smith from *The Fatal Environment*, where New Americanists construct their field identities, Crews indirectly discloses the rationale for his own misrecognitions: for Crews, New Americanists quite literally exist outside the assumptions constitutive of his field. Their externality to Crews's field and their construction within another indicates both that a crisis in the field-Imaginary (its common sense) is taking place and that this crisis is becoming apparent in the war of paradigms.

New Americanists and New Historicists from the Outside/In

So far Crews's review has proven useful in several ways: in defining a shift in the orientation of the field, in exemplifying the crisis in identity produced by this shift, and in the correlation between these crises and the liberal end of ideology consensus. Stated differently, Crews's discussion of New Americanists indicates the intimate relationship between the paradigms within American Studies and the dominant myths about the nature of the American character. These paradigms do not refer to existing facts, but are constituted out of the field-Imaginary of American Studies whose

15. Crews, "Whose American Renaissance?" p. 74.

primal scene they constitute. When a critic, such as Slotkin, offers an alternate Imaginary out of which to constitute the field of American Studies, he threatens the identity of those constituted in the previous field-Imaginary. In reaction to this (imaginary) threat, Crews recovers the America produced out of the cold war consensus.

Throughout his review, Crews differentiates his field's practices from those of the New Americanists' by the difficulty he displays in placing them. That he places them within the academy, yet outside his field, is significant for Crews's having misrecognized the separation (on which he bases his identity) between the cultural and the political. Crews fails to acknowledge New Americanists as members of his field because they insist on literature as an agency within the political world and thereby violate the fundamental presupposition of the liberal imagination. In returning a historical context to American Studies, New Americanists have developed a subfield within American Studies called New Historicism. The New Historicism constructs for New Americanists an ideological agency which returns questions of class, race, and gender from the political unconscious of American Studies. That agency depends for its effectiveness upon the skill in close reading developed by the previous generation of Americanists: their new critical ability to convert even the most incoherent of texts into an apparent unity. Such New Historicists can turn the raw materials of history (chronicles, unofficial memoirs, fashions, economic statistics, anecdotes) into objects of New Americanists' attention by reconstructing these texts' relations with canonical works. Since these constructions address the ways in which New Historicists and professional historians treat historical materials differently, I will, before defending them, restate the most frequent criticisms professional historians have directed against the New Historicists—that they are unable to follow the rules of disinterested inquiry and that they formulate arbitrary connections between text and context.

In relating the otherwise forgettable objects of everyday life to historical meta-narratives, New Historicists turn one of the prerogatives of a close reader into an historical agency. Like the close reader, the American New Historicist constructs relations between otherwise unrelated political, economic, and historical materials and the meta-texts of American Studies. They remake American history by making it seem in need of a field made up of close readings. When official history is written after the manner in which New Americanists read texts, that history no longer remains beholden to the strictures of empiricist or realist or conventionalist historiography—any more than a close reading does. By reading into archival materials the mediations necessary for historic placement, American New Historicists have substantially revised the textuality of American history.

As Paul Bové has persuasively demonstrated, their newly discovered power over history has led some New Historicists to inflated claims about literature's effect on political change.[16] One familiar version of these claims depends upon the homologous relationship between the "textuality" of history and the "historicity" of the text. Now on one level this homology and the claim dependent upon it are simply true. For, even if the New Historicism had not led to changes in the practices of professional historians, or effected any great change in the culture at large, it has, in the practices of the New Americanists, significantly changed the field of American Studies. Having interpellated historical documents and related interpretive constructions into the textuality of American literature, the New Historicist has in fact historicized the literary text. But the culture in which these historical changes have taken place remains the relatively restricted field of American Studies, a field, as Crews's review indicates, particularly volatile at the present time, with a number of divergent practices in the process of emergence. Given its resourcefulness in the production of new relations, the New Historicism provides New Americanists with a way of affiliating their emergent disciplinary practices with emancipatory social or political movements. But the relationships American New Historicists establish between those social movements and their emergent practices are, as I hope to demonstrate, quite complicated.

When New Americanists read the relations between social movements and their own emergent practices, their readings sometimes turn the structural unit of signification for a disciplinary practice—displacing the preceding unit with one significantly different—into a homology for the basic reflex of an emancipatory social or political praxis—the opposition of a dominated group to an oppressor. When they articulate their new practices in terms of this homology, but without nonacademic political associations, New Americanists activate what we might call the ideology of discipline formation. That is, they identify and symbolically affiliate what is innovative in their disciplinary practices with a social movement's opposition to an oppressor. This identification is ideological in the sense that it constitutes for the New Americanists an imaginary scenario about what actually takes

16. See Paul Bové, *Intellectuals in Power: A Genealogy of Critical Humanism* (New York: Columbia University Press, 1986), particularly "Intellectuals at War: Michel Foucault and the Analytics of Power."

place when someone learns a new discipline. Reconstructed out of the imaginary relations within this scenario, the rigorous methodology, while being learned, occupies the position of the oppressor, but after the discipline's methods are thoroughly learned, that same rigorous methodology occupies the position of the emancipator. The release is as much a part of the structure of disciplinary instruction as is the oppression. It is only when the ideology about the instruction takes precedence over its actual content that the scene of disciplinary instruction turns into a generalized opposition directed against an oppressive power.

Thus far, this account legitimizes New Historicism's claim to cultural power, but it questions the generalized oppositional context within which some American New Historicists have described their discipline. This delegitimation partially corroborates, but also importantly revises, Crews's claim that their ideology should exclude the New Americanists from academic fields. As Gerald Graff has reminded us,[17] American Studies followed English Studies in assigning academic status to the demands for equality and justice of disenfranchised social groups. By redefining them within the terms of their field, previous Americanists fulfilled these political demands but only in the idealizing terms of the liberal imagination. This liberalization from *within* the field of American Studies, as Allen Grossman has pointed out, compensated for the diminution of progressive political programs outside the academy.

> The acceptance of modern letters in the mother tongue as a university subject runs fairly parallel, as is obvious with the liberalization of the polity in England and America and particularly with the emancipation of women, so far as it occurred. Where the university could not ignore a class or group, it was inclined to offer it a pathway to academic legitimacy that satisfied claims upon status but excluded from the means to rule.[18]

If American Studies redefined liberty as a freedom from emancipatory demands, the liberal imagination, in its exercise of negative capability, denied those demands any specific political representation. Demands for women's or Blacks' rights became identified instead with all the other public

17. See Graff, *Professing Literature*, pp. 209–25.
18. Allen Grossman in "Criticism, Consciousness and the Sources of Life: Some Tasks for English Studies" in *Uses of Literature*, ed. Monroe Engel (Cambridge: Harvard University Press), p. 25.

matters from which the liberal psyche should separate itself. But the New Americanists' inclusion among their ranks of representatives from newly enfranchised political groups refuses the reduction of real political gains into the symbolic attitudes struck by the liberal imagination. Insofar as the liberal imagination represents the denial of political questions, the academic field it supervises becomes, for the New Americanists, an appropriate battlefield to fight for the return of these questions to the literary imagination.

As we have seen, the New Historicism enables New Americanists to reconstruct the relation between public and cultural matters previously denied. When a New Historicist makes explicit the relationship between an emancipatory struggle taking place outside the academy and an argument she is conducting within the field, the relationship between instruction in the discipline's practices and participation in emancipatory political movements can no longer be described as imaginary. Such *realized* relations undermine the separation of the public world from the cultural sphere and join, as Jonathan Arac puts it, "the nexus of classroom, discipline and profession to such political areas as those of gender, race and class as well as nation."[19]

From the Cold War Consensus to the New Dissensus

In their representations of public questions and political groups previously excluded from their field, New Americanists can be—they are by Crews—described as external to American Studies. When their work continues the struggles taking place outside the academy or realizes the connection between their disciplinary practices and oppositional political movements, New Americanists separate their discipline from the liberal consensus.

In characterizing the difference between the liberal "end of ideology" consensus represented within his field and the New Americanists' oppositional practices, Crews turns to Sacvan Bercovitch, whose notion of "dissensus" politics at once discriminates New from previous Americanists and designates their pluralistic project as unassimilable to any consensus. Since any consensus, in Bercovitch's estimation, reproduces the cold war ideology, only a dissensus view will counter that ideology.

To discriminate among New Americanists and distinguish their op-

19. Jonathan Arac, *Critical Genealogies: Historical Situations for Postmodern Literary Studies* (New York: Columbia University Press, 1987), p. 307.

positional practices from Bercovitch's notion of dissensus, I now turn to that notion. While he never explicitly defines dissensus, Bercovitch uses the term to convey the discontinuity between generations—setting the heterogeneity of his contributors' dissenting opinions about American literature against that generation's liberal consensus. Used to indicate a gathering of diverse views, Bercovitch's term tacitly corroborates the cold war consensus it explicitly opposes. Yet Bercovitch's dissensus restores value only to the principle of dissent. For this dissensus does not emerge out of his contributors' resistance to specific cultural arrangements or presupposition of a prior consensus. It is not a further development of political arguments only partially pursued by the preceding generation of Americanists or of residual forces needing realization. Neither is it an inclusion of contexts or historical facts missing from the prior history, yet crucial for adequate historical understanding. It is not any of these things because such contestatory relations between the new dissensus and the old consensus would do just what Bercovitch insists can (must) never be done, that is, argue for the effectiveness of an oppositional movement. Instead of proposing a description of his Cambridge project in New Americanist literary history as the history of an oppositional consensus in the process of formation, Bercovitch identifies any consensus derivable from his dissensus as the characteristic work of American Ideology. Previous efforts at a literary history (whether by Spiller, in the forties with fifty-five contributors, or by Parrington, in the twenties with one) resulted, Bercovitch claims, in a "consensus about the term 'literary' that involved the legitimation of an entire canon, and a consensus about the term 'history' that was legitimated by a certain concept of America."[20] The consensus about both terms was best expressed, Bercovitch agrees with Crews, by F. O. Mathiessen in his landmark study *American Renaissance*, where he explained that Whitman, Thoreau, Melville, Hawthorne, and Emerson all "felt it was incumbent on their generation to give fulfillment to the potentialities freed by the Revolution, to provide a culture commensurate with America's political opportunity."[21]

In fact, the consensus Matthiessen represented (which, as we have seen, included R. W. B. Lewis, Trilling, Smith, Chase, Marx, Poirier, Fiedler, Anderson, and, in complicated ways, an earlier cultural version of Bercovitch) emphasized *strains* in the American literary impulse that led out of

20. Sacvan Bercovitch, "The Problem of Ideology in American Literary History," *Critical Inquiry* 12, no. 1 (Summer 1986):632.
21. Bercovitch, "The Problem of Ideology," p. 633.

Parrington's notion of history and into alternative worlds organized by romance, style, cultural heroism, and (in the case of Fiedler's *Love and Death in the American Novel*) neurosis. Considered from one perspective, all the practitioners of American New Historicism are in revolt against the ahistoricism of the preceeding generation's consensus. Given his ground-breaking study of the monologic effect in both American literature and culture of the revolutionary mythos, however, Bercovitch cannot affiliate himself with the new generation's revolt nor indeed any oppositional model. He believes that the *mythos* of the revolution supported the cultural form he calls the American Jeremiad, which functions at times of organic crises (like the present) as a force for social integration in American society. Bercovitch also believes that any oppositional movement is, of necessity, both structured in this revolutionary mythos and dependent upon that mythos for cultural power. And having, in *The American Jeremiad*, rejected in advance any possible grounds for the conversion of dissent (whether expressed implicitly by literary works or explicitly by political groups) into the bases for actual social change, Bercovitch observes that American radicalism is always represented in ways that reaffirm the culture rather than undermine it. For Bercovitch, the history of American radical movements only reveals the incomparable cooptative power of American ideology rather than the movement's power to effect social change. American ideology refutes and absorbs subversive cultural energies, Bercovitch cogently observes, "harnessing discontent to the social enterprise" by drawing out protest and turning it into a rite of ideological assent.[22]

While Bercovitch proposed this description of American culture quite early in his career—as an expert in Puritan literature—the claim did not command the recognition from the field of American Studies until he used the writings of American Renaissance authors, Melville, Hawthorne, Thoreau, Emerson, and Whitman, as examples of the rhetoric of the American Jeremiad. In keeping with his understanding of the subsumptive power of an explanation borrowing on the revolution for its authority, Bercovitch cannot describe the new dissensus in terms of an opposition to the old consensus, but rather as the result of its breakdown. The old consensus no longer seems to account for the evidence, Bercovitch sensibly explains; hence, the context it once provided now conceals more than it reveals. In American Studies what we have instead of this context, Bercovitch contends, "is a Babel of contending approaches, argued with a ferocity reminiscent of

22. Bercovitch, "The Problem of Ideology," p. 644.

the polemics that erupted in the last great days of Rome."[23] However, insofar as it correlates the work of his twenty-one contributors with the end of an Empire, Bercovitch's New Cambridge History project not only does not eradicate but actively deploys the rhetoric of revolution. More significantly, Bercovitch welcomes the breakdown that the pervasive interpretive confusion resulting from this Babel forebodes.

In related observations about New Historicism, Stephen Greenblatt has recently argued that mainstream literary history produced a prevailing consensus quite similar to the one Bercovitch claims was at work in the old American literary history. Mainstream literary history, Greenblatt remarks, tends "to be monological, that is, it is concerned with discovering a single political vision, usually identical to that said to be held by the entire literate cultural class."[24] But Greenblatt then describes the old version of literary history in a way significantly different from Bercovitch. This old historicist version is old, Greenblatt claims, because it accepted historical fact as a phenomenon to be observed rather than to be produced by particular social groups in conflict with other social groups—as it is by the New Historicists. Whereas for Bercovitch the elaboration of conflict always works in the service of an American ideology, always able to find unity in diversity, for Greenblatt the New Historicists' multiplication of irreconcilable conflicts produces a context for their mutual contestation. Against Bercovitch's notion of an expressive unity in the old consensus, Greenblatt views literary works themselves as sites of internalized political conflict, "fields of force, places of dissension and shifting interests, occasions for the jostling of orthodoxies and subversive interests."[25]

Following Greenblatt's line of thought, we can begin to consider the limitations in Bercovitch's model of dissensus by noting the context for contentious dialogue he eliminates from consideration. By defining the new dissensus solely in terms of the breakdown of the old, Bercovitch relegates any of its political effectiveness to signs of this breakdown. Without any context within which dissensus Americanists can argue among themselves over the outcomes of the conflicts among dominant and subordinate social groups, among the rhetorics most effective for the reconstruction of American history, or among the shapes emergent historical forces should

23. Bercovitch, "The Problem of Ideology," p. 633.
24. Stephen Greenblatt, "Introduction," *Genre* 15, nos. 1–2 (Spring and Summer 1982):5.
25. Greenblatt, "Introduction," p. 6.

assume, the new dissensus only continues the old consensus—but under the displaced form of its breakup into unrelated fragments.

To give the new dissensus political effectiveness, Bercovitch should re-evaluate his oppositional model, beginning with his notion of the Jeremiad. For, at the time Bercovitch claims for it greatest cultural power, the pre-Civil War years of American Renaissance, it was, in fact, breaking apart as an adequate consensus formation. During the debates over the conflicted, highly charged, and mutually contestatory issues of expansionism, the national bank, slavery, and secession, the revolutionary mythos was put into service differently by each interest group—thereby losing its power to reconcile their disputes and integrate the factions. Unlike either the old consensus or the present dissensus, the oppositional movements which then formed had great political effectiveness. Their political means of continuing their rhetorical arguments, the Civil War, resulted in a transformation of the nation's polity—slaves were set free and the South underwent radical reconstruction, as did various previously disenfranchised groups in the North. Bercovitch's notion of dissensus, insofar as it is structured by the *separation* of the politics of dissent from the already established consensus, represses the social change an oppositional movement can produce. If, in his commentary on writers from the pre-Civil War era, he at times imposes his notion of the ideology of consensus onto American writers in his overseeing of the Cambridge project, he uses his prior description of the American Jeremiad to subsume and co-opt the differences among his contributors. In pre-designating any coalition of dissenters to be complicit with the integrative function in American ideology, Bercovitch proposes as the basis for his dissensus the breakdown of the ideology. But that breakdown, insofar as it presupposes *The American Jeremiad* as the source of integration, only signifies the historic effect of that work on the Cambridge project. As the *unity* the dissensus Americanists corroborate, *The American Jeremiad* provides their project with a tacit consensus. That tacit consensus in turn continues the work of ideological separation effected by the liberal consensus.

From the Cold War Dissensus to a New Americanist Counter-Hegemony

To understand what is politically effective about the cultural conversation initiated by the New Americanists and what differentiates that

conversation from dissensus, we need to consider the conversation it displaces. As we have seen, that conversation in the cold war epoch explicitly
related the construction of the field of American Studies to liberal anticommunist consensus. Lionel Trilling began this cultural conversation when he
used his reading of America's canonical writers to enforce that consensus:

> The fact is the American writers of genius have not turned their
> minds to society. Poe and Melville were quite apart from it; the reality
> they sought was only tangential to society. Hawthorne was acute
> when he insisted that he did not write novels but romances—he thus
> expressed his awareness of the lack of social texture in his work.[26]

Richard Chase, in a book published seven years after *The Liberal
Imagination*, explicitly relates Trilling's distinction between the romance and
the novel to the politics of the cold war consensus. For Chase, the romance, insofar as it represents the difference between negative capability
and ideological structures, is representative of America's cultural capital.
Chase reproduces this cultural capital by deploying the romance as his
means of constructing canonical texts. But then Chase advances Trilling's
hypothesis another step by asserting that "the abstractness and profundity of romance allow it to formulate moral truths of universal validity."[27]
And once he has identified the function of the romance with the cultural
entitlement to speak universal truths, Chase assigns this power not to the
romances themselves but to the liberal imagination capable of claiming this
power as its own. The liberal imagination recognizes in the romance

> an assumed freedom from the ordinary novelistic requirements of
> verisimilitude, development, and continuity; a tendency toward melo-
> drama and idyl; a more or less formal abstractness and, on the other
> hand, a tendency to plunge into the underside of consciousness;
> a willingness to abandon moral questions or to ignore the specta-
> cle of man in society, or to consider these things only indirectly or
> abstractly.[28]

In an intervention which significantly changes the terms of this conversation, Russell Reising, in one of the books Crews reviews (*The Un-*

---

26. Trilling, *The Liberal Imagination*, p. 212.
27. Richard Chase, *The American Novel and Its Tradition* (Garden City: Doubleday,
1957), p. xi.
28. Chase, *The American Novel*, p. ix.

usable Past: Theory and the Study of American Literature) underscores the relationship between Trilling's work and the liberal anti-Stalinism of consensus historians. Their embattled relationship with progressive liberal historians led anti-Stalinists to two fundamental strategies:

> (1) They replaced the progressive dualistic line up of historical forces with a triadic (sometimes called dialectical) model that postulated some "middle landscape" which synthesized various oppositions and (2) they rejected a materialistic emphasis on economics for an analysis of culture, focusing on human expression in psychology, art and literature. Whereas Progressives wanted to understand what in fact was the reality of history, counter-Progressives stressed the primacy of how people felt about reality and how their myths, images and symbols dramatized these feelings.[29]

Through his analysis of the relationship between Trilling's literary project and the more or less contemporary work of the consensus historians, this New Americanist underscores the ideological work the liberal imagination effected in the political world.

Following Trilling, Chase identifies this ideological work with the genre of the romance, then internalizes this separation as the regulative norm of American Studies. Geraldine Murphy, a New Americanist Crews does not mention in his review, has usefully identified Chase's development of Trilling's consensus with the "vital center" hypothesis of such cold war consensus historians as Arthur Schlesinger. In the cultural contradictions Chase isolated as the chief canonical feature in the American romance, Murphy discerns the construction of an American cultural front united against communism:

> the cultural front of this apocalyptic struggle between East and West pitted a socialist realism controlled by the State for its own propagandistic purposes against a subjective symbolistic, abstract modernism —the kind of art that readily symbolized the independent critical role of the artist in democratic society.[30]

In Murphy's reading of the liberal consensus, this opposition to communism produced a united cultural front in the fifties, but a cultural front that, follow-

---

29. Russell Reising, *The Unusable Past*, p. 95.
30. Geraldine Murphy, "Romancing the Center: Cold War Politics and Classic American Literature," *Poetics Today* 9, no. 4 (1988):738.

ing the disapperance of Stalinism as a vital opponent, was destined to lose any political effectiveness. Following the heating up of the Vietnam war in the sixties, the cold war itself, as the unquestioned basis for articulating the cultural capital of America, became the object of political opposition. And following the emergence of civil rights, women's rights, and student movements throughout the country, the cold war consensus lost its power to contain opposition.

The selves American citizens constructed out of the emancipatory politics of the sixties desublimated the political energies the liberal imagination had previously held in check. But their previous containment within a separate cultural sphere significantly qualified the effectiveness of these desublimated energies. Having been held in check by an *imaginary separation*, these energies were initially expressive of the power to break through imaginary barriers. The students' demands for political arrangements organized around the fulfillment of libidinal drives resulted in part from the transference into the political sphere of the impulses and drives previously identified as those experienced within the realm of the American romance. When students formulated demands within a political world that Ahab and Ishmael and Natty Bumppo and Emerson and Whitman had previously voiced only within the realm of the literary romance, they voiced their refusal to acknowledge the difference between the cultural and the public realm.

By insisting that the inner aspirations developed through their reading of the American romance should be realized within the public world, these students undermined Trilling's central premise of "Reality in America." In this essay, Trilling definitively separated the realm of the literary romance, where desire for wholeness could be fulfilled, from the realm of politics, where it could not. By breaking down the imaginary barrier separating the romance they had internalized from the external norms of American *Realpolitik*, the students desublimated the powerful energies produced as the ideological work of the liberal imagination, but in a political realm that had become for them indistinguishable from a utopian romance. The sixties, in other words, turned the politics of the forties inside out. Not Stalinism but liberal consensus became the threat to the whole self. And the response to this threat was the appearance, within the public world, of the primal scene of the American Romance. When students demanded from their public world what American characters had demanded in romance, they denied the imaginary separation, predicated by the Liberal Imagination, between the cultural and the political. Consequently, their politics literalized, in the public world, the imaginary of the American Romance.

In partial recognition of the need to restore the barrier separating these realms, Quentin Anderson, in a book published three years after the student riots of 1968, redesignates Trilling's liberal imagination *The Imperial Self*.[31] This change in the name of the self who acts from within the cultural sphere adapts the students' ideological critique of America's foreign policy in the Vietnam era to the characterization of the self constituted within America's foundational literary texts. In conscripting the name that had united various oppositional political groups against American foreign policy to describe the self produced out of the American Romance, Anderson reinstates the barrier separating cultural from political matters. But this time, the divisions appeared within the psyches of students who had previously refused to acknowledge the difference between the public and private realms. However, following the publication of *The Imperial Self*, Anderson's Columbia students, at any rate, would recognize a homology between the selves produced within American romances and within American foreign policy and would understand, as the rationale for this identification, a hypertrophy of narcissistic impulses productive of imperialism:

> I believe that the habit scholars have of calling Emerson misty or abstract, calling Whitman a successful charlatan, calling Henry James ambiguous, are but ways of referring to an inchoate perception of the absolutism of the self which is described in this essay. This absolutism involves an extreme passivity, which is complemented by, must be complemented by, the claim of the imperial self to mastery of what has almost overwhelmed it.[32]

In this passage, Anderson does not bring Trilling's and Chase's prior formulations into consideration for explicit revision, nor does he explicitly identify the liberal imagination as a version of the imperial self. Instead, he produces a protocol for relearning Trilling's instruction as the difference between the imperial self within the American Romance and America's imperialist foreign policy. But the imperial self produced out of the absolutist demands for mastery of previously unmastered materials differs crucially from the imperialist policies of a government. The cultural imperial ego is produced out of an extreme passivity designed to "suffer" the unmastered materials of a world external to the creative imagination. Following this act

---

31. Quentin Anderson, *The Imperial Self: An Essay in American Literary and Cultural History* (New York: Random House, 1971), pp. ix–x.
32. Anderson, *The Imperial Self*, p. 14.

of passive aggression, the material so suffered ceases to remain external and turns instead into the fluent and circumambient energies of the creative self.

Redefined as an unrealizable inner drive to master external matters, the imperial ego, for Anderson, rules the difference between its inner America and the rest of the world. The imperial ego *within* at once depends upon the public policy of U.S. imperialism for its definition, yet negates such a policy as antithetical to its authentic (real cultural) interests. And self-ruled rather than interested in ruling others, Anderson's imperial self overrules the need to materialize any other political interests. It restores the private cultural realm as the appropriate domain of the liberal imagination and condemns any realization of that imagination in the public world as a version of plain old U.S. imperialism.

In the Vietnam era of liberationist politics, Anderson's *Imperial Self* worked as an exemplary version of the American Jeremiad. In his critique of the nation's founding works, Anderson engages the oppositional energies released within the student counterculture, but then subsumes them within the dominant cultural realm that Trilling and Chase had previously cordoned off from politics. In the absence of any American Stalinists or communists or Marxists for liberal consensus critics to oppose, the liberal subjects Americans constructed out of the liberationist movements of the day become the implicit object of Anderson's liberal critique. Instead of proposing exemplary representations within past American literature for these counter-consensus movements, Anderson as a representative of the liberal consensus rediscovers within them the symptoms of absolutist drives, which, when acted upon in the public world, turned counter-imperialism into imperialism.

Published at the outset of the post-Vietnam era (and revised after his move to Columbia), Sacvan Bercovitch's *American Jeremiad* constructs a totalized cultural domain for Anderson's *Imperial Self* to supervise when he designates all oppositional political forces as figurations of the oppositioned structure at work in a pervasive revolutionary *mythos*. Daniel T. O'Hara cogently describes the collusion between Bercovitch's Jeremiad structure and the cold war consensus as a

> scene of Cold War cultural persuasion . . . the latest in a series of collective mythic acts of national self-definition that go back to the formation of the revolutionary ethos and before that to the Puritans' compact on *The Mayflower* to found a brilliant city on the Hill. The Soviet Union replaces Satan and his snares, the imperial British,

and the slave-holding secessionists as the latest cultural Other, the always already potentially present Enemy Within against which the authentic American must strive to create a distinctive identity.[33]

Thus, for Bercovitch every oppositional movement is susceptible to cooptation within what we might call the "surplus opposition" of the cold war consensus. Because he cannot envision any political culture in the United States other than one organized according to the supernumerary binarity of the cold war consensus, Bercovitch, as we have seen, proposes a dissensus politics. But, as his placement within this cultural conversation makes clear, Bercovitch's politics of dissensus only elevate *The American Jeremiad* into the consensus principle of the cold war liberals. And when, in the Cambridge project, it becomes the anthology's principle for the reorganization of American literary history, it continues the cold war consensus by taking opposition to a point of powerless dissensus. Without any arena for articulating different, dissenting voices into an empowering reconstruction of the field of American Studies, these individual, dissenting voices become simulacra of the structuring oppositions that articulated the cold war. Whereas, for Bercovitch, there was no way outside oppositional containment, for many New Americanists at work in his Cambridge History project (and elsewhere), there exists the possibility of countering the hegemony. Frederick Crews's review testifies to the New Americanists' effectiveness in reorganizing the field of American Studies.

New Americanists and the Counter-Hegemony

To understand what's at stake in the New Americanists' counter-hegemony, we need to turn first to Gramsci, who formulates the dynamic "wars of position" in which counter-hegemonic forces can be successfully mobilized against hegemony. A war of position takes place, as Joseph Buttigieg has pointed out, during periods of organic crisis, when the collective will organized according to one interpretation of reality gives way, after years of struggle, to alternative interpretations.[34] Gramsci locates the origin of organic crisis in moments of drastic cultural change which illuminate the incurable contradiction at work within prevailing organizing prin-

33. Daniel T. O'Hara, "Socializing the Sublime in American Renaissance Writers," *SAQ* 88, no. 3 (Summer 1989):701.
34. See Joseph A. Buttigieg, "The Exemplary Worldliness of Antonio Gramsci's Literary Criticism," in *boundary 2* 11, nos. 1–2 (1982–83):21–39.

ciples. Gramsci is as interested "to research into how precisely permanent collective wills are formed" out of a "concrete fantasy" as he is to study where "there exists in society the necessary and sufficient conditions for its transformation." To overturn the hegemonic successfully requires that oppositional forces construct their own version of a "concrete fantasy" whose "level of reality and attainability" will elicit identification from previously disadvantaged minority groups and will enable the construction of a prevailing alternate interpretation of reality able to turn the pervasive conflict of interpretations to the use of certain groups.[35]

Throughout this discussion of the New Americanists, I have argued the relationship between their emergence and the change in what Gramsci calls the "concrete fantasy" (what I have described as a crisis in the field-Imaginary) of American Studies. I depend upon this category because it accounts for both the remarkable integration in the meta-narrative thematic of American Studies and for the psychological resistance to any counter-hegemonic critique of the tacit assumptions at work in those narratives. Descriptive of the pre-linguistic identification of the field practitioner with the field's assumptions, principles, and beliefs, the field-Imaginary designates the place in American culture for the overdetermination of "romance." Naming at once the genre within the field, the means of producing and interpreting its canonical objects, the relations between the field's practitioners, the mediation between the field and the culture, and the means of separating culture from politics, the romance overdetermines the field of American Studies.

In *Professing Literature*, Gerald Graff discusses the historic role in the construction of American Studies of symbolic-romance theory in terms compatible with my own:

> The symbolic-romance theory, stressing as it did the inability of American narratives to resolve their conflicts within any social form of life, provided expression for disappointments left over from the thirties toward a society that had failed to fulfill its ideal image of itself but evidently could not be righted by social action.[36]

When transferred onto the field of American romance, these unresolved conflicts become the pure potentialities and infinite capabilities of the whole

35. Antonio Gramsci, "The Modern Prince," in *The Modern Prince and Other Writings*, ed. Louis Marks (New York: International Publishers, 1957), pp. 169, 184, 166, 174, and 154.
36. Graff, *Professing Literature*, p. 219.

self. And following Graff, what might be called the field-Symbolic of American Studies, the codification by its practitioners of primal scene materials into disparate interpretations and close readings, produces a thick description for this symbolic romance. When translating field-Imaginary materials into their interpretations, Americanists have enforced the field's tacit assumptions that their primal identities have internalized. In their secondary elaborations of their disparate critical practices, these Americanists have rationalized their tacit assumptions into the common sense of the field, thereby disseminating signs and codes in terms of what counts as legitimate knowledge. In their readings, then, Americanists like Crews, have simply recirculated the assumptions, norms, and beliefs which they have internalized on the primal scene as beyond question. And the central practices of these older Americanists have turned their romance with the primal scene of American Studies into what Daniel T. O'Hara called the romance of interpretation.[37] So, whereas the primal scene of the romance is predicated upon the separation of an internal from an external realm, O'Hara's romance of interpretation translates the power to separate from a public realm into the power to dominate a text, external nature, previous interpretations, a former self, in a relentlessly circular psychic economy.

In denying the separation constitutive of the field, however, New Americanists have changed the field-Imaginary of American Studies. The political unconscious of the primal scene of their New Historicist readings embodies *both* the *repressed relationship between* the literary and the political and the *disenfranchised groups previously unrepresentable in this relationship*. And as conduits for the return of figures and materials repressed through the denial of the relationship of the field to the public world, New Americanists occupy a double relation. For as *liaisons between* cultural and public realms, they are at once within the field yet external to it. Moreover, as representatives of subjects excluded from the field-Imaginary by the previous political unconscious, New Americanists have a responsibility to make these absent subjects representable in their field's past and present.

Predicated upon the linkage between the cultural and the public, the

---

37. In *The Romance of Interpretation: Visionary Criticism from Pater to de Man* (New York: Columbia University Press, 1985). O'Hara revises the interpretive romance hypothesis—which analyzes the ways in which the literary critic's transferences and countertransference with literary texts produce an inflationary critical self—in *Lionel Trilling: The Work of Liberation* (Madison: University of Wisconsin Press, 1988), which is simply the best interpretive study of Trilling's entire career available.

New Americanists' field-Imaginary correlates cultural with political materials in the primal scene. A brief list of New Americanists' titles should indicate this shift. Smith's *Virgin Land* gives way to Annette Kolodny's *Lay of the Land* and Slotkin's *Fatal Environment*; R. W. B. Lewis's *American Adam* becomes Myra Jehlen's *American Incarnation*, Carolyn Porter's *Seeing and Being*, or Henry Louis Gates's *Figures in Black*; Chase's *American Novel and Its Tradition* ends up Russell Reising's *Unusable Past*; Roy Harvey Pearce's *Continuity of American Poetry* translates to Paul Bové's *Destructive Poetics*, while Bercovitch's *American Jeremiad* finishes as Frank Lentricchia's *Criticism and Social Change*. All of these titles restore in their primal scenes the relations between cultural and political materials denied by previous Americanists. These recovered relations enable New Americanists to link repressed sociopolitical contexts *within* literary works to the sociopolitical issues *external* to the academic field. When they achieve critical mass, these linkages can change the hegemonic self-representation of the United States' culture.

Revisionist Interventions into the Canon

Throughout this discussion, I have used Crews's review essay to register the differences between New Americanists and their predecessors. To bring this discussion to a conclusion, I want to recall the review's final paragraph in which Crews surrenders to the New Americanists' authority over the field. Because Crews, in that final paragraph, does not remain beholden to the self-evident principles in his field, but rather acknowledges the counter-hegemonic authority of the New Americanists, I recall Crews's acknowledgment as an appropriate introduction to this collection of essays by New Americanists. To emphasize their counter-hegemonic effect, I have organized this volume in terms of changes in the materials in the field-Imaginary of American Studies: the recovery of the relationship between the cultural and the political sphere, the desublimation of romance, and the New Historicist return of the repressed context.

To reflect critically upon what is at risk culturally in the restored relation between the field of American Studies and the public sphere, the volume begins with Michael Warner's "*Res Publica* of Letters." In that essay, Warner is interested in the historic difficulties in effecting the conjunction of the print media and the public sphere. According to Warner's account of their mutual constitution, the public sphere's demand for disinterested citizens, for mutuality of conversation, and for public good significantly redefined the abstract generality and limitless exchangeability of the print media, its surplus relationality. In naming "supervision" and "negativity" as the two procedures redefining the print media into the assumptions of civil conversation, Warner, in his New Historicist analysis of the early American Republic, emphasizes (after Foucault) the disciplinary effect of the ideology of civic republicanism within the public sphere. By reading the public-oriented placement of printed materials in the early republic as the loss of the limitless discursiveness and abstract generality of writing as such, Warner isolates within writing itself the negative capability of the liberal imagination. For without the demands imposed on the *res publica* of letters by the public sphere, Warner observes, no subject can appear other than this surplus relationality.

The Desublimation of Romance

If Warner provides a New Historicist account of the difficulty in relating the Republic of Letters to the public world, John McWilliams supplies a genealogical account, different from that of the liberal consensus, of the origins of the romance within America's Republic of Letters. Instead of accepting Chase's explanation of the romance as his rationale for its dominance within the field, McWilliams finds in the romance genre a jeremiad-like surplus generalizability—a way to co-opt the terms of the literary value constitutive of the Tradition of British Literature and to subsume any other account predicated upon the difference between literary text and social context. Chase turned to Hawthorne, McWilliams argues, for his definitive conflation of America and Romance, but he did so in a period of "definitional chaos" when no one else insisted much upon the distinction between the novel and the romance. Chase's readings of Hawthorne legitimized the romance as the dominant literary genre, but in the timeless context of the canonical work rather than history.

McWilliams's New Historicist rationale for the romance recovers the historical context which explains the genre's effectiveness as well as its vulnerability. However, the other critics within this section will, in choosing noncanonical authors and texts, deny the romance its traditional effectiveness. In "Scarcity, Subjectivity, and Emerson," for example, Wai-chee Dimock reads Emerson's "Experience" without the support of the American romance tradition. This tradition reads the losses Emerson recorded to corroborate the essay's organizing thematic—alienation from a public world. Instead of continuing the terms of that reading, Dimock brings Emerson's essay into relationship with the otherwise unrelated field of political economy. In so doing, she turns political economy into an analytic category appropriate for an understanding of Emerson. By reading the essay as expressive of Emerson's internalization of a general economy, Dimock significantly expands the context for American Studies even as she significantly devalues the literary property of the romance. No longer can the romance remain a unit of reproducible cultural capital.

In "Hearing Narrative Voices in Melville's *Pierre*," Priscilla Wald takes up a romance, usually excluded from the canon as a literary failure, to make discernible the paradoxical relations the romance genre produces within an American writer. Wald argues that Pierre wishes to author himself but is compelled to recognize this self-authoring as a plagiarism of a pre-existing romance's text, the *Declaration of Independence*. In her subtle reading, Pierre's narrative registers his need for the authoritative voice he lacks. Wald's critique recalls Warner's emphasis on the negation of the self presupposed by the subjection to print and recalls McWilliams's cooptation of romance. In designating Americans' rivalry with their founding documents as the constitutive cultural location for this crisis in self-authorization, Wald, however, removes Melville's romance from the abstract generalities of writing as such and brings it into uneasy relationship with a specific American text in need of specific negotiation.

Steven Mailloux continues this re-situation of figures from literary romance into socioeconomic contexts by reading Mark Twain's *Adventures of Huckleberry Finn* from within the cultural rhetorics productive of child discipline. In "The Rhetorical Use and Abuse of Fiction: Eating Books in Late Nineteenth-Century America," Mailloux analyzes how the reading of books became functions of a more pervasive "technology of the self," relating reading habits with inner discipline and self-transformation. By highlighting the physicality of the rhetorical tropes used to relate reading and personal growth, he illuminates the ways in which consuming books and eating food both became aspects of cultural nurturing.

In Mailloux's reading of *Huckleberry Finn*, Twain isolates the delinquent in need of supervision by a culture he dispossessed. But Huck's dispossession of this culture, Ivy Schweitzer cogently observes, was revised by later Americanists into a romance of self-possession. In "Maternal Discourse and the Romance of Self-Possession in Kate Chopin's *The Awakening*," Schweitzer, then, reads Edna Pontellier in terms previously reserved for the male protagonists of American romance. Like Huck, Edna challenges the presuppositions organizing her culture and refuses to be regulated by them. In representing a female protagonist in a literary realm dominated by males, Kate Chopin returns to Hawthorne's Hester Prynne for a literary precursor. Schweitzer argues that Edna recapitulates for Chopin the contradictions in the character of Hester but also makes audible the conflicts silenced by Hawthorne's romance. Like Hester's, Edna's maternal role enables her to experience the romance of liberal individualism as a restraint upon as well as a retention of the self. Unlike Hester, however, Edna rebels in her feminine romance against the maternal role and experiences liberal individualism as the suppression of an alternate selfhood. Edna represents her experience of this alternate construction as a rebirth within a maternal realm, a rebirth in which merger is valued over resistance and reciprocity over solitude. But this rebirth does not take place within any available cultural location, but rather at her suicidal recognition of her culture's limits.

The New Historicist Return of the Repressed Context

That Schweitzer's Edna could merge with this alternate self, but only in a maternal realm of suicide by drowning, underscores the difference between her romance of self-possession and Robert Weimann's "internalized critique" in the nineteenth-century novel. In "Realism, Ideology, and the Novel in America: Changing Perspectives," Weimann argues that nineteenth-century novelists questioned the validity of the liberal assumptions organizing American culture. According to Weimann, Howells, Twain, Norris, London, and Dreiser constructed, in their novels, a critical consciousness able to assimilate the crisis in the dominant ideology into a narrative representation. The direct result of this internalized crisis was a critique of nineteenth-century liberal consensus. In elaborating this critique of liberalism, Weimann takes repossession of James, who represented Trilling's *Liberal Imagination*, as an example of liberalism's critique. The New Americanists who follow him in the volume explore the implication of this insight.

Warner, McWilliams, Wald, Mailloux, Dimock, and Schweitzer expose the cultural contradictions masked by the ideology of the literary romance. By turning for their analyses of the problematic of literary authority to noncanonical texts, to previously ignored authors for examples of the limitations in canonical assumptions, to economic categories for an understanding of the transcendental experience, and to diet regimens to explain the cult of reading, all of these New Americanists desublimate the romance's function within American Studies and affiliate the literary romance with previously unrelated cultural rhetorics and materialist logics.

In "American Literature and the New Historicism: The Example of Frederick Douglass," Gregory Jay uses Douglass's three autobiographies to argue that the return of such unrelated contexts to literary texts results in the alienation from them of romance elements. Jay's essay provides a significant critical reflection on the desublimation of romance. Here Jay indirectly associates the rise of New Historicism with this desublimation and finds in the historical agencies that American New Historicists construct a release from the constrictions of the white, eurocentric male subject reproduced within the romance of American Studies.

Howard Horwitz, in "'Ours by the Law of Nature': Romance and Independents on Mark Twain's River," relocates the romance of self-possession within the field of political economy. Like Wai-chee Dimock, Horwitz treats the romance as an ideological construct rather than a literary form. In elevating the independent selfhood of the riverboat captain to a romantic construction, Twain, Horwitz argues, idealizes the competitive relations of market capitalism. As a result of this idealization, the riverboat captain can lay claim to an authority unwarranted by his location within the commercial world.

Horwitz and Jay deploy their desublimation of the romance to empower their New Historicist readings. By disabling its ideological reflex—the romance's disconnection of realms—Horwitz and Jay restore as valid socioeconomic questions and political figures previously unrepresented within these narratives. In subjecting his restoration of these figures to a poststructuralist critique of representation, Jay devises a strategy to interrogate the rhetorics of self-production that take place *within* Douglass's autobiographies as well as *between* those works and the institutions conditioning their reception.

As Jay completes the desublimation of what McWilliams identifies as romance's surplus cooptative power, he replaces the romance with what Weimann refers to as the internalized critique of the nineteenth-century novel. Susan Mizruchi, in "Cataloging the Creatures of the Deep: 'Billy Budd, Sailor' and the Rise of Sociology," contrasts the heightened critical consciousness she (along with Weimann) finds in nineteenth-century realist novels with the regulatory social models she finds in the New Historicism. The rise of sociology and the writing of "Billy Budd," Mizruchi argues, are partially the results of the expansion, in the nineteenth century, of the number of potential social subject positions available for American citizens. This hypertophy in social roles produced, in America's citizenry, two antithetical reactions—the drive to generalized supervision of a heterogeneously organized society and the urge to be unconsciously positioned within structures of social control. Her careful reading of "Billy Budd" affiliates these two urges with questions of social visibility and with the rise of sociology as a discipline for social engineering.

In historicizing the differentiation of the fields of sociology and literature, Mizruchi is interested in recovering the problematic they shared as well as the differences in their engagement of it. In "Violence, Revolution, and the Cost of Freedom: John Brown and W. E. B. DuBois," William E. Cain considers the ways in which W. E. B. DuBois, by writing about John Brown, took possession of Brown as a sociopolitical symbol at a time when he urgently needed that symbol for the Civil Rights movement. DuBois's historical inquiry into Brown's biography cannot, according to Cain, be truly distinguished from the usage to which he put that biography.

In emphasizing the linkage DuBois established between historical analysis and an emancipatory political praxis, Cain quietly turns DuBois into a New Americanist. If the New Americanists' revisionist intervention into the canon presented here helps change American Studies into a field that can include W. E. B. DuBois's works, such inclusions speak powerfully to what changes still need to be effected in U.S. culture.

The *Res Publica* of Letters

Michael Warner

In *The Structural Transformation of the Public Sphere*, Jürgen Habermas shows that one of the most momentous developments in the political life of the West emerged as a new practice of reading.[1] In his view, from late in the seventeenth century until early in the nineteenth century, a set of institutions developed in which politics could be separated both from the state and from civil society. He calls that set of institutions the bourgeois public sphere and argues that its independence has since eroded. What I wish to take up here, however, is the place of reading in his narrative. Habermas tells the story of an increasing differentiation of a public sphere from state and civil society as primarily a story about new uses of texts. Newspapers, literary salons, coffeehouses, novels, art criticism, and magazines all play an important role in his account of how the fundamental structure of politics changed.

In this essay I want to pursue the untheorized implications of that

1. Jürgen Habermas, *Strukturwandel der Offentlichkeit* (1962), available in English as *The Structural Transformation of the Public Sphere*, trans. Thomas Burger (Cambridge: MIT Press, 1989).

account by arguing that, in the American case, the transformation of power came about not merely by an increased volume of print, but also by a new construction of the textuality of print. I will take up three instances where a conflict over emergent ways of using print took place: a Maryland tobacco controversy, a Boston currency crisis, and New York's famous Zenger case. In each case what happened was not simply a material change (more printing) with political consequences, but rather a fundamentally cultural change (as, indeed, all political formations are). By saying that the deployment of reading in the formation of the bourgeois public sphere was a cultural transformation of textuality, I mean that it required a new but tacitly symbolic vocabulary for understanding printed texts. So that after describing the three cases, I shall argue that the language of republicanism can be interpreted as just such a metadiscourse.

Before the middle decades of the eighteenth century, and also in ongoing contexts of customary law, the political sphere of the colonies depended on its continuity with common social exchanges. This model of the public as continuous with custom and natural order can be seen in a sermon preached in 1731 by Samuel Whittelsey, *A Public Spirit Described & Recommended*. Not untypically, Whittelsey defines a public spirit as one "that is truly & heartily Concern'd for the good and welfare of others."[2] The sphere in which this kind of public spirit functions is daily life, and although Whittelsey goes on to discuss the specialized business of government, his central premise is always a continuity between that business and common interactions, between public and spirit. For him, the exemplary case of the public sphere is the daily practice of religion: "It is Religion that unites and ties the several members of the Society together" (*PSDR* 9). Far from being an impersonal sphere of political decisionmaking, publicness is a mode of sociability as subjection in an ideally nonnegotiated social order, allowing judgment, in Whittelsey's words, to "run down as a River, and Righteousness as a mighty Stream" (*PSDR* 11).[3] And whereas, for later thinkers such as John Adams, public activity always has a critical intention with regard to power, for Whittelsey, public activity and critical intentions are categorical opposites: "A Contrary Spirit is a Base Spirit" (*PSDR* 29).

2. (New London, 1731), p. 7. Further references to this text will be made parenthetically (*PSDR*). See also similar sermons by Timothy Cutler, *The Firm Union of a People Represented* (New London, 1717) and William Balch, *A Public Spirit* (Boston, 1749).
3. The metaphor of the fountain is closely associated with this model of society and is analyzed in a brilliant turn by Louis Althusser in *Montesquieu, Rousseau, Marx: Politics and History*, trans. Ben Brewster (London: Verso, 1982).

To a public sphere of such a customary type, printed discourse holds a more or less arbitrary relation, capable equally of confirming or distorting the norms of public spirit. So for the early colonists, being public did not entail a special communicative context such as publication, and publishing did not have the meaning of making things public. In 1709, for example, when Cotton Mather drew up in his diary a list of resolutions for himself, he included a set of resolutions to perform "In my public Circumstances." He resolves, under that heading, to pray and to make "careful Visits, in my Flock." It is also in this context that he writes, "And I would compose and publish many *Essayes*, accommodated unto the Interests of Christianity in the Land; such as may find out all Sorts of People, in the several Wayes, wherein they may be sett athinking on such Things, as may be for the Glory of God."[4] Insofar as publishing is public, it is an extension of personal visitation; what marks Mather's entry into his public capacity is not writing as such, but rather his authoritative ministrations of which writings are only instruments. And since publication is as remote as possible from collective decisionmaking, political debate does not appear as an appropriate genre for Mather's writing.

Indeed, expressly political publications were virtually unknown in the print discourse of the colonies before 1720. One of the rare exceptions can reinforce the point: I refer to a pamphlet precipitated by the 1689 revolution against the Andros regime in Massachusetts. It begins by wishing its nonexistence: "It is the Unhappiness of this present Juncture, that too many Men relinquish their Stations of *Privacy* and *Subjection*, and take upon them too freely to descant upon affairs of the *Publick*."[5] Citizenship, ideally identical here with an adherence to stations of privacy and subjection, would not in its normal course involve political publication. Of course, Puritan Massachusetts did have institutions and modes of discourse for political affairs: town meetings, magistracy, sermons, and the like. But the structure and legitimacy of these institutions depended on their continuity with the mode of sociability called "public spirit," and thus on their *not* taking the form of interested debate or collective conflict resolution. Published debate could only be an index of failure in public affairs, a poor substitute for a public spirit strangely forgotten in a moment of crisis.

4. *Diary of Cotton Mather* (New York: Ungar, 1957), 2: 17.
5. *An Appeal to the Men of New England* (Boston, 1689), p. 1.

The Maryland Tobacco Controversy

Maryland had had printers as early as 1685, but not for political publishing. In fact, William Nuthead, who had already been forbidden to print in Jamestown some years earlier, was jailed in Maryland in 1693 for printing the proceedings of the legislature. He was then ordered never again to print anything relating to public affairs, so that he and, subsequently, his widow printed mostly blank legal forms. (When William Nuthead died in 1695, his debtors, some sixty in number, were almost all sheriffs, clerks, or justices.)[6] By 1725, however, it had come to be understood—at least by some in Maryland—that the establishment of a public discourse would be a good reason for bringing another printer to Maryland. In that year, the Assembly decided to print its own proceedings, a task which necessitated going to Philadelphia. The book, when it appeared, bore a preface complaining that without a press Marylanders "have scarce had any Opportunity of Judging whether they were Served or Prejudiced by their Representatives; whether their Constitution was maintained or prostituted, whether their *English* Liberties were Asserted or Neglected by them." Indeed, the preface continues, many delegates "who have, by an Ingenuous Honest Conversation, justly Recommended themselves to the Choice of the Electors, have not known what was the Constitution of their Country." The preface here establishes a double perspective for the utility of public discourse: print will function for freeholders as activity in the civic sphere and for representatives as the medium of authoritative instruction. "But 'tis hop'd from this beginning and the provision that is made for having a Press amongst us, the Gentlemen of the Country will more readily fall upon this useful kind of Learning."[7] William Parks, the English provincial printer who was brought to the colony shortly thereafter (and who later moved on to Williamsburg and printed *Typographia*), depended on the political value of such thinking for the success of his press.[8]

In 1727, shortly after Parks's establishment in Annapolis and early

6. On Nuthead, see Lawrence C. Wroth, "The St. Mary's City Press: A New Chronology of American Printing," *Colophon* n.s. 1 (1936): 333–57.
7. "An Epistolar Preface to the Maryland Readers," in *The Charter of Maryland*, with *The Proceedings and Debates of the Upper and Lower Houses of Assembly in Maryland* (Philadelphia, 1725), p. iii–iv.
8. On Parks, see J. A. Leo Lemay, *Men of Letters in Colonial Maryland* (Knoxville: Univ. of Tennessee Press, 1972) and Lawrence Wroth, *A History of Printing in Colonial Maryland 1686–1776* (Baltimore, 1922).

on in the tobacco controversy, he printed a pamphlet called *A Letter from a Freeholder*, responding to a letter in the *Gazette*. (Unfortunately, the early issues of the *Gazette* itself are not known to have survived.) As though to register resistance to the idea of public, printed discourse, the tract opens with an apology for its publication:

> I am very glad that a Gentleman who is a Friend to his Country, (as I am firmly perswaded the Author of the late *Letter to the Printer* really is) has communicated his Thoughts to the Publick, concerning a thing so much desired and so much wanted as a *Tobacco-Law* . . . And I am in Hopes that others, excited by the same generous Motive, will follow so laudable an Example, that by the Communication of Mens Thoughts and Sentiments to each other, such Methods may be taken for the Regulation of our Staple of Tobacco.[9]

For the author of the pamphlet, communication in print is not ancillary to a public sphere or a reflection of it, but rather is its ideal version. Apparently taken with the novelty of the pamphlet's form, the author goes on:

> As I am of Opinion with the Author of the Letter, that aiming at the Good of ones Country, is a sufficient Apology for publishing a Man's Thoughts; so am I clearly of Opinion that it is the indispensable Duty of every Man to do it, with Sincerity and Freedom; and that he ought not to suffer any private Views or Ends (inconsistent with the common Good) to byass or influence him; and that not being Master of a correct Stile, or Propriety of Expression, is no Excuse for being silent on so important and pressing an Occasion. (*LF* 4)

Here the notion that every man ought to publish reveals, of course, that the author assumes that he writes to a restricted community of white, propertied males. But in this scenario he also imagines a new set of relations among persons, discourse, and the political order, though many of these new relations are necessarily assumed rather than explicit.

Most obvious is the notion that men, who had, after all, been exchanging opinions all along in other formats, should now have a specialized discourse for that purpose. What would be the advantage of such a (meta)linguistic codification? How and to what purpose shall a public discourse be demarcated from other cultural forms and linguistic environments? The pamphlet's rhetoric shows us first that, purged of "private

9. *A Letter from a Freeholder, to a Member of the Lower House of Assembly* (Annapolis, 1727). Further references to this text will be made parenthetically (*LF*).

Views or Ends," publicity in such a discourse will be impersonal by definition. Persons who enter this discourse do so on the condition that the
validity of their public utterance will bear a negative relation to their persons.
These perspectives could not be separated: the impersonality of public discourse, in other words, is seen both as a trait of its medium and as a norm
for its subjects. Moreover, a special feature of the political order will follow,
since the government could no longer remain indifferent to this independent
public discourse, but rather must regard its relation to the public discourse
as a criterion of its own legitimacy. A complex network of assumptions appears here in order to render the printing of this pamphlet normal, and for
the rest of the century the presses would creak in its elaboration.

This new set of assumptions exemplifies the transformation of the
public sphere. It was not simply a matter of an emergent reading audience
or a new genre; the people who read these pamphlets, after all, were presumably the same people who read other things, such as bills and Bibles,
before. And the political tract as genre antedates printing, as was understood by its many eighteenth-century practitioners, who never tired of invoking their classical and early modern predecessors. What is more to the
point is that the public sphere required a special set of assumptions about
print. Indeed, it required an articulated relation between assumptions about
print and norms of a specialized discursive subsystem. For the Maryland
author and other contributors to the public discourse, the very printedness of that discourse took on a specially legitimate meaning, because
it was categorically differentiated from personal modes of sociability. Mechanical duplication equalled publishing precisely insofar as public political
discourse was impersonal.

Before examining the principles of this discourse in detail, let us continue to pursue the Maryland author's own understanding of the new public
order. He depicts the conditions of his pamphlet's utility, appealing jointly to
the nature of representative government and to the act of printing:

> It is the Opinion of some very learned Men, that something useful
> and improving may be collected from the meanest Productions: The
> Bee gathers honey from all sorts of Flowers to encrease the com-
> mon Stock, and our Assembly is the common Hive into which every
> Man's Thoughts and Sentiments ought to be carried, and in which
> those that are good and useful in themselves ought to receive Life
> and Vigour. . . . The Usefulness of Mens publishing their Thoughts
> with Candor and Sincerity on the present occasion, will further ap-
> pear by this consideration, that the Legislators may by examining

and comparing Mens Notions and Sentiments, find out all or the chiefest Advantages and Inconveniencies to the People attending a Tobacco-Law. (*LF* 4)

As in the 1725 preface quoted above, published debate is here presented as public from two different perspectives: freeholders are seen as actively engaged in the civic sphere by their participation in discourse, and legislators find their representative functions in that same discourse. The pamphlet claims the relevance of both perspectives in its full title: *A Letter from a Freeholder, to a Member of the Lower House of Assembly*. These twin perspectives of participation determine the text as an exchange between identifiable persons. Indeed, in the colonial period the most popular genres for political debate, by far, were the epistolary pamphlet and the dialogue.

Yet it should be noted that an indispensable tension is visible in the pamphlet's rhetoric. The important thing about this pamphlet and others of its genre is that although the relation between two correspondents defines the value of participation, nevertheless, that relation cannot be adequate to the medium. The pamphlet, for example, is not a personal letter and *must* not be, in the conditions of the public sphere of representational politics. Writing's unrestricted dissemination appears here as the ground of politics because in its very contrast with personal presence it allows a difference between public discourse and private correspondence. Freeholder and member alike encounter the exchange *not as a relation between themselves as men, but rather as their own mediation by a potentially limitless discourse*. That is why their exchange is not just written, as the pose of correspondence already implies, but also printed in the form of a pamphlet. A consciousness of the medium is carefully sustained, not only in the explicit metacommentary here, but equally in the formalized diction and mode of exposition. And that consciousness of the medium is valued precisely because it remains unreconciled with the conventions of personal exchange.

The meaning of public utterance, for both men, is established by the very fact that their exchange can be read and participated in by any number of unknown and *in principle unknowable* others. No catalogue of empirical readers will exhaust the implied sphere of this discourse. The resulting form of mediated relations (which is not to imply that other relations are *un*mediated) was to become the paradigmatic political relation of republican America. The assumptions that made it possible could doubtless be translated to oral settings, as long as people agreed to behave as though they were being supervised by an indefinite number of others, any one of whom might occupy their own position irrespective of status. This universalizing mediation of publicity, though possible in any number of contexts, would, nevertheless, continue to find its exemplary case in printed discourse. The more powerful the political norms of the relation became, the more print discourse would seem special and important.

The surplus of the letter over the relation of correspondents is determined not as the free play of language—indeed, it requires a perfect faith in the determinacy of meaning—but as the condition of a norm. Following Habermas, we may call this norm the principle of supervision, "that very principle which demands that proceedings be made public." [10] On the basis of this principle, and in the understanding that its address is a spectacular transaction, the *Letter* is able to conclude with a reference to communication that has the force of a threat:

> Thus, Sir, I have given you very candidly my Thoughts on the Proposals for a *Tobacco-Law*; and I am so far from making any Apology for the Trouble I have given you, that I tell you in plain and honest *English*, that it is your Duty (if you find any Thing in these my Notions, or in those of any other Persons, that shall be communicated to you, useful to the Publick,) to endeavour to the utmost of your Power, that the Publick may receive the Benefit of 'em; And, that if you are byass'd by any private or partial View, prejudicial to your Country's Service, you betray the Trust those you represent have reposed in you; but I hope for better Things from you, and that you'll behave your self as becomes a good Patriot, and an honest Man; upon which Terms, and no other, You may always depend on the Vote and Interest, as well as the sincere, and hearty good Wishes of, Sir,
>
> Your most humble Servant,
A Free-holder.
>
> (*LF* 4)

There is more involved here than the cantankerousness of an anonymous author. The avoidance of privacy in the closing remarks is authoritative be-

---

10. Jürgen Habermas, "The Public Sphere: An Encyclopedia Article," trans. Sarah Lennox and Frank Lennox, *New German Critique* 3(1974): 49–55. "To the principle of the existing power, the bourgeois public opposed the principle of supervision—that very principle which demands that proceedings be made public. The principle of supervision is thus a means of transforming the nature of power, not merely one basis of legitimation exchanged for another" (52).

cause of the principle of supervision that conditions the public sphere of print discourse. Supervision, in this cultural context, is both a legitimate threat and the immanent meaning of printedness.

The principle of supervision is a paradoxical kind of discipline. In an important sense, the public official cannot answer to it as a person by proving his godliness or his gentlemanliness, because validity in the public sphere of print discourse holds a negative relation to persons. The *Letter* does not threaten the Assemblyman in his person—indeed, it warns him to discount "any private or partial View." But because of this abstractness defining the norms of publicity, the same principle of supervision that disciplines the public official also appears as empowering. It gives the legislator his capacity to represent the whole of the public rather than persons. At the same time, it is balanced by a contradictory emphasis on participation. The pamphlet depicts a freeholder instructing a representative and a representative legislating for the freeholder; this component of individual participation does not disappear from the pamphlet's rhetoric even though instruction and legislation are only valid to the extent that they are distinguishable from the personal dimension. The generic pose of correspondence maintains that dimension, while the recognition of printed dissemination (i.e., the recognition that this correspondence is only a pose) expresses the negation of persons necessary for legitimacy.

As a condition of legitimation, the negation of persons in public discourse is equally important as the principle of supervision. To distinguish this specifically political assumption from the negativity of the symbolic in general, or the universality of truth claims in general, I shall call it the principle of negativity.[11] This principle is a ground rule of argument in a public discourse that defines its norms as abstract and universal, but it is also a political resource available only in this discourse and available only to those participants whose social role allows such self-negation (i.e., to persons defined by whiteness, maleness, and capital). And although the negativity of persons in the public sphere appears in the form of a positive trait— namely, virtue—it is at this point in the republican tradition that virtue comes to be defined by the negation of other traits of personhood, in particular as a rational and disinterested concern for the public good.

We may find the principle of negativity explained in the language of

11. This principle may be described as a form of the negativity of democratic politics in general, as explained by Ernesto Laclau and Chantal Mouffe in *Hegemony and Socialist Strategy* (London: Verso, 1985).

the time by a later contributor to the same tobacco debate. Writing in the pages of Parks's *Maryland Gazette*, one "P. P." defends himself for having published anonymously in the public controversy. He had been accused of cowardice and of insolence because he had brought forth, in what is called an "unprecedented Method," accusations against "a Gentleman"—and that "before the whole Country, in the most public Manner."[12] In a social order of deference and customary law, such action would be scandalous indeed. But "P. P." argues that persons are irrelevant in the discourse of the public sphere where, he says, assertions are assessed by readers for just reasoning. Public writing can therefore be contrasted with personal testimony, in which "it is absolutely necessary to know the Person of the Witness." "Now P. P. does not pretend," he says of himself, "to know any thing, of his own Knowledge, of the Conduct of any of the [tobacco] Merchants; what he chiefly relies on, is what is publish'd, and has been seen by the Generality of People, as have his Inferences."[13] "P. P." here validates his writing by exempting it from any link to himself, a tactic nicely amplified by the use of the third person in naming himself. It is nonetheless a personal tactic and claim, a skillful posture that can be described as a kind of cultural capital. This personal tactic of depersonalization both requires and enables a specialized subsystem of public discourse.

Curiously, "P. P." also recommends that his accuser read several publications, published under fictitious names, that, by means of their fictive personae, were able to avoid the resistance of "Personal Prejudice." This extra detail about pseudonyms reminds us of the importance of print, as it is here construed, in enabling the virtue of the citizen by the very fact that writing is not regarded as a form of personal presence. The difference between the private, interested person and the citizen of the public sphere appears both as a condition of political validity and as the expression of character of print. We have already seen that the illimitable readership of print discourse becomes important as the correlative of public supervision; here the apparent absence of a personal author in printed language has become important as the correlative of the principle of negativity.

"P. P." was forced to articulate and defend these constructions because the emergent public discourse of print was still in conflict with other determinations of the public, of personhood, and of language. Many Marylanders were newly encountering such norms of policy and discourse while

12. *Maryland Gazette*, 29 April 1729.
13. *Maryland Gazette*, 6 May 1729.

those norms were still being clarified in the course of the tobacco debate and while the institutionalization of print discourse there was not yet secure. Neither the new paradigm of print nor the new paradigm of politics took the field instantaneously, although they appeared together as they made each other mutually intelligible. Moreover, as we might guess from the prominence of imperial and commercial issues in the Maryland public debates, the emergence of the public discourse was not simply a local phenomenon. In the same period, similar events were taking place in cities such as Philadelphia and Charleston. For the gentry of the southern colonies in particular, the development of public debate in print was a way of keeping in contact with the English, and so its spread was unimpeded though gradual.

The Boston Currency Crisis

In Boston, however, where the customary public sphere of Puritan society was more intensely organized and where a corresponding tradition of printing was already established, the emergence of printed debate took place only in struggle. Since the brief crisis following the dissolution of the Andros regime, manifestly political printing in Massachusetts had consisted almost entirely of the governor's edicts. A newspaper was established in 1704; bearing the bold legend "Published by Authority," it reproduced edicts of the governor and his imperial superiors, but contained virtually no local political news, much less debate. In 1714, however, a conflict arose that suddenly veered into print with the publication of a handful of pamphlets. It subsided only temporarily and returned in a more critical form by 1720, when political pamphlets were published in then-undreamed-of numbers and occupied the town's attention. Late in 1719, a second Boston newspaper was founded, followed in 1721 by a third (although it was only the fourth in all of colonial America). One writer in the latter paper observed, early in 1722, "Letters (I don't mean Learning) grow upon us daily; we have Weekly three News-Letters, and sometimes as many little Books or Pamphlets (I don't say Sermons) published."[14] These developments institutionalized the public sphere of print discourse, although of course that discourse continued to compete with other modes of legitimation.

As in Maryland, the transformation of the public sphere in Boston began in relation to the market. The central dispute in the Boston crisis was the creation of a currency; a group of merchants, plagued by a chronic

14. *New England Courant*, 12 March 1722.

monetary shortage that imperial policy had long aggravated, were struggling to establish a new currency of either private or colonial issue. When
the Boston merchants first began planning a private bank for the issue of a
currency in 1714, the attorney general viewed their project as that of an illegitimate body politic. He accordingly filed a brief in council in August of that
year that produced an order that "the Projectors or Undertakers of any such
Bank, do not proceed to Print the said Scheme, or put the same on Publick
Record, Make or Emit any of their Notes or Bills, until they have laid their
Proposals before the Generall Assembly of this Her Majesties Province . . .
And that this Order be Printed in the Weekly News Letter."[15] For the council, the control of commerce belonged to customary authority. And so did
print: the interdiction against printing assumes an official status for printed
texts such as that of the interdiction itself. When the merchants continued
to meet and discuss their plans, the attorney general published a pamphlet
denouncing the scheme. Indignant that the merchants were "openly carrying on their *Bank*," he argued that all such authority must derive from the
crown.[16]

The merchants, who had already reprinted a pamphlet describing
a currency scheme, began writing their own pamphlets, thus treating print
discourse not as an official channel of customary authority but as a second
dimension of the political—an arena of debate distinct from the constituted
authority of office. In one pamphlet, they describe the interdiction against
printing their scheme as "very hard, in that they were denied the benefit of
the Press," but they maintain that the ban applied only to the final proclamation of the scheme and not to the debate of its formation.[17] Thus was
inaugurated a new public debate in Boston; of the pamphlets that followed,
many were distributed free by their sponsors and most were circulated
aggressively. One pamphlet plays on that fact by beginning with a comic
scene: "My good Neighbour *Rusticus* quite tir'd out with the *dispersion* of
the *Distressed State* from Vill to Vill (like the Circulation of a Country Brief
for the Common Charity) cameat last puffing to my door, and desired me
to Read, and give my thoughts upon it."[18] Another writer claims to have
had someone else's pamphlet thrust into his hands on the Exchange.[19] It

15. *Boston News-Letter*, 23 August 1714.
16. [Paul Dudley], *Objections to the Bank of Credit* (Boston, 1714), p. 3.
17. *A Letter, from One in Boston, to his Friend in the Country* (Boston, 1714), p. 6.
18. *The Postscript* (Boston, 1720).
19. *Reflections upon Reflections: Or, More News from Robinson Cruso's Island, in a Dialogue Between a Country Representative and a Boston Gentleman* (Boston, 1720).

became common for each pamphlet to review its predecessors. By 1720, a pamphlet called *Reflections upon Reflections* could be stating the obvious when it said that "various Schemes, & projections, and Sentiments of Men (as their particular Interests, and private views have led them) have been exhibited, and almost an infinite number of Pamphlets dispersed thro' the Country."[20]

That same pamphlet, however, goes on to lament the debate which its author attributes to "such *furious Zeal*, and *Party warmth*, as has ended in Enmity." The idea of a political public of readers still seemed highly problematic. Indeed, nothing is more common in the pamphlets of the currency crisis than the theme that the debate itself manifests private and factional interests incompatible with the public good. The attorney general's argument, for example, is dismissed by one pamphlet as representing only the "Court interest."[21] Another appends cautionary postscripts defining "A Character of a Publick Spirit" as disinterested and "A Character of a Private Spirit" as selfish.[22] Each author denies having personal interests in the outcome. Moreover, each author strikes a defensive posture against the charge of party-mongering. John Colman, leader of the merchants, concludes his major pamphlet with the assertion that he is "prejudiced against no Man": "It is the good & Happiness of my Country that lies upon my Spirits and hath Influenced me hereunto. I have no private *sinister* aim in pursuit separate from the good of the whole, but am animated only by a sense of the distresses of the Town and Country, for want of a Medium of Exchange."[23] A respondent felt similarly moved: "Thus, Sir, I have given you my Thoughts with a sincere aim at the Good of my Country; and without prejudice or affection to any Man, or Party of men."[24]

The anti-party theme, which was as prominent in Maryland or South Carolina or Pennsylvania as it was in Boston, has to be distinguished from the norms of a customary public. The latter were invoked by the *Boston News-Letter*'s appeal for people to shut up and lead "quiet and peaceable Lives."[25] Such anti-party rhetoric would seem to be a version of the same appeal, but it is peculiarly double-edged. Anti-party rhetoric appears

20. *Reflections upon Reflections*, p. 5.
21. *A Letter from One in Boston to his Friend in the Country*, p. 1.
22. *Some Proposals to Benefit the Province* (Boston, 1720).
23. [John Colman], *The Distressed State of the Town of Boston, &c. Considered in a Letter from a Gentleman in the Town, to his Friend in the Countrey* (Boston, 1720), p. 9.
24. *A Letter from One in the Country to his Friend in Boston* (Boston, 1720), p. 22.
25. *Boston News-Letter*, 18 August 1720.

to invoke the earlier, customary norm of subjection insofar as it appears to oppose the existence of the debate itself. In actuality, however, it sustains the debate by providing the categories that would make an ongoing public debate thinkable. The language of resistance to controversy articulates a norm for controversy. *It silently transforms the ideal of a social order free from conflictual debate into an ideal of debate free of social conflict.* One pamphlet puts it this way:

> I wish from my heart that some Method may be found for our relief to prevent Party-making amongst us; it grieves me to see our Divisions which are daily increasing, and which tend only to our ruin; whereas if we would but Unite, and bare with one another in our different Apprehension of Things, debate Matters fairly, and lay aside all private designs, and Animosities, and believe that every Man's particular Interest is comprized in the General, and study sincerely the Publick Good, I am fully perswaded we might contrive ways to Extricate our selves out of these Difficulties, and be as flourishing a People as ever.[26]

This argument, apparently directed against public polemic, already presupposes the norms of public discourse—especially the principle of negativity, which appears here in the call to "lay aside all private designs and animosities." The tone suggests a conservative effort: divisions are increasing, but it is still possible to be "as flourishing a People as ever." The conservative posture, combined with the norm of unity, conceals the innovative character of the ideal of debate. The unity of this debating community will not, after all, be the same as the unity of the past society, since that society had been understood as unified only insofar as it was free of the "Divisions" that created debate.

Similarly, another pamphlet has it:

> The Gentlemen who have Printed their Thoughts on this Occasion, do (as far as I can discern) desire to see their Country in a Flourishing Trade, & Prosperous Condition, as they have seen it formerly; They differ indeed in their Conjectures about the Measures proper to be taken at this Juncture for this End; But its much to be Lamented, that Gentlemen who desire the good of their Country, can't declare their differing sentiments, about the best Means to promote

26. *A Letter From a Gentleman* (Boston, 1720), p. 13.

it, without falling under the Displeasure of those whom they study to serve.[27]

Though intelligible in a social order in which the debate seemed, at least to the governor and council, to be the loss of all public spirit and the degeneration of authority, anti-party rhetoric bore witness to the new discursive norms that constituted both a public sphere and an understanding of print. The use of certain kinds of texts had become natural to the political world.

The restructuring of power in the struggle over models of legitimation and discourse raises the question of who the agents in the struggle were, and what their interests in it might have been. In the eyes of the governor's party, the debate was a class problem, a view shared by the historian Gary Nash, who lays great stress on the episode. Nash sees in the currency crisis a turn toward populist politics; the pamphlets, he writes, "made direct appeals to the people, both those who enjoyed the vote and others who participated in the larger arena of street politics," and "were intended to make politics everyone's concern." According to Nash, print discourse was consumed by an artisan class that was not otherwise accustomed to adjudicating political affairs. "It was testimony to the power behind the printed word," he writes, "that even those who yearned for a highly restricted mode of politics were compelled to set their views in print for all to read. For unless they did, their opponents might sweep the field."[28]

Yet the difference between the old and new modes of politics was more than a matter of degrees of restriction. The pamphlets enact not so much a liberalization as an *abstraction* of the public, establishing the impersonality of its norms and the negativity of its citizens. Doubtless the transformation was motivated rather than arbitrary, and doubtless the self-understandings of economic classes were elements of its motivation. At the same time, the self-understanding of those classes—and thus their interests and nature—were at stake in the transformation. The currency dispute in Boston, like a similar dispute in Philadelphia, or like the tobacco-regulation debate in Maryland, gave a new identity to market society and legitimated new organizations of economy.

By seeing the debate as a turn toward populist politics, Nash also observes that the generalized public discourse potentially legitimated the participation of any class. This potential lay in the negativity that defined

27. *Reflections on the Present State of the Province of Massachuset-Bay in General* (Boston, 1720), pp. 3–4.
28. Gary Nash, *The Urban Crucible* (Cambridge: Harvard Univ. Press, 1979), p. 86.

the citizen in the printed public discourse, since participation could be legitimated despite personality, faith, class, or other criteria of validity. Yet it would be easy to be misled by the potential of this principle of negativity, as it was incapable of extending itself by its own dynamic. Radical though the principle seems in retrospect, it did not in practice allow access to the public arena for women, or blacks, or Indians, or the unpropertied, or various persons classed as criminal. Indeed, it was only because of the covert identification of print consumption with the community of propertied, white males that public discourse came about in the first place. Because the same differentials of gender, race, and class allocated both citizenship, on one hand, and active literacy, on the other, freehold and discourse could coincide *without* necessarily entailing a liberalization of power. The posture of negation that served as the entry qualification to the specialized subsystem of public discourse remained a positive disposition of character, a resource available only to a specific subset of the community.

The principle of the citizen's negativity, then, was not necessarily liberalizing as long as the covert distinction of the print community could be maintained, since in the new paradigm the print public could be equated with the political public. The principle of negativity, however, did mean that the constitutive distinctions of the political community had to *remain* covert. In situations where excluded groups were able to sustain a claim to discursive participation, the principle of negativity could be a powerful legitimating standard. In the case of Boston, the currency crisis articulated the (white male) community of the market as society; in that situation, therefore, (white male) artisans were politicized by print discourse, even though the abstraction of print remained incapable, by itself, of materially affecting lines of race and gender except by reproducing them in a masked form.

New York and the Zenger Case

As in Boston, the transformation of the public sphere in New York came about through the difficult emergence of a local print discourse, the difficulty of which was dramatized in a hotly contested political trial. What is particularly revealing is that it was the trial of a printer, John Peter Zenger, for seditious libel. The case has a certain notoriety in American legal history because it became the subject of nationalist legend in the nineteenth century. In this legendary history, Zenger appears as a patriotic hero fighting for American liberties and founding the principles behind the first amendment. More recently, the Zenger case has been the subject of revision among historians, who are now more likely to describe him as a poor pawn in a civic feud, a tradesman hired by the Morris faction because he was convenient, but who played little more than a mechanical role in the events that now bear his name. In the old Whig legend, Zenger's lawyer, Andrew Hamilton, was thought to have revolutionized liberty if not by inventing the freedom of the press then at least by securing it on these shores. In the current historical literature, it is sadly pointed out that prosecutions for seditious libel continued to occur on a regular basis. As late as 1798, the Alien and Sedition Acts could be passed without being impeded by the precedent of the Zenger case.[29]

Both the legendary history of the Zenger case and its debunking counterhistory share a set of modern liberal assumptions about the relation between the press and the law as well as about the relation between persons and political discourse. It is assumed on both sides that the moral consciences of the colonists were equipped with an idea of free and unbiased mass media. In the Whig version, the colonists are thought to have acted heroically on the basis of conscience by establishing the Zenger case as a precedent; while in modern legal history, they appear to have betrayed their shabby ignorance and moral cowardice in failing to sustain the precedent. And for both Whig history and libertarian lament, freely competitive public debate is assumed to be the natural expression of political personhood. Because of such assumptions, the historical literature typically misses the important developments in the public sphere that are exemplified in the Zenger case. If we stand back from the nationalism and preoccupation with precedent that have dominated this disagreement, it is possible to see the trial as an especially illuminating crisis in the joint transformations of print discourse and the public sphere. In particular, the trial reveals the stakes of power involved in that transformation.

The conflict leading up to the trial was one over the sources of law. William Cosby, in his turbulent and relatively brief career as governor of

29. The main treatment of the case is Stanley Katz's introduction to James Alexander, *A Brief Narrative of the Case and Trial of John Peter Zenger* (Cambridge: Harvard Univ. Press, 1963). See also Livingston Rutherfurd, *John Peter Zenger: His Press, His Trial and a Bibliography of Zenger Imprints* (1904; repr. Johnson Reprint Corp., 1968); Paul Finkelman, "The Zenger Case: Prototype of a Political Trial," in Michal R. Belknap, *American Political Trials* (Westport CT: Greenwood Press, 1981), pp. 21–42; Leonard W. Levy, *Emergence of a Free Press* (New York: Oxford Univ. Press, 1985); and Stephen Botein's introduction to *Mr. Zenger's Malice and Falshood: Six Issues of the New-York Weekly Journal* (Worcester MA: American Antiquarian Society, 1985).

New York in the early 1730s, seemed, to the colonials, determined to play the role of the despot. He laid absolute claim to the spoils of his office; he treated the courts as administering justice at his pleasure, dismissing recalcitrant justices; he tried to avoid dependence on the General Assembly and even attempted to rig elections; and he invoked imperial authority whenever customary legal and judicial procedures obstructed his plans. Such actions depended on a status-based model of legitimation that posited ultimate sovereignty in the crown—a model that until recently had been dominant in England and continued to organize many parts of the imperial administration despite the increasing importance of Parliament in English affairs. Local leaders in New York, however, had different allegiances: in part, to the traditions of common law which gave them a high degree of local autonomy and which made state administration dependent on local custom and, in part, to the abstract norms and procedures of predictability that organized the emerging society of the capitalist market. Both the norms of custom and the norms of the market conflicted at times with the status model of legitimation on which the imperial administration rested.[30]

To the influential group of New Yorkers led by Lewis Morris, a Supreme Court justice whom Cosby had replaced, Cosby was a threat to their own local power and, more generally, to the system of customary law on which their power was based. Morris organized an opposition and sailed for London to plead for Cosby's removal. More consequential was the strategy of Morris's associates, the lawyers James Alexander and William Smith: in the fall of 1733, they hired the almost unknown printer John Peter Zenger to establish a newspaper. Until that point there was only one newspaper in New York, and that was William Bradford's *New York Gazette*. A contributor to Zenger's new paper, the *New-York Weekly Journal*, would soon describe Bradford's *Gazette* as "a paper known to be under the direction of the government, in which the Printer of it is not suffered to insert anything but what his superiors approve of, under the penalty of losing £50 per annum salary and the title of the King's Printer for the Province of New York."[31] Implicit in this kind of language, of course, is a norm of public discourse, and in the long run the development of the emergent model of the public sphere would make far more difference in the structure of power than would Morris's London lobbying efforts.

30. For general background see Gary Nash, *The Urban Crucible*, and Patricia U. Bonomi, *A Factious People: Politics and Society in Colonial New York* (New York: Columbia Univ. Press, 1971).
31. *New-York Weekly Journal*, 17 December 1733.

Conscious of the novelty of their opposition paper in New York, Alexander and Smith began in the *Journal*'s first essay to offer a theory of print that would be at the same time an anti-dynastic theory of legitimacy. "The liberty of the press," they announced in the first sentence, "is a subject of the greatest importance, and in which every individual is as much concerned as he is in any other part of liberty."[32] "Liberty," it should be noted, in the eighteenth century meant, specifically, civic liberty—not just freedom from restraint of any kind, but rather the power of exerting oneself in the civic sphere. The word resonated with the whole of republican political thought; even to speak of "the liberty of the press" was to treat print within a highly charged political language. The local appeal of this language was that it could articulate colonial resistance to administrative power. Alexander and Smith therefore stress that the utility of the press lies in its ability to challenge administrative abuse. Depicting an "evil minister," they argue that published reports of his actions, "by watching and exposing his actions," will bring him into censure.

What is transparent to us, but scandalous to contemporaries, is the assumption that the censure of readers is a legitimate way to coerce officials. Governor Cosby himself, in a letter to the Duke of Newcastle, referred to the "paper warr" launched by Alexander and Smith as an attempt to have the government "prostituted to ye censure of ye mob."[33] One hostile writer commenting on the Zenger case condemned those New Yorkers who mistook "the liberty of the press for a license to write and publish infamous things of their superiors."[34] The disagreement here discloses a structural conflict between two sets of assumptions: on one hand, a social order in which "superiors" has a referent; on the other hand, a discursive order in which the act of reading can be equivalent to the political act of censure.

In a social order based on status, such as that of colonial New York, it did not strictly matter whether the published censure of an official were true or not. Even if true, such publication would be regarded as the defamation of a superior. Indeed, as John Peter Zenger would find out, English law held the truth of an accusation to be an *aggravation* of libel rather than a defense against it: since more people would believe a true libel than a false one, it would do greater damage to the esteem in which officials must be held. Long before charges of libel were filed, however, Alexander and

32. *New-York Weekly Journal*, 12 November 1733.
33. Quoted in Botein, *Mr. Zenger's Malice*, p. 7.
34. *Barbados Gazette*, July 1737, reprinted in Katz, ed., *Brief Narrative*, p. 154.

Smith were elaborating a concept of the social use of publication that would not only legitimate but also require defamation. "When did calumnies and lies ever destroy the character of one good minister?" they ask. "If their characters have been clouded for a time, yet they have generally shined forth in greater luster."[35] The scrutiny brought about by critical publication validates the good official.

Clearly, the assumption behind this concept of publication is the principle of supervision, and the *Journal*'s authors express it in a remarkably revealing sentence: "The facts exposed are not to be believed because said or published; but it [i.e., publication] draws people's attention, directs their view, and fixes the eye in a proper position that everyone may judge for himself whether those facts are true or not."[36] While this sentence takes the principle of supervision as a presupposition, on the level of explicit content it also offers a strikingly literal trope of supervision: a drawn attention, a directed view, and a fixed eye. The sense of sight is of course not necessarily more appropriate to the public world than any other sense is; yet the optic and spatializing metaphor of supervision became, in eighteenth-century America, the dominant way of conceptualizing the public. The *Journal*'s metaphorics of supervision refers to a disposition of character that makes reading a valuable action. It is the specificity of *reading* as the paradigmatic public action that lies behind the literalizing trope of supervision. The sentence unwittingly implies that when the virtuous citizen fixes his vigilant eye upon the civic scene, what he is looking at is a printed object. And because his gaze upon the material artifact of print is equivalent, in Alexander's words, to the "popular examination" of officials, it follows that the press in a republic with corrupt leaders is naturally an oppositional press (or, more generally, a regulative press).

The same sentence, it should be noted, exemplifies the principle of negativity, to which the principle of supervision is closely related. "The facts are not to be believed because said or published. . . ." The authority of published assertions is deferred to the validating inspection of the reading citizen. And because their authority is deferred, so is the responsibility for them. The *Journal*'s authors did not deny that there could be an abuse of the press, but they ambiguated the relationship between such abuse and the responsibility of particular, authorizing persons. "I agree with [Bradford] that it is the Abuse, and not the Use of the Press, [that] is blameable," one

35. *New-York Weekly Journal*, 12 November 1733.
36. *New-York Weekly Journal*, 12 November 1733.

Journal essay says. "But the Difficulty Lies who shall be the Judges of this Abuse. . . . I would have the Readers Judges: But they cant Judge, if nothing is wrote."[37] The same deferred authority that results in the principle of supervision here implies the principle of negativity: political assertions can be made neutrally, since their validity will be determined by the impersonal judgment of the general readership. In this important sense, publication is no longer to be considered as personal utterance.

Bradford's *Gazette* was quick to challenge these implications. "Is the Art of Printing less criminal than Natural Speaking?" a *Gazette* author asked rhetorically. "Nature has given us the Liberty of Speech, but that will not protect a Man from having his Head broke, if he gives ill Language."[38] The governor, sharing the desire to have somebody's head broken after the *Journal* printed some harsh criticism of his administration and sharing the same skepticism about the negativity claimed by the *Journal*'s authors, had a charge of seditious libel filed against the printer. Zenger was accordingly taken to prison, where he remained for a full eight months before his case came to trial. The trial itself seemed destined to uphold the governor. The judges, to begin with, were his hand-picked dependents. When Alexander and Smith, acting as defense counsel, challenged the legitimacy of the judges' commissions, the judges responded by disbarring them. Moreover, the legal case lay against Zenger. English law not only forbad evidence of truth as defense against libel charges, it decreed that the libelousness of a text was to be determined by the bench. Only the facts of printing or writing were to be determined by the jury, and Zenger's own journeyman and two sons were waiting in the court to testify that he had in fact printed the *Journal*. (Their testimony in any case would have been a formality; it is recorded that the jury knew Zenger to be the printer already, having themselves bought the *Journal* in Zenger's shop.)[39]

Zenger's new lawyer, the Philadelphian Andrew Hamilton, in the face of this seemingly closed case, pursued an entirely different line of defense. Rather than defend Zenger on the terms constructed by the law, he conceded the relevant facts at the opening of the trial. Then, after the prosecution's witnesses had been dismissed, he began an argument that, in effect, challenged the construction of political utterance that the prose-

37. *New-York Weekly Journal*, 18 February 1734.
38. *New York Gazette*, 4 February 1734.
39. This is recorded in James Alexander's preparatory brief, which can be found in Katz, ed., *Brief Narrative*, p. 139.

cution's case assumed. The first step in the defense was to introduce evidence about the truthfulness of the *Journal* articles named in the charges against Zenger. In doing so, he invoked the republican political principle that censure of an official is an exercise of virtue rather than a violation of status. But this line of defense was rejected by the court. Hamilton next turned to the jury, to whom he delivered a forceful appeal to decide not just the facts of the case, as precedent prescribed (and which he had already admitted), but the law of the case as well.

Hamilton's turn to the jury was powerfully overdetermined. Part of its strength lay in the appeal to custom and to local tradition. The jury system, derived from the common law and allowing a high degree of local, consensual autonomy in the use of coercion, represented exactly the forms of power threatened by the growing imperial bureaucracy. Appealing to the jury to set the law, Hamilton was also appealing to the socio-political base of the original conflict with Cosby. But Hamilton's arguments to the jury superimposed, on this appeal to custom and to local autonomy, the substantially different discursive norms of the new public sphere. He justified the appeal to the jury in the same language of deferred authority, supervision, and negativity with which Alexander had described print. The exchange is worth following in some detail in order to see how this double appeal to custom and to publicity came about.

First, Hamilton baited the prosecution by asking for a definition of libel. The prosecutor's definition emphasized defamation, including that of language understood to be "ironical or scoffing." Hamilton responded by seizing on the word "understood" in the prosecutor's definition:

> Here it is plain the words are scandalous, scoffing and ironical only as they are UNDERSTOOD. I know no rule laid down in the books but this, I mean, as the words are *understood*.

None of Hamilton's argument so far did anything obvious to advance Zenger's defense, and Chief Justice De Lancey conceded the apparently trivial point:

> *Mr. Chief Justice*. That is certain. All words are libelous or not, as they are *understood*. Those who are to judge of the words must judge whether they *are scandalous* or *ironical, tend to the breach of the peace*, or are *seditious*: There can be no doubt of it.[40]

40. Katz, p. 78.

This exchange about interpretation set the stage for the climax of the trial. In the eloquent speech that followed, Hamilton took the already conceded point about the test of understanding for irony or for libel as an argument that the meaning of an utterance is deferred to its interpretation. He then, in effect, gave that principle a political meaning. Whereas Chief Justice De Lancey took the theoretical point to be consistent with his own role (he is clearly thinking about himself when he says "Those who are to judge of the words"), Hamilton argued that the only interpretation that could indicate irony or libel would be a socially general one. The relevant interpretation therefore had to be performed by the jury rather than the judge. "The law," he told the jury, "supposes you to be summoned *out of the neighborhood where the fact is alleged to be committed*; and the reason of your being taken out of the neighborhood is *because you are supposed to have the best knowledge of the fact that is to be tried*."[41]

Now in Hamilton's courtroom performance, the jury's being taken "out of the neighborhood" refers ambiguously to their immediacy and to their mediation. On one hand, he was clearly referring to their local roots, their embeddedness in the norms of custom and the politics of community. On the other hand, he was referring to their representative plurality; since the jury represents the neighborhood *in general*, their interpretation can be taken to indicate an accurately universalizable judgment. Only in this latter sense could Hamilton's appeal to the jury conceivably follow from his argument about interpretation, especially since De Lancey, a New Yorker, could claim as much local knowledge as the jury members. The dependence of meaning on interpretation was thus understood in the Zenger trial as requiring a universality of judgment that militated against hierarchy. The success of Hamilton's performance, however, depended on his ability to conflate that implicit norm of abstract universality with the customary norm of local consensus. This delicate overdetermination made localism and universality indistinguishable from each other and equally opposed to the hierarchy of imperial administration.

The rest is well known: the jury returned a verdict of not guilty, the courtroom broke into cheers for Hamilton, and he was carried jubilantly into the streets. (Zenger, meanwhile, had to return to prison for another night before he was released.) Regardless of whatever role it may have had in setting legal precedents, I take the Zenger case to be representative of prerevolutionary colonial politics in at least three ways. First, it

41. Katz, p. 75.

demonstrates with clarity how the discursive norms of the public sphere required a specific understanding of print. A writer for the *New York Journal* in 1770 would make the connection clear in a way that had by then become commonplace: citing the Zenger case as an illustration, he writes, *"Public grievances* can never be redressed but by *public complaints*; and they cannot well be made *without the Press."*[42] Second, the case shows that the new discursive norms of print were articulated as a model of legitimacy that had revolutionary potential. The universality claimed by print discourse could be extended to an understanding of society as the agent of supervision. Third, the Zenger case shows how the success of that articulation depended on an overdetermined relation between publicity and custom. For forty years after the trial, resistance to the crown would increasingly be legitimated in the abstract and universalizing norms of public print discourse, although that resistance would be mobilized in the local politics of custom—an unstable alliance that would break down after the Revolution.

Far from being a minor adjustment in the rhetoric of and about officials, the rise of public discourse was one of the decisive innovations of the modern era. It enabled nothing less than the newly important differentiation between society and the state. This distinction, the premise of so much eighteenth-century social thought, carried with it the set of related distinctions classically studied by Weber, distinctions such as that between officer and office. It is no doubt one of the main reasons why modernity and printing have been associated ever since. Yet the decisive factor was not printing in general, but rather the specialized discursive subsystem that was articulated through special conventions for print. Only by means of a public discourse could the bureaucratic institutions develop, because state and society became differentiated in the appearance of the principle of supervision, which was imaginable only when a supervising agency could be given definition in distinction from the appointed and elected officials whom it would supervise. In the juridical practices of common law, where legislative and coercive power lay in a jury system predicated on ethical unity, no such boundary could be drawn.

What is this supervising agency? The literal answer might be the freeholders, except that as the occupants of the perspective of public discourse any such freeholders are distinguished from the exercise of public office which is otherwise their capacity. In this sense, the "public," "society," or "the people" have only a negative existence in relation to the official

42. *New York Journal*, 15 March 1770.

embodiment of power. Subjects find themselves as private persons within these large categories to the extent that the public discourse makes available to them their privative relation to the state.

Yet in another sense society and the public acquired a positive—though unrecognized—identity in the transmission of print. That is to say, the public was constructed on the basis of its metonymic embodiment in printed artifacts. That is how it was possible to imagine the public supervising the actions of officials even when no physical assembly of the public was taking place. By mid-century, newspapers were being published regularly in the major towns and were sustaining abstract, but local, political discourse. Pamphlets and broadsides were a familiar and normal feature of politics. In their routine dispersion and in the conventions of discourse that allowed them to be political in a special way, these artifacts represented the material reality of an abstract public: a *res publica* of letters. Important consequences followed both for the public and for print: unlike the public of the customary order, which was always incarnated in any relation between persons and which found its highest expression in church and town meetings, the public of print discourse was an abstract public, *never localizable in any relation between persons*. By the same token, print became publication in a newly privileged way, since it was only in print discourse that one could make things public for the now abstract public.

Printed artifacts, however, were not the only metonym for an abstract public. Also important were currency and commodities in general. For this reason it was not accidental that the public debates of print discourse took shape in relation to emergent forms of currency and commerce; public discourse articulated a society of which the North American colonies were only the furthest periphery, a society of commerce and regulation that had developed from the great early Renaissance fairs to the markets of international commerce. Printing in Western culture has always owed much of its character to the fact that it developed as a trade within this world of the fairs and the markets. Printers, of course, sold their products as goods and advertised other goods. They also printed the experimental new paper currencies of the eighteenth century, as well as the increasingly detailed public trade reports. Early colonial newspapers were often frankly founded for the promotion of trade, and most of the early public discourse of print is devoted to the regulation of trade.[43]

43. The *Boston Gazette* of January 4, 1720, for example, asserts that the paper's purpose is "to endeavour to advance, but not prejudice Trade"; the Philadelphia *American Mercury* shortly thereafter declared that "The Design of this Paper" was "to Promote

As the public discourse developed, the market and the public came to be capable of mutual clarification. The value of print and the value of currency equally required the potential for inexhaustible transmission, while the character of publication and the character of economic exchange equally required norms of impersonal relations. Public discourse and the market were mutually clarifying, then, in both their positive and negative characters: positive, because both public and market were metonymically realized in printed, mass-produced artifacts; negative, because the private subject finds his relation to both the public and the market only by negating the given reality of himself, thereby considering himself the abstract subject of the universal (political or economic) discourse.

The economy of discourse resulting from this mutual articulation, I would suggest, was the decisive feature of print capitalism. I take the term "print capitalism" from Benedict Anderson's admirable and provocative study of nationalism; unfortunately, Anderson's brief book leaves his suggestion relatively undeveloped and the term undefined. For Anderson, print capitalism was the historical development that made possible the emergence of transcendent, imaginary communities of nations.[44] Observing that books were the first capitalized commodities, Anderson argues that their readers—especially the readers of novels—labor to imagine a community of which they are a part even though the identity of that community does not allow a local proximity. The community of readership is a corporate body realized only metonymically, and this imaginary community, in Anderson's view, is the elemental form of the nation. In the articulated relation between print and capitalism that the Boston and Maryland debates illustrate, we can see that Anderson's term is more apt than he has himself shown. The imagination of community constructs the political nation not just indirectly, through novels, but directly, in the creation of the public sphere.

Republicanism as Metadiscourse

It will have struck any historian of the period that the examples of public discourse that I have given all happen to be examples of republican rhetoric as well. In the practices of print discourse, the American creoles elaborated a public sphere by means of their elaboration of the conceptual

Trade" (quoted in Anna DeArmond, *Andrew Bradford, Colonial Journalist* [Newark: Univ. of Delaware Press, 1949], p. 41).
44. Benedict Anderson, *Imagined Communities* (London: Verso, 1983).

vocabulary of republicanism and vice versa. Elaborating the republican vocabulary filled the need to make and remake continually a fit between the public discourse and the social world. Republicanism in this context means rather more than the republican political arguments advanced in printed debates. It is what J. G. A. Pocock calls "the language of republicanism": a conceptual vocabulary that made the whole range of republican political arguments possible.[45] By the same token, republican ideology was also an ideology of print in that its central categories—at least in the colonial American version of republicanism—were articulated in, and thus given meaning within, the symbolic practices of publication. We have already seen several examples: the anti-party rhetoric of the Boston currency crisis, for example, simultaneously gave meaning to the practice of publishing and to the republican norm of disinterest. To honor the powerfully republican character of the arguments in the Zenger case, the city of New York gave Hamilton a gold snuffbox inscribed with republican mottoes (an act that was soon denounced from as far away as Barbados).[46]

Historians have observed, at least since Timothy Breen's *Character of the Good Ruler* and Bernard Bailyn's *Ideological Origins of the American Revolution*, that a powerful strain of republican rhetoric, associated in England with Whig or Country traditions, began to flourish in the colonies at about the same time as the Boston currency crisis.[47] Though the commonwealth tradition was scarcely unknown to the Puritans,[48] in the early eigh-

45. *Machiavellian Moment*. For an account of the differences between Pocock's approach and the model of historiography it has been replacing, see Joyce Appleby, "Republicanism and Ideology," *American Quarterly* 37 (1985): 461–67. To say that the language of republicanism was to be found on such a fundamental ideological level is not, of course, to deny that there were variations and conflicts within republicanism, nor to deny that other conceptual vocabularies were lingering or emerging in the cultures of the American colonies. No reader of Pocock's work, for example, can fail to notice the ceaseless transformations of even the most central terms he studies. It is to say what is now relatively uncontroversial among historians: that for the colonists, the intelligibility of the political world and the possibility of action in it were constituted by the categories of a broad republican tradition.

46. Katz, ed., *Brief Narrative*, pp. 101–5, 155.

47. Timothy Breen, *Character of the Good Ruler* (New Haven, CT: Yale Univ. Press, 1970); Bernard Bailyn, *Ideological Origins* (1967; rpt. New York: Vintage, 1970). Both historians have also registered, at least indirectly, the close relation between republicanism and print discourse. Breen, for example, writes that the Country party's "most important contribution to the political life of New England may well have been the way it used the printing press to educate the public" (247). See also Caroline Robbins, *The Eighteenth-Century Commonwealthman* (Cambridge, MA: Harvard Univ. Press, 1959).

48. Thus Governor Dudley of Massachusetts could complain in 1702 of the "Common-

teenth century the republican categories of Country politics rapidly took hold throughout the colonies to organize political interests and conflicts. Politics came to be conceptualized increasingly in terms of virtue and corruption, interest and disinterestedness, public and party, liberty and power. These categories were not simply those of learned argument, but, more powerfully, those of cliche and common sense.

For this reason, nearly any example from the printed debates will also illustrate republicanism; let us take a pamphlet entitled *English Advice to the Freeholders, &c. of the Province of the Massachusetts-Bay*. Signed "Brutus and Cato," the pamphlet was printed in 1722 by James Franklin (no doubt with the assistance of his then apprentice brother), and is a prime instance of print supervision in the emergent republican paradigm. It begins by noting the upcoming May elections and appeals with a rhetoric of urgency for the election of "Patriots," "especially in the *House of Representatives*, who are the *Guardians of the People's Liberty*." The author is then able to add: "Remember (Countrymen) that Liberty is a Jewel of an inestimable Value, which when once lost, is seldom recovered again. . . . One way to keep it, is, to chuse good Men to *represent* you; such as dare boldly exert themselves for the *publick Good*, by making Laws that will secure you from any Attempts that may be form'd to your Prejudice by succeeding Rulers" (3–4).

The general republican sentiments are presented as obvious and nonargumentative. Even supporters of the incumbent officials could concede the praise of active liberty and the ideal of the public good. Thus the speaker says only, "Remember . . ." Within this profession of the obvious lies a whole set of interpretive categories and normative assumptions about power and personhood. To begin with, the cliché represents liberty as imperiled by rulers and requiring rigorous civic exertion against their ever-threatening encroachment. The assumptions that make this cliché intelligible include the notions of place-holding as corruptive, of virtue as active but disinterested participation in the civic sphere, and of the opposition between general concerns and private interests. Where such rhetoric had been traditionally oppositional in the English context, for the North American creoles it could define the colonial situation in the administrative empire generally, a fact that would later be of some consequence.[49]

In this context, referring to the civic exertions that preserve liberty

---

wealthmen" in the Assembly who "so absolutely Depend for their Station upon the People, that they dare not offend them" (Breen, *Character of the Good Ruler*, p. 321).
49. This point is amplified by Bernard Bailyn in *The Origins of American Politics*.

was also a way of thinking about the public discourse itself. Every citizen (read: white, landowning male) is assumed by the pamphlet's author to have an interest in monitoring the actions of rulers with a critical intention. Though ultimately this interest will require the election of public-minded representatives, an even clearer way of monitoring the ever-renewed threat to liberty is through discourse of the kind embodied by *English Advice* itself. This is how the principle of supervision comes into being. I have treated that principle as single principle; whereas in fact it was enunciated through a wide range of very different assertions about politics. There is a common element to these republican clichés about liberty, power, and corruption— a common element that allows us to summarize them as the principle of supervision: together they form a cultural understanding of the desirable uses of print. Republican rhetoric and the discursive conditions of the public sphere rendered each other intelligible. In the very act of giving advice about liberty and power, the pamphlet provides the categories of its own utility. In this sense, colonial republicanism can be described as a metadiscourse.

It is doubtless for this reason that the traditions of republican rhetoric most favored in the colonies were those that themselves developed as a metadiscourse of printed debate in England. The most popular republican texts in the colonies included works such as *The Spectator* and, perhaps, even more importantly, *Cato's Letters*.[50] Both were periodical series, and both incorporate their ongoing—even routine—appearance in print as an assumption about political legitimacy. For Addison and Steele and, even more, for Trenchard and Gordon, political publication is far from being a deviation from social order produced by crisis; indeed, what they fear is not a society riddled with political publications, but rather a society without them. This normative routinization of print discourse lies behind the very idea of the serial essay: the first *Spectator* boldly advertised, "To be Continued every Day." Even though colonial printers were limited to weeklies, the serial essay became almost universally adopted as the showpiece of American newspapers.

The authors of these British essays, like those of their American counterparts, devoted their labors to the elaboration of terms that would allow continuous, normal, normative publication. The character of the Spectator is himself designed for that function. Here is his famous introduction:

50. Gary Huxford, "The English Libertarian Tradition in the Colonial Newspaper," *Journalism Quarterly* 45 (1968): 677–86.

> I have observed, that a Reader seldom peruses a Book with Plea-
> sure, 'till he knows whether the Writer of it be a black or a fair Man,
> of a mild or cholerick Disposition, Married or a Batchelor, with other
> Particulars of the like nature, that conduce very much to the right
> understanding of an Author.[51]

Though no republican political arguments have yet been advanced, the
Spectator has already established the Country posture of disinterested
examination. Indeed, his *nom de plume* (one might as well say *nom d'impri-
merie*) makes him almost an allegorically literalized embodiment of supervision. The tone of the passage, moreover, is organized by the normative
implication that personal identity, in all of its contingent "Particularities,"
ought not to dictate the value of a writing. That implication is all the more
powerful insofar as we know the subsequent details of the characters' identity to be fictitious. The principle of the negativity of public discourse is
thus made available through the Spectator's ironic detachment from the
reader's curiosity and through the fictitiousness of the serial's characters.
And the normative character of that principle is made available in the form
of the disinterest of Country republicanism.

The first *Spectator* essay, with the introduction of the Spectator, appeared in 1711. Ten years later, on August 7, 1721, the first issue of the
New England Courant appeared, with its own introduction:

> It's an hard Case, that a Man can't appear in Print now a Days,
> unless he'll undergo the Mortification of Answering to ten thou-
> sand senseless and Impertinent Questions like these, *Pray Sir, from
> whence came you? . . . Was you bred at Colledge, Sir?*

The printer's apprentice brother, Benjamin Franklin, would repeat the same
theme yet again in his Silence Dogood papers of the following year, albeit
in a more graceful and inventive manner. The pressurized tone of the
Courant's introduction—the pertness of "Impertinent"—may be taken as
registering the resistance to civic discourse in Boston. James Franklin's
rhetoric is the Country posture without the Country; where Addison and
Steele could rely on the (assumed) class position of the gentry as a liberal
vantage on the political world, Franklin from the first was forced to validate
utterance in a world of print dominated by the Puritan clergy. His introduction comes into focus if we remember the swagger of the authors who

51. *Spectator* No. 1, quoted from Angus Ross, ed., *Selections from the Tatler and the
Spectator* (Harmondsworth: Penguin, 1982), p. 197.

defended Cotton Mather against Robert Calef in 1701: "It was highly re-joycing to us, when we heard that our *Book-sellers* were so well acquainted with the Integrity of our Pastors, as not one of them would admit any of those *Libels* to be vended in their shops." Franklin's opposition to the famil-iar pastors comes in the imagination of a different norm for the vending of what he prints. That imagination/action is made possible for him by the Addisonian model, but the model in turn is transformed in the articulation: it now refers not to a class position above concern—the concealed model of the gentry's liberality—but the market-society negativity which is now the condition of print and which the self-conscious artisan Franklin marshals more aggressively against social distinction than Addison and Steele would ever have done.

The Desublimation of Romance

The Rationale for "The American Romance"

John McWilliams

Richard Chase's claim that the social novel and the otherworldly romance are opposed forms dominating European and American fiction could not have been more timely. When *The American Novel and Its Tradition* first appeared in 1957, F. R. Leavis's imperious assurance that the British novel of manners, concerned with class, money, and marriage, had always been "The Great Tradition" of fiction, had enjoyed three years of wide currency.[1] Leavis's fictional preferences were sufficiently important to be vigorously contested, especially among American literary critics whose very subject matter was, *ipso facto*, excluded from greatness. The basis for a counter-assertion was, however, already in place. R. W. B. Lewis's *The American Adam* (1955) had recently aroused interest in images of an utterly unBritish world, one of classless national innocence, placeless New World paradises, and their impending corruption. Charles Feidelson's *Symbolism*

I am grateful to Nina Baym and George Dekker for criticisms which have improved this essay.
1. The Doubleday Anchor paperback edition of Leavis's *The Great Tradition* (1948) was published in 1954.

and American Literature (1953) had argued for the modernity and complexity of a symbolic mode of vision common among American writers as
diverse as Poe, Whitman, and Horace Bushnell. In a widely read essay entitled "Manners, Morals, and the Novel" (1947), Lionel Trilling had observed
that Americans are so habitually resentful of any discrimination based upon
social class that "the novel as I have described it has never really established itself in America."[2] Behind the claims of Lewis, Feidelson, and Trilling
lay the authority of F. O. Matthiessen's American Renaissance (1941), in
which Emersonian self-reliance had been advanced as the controlling ideal
of America's great literature, while the stature of Hawthorne and Melville
had been associated with their skeptical distance from a culture already
committed to individual gain through social conformity.

Chase's formulation of the model of American Romance subsumed
as well as promoted important strands of American critical thought. Because the American Romance was defined as a form hospitable to both
"pastoral" and "melodrama," it could accommodate the subject matter of
The American Adam, or even of Henry Nash Smith's Virgin Land (1950), as
well as the influence of the gothic novel upon Romantic writers presumably
exhilarated by Lawrencian probing into America's outer and inner spaces.[3]
The symbolic mode of American Romance allowed for modernist ambiguity,
while also arguing for its emergence from America's Puritan or "Manichean"
proclivity for allegorical absolutes. For Chase, America's great tradition of
Romance, from Brockden Brown to Faulkner, could be claimed to have
been historically central because it had been sustained by writers whose
devotion to an art about the inner self had left them skeptical of communal values based upon material progress. The theory of the Romance thus
allowed America's nineteenth-century novelists to be seen as prototypes of
alienated modern artists concerned with the deeper psychology.

"The American Romance" has proven to be, in many ways, an ad-
mirably capacious theory. Harry Levin's The Power of Blackness (1958),
Leslie Fiedler's Love and Death in the American Novel (1960), Richard
Slotkin's Regeneration Through Violence (1979), and John Irwin's American Hieroglyphics (1980), to cite just four prominent examples, have little
in common except their fascination for all those dark, inner, asocial drives
of the self which the very notion of the "American Romance" has encour-

2. The Liberal Imagination (New York: Viking Press, 1950), p. 212.
3. Richard Chase, The American Novel and Its Tradition (Baltimore: Johns Hopkins University Press, 1980), p. 1.

aged us to ponder. Chase's book has also provoked complex and subtle refinements of its own theory of American fiction, notably Joel Porte's *The Romance in America* (1969) and Michael Bell's *The Development of American Romance* (1980). Whereas Porte saw the romance as a means of disguising subversive psychological truths, Bell focused on "the sacrifice of relation," the eventual cutting of the Jamesian cable, which is implicit in the Romance's abandoning of community. Critics such as Jane Tompkins, who have opposed the theory of American Romance in order to emphasize fictions that more directly perform what she calls "cultural work," are nonetheless affirming in another way the truth of Chase's opening sentence: "The imagination that has produced much of the best and most characteristic American fiction has been shaped by the contradictions and not by the unities and harmonies of our culture."[4]

Adaptable to different scholarly interests, the theory of American Romance has also had strong institutional reasons for its persistence. A professional reason closer to hand than Cold War nationalism explains why *The American Novel and Its Tradition* had sold more than 100,000 copies by 1980. Chase's model of the Romance gave Americanists a counter-theory of the American novel which justified the separate study of American fiction at a time of great expansion in higher education, including Ph.D. programs with increasing specializations in English or American literature. Although the theory of the American Romance defines the fictive world as some variant of a "neutral territory" halfway between fact and fancy, town and wilderness, the institutionalizing of the American Romance in higher education led to claims upon a curiously vacant kind of literary *patria*. The truth of the imagination was said to reside in a placeless American domain of the spirit, as for example in Richard Poirier's *A World Elsewhere* (1965).

On the one hand, such critical interest in the otherworldly solitudes of Romance must be seen as an appropriate study of the various Glimmer-glasses, insular Tahitis, directionless rafts, initiatory hunts, and green lights with which our canonized literature clearly abounds. Seen in this way, the theory of American Romance is a scholarly reenactment of Francis Grund's insight that, for citizens of these new United States, "America" is always a place yet-to-be, not the compromised reality immediately around us.[5] On

4. *The American Novel and Its Tradition*, p. 1; Jane Tompkins, *Sensational Designs: The Cultural Work of American Fiction 1790–1860* (New York: Oxford University Press, 1985), pp. xiii, 102, 103.

5. *The Americans in Their Moral, Social and Political Relations* (Boston: Marsh, Capen & Lyon, 1837), pp. 149, 151.

the other hand, however, there has been much that is tacitly exclusive about the theory of American Romance. Just as *American Renaissance* made no room for Mrs. Stowe, Emily Dickinson, or Frederick Douglass, so Chase's formulation of the American tradition allowed entrance only to the less worldly fictions of certain white male novelists: *Wieland*, but not *Modern Chivalry*; *The Prairie*, but not *The Bravo*; *The Blithedale Romance*, but not *Uncle Tom's Cabin*; Henry James, but not Edith Wharton; Frank Norris, but not Theodore Dreiser; Scott Fitzgerald, but not Willa Cather; William Faulkner, but not Richard Wright.

To imply any deliberate racism or sexism here would be a foolish anachronism. Although Stowe, Wharton, Dreiser, Cather, and Wright were all highly regarded, widely read novelists in the late 1950s, Chase's primary reason for ignoring them was the widespread assumption that novels of direct moral persuasion and/or social determinism were somehow unliterary, almost illiberal. Because Chase had developed an *a priori* theory of an American fictional genre, he chose to study those authors and works best suited to exemplify it. Nonetheless, the consequence of his selectivity would prove to be increasingly binding. Even if one grants that Cooper, Hawthorne, Poe, Melville, and James are the most accomplished artists among nineteenth-century American writers of fiction, the Romance theory concentrated upon one or two dimensions of the same few authors with inevitably diminishing returns. Insisting upon the removal of the Romance world from political and social contexts, Chase's followers treated American Romances as instances of psychological modernity, thereby slighting their historical import for the world around them. In scholarly practice, the term "Romance" was thereby freed from its undeniably nineteenth-century origin in Scott's "historical romance," and then elevated into a universal, fictional type with a particular American application. Many historically or culturally oriented studies of individual authors would, of course, continue to appear, but the governing theory of American fiction abstracted the "Romance" from the cultural contexts in which it had been written.

Because a fair judgment requires clarity about its implications, the limit of this charge should be declared. Despite inevitable differences of interpretation, the quality of Chase's analyses of individual novels surely cannot be at issue. Although Chase was no devotee of the New Criticism, his New Critical readings of works as dissimilar as *Satanstoe*, *The Portrait of A Lady*, and *Light in August* remain as lively and cogent today as they were in 1957. The longstanding authority of *The American Novel and Its Tradition* must be partly credited to these strengths, especially to Chase's remarkable sensitivity to characterization and to the significance of tonal inconsistencies. It is rather Chase's theory of American fiction as a whole that needs, at the very least, skeptical scrutiny. Robert Spiller, a scholar whose work is now discredited in many circles, warned against the seductiveness of Chase's theory, quite perceptively, in a review of 1959:

> Mr. Chase's method is to set up a thesis which may serve as an hypothesis of historical development of a literary form. He then selects what he believes to be the few best works of major American authors in this form and proceeds to an analysis of these texts by application of the thesis to them. . . . By a circular argument, he builds an increasing conviction on the part of the reader in the validity of the original thesis so that, at the end, he has defended rather than proved his case.[6]

Spiller does not predict the likely effect of Chase's having made a circular argument from his particular paradigm of the American Romance. To accept Chase's theory of American fiction because of his persuasive explications would be to assume that, in fact, American culture has always been so impoverished that major artists could only choose to write Romances about it. That assumption has always been patently false.

Upon what foundation does the supposed nineteenth-century distinction between the British novel and the American Romance actually rest? At stake here is a matter even more fundamental than the many troubling anomalies posed by British romances such as *Wuthering Heights* and American social novels as different as *Home as Found* and *Uncle Tom's Cabin*. Did the generic distinction so important to Chase actually exist in nineteenth-century literary discourse? Nina Baym's detailed study of the language of American periodicals from 1820 to 1860 shows that the terms "novel" and "romance" were so regularly interchangeable among reviewers that their usage amounts to a "definitional chaos."[7] "Romance" was both a diachronic term applicable to all fiction and a synchronic term referring to historical fiction; yet, it was also a catch-all word for fiction of any kind that seemed adventurous or thrilling.[8] Chase's assumption that the word "Ro-

---

6. Review of Richard Chase's *The American Novel and Its Tradition*, AL 31 (1959): 82–84.
7. "Concepts of the Romance in Hawthorne's America," NCF 38 (1984): 439.
8. Baym, "Concepts of the Romance in Hawthorne's America," pp. 426–43, especially p. 437. Baym develops this argument in chapter eleven of *Novels, Readers, and Reviewers: Responses to Fiction in Antebellum America* (Ithaca: Cornell University Press, 1984).

mance" had a distinct integrity in antebellum literary practice clearly cannot be sustained.

The defense one might offer against Baym's findings would be to contend that these reviewers were, after all, only hasty magazine hacks who misunderstood the achievement and purpose of America's great Romancers. Such a defense, however, is simply not tenable as soon as we even briefly recall the terms the canonized "romancers" actually applied to their novels. A few examples: *Wieland* is subtitled "An American Tale"; *The Pioneers*, "A Descriptive Tale"; *The Last of the Mohicans*, "A Narrative of 1757"; and *The Prairie*, "A Tale." *Pym* is a "Narrative"; Poe chose the title *Tales of the Grotesque and Arabesque* for his delvings into the terror of the soul. None of Melville's novels is identified in the text as a Romance. Even "The Turn of the Screw," which is surely the quintessential Romance as Chase conceives of the term, is referred to in James's preface as a "story," a "romance," and a "tale." Near the century's end, the narrator of "Billy Budd" was to insist that his tale is "no romance"; the subtitle Melville seems to have chosen was "An Inside Narrative."[9]

Such recurrence of terms like "tale" or "narrative" suggests that the connections between the characters and the culture in which their lives were led were far more central to these writers' purposes than any elaboration of psychological symbols. One may, of course, allege that the frequency of the words "tale" and "narrative," rather than "romance" or "novel," was merely incidental—too much can surely be made of subtitles. When we consider the same novelists' extended remarks on genre, however, the "definitional chaos" seems only to increase. In 1828, Cooper identified himself in public print as "a gentleman who is the reputed author of a series of tales, which were intended to elucidate the history, manner, usages, and scenery of his native land," while saying nary a word about the Romance.[10] Cooper's association of the Leatherstocking series with the "Romance" became explicit only at the very end of his life, in the 1850 Preface, where it is applied to his characterization of the Indians and of Leatherstocking, but not to the five *Tales* as a whole. It is only in his letters that Melville fleetingly refers to *Mardi*, *Moby-Dick*, and *Pierre* as Romances, be they of a regular or irregular kind. While planning *Mardi* and *Moby-Dick*,

9. Ed. Harrison Hayford and Merton M. Sealts (Chicago: University of Chicago Press, 1962), p. 53.
10. *Notions of the Americans*, ed. R. E. Spiller (New York: Frederick Ungar, 1963), pp. 1, 254.

the term "romance" seems to have connoted to Melville an open, improvisational, and "diving" form of philosophic writing which both attracted and repelled him. Yet, while planning *Pierre*, the term "romance" seems to have referred to the domestic fictions he intended to parody. In neither usage, however, does Melville accept "romance" as a term adequate to describe or contain his fiction. *Moby-Dick* is clearly a work which assimilates and then transforms all genres, including the Romance.

In "The Art of Fiction" (1884), Henry James was to dismiss the "celebrated distinction between the novel and the romance" as a matter of labels that create "clumsy separations."[11] Although James probably used the term "romance" as often as "romantic" in his criticism, the defining of the Romance as a separable kind of fiction was of concern to him only in the Preface to *The American*, written at a time when James was seeking to identify the reasons for an early novel's presumed failure. Henry James is the only author claimed by the opposing traditions of both Chase and Leavis, yet James's critical writings contend that romance and realism should not be regarded as separable fictional genres, but as different and differing ways of apprehending reality that coexist in any great novel.

An inconsistency in my argument seems to have arisen at this point. If Nina Baym's claim for a mid-century definitional chaos is accurate, how could Henry James have casually referred to the "celebrated distinction between the novel and the romance" as if it were common knowledge? The answer certainly cannot be sought in any systematic study Henry James had made of the near contemporary usage of generic terms; the counting of evidence was not his practice. The probable source of James's phrase is his rereading of Hawthorne for the critical biography he had published five years before "The Art of Fiction." Surely it was in the prefaces to Hawthorne's four novels, all of them titled or subtitled a "romance," that James found the "distinction" he would soon claim to be "celebrated." It was Hawthorne who had clarified and deepened the tentative distinctions

11. In *The Art of Criticism: Henry James on the Theory and Practice of Fiction*, ed. William Veeder and Susan M. Griffin (Chicago: University of Chicago Press, 1986), p. 174. To Nicholaus Mills, the various separations of novel and romance have proven so clumsy that discriminations among fictional genres are to be abandoned (*American and English Fiction in the Nineteenth Century: An Antigenre Critique and Comparison* [Bloomington and London: Indiana University Press, 1973]). The authors Mills chooses to compare, however, did not reject the possible utility of considering the varying kinds of fiction. Mills's opposition to genre becomes so polemical that it makes Chase's applications of his dichotomy seem remarkably subtle.

between the novel and the Romance that go back through Cooper and Scott to Horace Walpole and Clara Reeve. But Hawthorne's influence upon James, no matter how deep or lasting, proves nothing about any predominance of the Romance in "the American novel and its tradition." Among the canonized American writers of fiction before James (Brockden Brown, Cooper, Poe, Hawthorne, Melville), the distinction between the novel and the romance continued to be of importance only to Hawthorne, for whom it came to be crucial. Ultimately, it was Hawthorne who had created James's "celebrated distinction," who had used generic terms consistently, and who had repeatedly redefined the meaning of "Romance" as it applied to the subjects of his longer fictions.

For American literary scholarship more is at stake here than the use of particular terms by nineteenth-century authors. For at least thirty years, whenever scholars, critics, and prospective student-teachers have read that the American Romance is our prevailing fictional mode, they have been drawn to regard Hawthorne as the central figure in the tradition's carpet. Hawthorne has served as the link between Brockden Brown and James, between Cooper and Faulkner, between Poe and Flannery O'Connor. His centrality for the study of American fictional and literary traditions has been assumed in books by all of the following writers and scholars: D. H. Lawrence, F. O. Matthiessen, Charles Feidelson, R. W. B. Lewis, Richard Chase, Marius Bewley, Joel Porte, Michael Bell, Richard Slotkin, Larzer Ziff, and, more recently, John Irwin, Richard Brodhead, Michael Gilmore, Donald Pease, and George Dekker. In their critical studies, one or another of the canonized writers need not appear, but at least one chapter on Hawthorne is common in all.

Hawthorne's centrality has, to be sure, reasons beyond his indispensability to the theory of the American Romance. As long as scholars and readers care for psychological subtlety, for New England historical literature, for New and Old World literary relations, and for artistic control, Hawthorne's achievement will be impossible to deny. Chapters in Richard Brodhead's The School of Hawthorne (1986) and in Jane Tompkins's Sensational Designs (1985) have demonstrated how Hawthorne became, in the late nineteenth century, America's one widely praised and even institutionalized novelist, thus confirming his prominence. But we also need to recognize that, since Richard Chase's time, we have readily granted Hawthorne's centrality as the architect of a theory of Romance fiction which has been assumed to be indigenous and widely applicable.

Chase's justification for the paradigm of the American Romance, offered in his first chapter entitled "The Broken Circuit," rests on three passages. In both its 1835 and 1853 versions, William Gilmore Simms's "Preface" to *The Yemassee* contrasts the British novel to the American Romance through the use of terms very similar to those both Chase and Leavis would later employ. The difficulty with Chase's use of *The Yemassee*'s "Preface," however, is that the contrast between the novel and the Romance is subordinate to Simms's contention that "the modern Romance is the substitute which the people of the present day offer for the ancient epic."[12] This particular generic transformation—the verse epic into the historical prose romance—would prove to be at least as crucial to Cooper, Simms, Melville, Prescott, Parkman, and Norris as the distinction between the novel and the romance.

Similarly, Chase's rendering of James's definition of "projected romance" in the "Preface" to *The American* ("experience liberated, so to speak; experience disengaged, disembroiled, disencumbered"[13]) exaggerates both the degree to which James accepted "novel" and "romance" as distinct critical terms and the degree to which James embraced "experience liberated" as a desideratum for his own fictions. The crucial passage for Chase's purpose, however, is, of course, the "Preface" to *The House of the Seven Gables*, in which "the truth of the human heart" is retained for the Romance under an "atmospherical medium" which admits both the Marvelous and life's "deeper shades."[14] It is essentially upon this passage, together with Hawthorne's remarks in "The Custom-House" on the Romance's neutral territory, that the plausible justification for Chase's theory of the American Romance must finally rest.

Anyone who continues to presume the existence of an American Romance tradition must at least acknowledge that, although Hawthorne's fiction may be the exemplar of the Romance, he was not its continuing advocate. Chase treats the prefaces to *The Scarlet Letter* and *The House of the Seven Gables* as if they represented Hawthorne's unchanging commitment to the literary promise of Romances that deal with American materials. Hawthorne, however, steadily shifted his idea of how the Romancer's imagination functioned. The scarlet letter is a very tangible object in a very real custom house; the union of moonlight and firelight enables existing physical objects ("a child's shoe; the doll, seated in her little wicker carriage;

12. As quoted by Chase in *The American Novel and Its Tradition*, p. 16.
13. As quoted by Chase in *The American Novel and Its Tradition*, p. 26.
14. As quoted by Chase in *The American Novel and Its Tradition*, p. 18.

the hobby horse") to be transformed and "spiritualized" into a neutral territory that partakes of both the actual and the imaginary. The world of Hester Prynne is one in which historical actualities and imagined emotions are indivisible, where each may "imbue itself with the nature of the other."[15] The house of the seven gables seems to function in a similarly integrative way, except that the "Preface"'s last words surprisingly contend for a separation: "He [the author] would be glad, therefore, if—especially in the quarter to which he alludes—the book may be read strictly as a Romance, having a great deal more to do with the clouds overhead, than with any portion of the actual soil of the County of Essex."[16] The "Preface" to *The Blithedale Romance* widens the distance between romance and reality still further. Hawthorne chooses to write a Romance about Blithedale because Brook Farm offers a world apart from American daily reality. Blithedale can readily become "a theatre, a little removed from the highway of ordinary travel," a place where the Romancer's characters, now defined as "the creatures of his brain," "may play their phantasmagorical antics."[17] By the time Hawthorne wrote the "Preface" to *The Marble Faun*, his avowed purpose was "merely to write a fanciful story, evolving a thoughtful moral," without attempting any "portraiture of Italian manners and character." Evidently, the world suitable to Romance writing was no longer even a removed theatre within America. The writing of a Romance finally needed shadowy antiquities and gloomy wrongs associated with old world ruin and now explicitly disassociated from "the annals of our stalwart republic."[18]

The settings of the four Romances suggest Hawthorne's increasing removal from the historical actualities of American life, together with his growing belief that a Romance was only an artifice of the fancy anyway. As the Romance became more and more the place where the imagined never meets the actual, the Romance became ever further removed from the shaping realities of New England's past. Ultimately, Hawthorne reached two complementary conclusions: the only true subjects for a Romance lie in Europe and "my own individual taste is for quite another class of works than those which I myself am able to write."[19] In preferring the beef and ale

15. Nathaniel Hawthorne, *The Scarlet Letter*, the Centenary Edition, ed. William Charvat et al. (Columbus: The Ohio State University Press, 1962), 1: 35, 36. Future references to Hawthorne's writings will be to the appropriate volume of the Centenary Edition.

16. Hawthorne, *The House of the Seven Gables* 2: 3.

17. Hawthorne, *The Blithedale Romance* 3: 1.

18. Hawthorne, *The Marble Faun* 4: 3.

19. Hawthorne to James T. Fields, February 11, 1860, *The Letters of Nathaniel Hawthorne* 18: 229. Pursuing the logic of the "Preface" to *The Marble Faun*, Nina Baym has

"novels" of Anthony Trollope to his own self-disparaged romances, Hawthorne had arrived at a judgment that fits Leavis's model of a great tradition, but not Chase's.

It is hardly surprising that Richard Chase did not consider *The Marble Faun* in *The American Novel and Its Tradition*. Its very existence poses an insoluble problem to his thesis. Hawthorne, the chief exemplar of the writer of the American Romance, had ended his authorial career contending that "America" and "Romance" were discrete entities. His last Romance was published under a premise that denied the grounds of his former achievement. One may, of course, discount the "Preface" to *The Marble Faun* on the shaky logic that the novel itself, compared to *The Scarlet Letter*, is artistically negligible. The fact remains, however, that Hawthorne finally vitiated the very theory Richard Chase would choose him to exemplify.

Recent studies that accept both "the American Renaissance" and "the romance" as still useful terms have opened up the ultimately circular quality of Chase's theory. Donald Pease's idea of the "visionary compact" challenges the assumption that Hawthorne and Melville sought sources of power and insight in the lonely marginality and "negative freedom" of representative American selves.[20] Evan Carton has sought to break through the generic limitations of the word "romance" by studying Emerson, Dickinson, Poe, and Hawthorne as Romancers who both mistrusted and exulted in the transformative power of language.[21] George Dekker has provided "the American romance" with much needed literary origins and access to cultural conflicts by insisting upon the source of the term "historical romance" in Scott's fiction and by studying how American historical fictions have altered their *Waverley* prototype.[22] All three approaches, different though they are, have in common an implicit challenge to the boundaryless and abstract qualities of the older idea of the Romance's neutral territory.

What can we surmise about the future utility of the term "Romance"?

---

suggested the "possibility" that "the novel rather than the romance (insofar as the two forms are distinguishable) is the form appropriate to American experience" ("Concepts of the Romance in Hawthorne's America," p. 443). Another possibility is that the example of Scott compelled all American authors interested in creating "associations" for the nation's past to situate their writing somewhere along a spectrum between "history" and "romance."

20. *Visionary Compacts: American Renaissance Writings in Cultural Context* (Madison: University of Wisconsin Press, 1986), p. x.

21. *The Rhetoric of American Romance* (Baltimore: Johns Hopkins University Press, 1985), pp. 1, 21.

22. *The American Historical Romance* (Cambridge: Cambridge University Press, 1987), pp. 20, 29–54.

It will surely always be important to everyone interested in Hawthorne's fiction as literary art, as a rendering of the New England past, or (hopefully) as both together. Because of its links to the epic and history, the Romance must be seen as a vital influence on the frontier novels of Cooper and Simms and the heroic histories of Parkman and Prescott. The American developments of Scott's "historical romance," as Michael Bell and George Dekker have shown, offer real and nearly inexhaustible subjects for inquiry.[23] An hour or two spent with Lyle Henry Wright's bibliography will convince scholars interested either in Romantic art or in "cultural work" that there were even more "historical romances" written about the American Revolution than there were about Puritan New England. These generic developments collectively suggest that, despite Richard Chase, the many forms of the prose Romance throughout the early nineteenth century were driven by an intense concern with the ways in which the past has made the present. The alleged poverty of American materials, it seems, prompted authors to imagine a richer past, rather than to escape to worlds elsewhere.

Whether or not the term "romance" can be plausibly applied to genres of American literature other than that of historical prose remains more problematic. Evan Carton's *The Rhetoric of American Romance*, for example, is remarkably acute in showing how aware Emerson, Dickinson, Poe, and Hawthorne were of the transformative power of words, especially their own. Carton's retaining of the term "romance" to describe this process, however, is somewhat less than convincing, not only because Emerson and Dickinson rarely used the word, but also because Carton's whole endeavor more closely resembles Derrida's ideas of structure, sign, and play than it does any of the nineteenth-century connotations of "romance." Ways will probably be found by which the word "romance" can be successfully adapted to new critical concerns we cannot predict. Only one conclusion seems wholly tenable: Chase's notion of the timeless Romance as a generic term broadly applicable to American fiction from 1780 to 1860, let alone to all of "the American novel and its tradition," should be now and finally abandoned. Chase's book was the perfect product of its scholarly —critical—moment, but Chase cannot tell us why both *The Pioneers* and *Uncle Tom's Cabin* unfold their narratives in socially descriptive ways that William Dean Howells would surely have appreciated, had he paused long enough while championing realism to reread them.

23. George Dekker, *The American Historical Romance*; Michael Bell, *Hawthorne and the Historical Romance of New England* (Princeton: Princeton University Press, 1971).

Scarcity, Subjectivity, and Emerson

Wai-chee Dimock

In the opening paragraph of "Experience," Emerson is eloquent (and perhaps eloquently misleading) in his complaint about the meanness of our lot and the meagerness of our constitution. "Did our birth fall in some fit of indigence and frugality in nature," he writes, that "we have health and reason, yet we have no superfluity of spirit for new creation? We have enough to live and bring the year about, but not an ounce to impart or to invest."[1] Emerson is obviously distressed by the situation, and yet his grounds for distress, if we take another look, might turn out to be, if not exactly specious, then at least puzzling. What Emerson is complaining about, after all, is not absolute lack, not a state of not having enough, but a state of not having something extra. Why is it so important to have, as he says, a "superfluity" of things? Why is "having enough to live" not enough for him? Why should excess be offered as the norm, against which mere sufficiency becomes, paradoxically, insufficient?

1. *The Collected Works of Ralph Waldo Emerson*, ed. Robert E. Spiller et al. (Cambridge: The Belknap Press of the Harvard University Press, 1971–   ), 3: 27. All further references to this essay will be included in the text.

As if this is not confusing enough, Emerson then goes on, in the rest of the essay, to turn his argument completely around, so that the very thing he started out longing for now becomes something that is all too prevalent. Excess, far from being a luxury that is desirable and unattainable, turns out to be the condition in which we all find ourselves, a condition that ensnares us and afflicts us. "Everything runs to excess," Emerson now laments. It is a kind of curse upon us because, in order to bring us "to the edge of ruin, nature causes each man's peculiarity to superabound" (38). Such an "unfriendly excess . . . neutralizes the promise of genius," and "makes a mischief as hurtful as its defect" (30).

It is possible to read these statements as another example of Emerson's famous "inconsistency" and to interpret them as a linguistic problem, a problem of elusive rhetoricity.[2] I would like to suggest, however, another approach, one that focuses instead on the shifting status of the three terms —"indigence," "sufficiency," and "superfluity"—as a problem of economics, a problem of designating a zero point, a standard of measurement that establishes not only what is sufficient, but also what goes beyond it and what falls short of it, what constitutes a surplus and what constitutes a shortage. Emerson's conflicting opinions, in other words, seem to reflect, at least in part, an uncertainty about his standard of measurement, an uncertainty which makes "less than enough" and "more than enough" highly unstable and highly reversible terms for him. What has to be resolved, then, in the course of "Experience," is just this uncertainty. As Emerson works his way from the essay's melancholy beginning to its triumphant conclusion, what he also needs to work out, I argue, is a new standard of sufficiency: a new and strategic placement of "enough" and, correspondingly, a new and strategic mapping of scarcity and superabundance, which will ultimately transform his former cause for complaint into a cause for celebration.

An implied standard of sufficiency is so central to "Experience" that it informs even its best-known passage, Emerson's lament about the death of his son. That passage, unlikely as it might seem, is actually a good example of the essay's obsession with measurement: measurement regulating what suffices and what does not suffice. Emerson's lament, we might recall, is occasioned not so much by the death of his son as by his own inability to

2. Two exemplary recent readings of Emerson from this perspective are B. L. Packer, *Emerson's Fall: A New Interpretation of the Major Essays* (New York: Continuum, 1982), and Richard Poirier, "The Question of Genius," in *The Renewal of Literature: Emersonian Reflections* (New York: Random House, 1987), pp. 67–94.

feel pain.[3] Or perhaps we should say that it is occasioned by his inability to feel *enough* pain, enough pain to match such a tremendous bereavement:

> In the death of my son, now more than two years ago, I seem to have lost a beautiful estate,—no more. I cannot get it nearer to me. If tomorrow I should be informed of the bankruptcy of my principal debtors, the loss of my property would be a great inconvenience to me, perhaps, for many years; but it would leave me as it found me,—neither better nor worse. So is it with this calamity; it does not touch me. (29)

As the repetition of the phrases "no more," "cannot get it nearer," and "neither better nor worse" suggests, what disappoints Emerson is, once again, not so much the absence of pain as its insufficient magnitude, its failure to exceed the usual limit. He feels some pain when his son dies, sure enough; but that pain turns out to be no more than what he would have felt had he lost a large sum of money. It is this—the fact that the pain is not greater, more acute, more shattering—that embitters Emerson. What bothers him, in short, is once again the absence of a "more than," the absence of something extra, which, paradoxically, is no more than what would have been just right. One ought to feel more pain losing a son than losing a lot of money. "More" here is a measure, not of superfluity, but of sufficiency.

What Emerson's famous lament invokes, then, is once again a standard of measurement that, by prescriptively locating sufficiency at the pole of abundance, in effect makes scarcity a descriptive given. Since the only way to have enough is to have more than enough, having enough would seem out of reach for most people. Scarcity is a foregone conclusion, a normative state of affairs, in an Emersonian economy. Described in this way, Emerson would seem to bear an interesting relation to the classic political economists—figures like Ricardo and Malthus—for whom scarcity is likewise the norm.[4] Emerson, of course, is known not to have liked either

---

3. For a reading that emphasizes the centrality of the son, see Sharon Cameron, "Representing Grief: Emerson's 'Experience,'" *Representations* 15 (1986): 15–41. Cameron's argument, though dazzling, seems to me ultimately so involved as to miss the force of the essay. For an alternate reading of this passage, one that interestingly contrasts Emerson's economy of mourning with Freud's, see Mark Edmundson, "Emerson and the Work of Melancholia," *Raritan* 6 (Spring 1987): 120–36.
4. For a succinct summary of the importance of scarcity to Malthus and Ricardo, see Harold J. Barnett and Chandler Morse, *Scarcity and Growth: The Economics of Natural Resource Availability* (Baltimore: Johns Hopkins University Press, 1963), pp. 51–64.

Malthus or Ricardo.[5] In "Plato," for instance, he alludes to "sinister political economy" and to the "ominous Malthus," whose teachings he associates with the "pitiless subdivision of classes, the doom of the pinmakers, the doom of the weavers, of dressers, of stockingers, of carders, of spinners, of colliers."[6] Such Malthusian horrors are obviously unacceptable; they are unnecessary as well, according to Emerson. And, to banish such horrors, he need look no farther than his native Massachusetts, whose drainage systems, in reclaiming the swamps, are "so many Young Americans announcing a better era,—more bread." Indeed, as he puts it, "these [drainage] tiles are political economists, confuters of Malthus and Ricardo."[7] Emerson himself is not above doing some "confuting" of his own, for instance, in an 1836 journal entry. "Malthus revolts us," he writes, "by looking at a man as an animal." Such a view, he goes on to say, is one "which I spit at."[8]

Emerson's sentiments on the subject cannot be clearer, it would seem. And yet, such clarity notwithstanding, it is instructive to put him momentarily in the company of those he so heartily dislikes. Such a move would not only contextualize Emerson, by foisting upon him an unexpected group of associates, it would also reconstitute political economy as an analytic category, by imagining its metamorphosis—its inflections and deflections—in a different field of action. Indeed, Emerson's experiments with "sufficiency" are such as to underscore not only an important continuity with the political economists, but also an intriguing pattern of transformation, a pattern that ultimately says as much about the *context* for ideas as about the ideas themselves. That "context" happens to be our "text" on this occasion, but it is useful to remind ourselves of its potentially contextual character, just as it is useful to recall Malthus and Ricardo, if only as an oblique way of engaging a text in which they obliquely figure.

For Malthus and Ricardo, of course, scarcity is very much a given, not so much a certified hypothesis as a self-evident fact. As Malthus ex-

5. As John C. Gerber observes, Emerson "thought their outlook limited, their writing unprovocative, and their conclusions inadequate." See "Emerson and the Political Economists," *New England Quarterly* 22 (1949): 336–57.

6. "Plato, or the Philosopher," in *Representative Men, Collected Works*, 4: 30.

7. "Farming," in *The Complete Works of Ralph Waldo Emerson*, ed. Edward Waldo Emerson, Centenary Edition (Boston: Houghton Mifflin, 1903–1904), 7: 150.

8. *The Journals and Miscellaneous Notebooks of Ralph Waldo Emerson*, ed. William Gilman et al. (Cambridge: The Belknap Press of the Harvard University Press, 1960–1982), 5: 227.

plains in his famous formula, "Population, when unchecked, increases in a geometrical ratio," whereas "subsistence increases only in an arithmetical ratio." It follows, then, that "a scarcity of provisions must fall hardest upon the least fortunate members of the society." "No possible form of society could prevent the almost constant action of misery," because it is "an absolutely necessary consequence."[9] This dismal outlook is shared by Ricardo as well, most notably in his rent theory. "On the first settling of a country, in which there is an abundance of rich and fertile land," Ricardo argues, "there will be no rent," for the same reason that "nothing is given for the use of air and water, or for any other of the gifts of nature which exist in boundless quantity." It is only "because land is not unlimited in quantity and uniform in quality . . . that rent is ever paid for the use of it." Thus, "with every step in the progress of population, which shall oblige a country to have recourse to land of a worse quality . . . rent on all the more fertile land will rise," and, as a result, "rent invariably proceeds from the employment of an additional quantity of labour with a proportionally less return."[10] In short, for both Malthus and Ricardo, resources are limited, diminishing returns are inevitable, and poverty is normative, given the unequal race between population and means of subsistence.

And yet, central as "scarcity" was to classical political economy, American exponents had also, from the very first, contested and qualified the Malthusian and Ricardian model.[11] For one thing, the geographical and demographic facts of the new nation were such as to make "scarcity" a highly unpersuasive supposition. Jefferson, writing to the French economist Jean Baptiste Say, suggested, for instance, that "the differences of circumstances between this and the old countries of Europe furnish differences of fact whereon to reason in questions of political economy," and went on to argue that, contrary to Malthus's predictions, American food supply would "increase geometrically with our labors," and that "its surplus [would] go to

9. Thomas Robert Malthus, *First Essay on Population* (1798; rpt. New York: Augustus M. Kelley, 1965), pp. 14, 51, 36, 15.

10. David Ricardo, *On the Principles of Political Economy and Taxation*, in *The Works and Correspondence of David Ricardo*, ed. Piero Sraffa (New York: Cambridge University Press, 1951), 1: 69, 70, 72.

11. See, for instance, Joseph Dorfman, *The Economic Mind in American Civilization, 1606–1865* (New York: Viking, 1946), vol. 2; Joyce Appleby, *Capitalism and a New Social Order* (New York: New York University Press, 1984), pp. 98–99; Edmund Cocks, "The Malthusian Theory in Pre-Civil War America," *Population Studies* 20 (March 1967): 343–63.

nourish the now perishing births of Europe."[12] In the same vein, Jefferson also tried to convince his revered friend, the economist Thomas Cooper, that "from the singular circumstances of the immense extent of rich and uncultivated lands in this country, furnishing an increase of food in the same ratio with that of population, the greater part of [Malthus's] book is inapplicable to us."[13]

The most comprehensive and ambitious refutation of Malthus and Ricardo, however, was left to Henry C. Carey, the most influential political economist in antebellum America (and later, the most ridiculed). In his popular work, *The Past, the Present, and the Future* (1847), and, in a later and somewhat repetitious volume, *The Harmony of Interests* (1852), Carey outlined an evolutionary theory which, if accepted as true, would have completely revised the foundations of political economy. Human beings, according to Carey, did not begin under optimal circumstances and were then driven, with growing population, to cultivate land less and less favorable, as Malthus and Ricardo asserted. On the contrary, they started out on barren hilltops, and, with every advance in civilization, moved closer to the rich bottomlands of the world. Given such a trajectory, "diminishing returns" obviously made no sense. Carey argued, in fact, for just the opposite. Human progress, as he saw it, was to be a story of ever *increasing* returns, a story beginning with scarcity and ending with superabundance.[14]

Such an evolutionary theory was clearly a partisan exercise. As it was, Carey's animus against Malthus and Ricardo was barely disguised. And yet, animus notwithstanding, his model remained a tribute to those he critiqued, because, far from being a radical departure, it was really no more than a "consistent inversion of Ricardo," as Paul Conkin points out.[15] As such, it also tended to replicate the Ricardian system in inconvenient ways. From the standpoint of social wellbeing, an unwieldy surplus might be just as bad as diminishing returns. Carey himself eventually sensed this, but

12. Jefferson to Jean Baptiste Say, Feb. 1, 1804, in *The Writings of Thomas Jefferson*, ed. Andrew A. Lipscomb and Albert Ellery Bergh (Washington, D.C.: Thomas Jefferson Memorial Association, 1903–1905), 11: 2–3.

13. Jefferson to Thomas Cooper, Feb. 24, 1804, Jefferson Papers, Library of Congress. Quoted in Drew R. McCoy, "Jefferson and Madison on Malthus," *Virginia Magazine of History and Biography* 88 (1980): 267.

14. Henry Carey, *The Past, The Present, and the Future* (1847; rpt. New York: Augustus M. Kelley, 1967), pp. 9–93.

15. Paul K. Conkin, *Prophets of Prosperity: America's First Political Economists* (Bloomington: Indiana University Press, 1980), p. 283.

others, more prescient than he, had already begun to diagnose it as a problem long before he tried to offer it as a solution. James Madison, writing to Jefferson in 1786, worried about just this problem, the problem created by nature's bounty. For Madison, surplus meant not only a surplus of *material* resources but also a surplus of *human* resources, and the consequences were bleak. "As there must be a great surplus of subsistence," Madison said,

> there will also remain a great surplus of inhabitants, a greater by far than will be employed in cloathing both themselves and those who feed them, and in administering to both, every other necessary and even comfort of life. What is to be done with this surplus? Hitherto we have seen them distributed into manufacturers of superfluities, idle proprietors of productive funds, domestics, soldiers, merchants, mariners, and a few other less numerous classes. All these classes notwithstanding have been found insufficient to absorb the redundant members of a populous society.[16]

For Madison, surplus, rather than scarcity, was the threat facing the new nation. And yet, surplus and scarcity were ultimately indistinguishable in his account, because surplus of resources must mean scarcity of employment opportunities. Where nature is too bountiful, there simply will not be enough jobs to engage the "redundant members of a populous society." Of those redundant members, then, "a large proportion is necessarily reduced by a competition for employment to wages which afford them the bare necessaries of life."[17] Far from being a source of felicity, natural abundance, in Madison's account, only led to general wretchedness, subsistence wages, and the elimination of "a large proportion" of people through ruthless competition.

Madison's fearful scenario vividly conjures up the perils lurking behind the fact of abundance. It also serves as a proleptic critique of Henry Carey, warning him that a simple inversion of Malthus and Ricardo might not work. What is needed, then, to avoid Carey's mistake, is a different style of response to the classic political economists, one that operates by a

16. Madison to Jefferson, June 19, 1786, *The Papers of Thomas Jefferson*, ed. Julian P. Boyd (Princeton: Princeton University Press, 1950–), 9: 660.
17. Madison, speech in the Virginia Constitutional Convention, December 2, 1829, in *Mind of the Founder: Sources of the Political Thought of James Madison*, ed. Marvin Meyers (Indianapolis: Bobbs-Merrill, 1973), p. 517.

more complex process than simple inversion. In this context, it is especially interesting to come upon Carey's name, mentioned with evident approval, in Emerson's essay "Farming," the same essay where Malthus is roundly dismissed:

> There has been a nightmare bred in England of indigestion and spleen among landlords and loom-lords, namely, the dogma that men breed too fast for the powers of the soil; that men multiply in a geometrical ratio, whilst corn multiplies only in an arithmetical; and hence that, the more prosperous we are, the faster we approach these frightful limits: nay, the plight of every new generation is worse than of the foregoing, because the first comers take up the best lands; the next, the second best; and each succeeding wave of population is driven to poorer, so that the land is ever yielding less returns to enlarging hosts of eaters. Henry Carey of Philadelphia replied: "Not so, Mr. Malthus, but just the opposite of so is the fact." [18]

On this occasion, Henry Carey is the one who actually "replies" to Malthus, but Emerson himself obviously has some interest in that endeavor too. Indeed, "Experience" can be read in just that light: as Emerson's "reply" to Malthus, a reply very much in Carey's spirit, though wilier and not so foolhardy. Like Carey, Emerson rejects the "nightmare" of a Malthusian economy; he does not make the mistake, however, of simply inverting its primary term. In fact, far from inverting "scarcity," he is pleased to find it anywhere he looks, or, more to the point, he is pleased to find it anywhere he chooses to look. It is the *placement* of scarcity, then, that constitutes the most important strategic move for Emerson. Instead of aligning scarcity with macroeconomics, as a problem between population and resources, he aligns it instead with subjectivity, as a problem between the self and its own experience. In short, what Emerson seems to have extracted out of the Malthusian economy is what we might call a "general economy" of selfhood, whose circulation is strictly internal and whose standard of measurement registers only subjective affect.[19] Such an economy not only enables Emer-

18. "Farming," p. 150.
19. For an interesting discussion of the relation between "general economy" and "economy" in the narrow sense, see Jacques Derrida, *Positions*, trans. Alan Bass (Chicago: University of Chicago Press, 1981), pp. 60–67. See also an earlier essay, "From Restricted to General Economy: A Hegelianism without Reserve," in *Writing and Difference*, trans. Alan Bass (Chicago: University of Chicago Press, 1978), pp. 251–77.

son to sidestep the empirical fact of America's abundance, it also more crucially enables him to posit something called the "self."

The "self" can be posited now, because, by the same motion that Emerson internalizes scarcity and removes it to a separate locale, in effect he authorizes a prior division—between outer and inner, between "objective" reality and "subjective" experience—the very division which allows the self to come into being. Subjectivity in Emerson, then, would seem primarily to be a structural effect: an effect of the spatial organization of scarcity and abundance. Imagined as a world apart, the site of "indigence" in a bountiful environment, such a self owes its very identity to the discrete distribution (and discrete segregation) of attributes. And it is within this topography that the self assumes its customary form: as a distinct entity, a figure integral unto itself and sovereign within itself. Self-sufficiency, for such a figure, is not so much an acquired virtue as a native birthright.

And yet, if self-sufficiency is a birthright, that birthright is predicated on grounds altogether curious, if not downright befuddling. For it is the self's felt lack—its experiential scarcity—that sets it apart from the world of abundance and, paradoxically, underwrites its autonomy. To make the paradox even more apparent, we might say that, for Emerson, subjective deficiency is the ground for self-sufficiency. The paradox is daunting, but it is a necessary one as well, I think, because it is just this paradox that connects the Emersonian self to the world from which it is by definition set apart and that makes its discrete existence a functional existence. Indeed, to the extent that the self embodies a separate economy, one of its chief functions is, no doubt, to body forth an alternative standard of sufficiency, an alternative ratio between "enough" and "not enough." We might think of the Emersonian self, then, as the scene for a highly unusual kind of accounting, where "sufficiency" and "deficiency" are ceaselessly adjusted and readjusted, measured and remeasured. And it is in that process—in going over the self's accounts—that Emerson comes to be aware of his grievous deficit, his lamentable shortage of pain.

In short, the Emersonian self, as the site of constitutional scarcity, would seem also to be the site of vigilant proprietorship. Such a model of selfhood, odd as it might seem, is, from one perspective, familiar. It is, quite simply, a Lockean model, one that, in proposing that each "man has a property in his own person," in effect, makes selfhood coextensive with ownership.[20] What makes Emerson's construct different—at once more subtle

20. John Locke, *The Second Treatise of Government* (New York: Bobbs-Merrill, 1952), p. 17.

and more extreme—is that he understands proprietorship not as jurisdiction over the world of things, but as jurisdiction over the self's affective terrain. If the self here stands as the *locus* of ownership, as with Locke, the *content* of ownership is nonetheless profoundly different. What this self lays claim to, after all, is nothing as crude or mundane as material goods, but something less tangible and more sublime. Its entitlements range over the world of sensations.[21]

Unpalatable as it might seem, pain is nonetheless to be claimed, but not because Emerson is a masochist. This is, rather, a matter of principle, a matter, that is, of the self's proprietary rights. One is entitled to feel pain, and not to feel it—a suitable amount of it—is to be deprived of something that is rightfully one's own. What we see in Emerson, in short, is what we might call the internalization of property: the reinscription of the will to own in a realm of privacy and inwardness.[22] To be a proprietor here one hardly needs a relation to something "out there." All one needs is a reflexive relation, a relation to one's own pain, for instance. Such an understanding of property not only revises the content of ownership, it also remaps the self's proprietary province.

To locate property inside the self, in the realm of subjectivity, would seem one way to safeguard that property. Surely, what is "inside" one cannot be so easily taken away. Internalization and security of title ought to go hand in hand. And yet this is emphatically not the case with Emerson. Quite the opposite is true, in fact, because, as we have seen, internalized *property* turns out also to mean internalized *poverty*. This is why the self in "Experience" is so volubly and obsessively deprived, and why it complains that its "birth" had coincided with "some fit of indigence or frugality in nature." Far from making ownership secure, the internalization of property only makes neediness ontological. This is a surprising development indeed; and because this is a juncture where things could have been differ-

21. For a brief but fascinating account of the "primacy of sensation" and its attendant "arithmetic of pleasure," see Jean Starobinski, *The Invention of Liberty*, trans. Bernard C. Swift (Cleveland: World Publishing Co., 1964), pp. 53–54. In Emerson, the primacy of sensation seems to have engendered an arithmetic of pain as well.

22. In this context, it is interesting to recall Michael Gilmore's remark that, for Emerson, "spirit functions exactly like the market to domesticate the world and make it portable" (*American Romanticism and the Marketplace* [Chicago: University of Chicago Press, 1985], p. 29). Also relevant here is Howard Horwitz's account of Emerson's "faith in the spiritual capacity of property." See "The Standard Oil Trust as Emersonian Hero," *Raritan* 6 (Spring 1987): 97–119. I would like to argue, however, that what the Emersonian spirit domesticates is not just commodity or property, but also scarcity.

ent—a juncture of rejected alternatives and enforced predicates—it is also a juncture that especially merits our attention.

In Emerson's case, since poverty is not a logical inference, but a prescribed term, we might also think of it as a functional term, an example of what Jean Baudrillard calls the "ideological genesis of needs."[23] Emerson seems compelled, for one reason or another, to insist on the primacy of poverty, to posit it and to uphold it, over and against other equally plausible alternatives. And, because he does so at some pains, one suspects that, for him, poverty is ultimately a strategic claim, an advantage rather than a setback.[24] Emerson himself says as much. Toward the end of "Experience," for example, he tells us (in his usual cryptic fashion) that "poverty" might not be so bad after all. Poverty is inescapable, he says, because we are all impoverished by our subjectivity, by "our constitutional necessity of seeing things under private aspects." Such privation is actually a good thing, however, because "That need makes in morals the capital virtue of self-trust. We must hold hard to this poverty, however scandalous, and by more vigorous self-recoveries, after the sallies of action, possess our axis more firmly" (46).

Why is an impoverished self an advantage rather than a setback? And why is such a self, a self that is nothing but needs, offered to us as a model of sufficiency? To make sense of this perverse logic, we have to look further, I think, than the immediate text of "Experience" and its array of pertinent terms. We have to look beyond its model of subjectivity and try instead to reconstruct its genesis, to investigate as contextual what is inscribed here as congenital. With this goal in mind, it is especially useful to read Emerson's impoverished self in the context of social psychology: in the context, that is, of the fears and passions that inspired nineteenth-century discourse about wealth and poverty.

Edward Everett (whose "beautiful elocution & rhetoric had charms for the dull," according to Emerson[25]) captured the headiness as well as the anxiety characteristic of such discourse when, in an 1831 Faneuil Hall

23. Jean Baudrillard, "The Ideological Genesis of Needs," in *For a Critique of the Political Economy of the Sign*, trans. Charles Levin (St. Louis MO: Telos Press, 1981), pp. 63–87.
24. Writing in the tradition of Marcel Mauss and Georges Bataille, Richard A. Grusin has called attention to the "economy of expenditure" in Emerson. See "'Put God in Your Debt': Emerson's Economy of Expenditure," *PMLA* 103 (1988): 35–44. And yet "expenditure" does not seem to be an autonomous category in Emerson. If anything, it seems more a means to poverty than an end in itself.
25. *Journals and Miscellaneous Notebooks* 8: 42.

speech, he asked his audience: "Is it not a notorious fact that every shop is employed,—every house occupied,—every mechanic overworked,—rents and wages high and rising,—the whole community in a state of exuberant prosperity? Will any body venture to deny it?"[26] As Everett's bullying tones suggest, hyperbole and hysteria were never far apart, even in the most determined advocate of prosperity. Nor was this simply an effect of the oratorial mode. In the privacy of his diary, the prominent New York merchant Philip Hone gave voice to the same uneasy jubilation that energized Everett's orations. "It is an interesting and gratifying subject of reflection," he wrote, "that our country at large, and particularly this city, is at this time prosperous beyond all former example, and somewhat remarkable that different interests, usually considered opposed to each other, are equally successful."[27]

Hone found it "gratifying" (as well as "remarkable") that prosperity brought none of its usual conflicts of interests. And yet those conflicts, happily absent on this occasion, were nonetheless real and much commented upon. As early as 1814, John Adams had expressed his fear to Jefferson that "Human Nature, in no form of it, ever could bear prosperity."[28] For the next forty years, ministers and concerned citizens echoed his sentiment. Professor Laurens Hickok of Union College, for example, thought that America was "endangered by nothing but our prosperity" and predicted that, should the national enterprise fail, it would "doubtless be because our prosperity is greater than our virtue can bear." He collected all these ideas into a book called *A Nation Saved from its Prosperity only by the Gospel*.[29] From the pulpit, Lyman Beecher made the same predictions. "The greater our prosperity the shorter its duration, and the more tremendous our downfall," he told his congregation, in a sermon called "The Gospel the only Security for Eminent and Abiding National Prosperity."[30] The 1836

26. Everett's speech was reported in the *Columbian Centinel*, October 29, 1831. Quoted in Edward Pessen, *Most Uncommon Jacksonians: The Radical Leaders of the Early Labor Movement* (Albany: State University of New York Press, 1967), p. 6.
27. *The Diary of Philip Hone*, ed. Allan Nevins (New York: Dodd, Mead & Co., 1927), 1: 41.
28. John Adams to Thomas Jefferson, July 16, 1814, *The Adams-Jefferson Letters*, ed. Lester J. Cappon (Chapel Hill: University of North Carolina Press, 1959), 2: 436.
29. (New York: American Home Missionary Society, 1853), pp. 8–9.
30. *The American National Preacher* 3 (March 1829): 147; quoted in Fred Somkin, *Unquiet Eagle: Memory and Desire in the Idea of American Freedom, 1815–1860* (Ithaca: Cornell University Press, 1967), p. 18.

Massachusetts Election Sermon put the case even more forcefully. "It is with nations as with individuals," the Reverend Andrew Bigelow told his audience, "that prosperity . . . is the parent of vice."[31]

Prosperity was the parent of vice, not just for John Adams, Laurens Hickok, Lyman Beecher, and Andrew Bigelow, but also for another group of orators and polemicists. Militant labor leaders, as it turned out, were equally emphatic on this point, although, as we shall see, the "prosperity" they denounced was significantly different—in structure, if not in substance—from the "prosperity" that worried their venerable compatriots. Here, prosperity appeared, not as an abstract danger, but as a concrete offense. What made it offensive, more specifically, was its placement within a particular tableau: an ever-recurring and ever-infuriating *mise en scène*. John Pickering's *The Working Man's Political Economy*, for instance, opened with a characteristic example of such a tableau. "Every where we [look]," Pickering said, we find two phenomena "star[ing] us in the face": "the rich few overburthened with wealth; the poor suffering with want." These were not separate incidents, he argued, but related events, because "the greater the amount of wealth in a country, the less is the poor man's share, and as the capitalist rises in riches, power and splendor, so in proportion the working man sinks into poverty, want, and wretchedness."[32]

In Pickering's account, prosperity is half the story, and only half the story. It cannot exist by itself, but always in conjunction with something that it engenders as complement and consequence. The polemical thrust of Pickering's account, in fact, lies precisely in this double focus, this refusal to give prosperity a separate representation. What it offers instead is a composite tableau, a tableau of two contrasting and yet related images. Split between prosperity and poverty, this tableau nonetheless dramatizes, in its very clarity of division, an equal clarity of relation between the divided terms. Such a scene obviously suggests a different reason why prosperity might be the parent of vice. Crucial to Pickering's argument, then, is the graphic representation of a "difference between," a representation that is both contrast and causality. This "difference between" animated virtually all working class polemics, but the most vivid example is perhaps afforded by

31. *God's Charge Unto Israel: A Sermon preached . . . at the Annual Election, on Wednesday, January 6, 1836* (Boston: Dutton and Wentworth, 1836), pp. 22–25.
32. *The Working Man's Political Economy, Founded Upon the Principle of Immutable Justice, and the Inalienable Rights of Man; Designed for the Promotion of National Reform* (1847; rpt. New York: Arno, 1971), p. 3.

Stephen Simpson, the flamboyant (and somewhat opportunistic) leader of the Philadelphia Working Men's Party:

> The slightest observation will satisfy the most prejudiced and scep-
> tical mind that nature has superabundantly supplied the industry of
> man with the means of universal comfort. . . . We behold the proof
> in the lord of ten thousand acres, tortured on his sick couch by the
> agonies of repletion, whilst the laborer famishes at his gate; we be-
> hold it in the luxurious capitalist, swelling with the overweening pride
> of overpampered opulence, whilst the hearts that labored to produce
> his wealth shiver and faint with misery and want or drag out a pro-
> tracted life of endless toil, blasting existence by the despair even of
> a bare competence.[33]

For Simpson, the landlord "tortured by the agonies of repletion" and the laborer "famish[ing] at his gate" logically (and literally) belong together, because the two are causally connected and mutually engendering. Neither is a separate entity, and both are necessary to make the picture complete. The difference between them—sharpened, dramatized, rendered graphic—serves not only to divide them but, paradoxically, also to conjoin them. For what Simpson offers is finally a relational model where "difference between" figures as both descriptive fact and causal logic. Indeed, it is the conflation of the two, the conflation of the descriptive and the causal, that gives Simpson's model its accusatory power. Where "difference between" figures as a *consequence*—a consequence of unequal distribution and unfair appropriation—causality itself becomes incriminating. To put this another way, we might say that what Simpson offers is a model of intersubjectivity, an adversarial model, where partners stand as the cause of each other's condition, and where one profits only at another's expense.

Described as such, Simpson's model bears an interesting resemblance to the model of intersubjectivity we find in Emerson.[34] That model is everywhere implicit, and, I would argue, it is present even in such an un-

33. Stephen Simpson, *The Working Man's Manual: A New Theory of Political Economy* (Philadelphia: Thomas L. Bonsal, 1831), pp. 8–9.
34. I use the word "intersubjectivity" here strictly to connote relations between selves. For a different use of the term, one that emphasizes the subject's ability to occupy successive discursive positions, see Donald Pease, "Emerson and the Law of Nature," in *Visionary Compacts: American Renaissance Writings in Cultural Context* (Madison: University of Wisconsin Press, 1987), pp. 232–34.

likely example as "Self-Reliance," which, in spite of its title, really bemoans what happens between selves as much as it celebrates the self in isolation. In the opening paragraph of that essay, for example, Emerson urges us to keep a jealous eye on our own thoughts, to "detect and watch that gleam of light which flashes across" our minds, because otherwise those thoughts will be taken away from us, since "tomorrow a stranger will say with masterly good sense precisely what we have thought and felt all the time, and we shall be forced to take with shame our own opinion from another." In fact, according to Emerson, "In every work of genius, we recognize our own rejected thoughts; they come back to us with a certain alienated majesty." [35]

Alienation of property would seem to be the standard occurrence when different selves come together, when ownership by one party deprives the other of what might have been his. Intersubjectivity is not a very pretty sight in Emerson, because it is the seamy side, as it were, of his model of selfhood. The Emersonian self, as the locus of ownership, is, as such, a candidate for dispossession: owning property that is infinitely alienable, perhaps already alienated, because the Other is always there, always eager as rival and usurper.[36] Such a model of intersubjectivity, with its sense of perpetual threat and endless appropriation, makes Emerson an exemplary figure for critics committed to the idea of poetic usurpation.[37] And yet Emerson might turn out to be even more exemplary than these critics suggest. Against the histrionic excesses of Stephen Simpson—against his portrait of overfed landlords and starving workers—Emerson might actually look like an unexcessive moderate, his view of human relations being no more than a mild transcript of a social hyperbole.

In representing the intersubjective as the realm of appropriation, Simpson not only offers an interesting parallel to Emerson, he also offers a clue, a genealogy, to the eventual erasure of the intersubjective in Emerson. "Experience" is a salient example here: the essay, we might recall, is

35. "Self-Reliance," Collected Works, 2: 27.
36. David Leverenz's discussion of male rivalry in Emerson is pertinent here. See "The Politics of Emerson's Man-Making Words," PMLA 101 (1986): 38–56.
37. Harold Bloom does not use the phrase "poetic usurpation," but his theory of repression seems very much predicated on this notion. See, for instance, his discussion of Emerson in Poetry and Repression: Revisionism from Blake to Stevens (New Haven CT: Yale University Press, 1976), pp. 235–55. For a sustained Bloomian reading of Emerson, see Julie Ellison, Emerson's Romantic Style (Princeton: Princeton University Press, 1984). For a specific instance of Emerson's appropriations, see Barbara Packer, "Origin and Authority: Emerson and the Higher Criticism," in Reconstructing American Literary History, ed. Sacvan Bercovitch (Cambridge: Harvard University Press, 1986), pp. 67–92.

not really about the son, but about Emerson himself—the man who does not feel enough pain and who resents that deficiency. The essay seems dominated exclusively by the intrasubjective, the relation between the self and its own pain, or its own lack of pain. And yet the intrasubjective is never an autonomous category in Emerson; it is, rather, a variable, related to the intersubjective by a ratio. The case here would seem to be one of utter asymmetry, a lopsided ratio resulting not only in the centrality of the former, but also in the marginalization of the latter. Why should Emerson favor such a configuration of selfhood? What is to be gained by making subjectivity strictly intrasubjective and not at all intersubjective?

Stephen Simpson's work embodies one answer to this question. As we have seen, he and other radical polemicists like him have made inter-subjectivity into a battlefield, the site of a vitriolic "difference between." Represented as the realm of inequity and injustice, intersubjectivity also becomes the realm of conflict. Indeed, to invoke this category at all is already to promote a style of explanation and a style of action. Against this background—against this militant view of intersubjectivity and this incrimi-nating placement of difference—we see why Emerson might want to dwell instead on the intrasubjective. Where Simpson represents difference as a "difference between," a difference between overfed landlords and starving laborers, Emerson represents it as a "difference within," a difference inher-ent in the self, inherent in its experiential deficit and ontological poverty.[38] The line of division is now drawn, not between selves, but within each and every self, a self eternally needy and eternally divided by the gap between what it wants and what it gets.

The internalization of scarcity, in short, enables Emerson to come up with a model of selfhood that marginalizes the intersubjective and, in the same gesture, collapses an antagonistic difference into an inherent dif-ference. Opulence and poverty, in this model, are no longer dangerous opposites, because there is no such thing as "opulence" any more. In-stead, poverty turns out to be universal, ontological, constitutive of the self,

38. My vocabulary here is meant to invoke Barbara Johnson's well-known essay, "The Execution of *Billy Budd*," which suggests that "Melville's story situates its critical differ-ence neither within nor between, but in the relation between the two as the fundamental question of all human politics." (*The Critical Difference: Essays in the Contemporary Rhetoric of Reading* [Baltimore: Johns Hopkins University Press, 1980], pp. 79–109.) Johnson's deconstructive procedure, however, invariably privileges "difference within" over "difference between." Such an emphasis—as my own reading of Emerson suggests —is not without its own problematics or politics.

and indeed, constitutive of *all* selves. Its ubiquity is such that no one, not even the overfed landlord, can escape its curse. But the curse of universal poverty is undoubtedly also a blessing. For if one is always subjectively poor—if poverty is congenital, universally inscribed in the gap between what one wants and what one gets—the landlord would seem no different from the laborer, whose poverty is likewise subjective and likewise congenital. In short, the primacy of "difference within" precludes any possibility for a "difference between." Where neediness is intrasubjective, questions of unequal distribution and unfair appropriation become immaterial, if not altogether moot.

The figure of the "impoverished self" reveals the rich and the poor to be unexpected equals. There is no culpable difference between them and no ground for incrimination. But the usefulness of such a self does not stop there. Given Emerson's model of intersubjectivity, what exonerates the self must empower it as well. A needy self is not only never guilty of appropriation, it is also equipped for doing just that. It is equipped, because, being the site of scarcity, it is logically also the site of accumulation. Always running on empty, it is always ready to receive more. That, surely, is what Emerson has in mind when he mysteriously announces, near the end of the essay, that "all I know is reception; I am and I have: but I do not get, and when I have fancied I had gotten anything, I found I did not. . . . My reception has been so large, that I am not annoyed by receiving this or that superabundantly" (48).

In these enigmatic assertions and discriminations, we are perhaps as close as we will ever get to the agency of the needy self. Emerson distinguishes between three terms: "am," "have," and "get." He embraces the first two, but rejects the third one. "Am" and "have"—being and ownership—are things he readily accepts; but "get" is not something he would admit to, because, according to him, even "when I have fancied I had gotten anything, I found I did not." He never "gets" anything, because his self never registers it. Blessed with an eternal neediness, functioning like some kind of human black hole, it can "receive" things, but always manages not to "get" them, because its constitutional poverty is such that nothing will ever add up, nothing will ever show forth, and so it can go on, receiving "superabundantly," but owning up to nothing. Forever unfulfilled and forever insatiable, it is forever equipped to take in something more. Here is a self destined to survive, a self that has nothing to lose and everything to gain, even in the no man's land that—for Emerson (as for Stephen Simpson)—marks the space of intersubjectivity.

Hearing Narrative Voices in Melville's *Pierre*

Priscilla Wald

Melville's *Pierre* inaugurates the tradition of author protagonists in American literature.[1] Pierre Glendinning's declaration of independence from an authorizing cultural discourse immediately precedes his resolve to write a novel that will "gospelize the world anew." But his narrative consciousness underwrites his apparently resistless damnation, as Pierre submits precisely to those self-evident truths that he has ostensibly rejected. Pierre, we learn, is actually writing two books, and the unconsciously authored narrative that dooms him deconstructs the narrative about Vivia, himself an "author-hero," to expose Pierre's "plagiari[sm] of his own experiences." The result, *Pierre*, is a compilation of unravelings that frustrates narrative expectations as it explores the impulse to narrativize.[2]

1. *Pierre*, in *Israel Potter, The Piazza Tales, The Confidence-Man, Uncollected Prose, Billy Budd*, with notes by Hamson Hayford (New York: The Library of America, 1984), pp. 2–421.
2. This claim runs counter to Richard Brodhead's assertion that a novel represents an author's "tacit commitment to the premise that the kind of world he wants to create can be articulated through a temporal narration, through an account of the progressive unfolding of sequential experience" (*Hawthorne, Melville, and the Novel* [Chicago: The

Pierre's "plagiarism" highlights his "characterization." His resistance to autonomy is apparent both in his life and in his earliest writings. Pierre is a scribbler whose "occasional contributions to magazines and other polite periodicals" bespeak his disinclination towards the rigors of authorship. He is lauded by critics for having "Perfect Taste" and being "unquestionably a highly respectable youth . . . blameless in morals, and harmless throughout" (287). In a chapter entitled "Young America in Literature," Melville parodically assigns Pierre archetypal status in an Emersonian vision; Pierre, like the nation, is reluctant to ruffle a surface beneath which "the world seems to lie saturated and soaking with lies" (244). He is unwilling, that is, to probe the contradictions that make his legacy intolerable.

Pierre turns to authorship when his discovery of an allegedly illegitimate sister shakes his faith not only in his family myth but in American society as well. Pierre's family is indeed rooted in American history; he is the grandson of two Revolutionary War heroes and heir to a "docile homage to a venerable Faith, which the first Glendinning had brought over sea, from beneath the shadow of an English minister" (11). He is, furthermore, the only living male surnamed Glendinning, from which he incurs sole responsibility for preserving the family line. At the commencement of *Pierre* there seems to be no problem, since Pierre is a remarkably dutiful nineteen-year-old with an appropriately tractable fiancée. But it is precisely his docility that makes him vulnerable to Isabel, a mysterious woman who claims to be his father's illegitimate daughter. Accustomed to submission, Pierre easily transfers his allegiance from his intractable mother to the equally potent Isabel.

Pierre discovers Isabel when she thrusts herself upon him, and the discovery leads him to question not only "the dear perfect father" that Mrs. Glendinning counsels him always to remember, but also the notion of legitimacy that he was raised to revere. The sullied "name of the father" calls the law itself into question, but Pierre's incapacity for ambiguity leads to his immediate reinstitution of the law; he vows to "legitimize" Isabel with a fictitious marriage that largely resembles his earlier relationship to his mother, and he leaves the idyllic Saddle Meadows for New York City where he intends to support himself by writing a novel that exposes the hypocrisy of social convention.

University of Chicago Press, 1976], p. 10). However, if the difficulty of *Pierre* stems from Melville's efforts to call the concept of narrative into question within a narrative form, then what Brodhead evaluates as a failed novel may in fact be a largely successful formal experiment.

Melville is not subtle about Pierre's textuality:

> So perfect to Pierre had long seemed the illuminated scroll of his
> life thus far, that only one hiatus was discoverable by him in that
> sweetly-writ manuscript. A sister had been omitted from the text. He
> had mourned that so delicious a feeling as fraternal love had been
> denied him. Nor could the fictitious title, which he so often lavished
> upon his mother, at all supply the absent reality. . . .
>
> "Oh, had my father but had a daughter!" cried Pierre; "someone
> whom I might love, and protect, and fight for, if need be. It must be
> a glorious thing to engage in a mortal quarrel on a sweet sister's
> behalf! Now, of all things, would to heaven I had a sister!" (11–12)

The passive voice of the passage emphasizes Pierre's "characterization";
the script is written that he need only enact. But the script is confusing,
even paradoxical. In the mid-nineteenth-century United States, the national
script of identity called at once for obedience and heroism. Pierre belongs
to what George B. Forgie calls "the post-heroic generation," which came
of age in the period preceding the Civil War, at a time when "[a]lmost all
important political, moral, and personal matters . . . were referred to, and
most policy choices measured against, the heroic standards of the founding period and the lives of the founders themselves."[3] Mrs. Glendinning's
consistent reminder of Pierre's ancestry is in keeping with the national
reverence of the founding fathers. The age invoked heroic models in a
generation to which heroism was forbidden. As Forgie notes, the founders
necessarily frustrated the heroic ambitions of their successors, who could
inherit the content of the rebellion, Union, only at the expense of its form,
revolution. Melville himself articulates (to Evert Duyckinck) the malaise of
the age in a letter written shortly before publication of *Pierre*: "We are all
sons, grandsons, or nephews, or great-nephews of those who go before
us. No one is his own sire."[4]

Mrs. Glendinning remarks on the paradox when she notices that
Pierre's docility, so admirable in its absence of challenge, is at odds with
the heroism that is also supposed to comprise his patrimony. Delighting in
Pierre's manageability, she "thank[s] heaven [she] sent him not to college,"
that is, to a place where he might learn to think independently, but she goes
on to muse that she would "almost wish him otherwise than sweet and

3. *Patricide in the House Divided* (New York: W. W. Norton and Co., 1979), p. 8.
4. *The Letters of Herman Melville*, ed. Merrell R. Davis and William H. Gilman (New
Haven: Yale University Press, 1960), p. 78.

docile . . . seeing that it must be hard for man to be an uncompromising hero and a commander among his race, and yet never ruffle any domestic brow" (27). Ultimately, however, Mrs. Glendinning favors her son's adaptation, as she "pray[s] heaven he show his heroicness in some smooth way of favoring fortune, not be called out to be a hero of some dark hope forlorn" (27).

It is characteristic both of the tragi-romantic dimensions of *Pierre* and of Pierre's reluctant authorship that both he and his mother are destroyed precisely by what "heaven" grants them in response to their invocations: Mrs. Glendinning, by Pierre's "heroism"; and Pierre, by his sister, Isabel.[5] In fact, in their fictional epithets of "brother" and "sister," both mother and son express their desire for Pierre's autonomy (by implication, from his father as well as his mother); yet, when Pierre declares his independence, both resort to madness and death. As a "fictional title" suggests, Pierre does not want to alter the text, but merely to modify it, and he is unprepared to re-write.

Endemic to Pierre's vision of his home is the inviolability of the family, particularly his dead father's perfection, and it is precisely the possibility of his imperfection that Isabel embodies and that Pierre's childlike fantasy cannot withstand. The deification of the father has an analogue in American nationalism, which Melville emblematizes in his use of "Young America," an epithet of national self-representation in the 1840s.[6] And Emerson's 1844 lecture, "The Young American," neatly fills out Pierre's Emersonian contours in the portrait of a nation so

5. Eric Sundquist similarly notes that "[i]ronically enough, the 'sweetly-writ manuscript of his life,' whose only flaw is the omission of a sister 'from the text,' is terribly disfigured by the correction of this detail" (*Home as Found: Authority and Genealogy in Nineteenth-Century American Literature* [Baltimore: The Johns Hopkins University Press, 1979], p. 171). Sundquist precedes the observation of this irony with the more general notation that "[i]rony invokes an object of reference only to call it into question; in extremity it mutilates its own discourse and hollows out its own authority, leaving a lacuna in the stead of signification" (171). Somewhat less violently, I am calling attention here to Melville's underscoring of Pierre's unwitting authorship; he is in fact destroyed less by his wish than by his interpretation of that wish. Perhaps, as Freud might suggest, his deepest wish is for self-destruction.

6. According to Michael Paul Rogin, "Young American" and "Manifest Destiny" were the two dominant political slogans of the 1840s. Significantly, both were coined by John L. O'Sullivan, an editor and journalist with whom Melville shared a number of acquaintances. (See *Subversive Genealogy: The Politics and Art of Herman Melville* [New York: Alfred A. Knopf, 1983]). Forgie discusses the psychological implications of this metaphor in the context of earlier and later "dominant metaphors" in *Patricide in the House Divided*.

newborn, free, healthful, strong, the land of the laborer, of the democrat, of the philanthropist, of the believer, of the saint, she should
speak for the human race. America is the country of the Future. . . .
it is a country of beginnings, of projects, of vast designs, and expectations. It has no past: all has an outward and prospective look.
And herein is it fitted to receive more readily every generous feature
which the wisdom or the fortune of man has yet to impress.[7]

An analogous denial of history is precisely what underwrites Pierre's authorial failure; the past rushes back, unperceived, to inform one's perception
of the present. Emerson returns, in this passage, to a Jeffersonian ideal,
an agrarian utopianism that in fact defines progress as a return to the past;
he celebrates the "happy tendency" of the young men "to withdraw from
the cities, and cultivate the soil," both because of the moral benefits they
will reap and because "this promised the conquering of the soil, plenty, and
beyond this, the adorning of the whole continent with every advantage and
ornament which labor, ingenuity, and affection for a man's home could suggest."[8] As Emerson frames conservation in progressive rhetoric, he blurs
the distinction between his utopianism and the industrialization that was
also hailed as utopian. "The conquering of the soil," similarly, could send
attentive youths not home to cultivate their gardens but westward under the
banner of "manifest destiny." Emerson and his "progressive" opponents,
like the North and the South, blur their distinctions in their use of a rhetoric
that summons in the same paradoxical past justification for the opposing
ideals of the present.

So, against Emerson's explicitly avowed ahistoricism runs a pre-
occupation with history that, as Ann Douglas has documented in *The
Feminization of American Culture*, characterized mid-nineteenth-century
America.[9] Emerson's denial of America's past in fact obscures the present

7. In *Essays and Lectures, Nature; Address, etc.*, with notes by Joel Porte (New York:
The Library of America, 1983), pp. 211–30.
8. Emerson, "The Young American," p. 227.
9. Again, Forgie's discussion of the preoccupation with the founding fathers during this
period is particularly illuminating in this context (see *Patricide in the House Divided*). In
effect, as Michael Kammen also observes, this age witnessed a kind of historical collapse
or conflation in which an ideal of the past was imposed on the present. The preoccupation
with history stems, in this formulation, from a "quest for republican legitimacy" and from
the desire for validation to be found in a "nostalgic vision of the Golden Age" that masks
the instability that actually characterized the goals and institutions of the past (*People of
Paradox: An Inquiry Concerning the Origins of American Civilization* [New York: Alfred A.
Knopf, 1972], p. 51).

as it invigorates the narrative of history, a progressive, resistless force that impels young Americans into the future while it justifies the growing nationalism that obscured difference and made invisible the atrocities committed in the name of "manifest destiny" (the heir of the Puritans' "divine mission") at home and of the Christian salvation (missionary movement) abroad. Isabel offers Pierre the chance to introspect, the potential to examine the resistlessness of the narrative of history in America.

Illegitimate Isabel, whose childhood memories are fragments of an ocean voyage, a madhouse, a house in the woods, and a gentleman whom she presumes to be her father, is a creature of boundaries, almost, in fact, supernatural. Brian Higgins and Hershel Parker call her "an embodiment of the Unconscious," and there is something undefined and primal about her.[10] Devoid of primary relationships, she is unformed humanity, the exact opposite of her pampered brother. Isabel is the alternate discourse, the outsider who transcends cultural norms and speaks, as her mystical music makes clear, from beyond language. She is civilized, brought into the cultural symbolic, after she has already begun, vaguely, to perceive; she is, that is, brought in relatively late and as an outsider, which privileges her perspective on the values and conventions of Saddle Meadows, a perspective to which the socially indoctrinated Pierre has no access. Isabel invites Pierre to the margins of his own discourse. And since "adultery," both word and deed, has consigned Isabel to the margins, Pierre can begin his heroic inspection of social convention with an exploration of this particular prohibition, specifically of the inviolability of the home and "the name of the father" (the law, in Lacan's formulation).

But, as the narrator alerts us from the onset, Pierre resists marginality, and Isabel promotes not inspection but submission. Pierre first encounters Isabel at a sewing circle that his mother patronizes; when they see each other, she faints. Pierre responds passionately but nevertheless passively: "A wild, bewildering, and incomprehensible curiosity had seized him, to know something definite of that face. To this curiosity . . . he entirely surrendered himself" (58). The narrator continues to insist on Pierre's passivity, suggesting that "the face . . . had . . . fully possessed him for its own" (66) with a "mystic tyranny" (63) that Pierre cannot question. The "tyranny" of Isabel's face derives in fact from the internalized source into which, as we have seen, Pierre eagerly incorporates her; it is that script, rather than its human embodiment, that dominates Pierre.

10. "The Flawed Grandeur of Melville's *Pierre*," in *New Perspectives on Melville*, ed. Faith Pullin (Edinburgh: Edinburgh University Press, 1978), p. 163.

The narrator offers an alternate narrative, a "history [which] goes forward and goes backward, as occasion calls" (67), that disrupts the progressive narrative of Pierre's discovery to propose an alternate narrative of his self-damnation. "Nimble center, circumference elastic you must have" (67), suggests the elusively unreliable narrator, presumably in order to understand the unperceived narratives that manifest themselves as resistless forces, like the resistless force of Emerson's disavowed historicism in the passage cited above. And it is precisely Pierre's failure to acknowledge this apparently ineluctable narrative of identity that leads him to "directly plagiarize[] from his own experiences" (352) in a text that was to mark his declaration of independence.

Isabel does not inaugurate Pierre's break with the past, with the arbitrary symbolism of Saddle Meadows, because he refamiliarizes her and draws her into the prewritten manuscript of his identity. She is, of course, the "sister [who] had been omitted from the text," the inscribed call to heroism that Pierre's legacy required him eventually to enact. But she also inherits the legacy of Pierre's interaction with his mother, who rhetorically prefigures Isabel with her fictional epithet of "sister." And, as the narrator stresses, Pierre rehearses even the pattern of his interaction with Isabel in his relationship with his mother.

What Isabel wills, though subtly articulated, replaces what Mrs. Glendinning demands; Pierre simply transfers his allegiance:

> Far as we blind moles can see, man's life seems but an acting upon mysterious hints; it is somehow hinted to us to do thus or thus. For surely no mere mortal who has at all gone down into himself will ever pretend that his slightest thought or act solely originates in his own defined identity. . . . [So Pierre's] nominal conversion of a sister into a wife . . . might have been found in the previous conversational conversion of a mother into a sister; for hereby he had habituated his voice and manner to a certain fictitiousness in one of the closest domestic relations of life. (209)

Pierre's relations with women appear to follow the pattern established by his mother, one that leaves no room for the autonomy that authorship requires. And Pierre is "no mere mortal who has gone down at all into himself"; he is neither perceptive nor analytical about his motivations. Mrs. Glendinning, we learn, returns Pierre's "romantic filial love . . . [with] triumphant maternal pride" precisely because "in the clearcut lineaments and noble air of the son, [she] saw her own graces strangely translated into the opposite sex"

(9), because, it seems, he is the reflecting pool to her Narcissus. And that is how Pierre learns to love, as we see in the opening scene with Lucy, in which "the two stood silently but ardently eying each other, beholding mutual reflections of a boundless admiration and love" (7). The only reflection of which Pierre seems capable is mirroring, and he never thinks to question the fictional self that he sees thus reflected.

Insofar as Isabel resembles their father, and presumably the resemblance is strong enough to convince an albeit receptive Pierre, she must resemble—or mirror—Pierre himself. Pierre, then, does not see difference so much as similarity when he looks at Isabel. His vision constitutes the dialectical identification with the other that, in a Lacanian formulation, is preformed in the mirror-stage. The narrator uses a literal mirror to suggest that Isabel's mirroring could still jar Pierre into a contemplation of the alienation implicit in the mirror-stage of identity-formation, an alienation, that is, that can potentially elucidate the contours of Pierre's cultural subjectivity. Pierre "started at a figure in the opposite mirror. It bore the outline of Pierre, but now strangely filled with features transformed, and unfamiliar to him" (76). But such heroism is not for Pierre, as he "vainly struggle[s] with the incomprehensible power that possessed him" (76). Pierre struggles in vain, a futile effort against the vanity and the narcissism through which he repossesses Isabel as a reflection of himself; he is, it seems, incapable of any more profound self-reflection. The narrator reduces Pierre to the "umpire" between "two antagonistic agencies within him" (77) and undercuts even this degree of psychological agency with the observation that "Pierre was not arguing Fixed Fate and Free Will, now; Fixed Fate and Free Will were arguing him, and Fixed Fate got the better in the debate" (216).

Pierre's decision to turn to authorship is intrinsic to the nature of his struggle. The impulse to write, to, as he conceives of it, "gospelize the world anew," has its psychological analogue in the impulse to define oneself, to be both original and authoritative. This notion of authorship charts a departure from the theological universe in which imitation enables one to approach the divinity; imitation becomes, in this secularized world, "plagiarism," a failure to resist the authorizing discourse. And yet, as we have seen, Pierre's rhetoric belies his intention to resist; his very conception of his struggle to possess his own narrative, to authorize himself, is paradoxical and self-defeating:

> Henceforth I will know nothing but Truth; glad Truth, or sad Truth; I will know what *is*, and do what my deepest angel dictates . . . Oh! falsely guided in the days of my Joy, am I now truly led in this night

of my grief?—I will be a raver, and none shall stay me! I will lift my hand in fury, for am I not struck? I will be bitter in my breath, for is not this cup of gall? Thou Black Knight, that with visor down, thus confrontest me, and mockest at me;—I will be impious, for piety hath juggled me, and taught me to revere, where I should spurn. From all idols, I tear all veils; henceforth I will see the hidden things; and live right out in my own hidden life!—Now I feel that nothing but Truth can move me so. (80–81)

Even at this moment, the height of his potential for self-authorization, Pierre imagines himself following "dictates," and no longer guided, he is nevertheless passively "led." Similarly, when he resolves henceforth to be impious, he juxtaposes impiety and piety in a dualistic opposition that affirms rather than negates the symbolic order from which he seeks his independence, as impiety assumes the very categories by which the culture defines "piety." In his transcendentalism, Pierre deifies "Truth," an absolute that he seeks as if it were a grail, and he resorts to images of madness, gall, and Black Knights that bespeak a marked tendency towards romanticism and that are perhaps even plagiarized from boyhood readings. His authorship has less than auspicious beginnings.

Pierre is, after all, fundamentally a believer, and he adheres fundamentally to the letter of the law. He believes the letter in which Isabel proclaims herself his sister, and he subscribes to what Donald Pease calls "the revolutionary mythos," the ahistoricism of the nation's perpetual breaking with the past.[11] Pierre removes his father's picture from the wall and, with an impressive faith in the power of the symbolic, declares, "I will no longer have a father" (Emerson's country with "no past"). But, from the first, Pierre's country was far more motherland than fatherland. The narrator again underscores Pierre's lack of preparation for the author's task:

Nor now, though profoundly sensible that his whole previous moral being was overturned, and that for him the fair structure of the world must, in some then unknown way, be entirely rebuilded again, from the lowermost corner stone up; nor now did Pierre torment himself

11. Kammen similarly observes that "the United States may very well be the first large-scale society to have built innovation and change into its culture as a constant variable, so that a kind of 'creative destruction' continually alters the face of American life." He counterposes such "constant breaking with the past" to the American tendency to "conform to transitory norms and fashions" (*People of Paradox*, pp. 115, 110), in order to outline a central dualism that underlies American ideology.

with the thought of that last desolation; and how the desolate place was to be made flourishing again. He seemed to feel that in his deepest soul, lurked an indefinite but potential faith, which could rule in the interregnum of all hereditary beliefs, and circumstantial persuasions; not wholly, he felt, was his soul in anarchy. The indefinite regent had assumed the scepter as its right; and Pierre was not entirely given up to his grief's utter pillage and sack. (113)

As the abundance of passive constructions and the imagery of monarchy make clear, Pierre chooses to substitute one absolute code for another rather than remain in doubt. He thus avoids the torment that he should inevitably feel under the circumstances. Pierre cannot tolerate the lack of structure implicit in his rebellion, and his metaphors belie his intention to create truly new forms in the place of the old, invalidating his declaration. Pierre, as a believer, must replace one faith with at least the "potential" of another. Insofar as Pierre is representative, Melville undermines the paradox evident in American rhetoric. The narrator makes apparent that the form of faith in the values of his inheritance belies the content of the legacy, as he rejects his Republican heritage in his preference of monarchy to self-government and his Puritan heritage in his failure to make the desert flourish.[12] In a time of profound need of cultural affirmation, the impending Civil War's threat to the Union, the cornerstone of national identity, Pierre stands only as a reflection of the nation's failure.

Discrepancies between beliefs and discoveries that contradict them, such as Glendinning Senior's adultery, precipitate psychological crises, which, in turn, potentially facilitate insight. But as Victor Turner has pointed out in his discussion of liminality, a cultural analogue of such individual

12. In underscoring distinctions here among Melville, the narrator, and Pierre, I want to stress my departure from a reading such as Pease's. It is not Melville but Pierre who returns to a past that, as Kammen suggests, exists more in rhetoric than in actuality. In my reading, Melville does not, as Pease suggests, return to an affirmative past; instead, he demonstrates that such a return is inevitable and the attempt to deny the past merely reenforces its authority. For Melville, we are rooted in a past with an authority that we cannot escape and must, therefore, strive to understand. With his political metaphor, Melville suggestively links the authority of the past to a political system that was consciously disparaged by that (American) past (Pease, *Visionary Compacts* [Madison: University of Wisconsin Press, 1987]).

Rogin similarly underscores the political significance of Pierre's failure when he observes that Pierre's "revolution is truncated, like the 1848ers', because he steps back from its consequences. Like them he is discredited and succumbs to royal power" (*Subversive Genealogy*, p. 169).

crises, the moment gives rise as well to the temptation to retreat more deeply into the sanctity of prescribed values.[13] As Nina Baym suggests, Pierre's crisis extends to grave "doubts about language" (910).[14] "Oh, hitherto," he laments, "I have but piled up words; bought books, and bought some small experiences, and builded me in libraries." Yet, just as his recognition of language and literature as the transmitters of his internalized script of cultural identity seems inevitable, Pierre again retreats into text, concluding his thought with "now I sit down and read" (110). And he similarly continues, "Oh, men are jailers all; jailers of themselves, and in Opinion's world ignorantly hold their noblest part a captive to their vilest; as disguised royal Charles when caught by peasants" (110). The metaphoric addendum, in which Pierre unconsciously preserves the equation of class distinction and nobility, distinctly undercuts the apparent sense of the initial observation, which, if followed logically, would have called the terms of the metaphor into question.

Pierre's susceptibility to Isabel is, as we have seen, not so much to Isabel as to the script into which he incorporates her. Consequently, he ignores the authorial challenge that she embodies. The social isolation of her formative years brings her acquisition of language into particular focus; she is conscious of the meaning of words and of her exclusion from meaningful discourse, especially from the narrative principles that provide coherence to the stories of more socialized selves. "I can not but talk wildly upon so wild a theme" (138), she explains, as she recounts the disjointed and impressionistic details of her strange autobiography. And her meditation on the word "father" illuminates the social contours of both the term and the role:

> . . . though at the time I sometimes called him my father, and the people of the house also called him so, sometimes when speaking of him to me; yet—partly, I suppose, because of the extraordinary secludedness of my previous life—I did not then join in my mind with the word father, all those peculiar associations which the term ordinarily inspires in children. The word father only seemed a word of general love and endearment to me—little or nothing more; it did not seem to involve any claims of any sort, one way or the other. (173)

13. *The Forest of Symbols: Aspects of Ndembu Ritual* (Ithaca: Cornell University Press, 1967).
14. See Nina Baym, "Melville's Quarrel with Fiction," *PMLA* 94, no. 5 (Oct. 1979): 909–23.

Isabel potentially affords Pierre the opportunity to examine social constructions that he had internalized unconsciously as truths. "[G]iven Melville's Emerson-derived notion of language as proceeding from a divine Author or Namer," argues Baym, "the loss of belief in an Absolute entailed the loss not only of truth in the universe but also of coherence and meaning in language."[15] Isabel actually goes further, as she points to a realm beyond language, a chaotic world that lacks coherence and meaning in general, a liminal space that temporarily illuminates the role of language in such social constructions.

At first, Isabel resists names. As she tells Pierre, "I did not ask the name of my father; for I could have had no motive to hear him named, except to individualize the person who was so peculiarly kind to me" (173–74). *"The gentleman"* and *"my father"* suffice as such particularizations for Isabel, who, furthermore, feels "there can be no perfect peace in individualness" (142). For Isabel, "individualness" means exclusion. She longs instead "to feel [her]self drank up into the pervading spirit animating all things" (142). Isabel speaks here for an alternate meaning of "union" in the "union of individuals" that United States ideology paradoxically espouses. Isabel's republic of spirit annihilates distinction; "union" means self-dissolution and is, clearly, incompatible with individualism. But "individualism," on the other hand, means exclusion and, for Isabel, has never translated even potentially into "opportunity." The will to belong, to be a part of society, supersedes even the desire to exist.

Significantly, "the gentleman's" absence prompts Isabel to forego her resolution and discover his name. Naming, and language in general, become presences that both signify and are initiated by absence.[16] On discovering writing on the handkerchief that "the gentleman" drops on his last visit to her, Isabel resolves to learn to read "in order," she tells Pierre, "that of [her]self she might learn the meaning of those faded characters" (175). Isabel's obvious social motivation again makes explicit the socializing quali-

15. "Melville's Quarrel with Fiction," 910.
16. The Lacanian concept of "desire" is related to this idea in interesting ways. According to Lacan (and to a Lacanian reading of Freud), an object's absence precedes its earliest constitution as an object. (See Juliet Mitchell's incisive discussion in her introduction to *Feminine Sexuality*, ed. Juliet Mitchell and Jacqueline Rose, trans. Jacqueline Rose [New York and London: W.W. Norton & Co., 1982.]) Isabel's exclusion from language makes the object status of language particularly apparent. Pierre's flaw stems partly from his tendency to regard language as a natural outgrowth rather than a cultural object (or artifact) that can be recontextualized and questioned.

ties of language as it bears witness to her susceptibility to socialization. Even her (suicidal) longing to dissolve into "the pervading spirit animating all things," as we have seen, attests to a desire to be included.

Thus socialized, Isabel surrenders her agency to become a conduit for "thoughts [that] well up in [her]." She protests:

> I can not alter them, for I had nothing to do with putting them in my mind, and I never affect any thoughts, and I never adulterate any thoughts; but when I speak, think forth from the tongue, speech being sometimes before the thought; so, often, my own tongue teaches me new things. (147)

What Pierre mistakes for mysticism is in fact Isabel's submission to the "pervading spirit," the social force. Her tongue teaches her new thoughts precisely because of her submission to the process of socialization. Language dictates thought. Isabel is not a teacher who can consciously lead Pierre to the margins of discourse; rather, she is an example who dwells on, and so illuminates, those margins. She apologizes for, rather than celebrates, the incoherence of her narrative. Initially, this incoherence disturbs Pierre, who

> [strives] to condense her mysterious haze into some definite and comprehensible shape. He could not but infer that the feeling of bewilderment, which she had so often hinted of during their interview, had caused her continually to go astray from the straight line of her narration; and finally to end it in an abrupt and enigmatical obscurity. But he also felt assured, that as this was entirely unintended and now, doubtless, regretted by herself, so their coming interview would help clear up much of this mysteriousness. . . . (162)

Pierre resists the discomfort of Isabel's "bewilderment" and seeks the familiar "straight line of . . . narration" just as he clings to his faith in the fundamental values that have been instilled in him. Such narration, as Hayden White suggests, privileges causality, a principle that is particularly suited to an ideology of individualism.[17]

17. See especially "The Value of Narrativity in the Representation of Reality," *On Narrative*, ed. W.J.T. Mitchell (Chicago: The University of Chicago Press, 1981), pp. 1–23. It is Pierre rather than Melville who demonstrates the "tacit commitment to the premise [of] . . . temporal narration" of which Brodhead writes (*Hawthorne*, p. 10). Melville—and the narrator—consciously seek to separate themselves from that commitment.

Gradually, however, the possibility of heroism tempts Pierre into an attraction precisely to the "bewilderment" that disturbs him. Pierre "saw, or seemed to see, that it was not so much Isabel who had by her wild idiosyncrasies mystified the narration of her history, as it was the essential and unavoidable mystery of her history itself, which had invested Isabel with such wonderful enigmas to him" (165). Unwittingly, Pierre is drawn to the paradox that Isabel embodies. The incoherence of her "narration" stems from her social exclusion; Isabel attempts to describe her experience, but there is no language that can convey the experience of illegitimacy in terms that are not social. Isabel makes every effort to use words to describe an experience that is beyond words. She attempts, in other words, to describe the outside (social exclusion) from within it, as Michel Foucault tries, with equal lack of success, to describe madness in its own terms rather than from within the language of reason.[18] Pierre has now reached the brink of another, perhaps the fundamental, social paradox; however, as we have seen, Pierre retreats from paradox. Isabel, or the experience of Isabel, "fill[s . . . Pierre] with nameless wonderings" (141), impels him beyond language. But instead of pursuing such wonderings to the margins of discourse, Pierre removes Isabel from the sphere of human experience. "[T]o him, Isabel wholly soared out of the realms of mortalness, and for him became transfigured in the highest heaven of uncorrupted Love" (170).

Pierre's idealization of Isabel also prevents his having to acknowledge his sexual attraction to her—and the incestuous implications of that attraction. Incest, which Freud and Lévi-Strauss both locate in the boundary between nature and culture, presents the possibility of ultimate defiance.[19] An incestuous relationship would allow Pierre to call into question the rudiments of civilization, the taboo from which all convention stems. But again Pierre retreats from the margins of discourse, this time into a veneration that enables him to deny his desire. Isabel, again, exists only as a character in a pre-written script. And Pierre rebels in accordance with

18. See *Madness and Civilization: A History of Insanity in the Age of Reason* (New York: Random House, 1965). Also see Jacques Derrida's critique of Foucault in "Cogito and the History of Madness," *Writing and Difference*, trans. Alan Bass (Chicago: The University of Chicago Press, 1978), pp. 31–63.

19. Fred G. See, "The Kinship of Metaphor: Incest and Language in Melville's *Pierre*," *Structuralist Review* 1, no. 2 (Winter 1978): 59. See has expanded these ideas in a fascinating study that historicizes certain aspects of contemporary critical theory (*Desire and the Sign: Nineteenth-Century American Fiction* [Baton Rouge and London: Louisiana State University Press, 1987]).

his two favorite texts, Dante's *Inferno* and Shakespeare's *Hamlet*. Significantly, the heroes of both these works end their political rebellion and their metaphysical quests in the self-surrender of either veneration or, literally, self-destruction.

The narrator makes apparent that Pierre's reluctance to venture to the margins of discourse has at its root his inability to recognize paradox. He[20] admonishes Pierre:

> Tear thyself open, and read there the confounding story of thy blind doltishness! Thy two grand resolutions—the public acknowledgement of Isabel, and the charitable withholding of her existence from thy own mother,—these are impossible adjuncts.—Likewise, thy so magnanimous purpose to screen thy father's honorable memory from reproach, and thy other intention, the open vindication of thy fraternalness to Isabel,—these also are impossible adjuncts. And the having individually entertained four such resolves, without perceiving that once brought together, they all mutually expire; this, this ineffable folly, Pierre, brands thee in the forehead for an unaccountable infatuate. (202–3)

The narrator counsels Pierre, first of all, to recognize his own textuality—and social identity—and hence to perceive the paralysis to which his denial of agency has consigned him. In other words, the narrator advocates a course that would lead to Pierre's self-authorization. Pierre, however, prefers to retreat not only from the margins of discourse, but also from Saddle Meadows, as though a physical rather than a mental space has entrapped him. "Henceforth," he declares, "cast-out Pierre hath no paternity, and no past; and since the Future is one blank to all; therefore, twice-disinherited Pierre stands untrammeledly his ever-present self!—free to do his own self-will and present fancy to whatever end!" (235). Pierre would rather be the victim, the cast-out, than accept responsibility for his leaving, and his third person self-reference further stresses his preference to be someone else's character.

20. My pronoun is admittedly somewhat arbitrary here. However, I justify my claim of a narrative "he" on the basis of two observations. First, the intensity of identification among Melville, the narrator, and Pierre suggests a male point of view, since Melville distinguishes sharply in this text—as in most, if not all, of his works—between a male and female perspective. Secondly, Melville's women in this text—again, as in most—are more dramatically self-revealing than the calculating narrator; they tend either towards passivity (Lucy) or mystical (or shrewish) attempts to control (Isabel and Mrs. Glendinning).

His flight to the city begins almost as an epic journey to the underworld, which, as in Dante (and his predecessors), frames the (ritualized) quest for identity in the inspection of the old order that leads to the institution of a new one. The journey begins in silence:

> All profound things, and emotions of things are preceded and attended by Silence. What a silence is that with which the pale bride precedes the responsive *I will*, to the priest's solemn question, *Wilt thou have this man for thy husband*? In silence, too, the wedded hands are clasped. . . . Silence is the only Voice of our God. . . .
>
> No word was spoken by its inmates, as the coach bearing our young Enthusiast, Pierre, and his mournful party, sped forth through the dim dawn into the deep midnight, which still occupied, unrepulsed, the hearts of the old woods through which the road wound, very shortly after quitting the village. (240)

The marriage imagery heightens the suggestions of incest and adultery that Pierre's companions, Isabel and Delly, an adulteress, embody. And Silence, perhaps actively resisting language at the margins of cultural discourse, suggests the possibility for speaking against the arbitrary terms of that discourse. Silence precedes marriage, the ritual that marks the assumption of a new role in the social order, as though possibility holds its breath before committing itself to the choice that marks participation in the social order, as though there were still some potential for resistance. But "Silence" becomes "no words," an alternate presence represented as absence, and the coach a prison whose "inmates" find no alternative to their captivity. "Silence is the only Voice of our God" suggestively intimates an absence that Pierre, and presumably his companions, cannot tolerate.

In fact, Pierre leaves precisely to maintain the symbolic order of Saddle Meadows. His fictitious marriage is not specifically intended as an act of defiance, but rather as an attempt to "legitimize" Isabel, to bring her into the realm of social conventions from which she has felt excluded. Pierre fails to recognize the potentially defiant implications of his departure; he leaves Saddle Meadows because to remain would be to leave Isabel outside society or to expose his father's adultery (itself a defiance of social conventions) or to commit the defiance of an incestuous marriage. His taking the adulteress, Delly, with him, in effect removes her from the eyes of Saddle Meadows. "Our young Enthusiast," ever the believer, is indeed an "inmate," imprisoned by his inability to transcend what he can no longer wholly accept, an inability that finds expression in an impotence extending as well to his inability to write.

Chaos and dream logic dominate the underworlds of epic. Apparently at the brink of the underworld, Pierre's "thoughts were very dark and wild; for a space there was rebellion and horrid anarchy and infidelity in his soul" (240). But, as the preceding paragraphs have made clear, Pierre cannot sustain such rebellion. Even here his thoughts appear to be at a distance from himself, almost as if the anarchy had invaded his soul, and he is not its source. Significantly, the narrator compares him to a priest of whom it is told that a "temporary mood . . . [once] invaded [his] heart. . . . The Evil One suddenly propounded to him the possibility of the mere moonshine of the Christian Religion. Just such now was the mood of Pierre; to him the Evil One propounded the possibility of the mere moonshine of all his self-renouncing Enthusiasm" (240–41). Like Pierre, the priest is the passive victim of a mood that he personifies as the devil. But the comparison further illustrates that Pierre has turned his self-renunciation into a kind of faith, that his actions are motivated by self-renunciation rather than self-assertion, and that he has therefore rejected psychological authorship.

The priest, who had been in the middle of administering the sacrament, "by instant and earnest prayer—closing his two eyes, with his two hands still holding the sacramental bread—. . . had vanquished the impious Devil" (241). In other words, the priest holds on to the symbol and so dispels his doubts, which he has already successfully projected onto a personified other. He applies a preexisting system to his situation and submits himself to it—"these [tenets] were the indestructible anchors which still held the priest to his firm Faith's rock, when the sudden storm raised by the Evil One assailed him" (241). The narrator frames Pierre's dilemma in the context of the priest's:

> But Pierre—where could *he* find the Church, the monument, the Bible, which unequivocally said to him—"Go on; thou art in the Right; I endorse thee all over; go on."—So the difference between the Priest and Pierre was herein:—with the priest it was a matter, whether certain bodiless thoughts of his were true or not true; but with Pierre it was a question whether certain vital acts of his were right or wrong. (241)

And "right or wrong" again images his dilemma as a dualistic opposition that depends on a given social order. Pierre is far more eager to read than to write.

As an act of reading (Isabel's letter) begins his challenge, so an act of reading accompanies his doubt. "When, first entering the coach, Pierre had pressed his hand upon the cushioned seat to steady his way, some crumpled leaves of paper had met his fingers. He had instinctively clutched them; and the same strange clutching mood of his soul which had prompted that instinctive act, did also prevail in causing him now to retain the crumpled paper in his hand for an hour or more of that wonderful intense silence . . ." (240). Again, Pierre longs to anchor his drifting mind; he receives the paper passively and then clutches it instinctively. Pierre prefers to surrender his subjectivity to whatever is available, and the paper suits his purposes. His lack of consciousness makes it seem as though the paper had arrived magically in his grasp; "[h]e knew not how it had got there, or whence it had come, though himself had closed his own gripe upon it" (242). The use of the objective "himself" further signals Pierre's characterization in a narrative he is unaware of authoring and so cannot resist. Pierre reads as an alternative to authorship: "more to force his mind away from the dark realities of things than from any other motive, Pierre finally tried his best to plunge himself into the pamphlet" (243).

Plunging, too, bespeaks a suicidal urge, an act of self-annihilation, an alternative to the self-reflection of which we have already seen Pierre consistently incapable. Here his plunge is clearly an attempt to escape from the questioning process that his emotional anarchy has begun to inspire rather than to continue to probe for truth. And plunging throughout the novel follows on turmoil, as after his first encounter with Isabel, "Pierre, gladly plunging into this welcome current of talk[,] was enabled to attend his mother home without furnishing further cause for her concern or wonderment" (60). Subsequently, plunging becomes an image of damnation in *Pierre*. Mrs. Glendinning, alarmed at the change that has come over Pierre consequent to his meeting Isabel, declares, "Let him tell me of himself, or let him slide adown!" (157). As if in fulfillment of her curse, the next section of the book begins, "Pierre plunged deep into the woods . . ." (157). And Pierre's efforts to convince Isabel to join him as his supposed wife in the city again instill plunging with forebodings of doom, "Already have I plunged! now thou canst not stay upon the bank" (227). Pierre opts continually for self-abandonment. His "plunge" into Plinlimmon's pamphlet becomes his Narcissus's dive, his unwitting attempt to possess himself which ironically results in his self-destruction.

And like Narcissus's pond, Plinlimmon's pamphlet casts back an image that Pierre fails to recognize as his own. Plinlimmon claims to have found "the talismanic Secret [that] . . . reconcile[s] this world with [man's] own soul" (244). The "talismanic Secret," as the narrator explains, is the solution to the paradox of idealism that underlies Christian society:

> Sooner or later in this life, the earnest, or enthusiastic youth comes to know, and more or less appreciate this startling solecism:—That while, as the grand condition of acceptance to God, Christianity calls upon all men to renounce this world; yet by all odds the most Mammonish parts of this world—Europe and America—are owned by none but professed Christian nations, who glory in the owning, and seem to have some reason therefor. (243)

"Solecism" subtly emphasizes the role rhetoric plays in this grand deception, in the resolution, that is, of a paradox. And this discovery, analogous to Pierre's discovery about his father's morality, provokes a quest that could well lead to authorship. The young enthusiast's uncertainty, according to the narrator, leads to an

> earnest reperusal of the Gospels: the intense self-absorption into that greatest real miracle of all religions, the Sermon on the Mount. From that divine mount, to all earnest-loving youths, flows an inexhaustible soul-melting stream of tenderness . . . sentences which embody all the love of the Past, and all the love which can be imagined in any conceivable Future. Such emotions as that Sermon raises in the enthusiastic heart; such emotions all youthful hearts refuse to ascribe to humanity as their origin. This is of God! cries the heart, and in that cry ceases all inquisition. (244)

Here the young enthusiast, like Pierre, refuses to probe and instead plunges into the text to find answers that will end the inquisition and, thus, any possibility of doubt and autonomy. Specifically, he turns to the Sermon on the Mount in which Christ speaks with authority, not as the scriber. And indeed it is as an author, through his sentences, that Christ seduces the Christian soul into submission. His sentences emblematize completion and contain the language of the potential author (rebel), who is condemned to repeat, or plagiarize, an authorizing discourse. One who repeats is, of course, reading and not writing a text.

The pamphlet portrays a provisional world and the arbitrariness of signification. Plinlimmon suggests that while attention to the ideals keeps man from "run[ning] into utter selfishness and human demonism" (251), absolute adherence to them requires that one "commit[] a sort of suicide as to the practical things of this world . . . and, finding by experience that this is utterly impossible; in his despair, he is too apt to run clean away into all manner of moral abandonment, self-deceit, and hypocrisy. . . ." (250–51). Plinlimmon elucidates the oppositional duality through which Pierre consistently affirms rather than questions, plunges into rather than probes, the symbolic order.

But Pierre, who even rebels "in obedience," albeit "in obedience to the loftiest behest of his soul" (245), reads the pamphlet "merely to drown himself" (245). Reading, "he felt a great interest awakened in him . . . but the central conceit refused to become clear to him" (245). Pierre waits for an illumination that would undermine the narrative principle that underlies his unwitting self-definition. Pierre's pamphlet, which is literally a fragment, offers fragmentation as an alternative to the inevitable plagiarism of a narrative identity. The uncertainty that Plinlimmon regards as a condition of earthly existence could easily translate into a rejection of the "truths" of social convention, prompting a rejection of the principle of coherence that governs Western identity and masks the experience of the fragmentation that promotes introspection.

The narrative, at this juncture, blurs the distinction between itself and Plinlimmon's pamphlet, as the narrator enters into a treatise in the first person:

> That profound Silence, that only Voice of our God, which I before spoke of; from that divine thing without a name, those impostor philosophers pretend somehow to have got an answer; which is as absurd, as though they should say they had got water out of a stone; for how can a man get a Voice out of Silence? (245)

The narrator's obvious subjectivity, which disrupts the text's narrative coherence, leaves the reader with an uneasy feeling, hinted at, but less dramatically presented elsewhere in the text. If the narrator has become so resolutely a character, then who is left to guide us through the profoundly disturbing collapse of Pierre? And what principle will ensure that the events of the text will eventually make sense to us? As Ahab's vision threatens to dissolve Ishmael, and as, in fact, Ishmael's ultimate internalization of Ahab does mark a sort of Pyrrhic victory for the captain's "madness," so Pierre's confused resolve seems to provoke the narrator into a narrative surrender. He exposes the relativity of the narrative consciousness by which he has both understood and undermined Pierre.

Insofar as we come to see the narrator's perspective as an alternate narrative (as, that is, *an* other, not *the* other narrative), then perhaps Silence can indeed speak to the attuned reader. The narrative unravelling that follows undermines narrative authority and alerts the reader to the possibility of an alternate discourse. Silence (and its counterpart, meaningless noise) emerges in resistance to narrative and meaningful language, not as an absence but as an alternate presence, the *embodiment*, perhaps, of possibility. "[E]verything written," writes Maurice Blanchot, "has, for the one who writes it, the greatest meaning possible, but has also this meaning, that it is a meaning bound to chance, that it is nonmeaning."[21] Silence presents the continuous possibility of an alternate meaning and so becomes itself an alternate meaning; it means that there are always other possible meanings. Insofar as the narrator's recovery of Pierre's unperceived narrative is itself a narrative act, *Pierre* opens itself to the possibility of a Derridean deconstruction, a reduction to noise. But as the narrator's narrative does succeed in recovering Pierre's self-annihilation in his narrative, and as Silence emerges as *a* and not *the* Voice in the text, and, finally, as Melville never fully undermines Pierre's representational status in "Young America," *Pierre* emerges as a multivocal critique of the resistless narratives that society and individuals unwittingly create and then live by.

Emblematic of such narrative reflexivity, Plinlimmon's pamphlet, which offers horological fragmentation as the earthly counterpart to chronometric silence, calls the implicitly progressive and causal form of narrative into question. Pierre is seduced by the apparent profundity of the reductive pamphlet and, especially, by the promise of consolation that the torn pamphlet never finally offers, but, as we have seen, Pierre is unable to break through the mirror image to the process of symbolization. The mirror is, for him, a Narcissus's pool in which he does not even recognize the image as himself. "For," as the narrator explains, "in this case, to comprehend, is himself to condemn himself" (246). The narrator's grammatical clumsiness itself mirrors the "highly inconvenient and uncomfortable" (246) task of such self-condemnation.

Pierre's "comprehension" (understanding) of the pamphlet would expose the futility of his quest for coherence and consistency, but "comprehension" also suggests engulfment. To "comprehend" anything is to enclose it, to impose coherence on fragmentation, and hence to "condemn" oneself to reject the possibility of self-authorization, which depends upon the perception of contradictions that disrupt coherence. The narrator con-

21. In *The Gaze of Orpheus and Other Literary Essays*, trans. Lydia Davis (Barrytown, NY: Station Hill Press, 1981), p. 19.

tinues his rhetorical performance as he retreats into the more "convenient" and "comfortable" narrative consciousness and reduces "comprehension" to the single sense of "understanding" with his assurance that "men are only made to comprehend things which they comprehended before" (246). To complicate this reading, to pause at the awkwardness that attests to textual mischief, to read, that is, in a way that is not governed by the rules of traditional narrative is to make visible the process of exclusion that is endemic to meaning and thus instigate self-authorization. Melville suggestively sends Pierre into New York wearing the pamphlet unwittingly in the lining of his coat.

Pierre's sojourn in New York is, appropriately, characterized by mirrors in which all difference is obscured beneath the unrecognized reflections of himself. The text itself mirrors earlier texts in an act of reflection that, the converse of Pierre's, elucidates rather than obscures. Pierre arrives in the city intending to find his cousin, Glendinning Stanly, whose name is the inverse of Pierre's ("pierre," French for stone; "stan," Anglo-Saxon). Lucy's predecessor in Pierre's affections, Glen even served as Pierre's earlier romantic mirror. As in Poe's "William Wilson," the double becomes increasingly the "conscience," or cultural voice (and Glendinning is even the name of one of Wilson's dupes). Whereas Glen Stanly is both real and villainous in *Pierre*, the allusion to Poe's story forces us to consider Pierre's role both in his own self-destruction and in, to some degree, his vilifying Glen. Nevertheless, Glen does assume Pierre's legacy, as he inherits Saddle Meadows and almost even Lucy. Both "stones" are, finally, equally unyielding, and the monuments of early friendship become, ironically, each other's tombstone. Pierre ultimately murders his cousin, ambiguously in self-defense, when the latter comes to retrieve Lucy, who has come to the city to join Pierre despite his "marriage" to Isabel. Like William Wilson's, Pierre's "murder" is equally a suicide. In murdering his counterpart, the cultural self he has rejected, he murders his whole self (literally, his ultimate suicide in prison).

It is tempting here to see in Pierre and Glen an analogue for the Confederacy and the Union, which, unable to compromise, face destruction and which, furthermore, fail to recognize their mirroring. What neither Pierre nor Glen can tolerate, it seems, is any violation of what Michael Kammen calls "the cult of consensus." [22] When Pierre, in quest of his kinsman, meets

22. Kammen sees the "cult of consensus . . . the desire for togetherness if not uniformity" as an outgrowth of "the quest for legitimacy and . . . the desire to reconcile our restless pluralities." He views the cult as a significant contribution to "the matrix of paradoxy

a "scarlet woman," Melville evokes Hawthorne's "My Kinsman, Major Moli-
neux," in which a youth in pre-Revolutionary America comes to the city
in search of his uncle, who he hopes will help him make his fortune. The
only person who accosts him is a prostitute in scarlet, who tempts him into
consensus, which he doesn't understand until his uncle passes, tarred and
feathered, and Robin finds himself laughing uncontrollably, caught up in
the contagion of "revolutionary" fervor. He also learns that "one man [may]
have several voices . . . as well as two complexions," a lesson that exposes
the ambiguity of the American Revolution to a listener who, like Pierre, does
not seem fully able to comprehend it but is in fact comprehended by it.

The narrator pauses, after Pierre's arrival in New York, to begin
"Young America in Literature" with a discussion of historiography:

> Among the various conflicting modes of writing history, there would
> seem to be two grand practical distinctions, under which all the rest
> must subordinately range. By the one mode, all contemporaneous
> circumstances, facts, and events must be set down contemporane-
> ously; by the other, they are only to be set down as the general
> stream of the narrative shall dictate; for matters which are kindred in
> time, may be very irrelative in themselves. I elect neither of these;
> I am careless of either; both are well enough in their way; I write
> precisely as I please. (286)

When the narrator classifies historiography, which he assigns to either of
two genres (what Hayden White would call the annals or narrative forms
of historical discourse), he both explains and illustrates how exclusion
underlies meaning.[23] Cultural convention is transmitted through the process
of categorization which organizes data into a coherent and "meaningful"
reality. Categories operate according to a principle of exclusion insofar as
"meaning" restricts the possibility of endless interpretation.[24] Even the form
of historical discourse, according to White, determines the extent to which

---

in American life—unstable pluralism" (*People of Paradox*, p. 92). As it is often difficult
to distinguish between—or among—political parties in the United States, it is similarly
difficult to separate Pierre's goals from what he claims to be fighting.

23. See Hayden White's classification, "The Value of Narrativity."

24. This observation is perhaps a commonplace of semiotic theory. I am particularly interested in Lacan's treatment of this subject. His theories of communication, meaning,
and interpretation are most pointedly articulated in this context in "The Function and Field
of Speech and Language," *Ecrits*, trans. Alan Sheridan (New York and London: W.W.
Norton & Co., 1977), pp. 30–113.

"reality wears the mask of a meaning, the completeness and fullness of which we can only *imagine*, never experience. Insofar as historical stories can be completed, can be given narrative closure, can be shown to have had a *plot* all along, they give to reality the odor of the *ideal*."[25]

Classification, while not itself a narrative act, is a restriction, a form of closure, and, as such, it anticipates Pierre's attempt to impose meaning on his life by narrativizing events. His effort thus to "gospelize the world anew" bespeaks the idealization that underwrites (and undercuts) his authorship. For Pierre, authorship is an absolute identity, a commitment or achievement which, therefore, entails a choice among rather than an inspection of the categories that are imposed on him through the internalized script of cultural identity. The narrator's transcendental ahistoricism, according to which his subjectivity organizes his data, recalls Pierre's declaration of independence in an act of mirroring that illustrates the failure to resist categorization, which is the goal of self-authorization.

This passage is a narrative "act" in another sense as well. It is a performance that enables the inspection that it apparently forestalls. Nina Baym views Pierre's authorship as a textual rupture in which "the uneasy union of narrator with tale dissolves." The fissure represents, in Baym's analysis, Melville's attempt to restore Pierre "to the center of the narrative."[26] Perhaps, however, as the reader is supposed to trip over such awkwardnesses as have previously been discussed, so the reader is meant to pause at the disruption marked by this juncture. The narrator willfully contradicts himself in his claim to transcendental ahistoricism in order to underscore the principle of exclusion by which Pierre converts the process of self-authorization into the ideal of authorship. Pierre's "authorship" is ˙neither sudden nor precipitous; the consequences of Pierre's obvious textuality have been, from the onset, the dominant subject of the narrative. The narrator's intrusion indeed disrupts the narrative flow, but the reader's discomfort should instigate a questioning process. The passage illustrates how Pierre symbolizes both the *process* and the consequences of his symbolization.

In addition, Baym attributes Melville's "generic drift" to his conviction that genre, as a manifestation of literary convention, restricted rather than expanded possibilities.[27] She reads the passage that introduces Pierre's

25. "The Value of Narrativity," p. 20.
26. "Melville's Quarrel with Fiction," p. 919.
27. This phrase was coined by Joseph Donahue of Columbia University in an American

authorship as evidence of one of the central problems of the text: Melville's "fiction got in the way of the direct statement that [he] was seeking to make" (919). Yet Melville's "generic drift" calls into question the principles of classification by which, as in the passage in question, we organize the data of our world. Melville's intentional disturbance of such boundaries forces a consideration—and a reconsideration—of the effect of those principles. Perhaps the chaos of Pierre, because of which a majority of the text's critics cite the failure of Melville's project, clarifies rather than obscures the central tenets of the work.

Pierre is not, as Richard Brodhead suggests, "a draught of a draught, in a . . . desperate sense"; it does not "trace its author's discovery of the impossibility of his own creative project . . . [nor] rule out even the minimal faith in his own work that the task of revision would require of him."[28] In fact, Pierre is an endless series of re-visions, that, as I have suggested, compel the reader's participation, and its open-endedness completes the task that Melville had begun in Moby Dick. Pierre is neither historical nor ahistorical, but in some sense the history of ahistoricism. What makes the text so difficult is Melville's struggle to expose, and so to check, the compulsion to repeat the unconscious narrative of one's identity that follows on a declaration of independence. For such repetition is, as we have seen, the "comprehension" (death) of the author. To turn comprehension/ engulfing into comprehension/understanding (mastery), requires repetition to bring the narrative of identity into consciousness. Undermining narrative authority, Melville does not, as Ann Douglas suggests, "allow[] his readers no real way into the novel," but in fact allows them no real way out.[29]

The narrator, in one of the more sardonic moments in the text, startles the reader with the impossibility of the whole project:

> The world is forever babbling of originality; but there never yet was an original man, in the sense intended by the world; the first man himself—who according to the Rabbins was also the first author— not being an original; the only original author being God. (302)

---

literature dissertation seminar, spring semester 1988. I have used the phrase because I think it aptly captures the almost paradoxical balance between intentionality and lack of control that Melville demonstrates here. See Baym, "Melville's Quarrel with Fiction," p. 918.

28. Hawthorne, pp. 189–90.

29. The Feminization of American Culture (New York: Alfred A. Knopf, 1977), p. 373.

As the narrator's theological stance should be, by this time, at least suspect, the sense of this declaration is unclear. But, psychologically, it re-visions authorship as a quest, an analytic process (rather than an end), to which the narrator opposes Pierre's pride, for "Pierre was proud; and a proud man . . . likes to feel himself in himself, and not by reflection in others" (304). As we have seen, a reflection in others, "mirroring," provides both the source of identity and the potential for its inspection. But as we have also seen, Pierre fails to recognize his mirroring and so succumbs to it.

Pierre declares, "I will gospelize the world anew, and show them deeper secrets than the Apocalypse!—I will write it, I will write it!" (319). His use of "gospelize" suggests that he cannot reject the basic tenets he thinks he has overthrown. Pierre wants to be the instrument through which an absolute eternal truth is filtered; he wants to transcribe rather than write. He is not only Ahab's heir, as critics have suggested, but Ishmael's as well.[30] When Ishmael ends *Moby Dick* with Rachel's searching for her children, he paraphrases a gospel that itself repeats Jeremiah in fulfillment of the prophecy. Repetition, in Matthew, is authorizing and authenticating. But in *Moby Dick*, it is a reflection of Ishmael's internalization of Ahab, his need, that is, to find meaning in chance events, such as his survival. Ishmael, traditionally considered a foil for Ahab's megalomaniacal acts of interpretation, is in fact finally, although subtly, seduced by Ahab's point of view; his mirroring ultimately submits, to a large extent, to a reflection of rather than on Ahab.

We can perhaps understand Pierre's plagiarism specifically in conjunction with his own desire for originality. The narrator opposes "plagiarism" not to originality but to conscious repetition. Edgar Dryden underscores "plagiarize" "because Pierre's experience is composed of a series of literary fictions,"[31] but it is more particularly a reference to the narrative of identity into which those fictions, along with all other cultural transmitters, have been incorporated. In his declaration of originality, Pierre denies the narrative that, as we have seen, consequently becomes a resistless force.

Pierre's text, which also features an author-hero, mirrors both Pierre and *Pierre*; the former is, again, not conscious of the full implications of reflection, whereas the latter exploits it. Melville ridicules Pierre, whose

---

30. See Brodhead, *Hawthorne*, pp. 170ff.
31. *Melville's Thematics of Form: The Great Art of Telling the Truth* (Baltimore: Johns Hopkins University Press, 1968), p. 138.

manuscript betrays not the darkness of his vision that horrifies his publishers, but the ludicrousness that undermines his tragedy. Goethe is an "inconceivable coxcomb . . . like a hired waiter" (352). The world could "spare a million more of the same kidney . . . crushed . . . like an egg from which the meat hath been sucked" (352–53). What Pierre's text tells us about *Pierre*, however, is to look to the most apparently ridiculous moments, the disruptions, in the text for access.

What seems most ludicrous and irrelevant, as Freud told his patients, is often what is most revealing. Pierre's unconscious desires, the narrative of which he is unaware, dominate his writing. Cold, hungry, and celibate, Pierre is preoccupied by questions of employment and images of food and of the body. Similarly, when the narrative dissolves into syllabic associations, Pierre's longings are more readily revealed: "—Nor jingling sleigh-bells, nor glad Thanksgiving, nor Merry Christmas, nor jubilating New Year's: —Nor Bell, Thank, Christ, Year;—none of these are for Pierre" (354). Striking in this catalogue is "Bell," Pierre's nickname for Isabel, the forbidden object; "Christ," too, alleges the importance of Pierre's cultural ties. "Thank" and "Year" denote cultural customs and categories of organization. But what is most important here is the reading lesson; association disrupts narration, imposing personal preoccupation on the events of the narrative.

Free association foregrounds the unperceived narrative that challenges the ostensible narrative. The two narratives promote a heteroglossia that can call narrative authority in general into question.[32] Language, too, unravels into its components during the free play of association. Language breaks down as Pierre is increasingly excluded from the world, as he

32. I am invoking Bakhtin here because of the exciting conjunction that I think remains to be developed between Bakhtin and psychoanalytic theory. These connections are rich enough to require a study of their own. Yet, I wish briefly to suggest that psychoanalysis operates by many of the principles of Bakhtin's dialogics; for example, the competing narrative voices, the heteroglossia that challenges narrative authority, are very much operative in Freud's concept of multi-determined symptoms. Schafer's competing narratives work even more directly in accordance with the concept of heteroglossia. A study of this sort could add a new voice to the growing dialogue between psychoanalytic and narrative theory.

In this context, it is interesting to note that Bakhtin, who did not have access to some of Freud's major works (including the more culturally oriented studies), attempted to restore a cultural/materialist perspective to psychoanalysis, which, he felt, was biologically reductive. See V.N. Volosinov (Bakhtin), *Freudianism: A Critical Sketch*, trans. I.R. Titunik (Bloomington and Indianapolis: Indiana University Press, 1976).

comes, that is, to share Isabel's alienation. As we have seen, Pierre cannot utilize his position to gain access to the margins of cultural discourse. Instead, it is a task left to the reader and the narrator, who, locating Glen's succession to Pierre's inheritance in "the hereditary syllables, Glendinning" (335), calls attention to the role of language in convention as well as to convention as a language, especially in reference to the name of the father and the authority of the law.

Without inspection, Pierre cannot change or resist the resistless force that he tragically (or pathetically) authors. His writing brings him to the precipitous discovery: "For the more and the more that he wrote, and the deeper and the deeper that he dived, Pierre saw the everlasting elusiveness of Truth; the universal lurking insincerity of even the greatest and purest written thoughts" (393). But Pierre has too much faith to make the necessary leap. If the elusiveness of Truth had led him to regard experience as relative and self-created, to perceive the terms of his unconscious narrative (the internalized script), Pierre would not have become the "most unwilling states-prisoner of letters." But his attachment to convention overpowers his authorship, as "he blindly [writes] with his eyes turned away from the paper;—thus unconsciously symbolizing the hostile necessity and distaste" (394). Necessity's "hostility" attests to the oppositional thinking to which Pierre surrenders his humanity, turning himself instead into a symbol and allowing himself to be written by a fate he authors and so potentially could alter.

Such alteration is, of course, no easy process; in fact it is, in Nick Carraway's words, "a matter of infinite hope." Typically coy, the narrator expresses a principle of interpretation that apparently chooses "the White Whale" and "the Ambiguities," over "Moby Dick" and "Pierre":

> Say what some poets will, Nature is not so much her own ever-sweet interpreter, as the mere supplier of that cunning alphabet, whereby selecting and combining as he pleases, each man reads his own peculiar lesson according to his own peculiar mind and mood. (397)

The narrator's claim, "I write precisely as I please," echoes through this passage. But "cunning" is disruptive; a "cunning alphabet" necessarily undermines linquistic free play. "Cunning" works against the narrator's claim as words signify against the intentions of their users. Language, a type of classification and cultural transmitter, organizes meaning, as "the Delectable Mountain," a mountain near Saddle Meadows rechristened by an old Baptist farmer, cast a "spell . . . [that], gazing upon [the mountain] by the light of those suggestive syllables, no poetical observer could resist" (397). The mood and the word, in intricate conjunction, conspire to mean.

Social terms invariably comprehend Pierre, organizing even—in fact, especially—his fantasies of rebellion, to which he is passive:

> one night . . . a sudden, unwonted, and all-pervading sensation seized him. He knew not where he was; he did not have any ordinary life-feeling at all. He could not see; though instinctively putting his hand to his eyes, he seemed to feel that the lids were open. . . . During this state of semi-unconsciousness, or rather trance, a remarkable dream or vision came to him. The actual artificial objects around him slid from him, and were replaced by . . . a baseless vision. (395–97)

Under the influence of and in conformity with "his Titanic soul" (396), his particular concerns, Pierre refashions Delectable Mountain into "the Mount of the Titans" (397):

> Stark desolation; ruin, merciless and ceaseless; chills and gloom, —all here lived a hidden life, curtained by that cunning purpleness, which, from the piazza of the manor house, so beautifully invested the mountain once called Delectable, but now styled Titanic. (399)

"Cunning," which recalls the "cunning alphabet," signals the projection onto the landscape with which Pierre denies his act of authorship. The narrator shifts rhetorically at this point from a description of what "the tourist" was and did to the direct second person address, "you still ascended . . ." (399), thus forcing the reader into a specific narrative perspective. This movement parallels Pierre's surrender to a narrative that he disowns as he abandons himself to the myth of Enceladus, which finally ends his attempt at authorship. Pierre returns home in his fantasy, and he overturns his mother's genteel Christianity, but only to replace it with a pagan and emphatically social ideal. Pierre imagines himself as Enceladus, the Titan child of incest, who led an assault on the heavens and was condemned by the gods to drag the earth on a chain around his ankle. The myth fits not only Pierre's unconscious concerns but, more potently, his unconscious desires:

> . . . Enceladus was both the son and grandson of an incest; and even thus, there had been born from the organic blended heavenliness and earthliness of Pierre, another mixed, uncertain, heaven-aspiring, but still not wholly earth-emancipated mood . . .—that reckless sky-assaulting mood of his, was nevertheless on one side the

grandson of the sky. For it is according to eternal fitness, that the precipitated Titan should still seek to regain his paternal birthright even by fierce escalade. Wherefore whoso storms the sky gives best proof he came from thither! (402–3)

The mytho-literary precedents for Pierre's rebellion again make clear that his "sky-assaulting mood," although directed against a paternal figure, is very much in accordance with a paternal tradition.

Most prominent, however, is the theme of incest. The monster, Enceladus, that springs from the seed of incest re-enforces the cultural prohibition. And yet, Enceladus enormously attracts Pierre in this vision. Incest has created a powerful hero, a replica of his heroic ancestors. Pierre's identification with Enceladus could foreground his attachment to his paternal ancestors, but, more important, his attraction to the myth borders on his acknowledgement of his desire for Isabel—inflamed, perhaps, by his celibacy—and, by implication, for his mother, and for himself. In other words, Pierre could potentially confront the desire through which he could shatter convention and the desire that prevents him from doing so. But his vision recovers that desire as it recovers it, and Pierre retreats for the last time from the cultural margins and the chance to resist the narrative of his identity.

Pierre seeks refuge from the intensity of his vision and from his struggle in an excursion to an art exhibit with Isabel and Lucy. Circumstances culminate his crisis as it began, in a wish that comes true—that Isabel is not in fact the sister for whom he had wished. A portrait of a nameless head in an art gallery casts doubt on Isabel and Pierre's familial ties. As Isabel's resemblance to Pierre's father's portrait convinces him that she is his sister, her resemblance to the stranger's portrait exposes the hastiness of his original conclusion. This time, however, "[t]he most tremendous displacing and revolutionizing thoughts [that] were upheaving in him, with reference to Isabel" (409), no longer pertained to heroism, but to his twin desires for Isabel and conformity. In the context of these desires, Pierre re-evaluates Isabel's story. The gallery portrait calls into question the symbol on which Pierre's chief evidence rested—the portrait of his father—and leads Pierre to wonder whether Isabel may have been consciously scripted: "By some strange arts Isabel's wonderful story might have been, someway, and for some cause, forged for her, in her childhood, and craftily impressed upon her youthful mind" (411). With no sister, Pierre has no excuse for heroism nor defiance (particularly the "danger" of incest); with no evidence of his father's adultery, he has nothing to define himself in terms of or against. Bewildered, Pierre must cast away his script and is temporarily reduced to wordless desire: "With such bewildering meditations as these in him . . . and with both Isabel and Lucy bodily touching his sides as he walked; the feelings of Pierre were entirely untranslatable into any words that can be used" (410).

Pierre, of course, is incapable of extending the limitations of language into an understanding of its inherent incapacities. And he is equally unwilling to act on his desire. But since he cannot relinquish the narrative of heroism, he channels his passion—composed of his frustrated rebellion and his desire for Isabel—into rage against the social institutions represented by the signatories of two letters he discovers on his return home. One terminates his contract with his publishing house, "Steel, Flint & Asbestos," a name that signifies impotence in its juxtaposition of fire-starters and fire-resistants. The other, from Glen Stanly and Lucy's brother, brands him "a villainous and perjured liar." Impotent against the social terms that he himself empowers, Pierre destroys himself, as we have seen, through Glen Stanly.

The final act opens on Pierre, whose metaphysical imprisonment has now taken literal form. In jail, Pierre finishes the second of his books, the one writ in blood, although his metaphors again consign him more to characterization than authorship:

> Here, then, is the untimely, timely end;—Life's last chapter well stitched into the middle! Nor book, nor author of the book, hath any sequel, though each hath its last lettering!—It is ambiguous still. Had I been heartless now, disowned, and spurningly portioned off the girl at Saddle Meadows, then had I been happy through a long life on earth, and perchance through a long eternity in heaven! Now, 'tis merely hell in both worlds. Well, be it hell. I will mold a trumpet of the flames, and, with my breath of flame, breathe back my defiance! But give me first another body! I long and long to die, to be rid of this dishonored cheek. *Hung by the neck till thou be dead*.—Not if I forestall you, though!—Oh now to live is death, and now to die is life; now, to my soul, were a sword my midwife! (418)

Pierre appears to want to act here, in fact, to believe that he is acting, "mold[ing] a trumpet of the flames . . . and breath[ing] back [his] defiance" (418). But he is only, again, enacting a script. Deluded, he believes that "now to die is life," and he refuses to accept the nothingness of reality in death even as he recoiled from the absence of certainty in life. Enter Isabel and Lucy to play out the full tragic scene: "Lucy shrunk up like a scroll, and noiselessly fell at the feet of Pierre." Enfolded in Pierre's destiny, Lucy has herself become a text in which Pierre reads his final line, "seizing Isabel in his grasp—in thy breasts, life for infants lodgeth not, but death-milk for thee and me!—The drug!" But Pierre's finale is pathetic rather than tragic. Even his death is plagiarized, this time from Socrates, with the notable difference that Pierre's makes no point and no sense. "Midwife" suggests that Pierre believes he is being somehow reborn; he rejects the reality of his death even as he has denied the reality of his life. Pierre dies not a tragic failure, but a failed tragedy.

The end of the novel reads as a parody of a Shakespearian tragedy, and, indeed, *Hamlet* runs throughout as a pre-text for Pierre's heroism and his paralysis.[33] The three main characters lie dead or dying and the only survivors are incidental characters, but no one pronounces the lesson to be learned or the principles on which the community may be rebuilt. The apocalyptic scene is relieved only by the archaic language that undercuts any vestige of the tragedy that may have remained, beginning with Lucy's brother's exclamation:

> "Yes! Yes!—Dead! Dead! Dead!—without one visible wound—her sweet plumage hides it.—Thou hellish carrion, this is thy hellish work! Thy juggler's rifle brought down this heavenly bird! Oh, my God, my God! Thou scalpest me with this sight!"
>
> "The dark vein's burst, and here's the deluge-wreck—all stranded here! Ah, Pierre! my old companion, Pierre; —school-mate—play-mate—friend!—Our sweet boys' walks within the woods!—Oh, I would have rallied thee, and banteringly warned thee from thy too moody ways, but thou wouldst never heed! What scornful innocence rests on thy lips, my friend!—Hand scorched with murderer's powder, yet how woman-soft!—By heaven, these fingers move!—one speechless clasp!—all's o'er!"
>
> "All's o'er, and ye know him not!" came gasping from the wall; and from the fingers of Isabel dropped an empty vial—as it had been a run-out sand-glass—and shivered upon the floor; and her whole form sloped sideways, and she fell upon Pierre's heart, and her long hair ran over him, and arbored him in ebon vines. (420–21)

Pierre here conforms to the pre-written script, and his apparent bent for playing out romantic scenes brings on his senseless and melodramatic

33. See also Sundquist's discussion of Melville's use of *Hamlet* in *Pierre* (Sundquist, p. 146).

demise. The ending is apocalyptic, but no Fortinbras or Edgar, Malcolm or Lodovico, survives to profit from his tragic errors and so institute a more just rule. The stakes are simply not that high. And we assume that Pierre's text suffers the same fate.

More than one of Melville's text's initial reviewers suggested that its author be institutionalized (rather than canonized). But the intensity of its critical reception, then and now, attests to the efficacy of its formal experimentation. A book about a writer's writing a book about a writer lends itself to the prismatic introspection that Brodhead sees as a failed novel, "a draught of a draught, in a . . . desperate sense."[34] *Pierre's* reflexivity inspects Pierre's internalization of a narrative identity that consistently foils his self-authorization, his inspection of the terms of cultural discourse, precisely because that internalization formalizes his declaration of independence. Melville's deconstruction of the national script of identity, which reads like the erratic disruptions of an unconscious, a cultural unconscious, insists on the reader's inspection of his/her own such internalization. *Pierre* confounds its readers' expectations by narrative disruptions that challenge fundamental (and internalized) assumptions about narrativity.

34. Brodhead is hardly alone in this response (*Hawthorne*, pp. 189–90). Critics, like the initial reviewers, tend towards vehemence, albeit often qualified by their acknowledgement of Melville's stature. Newton Arvin calls *Pierre* "one of the most painfully ill-conditioned books ever to be produced by a first-rate mind" (*Herman Melville* [New York: Viking Press, 1964]). Richard Chase calls it "a book that tries to be a novel of manners and turns into a ranting melodrama" ("Introduction," *Melville: A Collection of Critical Essays* [Englewood Cliffs, N.J.: Prentice-Hall, Inc., 1962], p. 9). F. O. Matthiessen offers the somewhat more qualified view that "if *Pierre* is a failure, it must be accounted a great one, a failure in an effort to express as honestly as possible what it meant to undergo the test 'of a real impassioned onset of Life and Passion'" (*American Renaissance: Art and Expression in the Age of Emerson and Whitman* [New York and London: Oxford University Press, 1941/1966], p. 487). Interestingly, I find myself most in accord with one of the earliest responses to *Pierre*—E. L. Grant Watson's view that it "is the story of a conscious soul attempting to draw itself free from the psychic world—material in which most of mankind is unconsciously always wrapped and enfolded, as a foetus in the womb" ("Melville's *Pierre*," *New England Quarterly* 3 (April 1930): 195–234). Among contemporary readings that I find most convincing, Richard Gray's "'All's o'er, and ye know him not': A Reading of *Pierre*" (*Herman Melville: Reassessments*, ed. Robert A. Lee [London: Vision Press, 1984], pp. 116–34) most persuasively argues for a revisionist reading of *Pierre*, which, he contends, anticipates the post-modern novel in "the subversive nature of its techniques, the self-reflexive character of its idiom" (117). It is primarily for its psychological depth and its fascinating narrative experimentation that I regard *Pierre* as a complete, successful, and brilliant work.

The Rhetorical Use and Abuse of Fiction:
Eating Books in Late Nineteenth-Century America

Steven Mailloux

Reade not to contradict, nor to belieue,
but to waigh and consider. Some bookes
are to bee tasted, others to bee swallowed,
and some few to bee chewed and digested.
—Francis Bacon, "Of Studies" (1597).

Do not read as a glutton eats. Digest your books, turn them into
nourishment, make them a part of your life that lives always.
—Annie H. Ryder, *Go Right On, Girls! Develop*
Your Bodies, Your Minds, Your Characters (1891).

In December 1884 the Philadelphia *Bulletin* published a letter from
a Texas correspondent. It began: "I am a young woman, twenty-one years

I thank the audiences at Duke University and the University of Toledo who responded to
early versions of this paper. I am also grateful to participants in the Rhetoric Colloquium
at the University of Toledo, especially Wallace Martin and Don Bialostosky, for their incisive criticisms and helpful suggestions. Above all, I thank my colleague John Crowley for
copies of *The Story of a Bad Boy* and *Peck's Bad Boy*, and Don Pease for his invitation
to contribute an essay to this collection.

old, and am called bright and intelligent. I fear I have seriously impaired my mind by novel reading. Do you think I can restore it to a sound and vigorous condition by eschewing novels and reading only solid works?" The editor responded to this letter first by commenting that the writer "proves herself a less hopeless case than most of her sisters in the east, who are not only saturated with the dilute sentimentality of fiction, but who also are completely satisfied with their condition." He then went on to advise these "young ladies who feed their brains with novels, and their palates with confectionery": Avoid "silly or pernicious trash"; shun "the monstrous volume of wishy-washy, sensational or at best neutral fiction which the reading public demands."[1]

A month after this exchange appeared, an early American notice of *Huckleberry Finn* began " 'Good wine needs no bush;' and a book by Mark Twain needs no beating about the bush. One takes it as children do sweetmeats, with trusting confidence."[2]

What I will try to do in this essay is tease out the cultural implications of the tropes used here to describe novel reading in late nineteenth-century America. This seemingly straightforward task will take me rather far afield as I examine two historical moments in the use and abuse of fiction: the late 1860s and, more briefly, the mid-1880s. The former period saw the enormous popularity of such children's fiction as Alcott's *Little Women* and Aldrich's *Story of a Bad Boy*, the development of the reformatory and placing-out movements in the disciplining of juvenile delinquents, and soon the publication of Abbott's influential child-rearing guide, *Gentle Measures for the Management and Training of the Young*. The latter years, the mid-eighties, witnessed the establishment of the Modern Language Association of America, the controversies over such juvenile fictions as *Peck's Bad Boy* and *Adventures of Huckleberry Finn*, the appearance of advice books such as *Hold Up Your Heads, Girls* and *Home, Health, Happiness*, and the introduction of literary study into the Elmira State Reformatory by the nation's leading reformatory theorist, Zebulon Brockway.

In my analysis, I will sketch out how American cultural rhetoric presented and orchestrated the effects of reading fiction for its audiences, whether white middle-class adult males or working-class female adolescents. This project grows out of a chapter in my book, *Rhetorical Power*, where I present a Foucauldean reading of the cultural reception of *Huckle-*

1. "Young Women and Novels," Philadelphia *Bulletin*, rpt. in Austin *Daily Statesman*, 28 December 1884, p. 2.
2. Detroit *Free Press*, 10 January 1885, p. 8.

berry Finn. There my goal was to explain why race or the "Negro Problem" played no explicit role in the reviews of Mark Twain's novel. I argue, in effect, that the cultural conversation of the mid-1880s demonstrated less anxiety about race relations then it did about juvenile delinquency and that the cultural censors reviewing *Huckleberry Finn* were preoccupied less with racist segregation practices than with the "Bad-Boy Boom" and the negative effects of reading fiction.[3]

The present essay takes up where this argument left off, not only by investigating other gendered assumptions about the bad effects of reading fiction but also by extending the analysis of how cultural rhetoric enables and constrains the interpretation and use of fiction at specific historical moments. Cultural rhetoric does this, I will show, by constructing and managing the effects of reading novels at various cultural sites: the home, the reformatory, and perhaps the university.

Taking up Louisa May Alcott's *Little Women* at the outset and Mark Twain's *Huckleberry Finn* near the end, I will argue that the cultural use of fiction involved, among other things, the circulation and transformation of particular tropes and arguments through various narratives of "evil reading," "juvenile delinquency," and "social disorder." I will focus on two special aspects of this cultural rhetoric: the materiality of its tropes and the disciplinary function of its arguments. In short, I will claim that the cultural talk about reading fiction was focused by an interpretive rhetoric of self-transformation and inner discipline, a late nineteenth-century American version of what Foucault called in his last works "technologies of the self."[4]

Because the historical argument of this essay gets rather detailed at times, I would like to lay out for you in rather rough form the results so far of this work in progress, my study of the cultural rhetoric of reading fiction. I have been struck most by the materiality, or better, the physicality of the tropes used for reading in the late nineteenth century: reading as eating, critical reading as an exercise in mental discipline, and evaluative reading as "moral gymnastics," in Twain's vivid phrase.[5] Such tropes and their ac-

3. *Rhetorical Power* (Ithaca: Cornell University Press, 1989), chap. 4.
4. Michel Foucault, *The Care of the Self*, trans. Robert Hurley (New York: Pantheon Books, 1986); and *Technologies of the Self: A Seminar with Michel Foucault*, ed. Luther H. Martin, Huck Gutman, and Patrick H. Hutton (Amherst: University of Massachusetts Press, 1988).
5. Samuel Clemens to Pamela Moffett, 15 April 1885, in *Mark Twain: Business Man*, ed. Samuel Charles Webster (Boston: Little, Brown, 1946), p. 317.

companying arguments assume the close cultural connection among moral order, mental development, and bodily exercise that I will make more explicit by examining late nineteenth-century rhetoric. These rhetorical interconnections, I claim, enabled not only the development of a new kind of children's literature after the Civil War but also reforms in the cultural management of delinquency and perhaps even the institutionalization of literary study in the university.

To start with, then, let me suggest two ways of interpreting the physicality of the tropes of reading. One way is to interpret the comparisons figuratively, as the nineteenth century sometimes did: reading as eating or gymnastics or discipline all symbolized the widely held social belief in the actual positive or negative effects of reading on the nineteenth-century reader, especially the vulnerable child, the malleable adolescent, and the potential criminal. But there is another way to read these tropes: interpreting the metaphors literally, again as the nineteenth century sometimes did. Literalizing these physical tropes means to institute practices that make reading itself part of the specific disciplinary targeting of the body. The rhetorical logic goes something like this: in the figurative meaning, reading is like eating in that both affect the individual though in very different ways, one mental, the other physical; then in the literalizing of the trope, reading and eating are viewed as only slightly different aspects of the same activity, the physical ingestion of nourishment (for mind and body); and what follows from this is that the regulation of reading and eating becomes part of the same material disciplining of individual subjects.

Because this distinction between figurative and literal interpretation is somewhat slippery in theory and always historically contingent in actual practice, I will present a concrete example of its functioning, an example that will introduce the first cultural sphere in which I want to locate the use of reading fiction: the social theorizing about child-rearing and juvenile deliquency.

1

By the early nineteenth century, the Enlightenment view of childhood exerted strong and steady pressure on the ideology of parenting throughout middle-class American society. An influential Lockean pedagogy advocated a balance between parental love and filial duty, an emphasis that shifted child-rearing toward less authoritarian and more child-centered practices and established a new preoccupation with affectionate discipline.[6] The Lockean view of successful childhood fostered a reconception of its opposite, juvenile delinquency. Beginning in the mid-1820s, new institutions emerged to deal with the problem of young law-breakers, separating them from adult criminals and prescribing different forms of discipline and punishment. In 1825 the Society for the Reformation of Juvenile Delinquents was organized, and it soon established the New York House of Refuge, the first of several such institutions founded before the Civil War.[7]

These houses of refuge built for handling juvenile delinquents were, in a sense, only miniature adult prisons. Though the managers of these institutions sometimes compared them to public schools, they also affirmed, as one historian has put it, that a refuge "was a 'juvenile penitentiary,' a prison scaled down to children's size and abilities. Of necessity, its officers were caretakers forced to regard inmates as potentially dangerous criminals with vicious habits requiring thorough eradication."[8] Built as large custodial institutions, refuge corrective practices often appeared to exemplify punishment rather than reform as their goal. But in the 1850s an anti-institutional rhetoric began influencing the theory and practice of delinquent management as preventative agencies and reform schools started replacing some houses of refuge.

One such preventative agency was the New York Children's Aid Society, founded by Charles Loring Brace in 1853. Brace studied at Yale in the 1840s, where he was inspired by the lectures of Horace Bushnell, author of the highly influential book *Views of Christian Nurture* (1847).

---

6. Cf. Steven L. Schlossman, *Love and the American Delinquent: The Theory and Practice of 'Progressive' Juvenile Justice, 1825–1920* (Chicago: University of Chicago Press, 1977), p. 50: "As in earlier periods, the ultimate aim of child rearing was to cultivate obedience and instill an unwavering moral sense. But now the motivational techniques were to be different: the stress was on persuasion, kindness, empathy—what I term affectional discipline—rather than on breaking a child's will through force." Also see the detailed analysis of advice manuals on child-rearing in Bernard Wishy, *The Child and the Republic: The Dawn of American Child Nurture* (Philadelphia: University of Pennsylvania Press, 1968), chaps. 1–8; and Richard H. Brodhead's discussion of "disciplinary intimacy" in "Sparing the Rod: Discipline and Fiction in Antebellum America," *Representations* 21 (Winter 1988): 67–96.

7. See Robert S. Pickett, *House of Refuge: Origins of Juvenile Justice Reform in New York State, 1815–1857* (Syracuse: Syracuse University Press, 1969); Robert Mennel, *Thorns and Thistles: Juvenile Delinquents in the United States, 1825–1940* (Hanover NH: University Press of New England, 1973), chap. 1; and Schlossman, *Love and the American Delinquent*, chaps. 2–3.

8. Schlossman, p. 28.

Bushnell emphasized the role of parents in using their sensitivity and feelings to shape their children's characters and to extend God's grace to the individual boy or girl. He used organic metaphors to describe the process of child-rearing, calling the parent "God's gardener," and he rhetorically reversed the institutional emphasis in dealing with juvenile delinquents by referring to the family as "God's reformatory."[9]

Brace literalized Bushnell's tropes by advocating that delinquents not be institutionalized in houses of refuge but be "placed out" with farm families whose influence would cultivate morality in the urban children who had gone astray. As he wrote in his 1872 book, *The Dangerous Classes of New York, and Twenty Years' Work Among Them*, "The founders of the Children's Aid Society early saw that the best of all Asylums for the outcast child, is the *farmer's home*. . . . [T]he cultivators of the soil are in America our most solid and intelligent class."[10] In Brace's rhetoric, farmers of the land become the best framers of the children.

The anti-institutional placing-out movement with its ideological rhetoric of the family had its institutional counterpart in the introduction of the "cottage plan" into state reformatories. Also called the "family system," this approach to rehabilitation differed radically from the old custodial model of the adult prisons and juvenile houses of refuge. Rather than one large building for incarceration, the cottage plan called for several smaller buildings each with its own family or group of inmates.[11] This new architectural organization of delinquents was coupled with a new style of management that followed from the rhetoric of affectionate discipline already at work in theories of child-rearing.

The first family plan in America was introduced into the first state reformatory for female delinquents, the Massachusetts State Industrial School for Girls in Lancaster. The trustees wrote in their first annual report in 1856 that the reformatory "is to be a *home*. Each house is to be a *family*, under the sole direction and control of the matron, who is to be the *mother* of the family. The government and discipline are strictly parental. It is the design . . . to educate, to teach [the girls] industry, self-reliance, morality and religion, and prepare them to go forth qualified to become useful and respectable members of society. All this is to be done, without stone walls,

9. Bushnell, *Views of Christian Nurture*, quoted in Mennel, p. 36.
10. Charles Loring Brace, *The Dangerous Classes of New York and Twenty Years' Work among Them* (New York: Wynkoop & Hallenbeck, 1872), p. 225.
11. Mennel, pp. 35–42, 52–56.

bars or bolts, but by the more sure and effective restraining power—*the cords of love.*" [12]

Even where the architecture remained custodial and the prison policy more authoritarian, the rhetoric of affectionate discipline—the cords of love —made headway at least in the case of antebellum prisons for women. For example, the first woman's prison in the United States was the Mt. Pleasant Female Prison at Ossining, New York, where beginning in 1844 the chief matron, Eliza Farnham, experimented with reform practices that emphasized education and sympathy rather than punishment. The techniques she introduced prefigured the post–Civil War reformatory movement and the gentler management techniques in dealing with juvenile delinquency. Among the practices Farnham initiated was the use of fiction for reformatory effect. In 1846 she added novels such as *Oliver Twist* to the prison library against the wishes of the Sing Sing chaplain who viewed all novel reading as irreligious.[13]

After the Civil War, Zebulon Brockway led the movement to replace the large impersonal custodial institutions like the New York House of Refuge with reformatories specializing in more individualized technologies of discipline. As superintendent of the Detroit House of Correction, he developed the educational practices that aimed to reform young male criminals, both adolescent and young adult. He visited the Lancaster Massachusetts Industrial School for Girls and was deeply impressed by its family system, its gentler disciplinary techniques, and its domestic training. Then in 1868 he helped establish the Detroit House of Shelter, affiliated with his House of Correction but restricted to female prisoners, including "wayward girls." [14] The institution's inspectors described the shelter's aims: "It is intended to receive here as into a home, women who . . . seem willing to accept a reform of life. It is intended that they should be received here into a family life, where they shall receive intellectual, moral, domestic, and industrial training, under the influence, example and sympathy of re-

12. Trustees, *First Annual Report*, p. 6, quoted in Schlossman, pp. 40–41. Also see Barbara M. Brenzel, *Daughters of the State: A Social Portrait of the First Reform School for Girls in North America, 1856–1905* (Cambridge: MIT Press, 1983), chap. 4.

13. Estelle B. Freedman, *Their Sisters' Keepers: Women's Prison Reform in America, 1830–1930* (Ann Arbor: University of Michigan Press, 1981), p. 48; and Nicole Hahn Rafter, *Partial Justice: Women in State Prisons, 1800–1935* (Boston: Northeastern University Press, 1985), p. 18.

14. Rafter, p. 26.

fined and virtuous women." [15] Describing one of the rituals that made up an important part of her reformatory routine, Emma Hall, the second matron, wrote in her annual report:

> [T]he most interesting feature of the house, and I am prone to say the most useful, is the Thursday evening exercise and entertainment. On this evening the whole family dress in their neatest and best attire. All assemble in our parlor . . . and enjoy themselves in conversation and needlework, awaiting the friend who week by week on Thursday evening, never failing, comes . . . to read aloud an hour entertaining stories and poetry carefully selected and explained.

The ritual of reading to the inmates was repeated in a more formal setting on Sundays when Brockway as superintendent would himself visit the shelter and would, in Hall's words, read "to the assembled family from suitably selected literature." [16]

2

Of course, these same rituals using literature for reformatory effect were repeated in other cultural sites outside reform school walls. Similar scenes are represented many times in a piece of fiction published in the same year as the founding of the Women's House of Shelter. In Louisa May Alcott's *Little Women*, the intended girl audience could read how the March daughters gathered each evening, talking and sewing together, often listening to their mother read from some suitable fiction or tell them some uplifting story. During a scene very much like that described by Hall, one of the March daughters exclaims: "Tell another story, mother; one with a moral to it. . . . I like to think about them afterwards, if they are real, and not too preachy." [17]

"Real and not too preachy" is an apt description of how Alcott's contemporary audience evaluated *Little Women* itself. The conservative Presbyterian periodical *Hours at Home* called the book a "capital story for girls" and later declared, "It will delight and improve the class to whom it is espe-

15. Detroit House of Correction *Annual Report* (1868), p. 7; quoted in Rafter, p. 26.
16. Hall's 1872 report quoted in Zebulon Reed Brockway, *Fifty Years of Public Service: An Autobiography* (New York: Charities Publication Committee, 1912), pp. 410–11.
17. Louisa M. Alcott, *Little Women, or Meg, Jo, Beth and Amy* (Boston: Roberts, 1868), p. 69. All further citations will be by page number in my text.

cially addressed." In a notice of the sequel, a reviewer for the *Common-wealth* wrote, *Little Women* "was one of the most successful ventures to delineate juvenile womanhood ever attempted." The sequel "continues the delight—it is the same fascinating tale, extended without weakening, loading the palate without sickishness."[18] As many literary historians have noted, Alcott's realistic characters represented a departure from the ideal-ized good girls and good boys in the dominant modes of didactic children's fiction.

Little Women, published in October 1868, tells the story of the family life of the four March daughters. Amy, Beth, Jo, and Meg range in age from 12 to 16, all at that stage of development the later nineteenth century came to call the period of adolescence. The popularity of this domestic novel among its youthful readers called forth a sequel almost immediately, and *Little Women, Part Second* appeared in April 1869, picking up the narra-tive three years later and telling the story of the courtship and marriage of the daughters. The first volume emphasized the perseverance of stable principle and the reading and imitation of books, while the second volume emphasized growth into early adulthood and the production of books and children. In the first, reading books is a synecdoche for adolescents gain-ing inner stability and self-discipline, while in the second, writing books is a metonomy for change and growth into maturity. Here I will discuss only the first volume and its relation to my essay's thesis.

In trying to decipher what effects reading *Little Women* had on some of its 1868 readers and to what uses they put the fiction, we might turn again to the contemporary reviews. A writer in *Arthur's Home Magazine* summarized both the plot and its "not too preachy" moral: "The father is in the army, and it is to please him that his daughters make an effort of a year to correct certain faults in their dispositions. In this they are quite successful, and the father comes home, after many sad war scenes, to find his little ones greatly improved in many respects, a comfort and joy to both their parents."[19] We might say that, at least for this reviewer, Alcott comes closest to declaring her message when she has the mother read aloud a

---

18. *Hours at Home* 8 (November 1868): 100, and *Hours at Home* 9 (June 1869): 196—both quoted in Richard L. Darling, *The Rise of Children's Book Reviewing in America, 1865–1881* (New York: R. R. Bowker, 1968), p. 242; and *Commonwealth* 7 (24 April 1869): 1—rpt. in Madeleine B. Stern, ed., *Critical Essays on Louisa May Alcott* (Boston: G. K. Hall, 1984), p. 82.
19. *Arthur's Home Magazine* 32 (December 1868): 375.

letter from the father, who, too old to be drafted, had volunteered as a chaplain during the Civil War. Referring to his four daughters, the father writes to his wife: "I know . . . they will be loving children to you, will do their duty faithfully, fight their bosom enemies bravely, and conquer themselves so beautifully, that when I come back to them I may be fonder and prouder than ever of my little women" (18).

This letter from an absent father both symbolizes and literally names the disciplinary strategy that is so much a part of this novel's rhetorical unfolding. First, in its consequent influence—despite its author's absence— the letter symbolizes the patriarchal power, off-stage though it might be, that continues to control the action of the story and the life of the family. Second, and more important, the letter explains how this power works, literally naming the strategy of familial love that fosters inner self-discipline.

It is this latter thematization that I wish to explore here in some detail. As we have seen, by the 1850s theories of child-rearing, educational practices, and institutional policies for dealing with juvenile deliquency had all been influenced by a rhetoric of affectionate discipline, which emphasized sympathy over severity, internal motivation over external control, shaping character through love rather than breaking will by punishment. By the late sixties, a cultural rhetoric circulated using images of the "family home" to represent this constellation of techniques for gentle management.

Throughout *Little Women*, the comforting, supportive home with its atmosphere of familial love remains a constant presence, a background against which all the individual problems are worked out. The Marches are a "happy family" (321) despite their lack of money. A dissatisfied daughter comes to realize that "home *is* a nice place, though it isn't splendid" (142). The mother warns her daughters about yearning after "spendid houses, which are not homes, because love is wanting" (146). And when the first daughter is about to leave the home, her sister exclaims: "I just wish I could marry Meg myself, and keep her safe in the family" (295).

But familial love is not represented as an end in itself. Remember the absent father's letter: he predicts and thus requests that his "loving children . . . do their duty faithfully." The mother takes special care to teach her daughters, by example and precept, the lesson of duty towards others. After letting them off their household chores for a week, she remarks on "what happens when every one thinks only of herself. Don't you feel that it is pleasanter to help one another, to have daily duties which make leisure sweet when it comes, and to bear or forbear, that home may be comfortable and lovely to us all?" (172). With the house in a shambles from neglect of their duties, the daughters learn their lesson.

Understanding one's duty is not, however, the most important lesson to be learned. Again the father's letter: his "loving children" must "fight their bosom enemies bravely, and conquer themselves so beautifully that when [he] comes home to them [he] may be fonder and prouder than ever of [his] little women." Being a little woman means gaining self-control—not by obeying external laws but through achieving inner discipline. Being a little woman means constituting oneself as a certain kind of subject, employing a particular technology of the self.

And how is this self-discipline to be achieved? For Jo March, the author's alter-ego, this self mastery must take place by fighting her "bosom enemy" within. In an early chapter, the narrator comments that "Jo had the least self-control" for "anger . . . her bosom enemy was always ready to flame up and defeat her; and it took years of patient effort to subdue it" (111). This patient effort demanded a self-surveillance that had to be constant: her mother, who had the same inner conflict, advised Jo to "keep watch over your 'bosom enemy' " (121). Jo's self-discipline was to earn her, in the narrator's words, "the sweetness of self-denial and self-control" (122).

And it is precisely here that the use of literature is employed just as strategically as it had been in girls' reformatories. Alcott uses Bunyan's *Pilgrim's Progress* to organize her narrative, inspire her characters, and figure their growth in self-discipline. Alcott's "Preface" adapts a passage from *Pilgrim's Progress* to express the wish that her own book would make her readers "pilgrims better, by far, than thee or me." It is Bunyan's book that Mrs. March cites to encourage her daughters on the path to reformation: referring to a children's game modeled on *Pilgrim's Progress* that they used to play, she says, "Now, my little pilgrims, suppose you begin again, not in play, but in earnest, and see how far on you can get before father comes home" (20). Meg comments that in "trying to be good . . . the story may help us," while Jo finds that reading her personal challenge as parallel to Christian's "lent a little romance to the very dull task of doing her duty" (20–21). For the rest of the novel, *Pilgrim's Progress* not only supplements the Bible as a "guide-book" (21) for the girls, but it also functions as an explicit gloss on their inner struggles. For example, the chapter describing Jo's battle with anger, her bosom enemy, is entitled "Jo Meets Apollyon." Other chapters have such titles as "Beth Finds the Palace Beautiful," "Meg Goes to Vanity Fair," and "Amy's Valley of Humiliation."

Thus, the reader of *Little Women* can use *Pilgrim's Progress* to interpret the girls' inner lives while they use it as a guide to self-discipline, for writing the selves they wish to be. Jo tells her friend Laurie to change his life, to "turn over a new leaf and begin again," but he responds: "I keep turning over new leaves, and spoiling them, as I used to spoil my copy-books" (314). Such new beginnings are many times more frequent for the daughters than for their young male friend. Their resolutions to try harder directly follow from their repeated examinations of conscience and their frequent confessions of failure to their mother. And this secularization of Christian self-disciplining through confession is aided by the reading of books like *Pilgrim's Progress*. Indeed, reading *as* self-reform takes place while the daughters read *about* self-reform. Consuming books like *Pilgrim's Progress* helps the girls re-figure the disorderly process of growing up as an orderly progression of moral development.

But such books are not all the daughters read. "Meg found her sister eating apples and crying over the 'Heir of Redcliffe.' This was Jo's favorite refuge; and here she loved to retire with half a dozen russets and a nice book" (42). Reading and eating are joined together in various ways throughout the story. At one point, Jo offers to read to Laurie and then brings food instead (74–75). While reading aloud to her aunt, Jo would nod off over a book she disliked and give "such a gape" that her aunt would ask what she "meant by opening [her] mouth wide enough to take the whole book in at once." "I wish I could and be done with it" was her reply (65). And then there was Scrabble, Jo's pet rat, "who, being likewise of a literary turn, was fond of making a circulating library of such books as were left in his way, by eating the leaves" (217). And, of course, Jo herself is called a "bookworm" (8) constantly feeding on romances and novels of her liking.

The use of fiction for female self-discipline and pleasure can be briefly contrasted to that found in a boy's book first published in the same year, 1869, as *Little Women, Part Second*. Here we will see not only the differences in how gender is rhetorically constructed in two popular children's novels but also the similarities in how reading fiction disciplines as it engenders action. Like Alcott's classic, Thomas Bailey Aldrich's *The Story of a Bad Boy* was viewed by contemporaries as a departure in children's fiction.[20] In this semi-autobiographical novel, Aldrich attempts a more realistic representation of boyhood, distinguishing his "bad boy" from "those

20. See, for example, William Dean Howells's review in *Atlantic Monthly* 25 (January 1870): 124.

faultless young gentlemen" usually represented in didactic Sunday School fiction.[21] Aldrich tells the story of a boy's pranks and adventures as he is growing up in small-town America, and his series of sketches begins the tradition of bad-boy books that Mark Twain's *Tom Sawyer* and *Huckleberry Finn* culminate. But it is not my purpose here to compare Aldrich's book to Twain's, a job ably done by recent Twain critics, but to use the book selectively to highlight the rhetorical strategies of *Little Women*.[22]

Tom Bailey, the author's alter ego, is, like Jo March, also described as a "bookworm" (45), but his appetite is more limited and his taste in books quite different from the romances Jo reads for entertainment or the books, like *Pilgrim's Progress*, she studies and tries to imitate. Of his first reading of the *Arabian Nights* and particularly *Robinson Crusoe*, the adult narrator says: "The thrill that ran into my fingers' ends then has not run out yet. Many a time did I steal up to this nest of a room, and, taking the dog's-eared volume from its shelf, glide off into an enchanted realm, where there were no lessons to get and no boys to smash my kite" (45). The young Tom later found a trunk full of more "novels and romances," which he "fed upon like a bookworm" (45).

What Tom learns in reading his books differs a bit from what the March girls learn in reading theirs. From Thomas Hughes's British boys' book, *Tom Brown's School Days at Rugby*, the American Tom takes the lesson "Learn to box . . . there's no exercise in the world so good for the temper, and for the muscles of the back and legs" (111–12). And the only duty that seems to concern Tom is the duty to be loyal to his secret gang and to have as many adventures and pull off as many pranks as possible with them. Besides standing by each other, the members of his secret society, the Rivermouth Centipedes, "had no purpose, unless it was to accomplish as a body the same amount of mischief which we were sure to do as individuals. To mystify the staid and slow-going Rivermouthians was our frequent pleasure" (103).

Like his more famous namesake, Tom Sawyer, Bailey's fancy is en-

21. Thomas Bailey Aldrich, *The Story of a Bad Boy* (Boston: Fields, Osgood, 1870), p. 8. All further citations will be made by page number in my main text.
22. On Aldrich, Twain, and bad-boy fiction, see especially Albert E. Stone, Jr., *The Innocent Eye: Childhood in Mark Twain's Imagination* (1961; rpt. [Hamden CT]: Archon Books, 1970), pp. 58–90; and Alan Gribben, " 'I Did Wish Tom Sawyer Was There': Boy-Book Elements in *Tom Sawyer* and *Huckleberry Finn*," in *One Hundred Years of Huckleberry Finn: The Boy, His Book, and American Culture*, ed. Robert Sattelmeyer and J. Donald Crowley (Columbia: University of Missouri Press, 1985), pp. 149–70.

flamed by the adventure books he reads. Moreover, he comments on how "hints and flavors of the sea . . . feed the imagination and fill the brain of every healthy boy with dreams of adventure" (147) and notes that "all the male members of [his] family . . . exhibited in early youth a decided talent for running away. It was an hereditary talent. It ran in the blood to run away" (236). Reading and imitating adventure books was as much a part of Tom Bailey's self-fashioning as those reading activities described earlier were a part of Jo March's self-disciplining. The different gender roles constructed by such narratives may be obvious, but it is only Alcott's more perceptive novel that explicitly marks these differences. Indeed, she ironically foregrounds them throughout her narrative by having Jo constantly allude to her preference for the opportunities available to boys but not to girls. To her best male friend, she laments: "If I was a boy we'd run away together, and have a capital time; but as I'm a miserable girl, I must be proper, and stop at home" (309).

Perhaps more important for my purposes here is the difference between the genres to which Alcott's and Aldrich's books belong. Alcott's is a female bildungsroman, with the adolescent girls molding their characters "as carefully as [Amy] moulds her little clay figures" (324), a simile used by Mrs. March to describe the growth of one of her daughters.[23] In contrast, Aldrich's book is finally only a series of sketches, more like a picaresque, taking his younger self through a series of adventures with no change in his character. But less apparent are the underlying similarities in the effects of the fictions, both as represented and performed. As represented in the two books, fiction affects internal motivation through imitation; and reading fiction has actual physical effects, whether in Jo's crying over *Wide, Wide World* or in Tom's thrilled finger tips in reading *Robinson Crusoe*. And as rhetorical performances themselves, both books, described as realistic by their readers, become useful as models for "appropriate" adolescent behavior. I have dwelt on the technologies of the self, the example of self-discipline offered by *Little Women*, but *The Story of a Bad Boy* also made for useful, that is safe, reading according to a new view of male youth then developing in the later nineteenth century.

Aldrich's book dramatized this emerging view that bad boys (at least

23. See Eve Kornfeld and Susan Jackson, "The Female Bildungsroman in Nineteenth-Century America: Parameters of a Vision," *Journal of American Culture* 10 (Winter 1987): 69–75.

middle-class bad boys) weren't doomed to become adult criminals. By telling his story as an adult looking back on his adolescent self, Aldrich makes it clear to his young and old readers that this sample of "delinquency" is only a temporary stage soon to be outgrown. No special intervention seems necessary. Sometime between the story told and its telling, the bad boy develops naturally into the respectable adult narrator. In this implication and the narrator's indulgent attitude toward the bad boy's pranks, we see a literary preview of G. Stanley Hall's later influential theory of adolescence, a scientific theory advocating a more tolerant attitude toward temporary youthful deviance. Hall suggested that "normal children often pass through stages of passionate cruelty, laziness, lying, and thievery" and that perhaps "a period of semicriminality is normal for all healthy boys." He argued that "magnanimity and a large indulgent parental and pedagogical attitude is the proper one toward all, and especially juvenile offenders."[24] Or as the town watchman puts it in Aldrich's story, "Boys is boys" (77).

Finally, as others have pointed out, Tom Bailey, like Tom Sawyer after him, is one of the "good bad boys," entertaining to his young male readership and non-threatening to his adult audience.[25] Even if there are few of the examinations of conscience and self-disciplining rituals that we find abundantly in *Little Women*, the adventurous spirit supposedly fostered by *The Story of a Bad Boy* certainly has its limits, as Tom refuses to disobey his guardian on more serious matters and, in one of the few self-examinations in the book, we see a boy motivated less by anxiety over a beating than embarrassment inspired by affectionate discipline: "It wasn't the fear of any physical punishment that might be inflicted; it was a sense of my own folly that was creeping over me; . . . I had examined my conduct from every stand-point, and there was no view I could take of myself in which I did not look like a very foolish person indeed" (249). Thus, Aldrich himself is most accurate when he concludes: "So ends the Story of a Bad Boy—but not such a very bad boy, as I told you to begin with" (261).

---

24. G. Stanley Hall, *Adolescence: Its Psychology and Its Relation to Physiology, Anthropology, Sociology, Sex, Crime, Religion and Education* (New York: D. Appleton, 1904), 1: 335, 404, and 339. In the first quotation Hall is speaking approvingly of a suggestion by Cesare Lombroso, and in the second he is repeating a claim of his own student, Edgar J. Swift.

25. See Leslie Fiedler, "Good Good Girl and Good Bad Boy," *New Leader* 41 (14 April 1958): 22–25; and Judith Fetterley, "The Sanctioned Rebel," *Studies in the Novel* 3 (Fall 1971): 293–304.

3

We must leave the late 1860s to find a bad bad boy. And in our move to the mid-1880s we will see further cultural permutations in the uses of fiction and the tropes of reading. A comic culmination of the bad boy book appeared in 1883, when George W. Peck published *Peck's Bad Boy and His Pa*. The central character, Hennery, is much more opposed to authority in his attitude and sadistic in his pranks, and readers are encouraged to laugh at the adult victims of the bad boy's cruel practical jokes. Peck's Bad Boy came to symbolize the worst fears of middle-class parents, as newspapers encouraged these fears with comments like the following from the Baltimore *Day*:

> When we speak of the pernicious influence of the dime novel or the Jesse James style of border drama we should not forget that there are other and more insidious ways of corrupting youth, and no better illustration of this could be given than the fact that when a number of boys in Milwaukee, of respectable parentage, were recently arrested for barn burning and other wanton outrages, the boast of one of them to the magistrate was: "I am Peck's bad boy, and don't you forget it." [26]

At stake here is the shaping of youthful identity, and this boy "of respectable parentage" boasts about the fashioning already accomplished. The disciplinary techniques of family and reform school are no match, it seems, for the rhetorical self-fashioning that produced this bad boy imitator. [27]

At least in this newspaper report, Peck's Bad Boy became a trope used by young law-breakers for self-definition. How widespread such molding of inner lives came to be remains problematic. But if 1880s juvenile voices are hard to hear, adult voices are not. Whatever juvenile subjects made out of Peck's Bad Boy, many adults were convinced that real bad boys were made out of juveniles subjected to bad boy fiction. Indeed, Peck's Bad Boy became a rhetorical figure marking a growing concern within the cultural conversation of the mid-eighties, a concern with the special dangers of adolescence and the perceived rise in juvenile delinquency.

26. Baltimore *Day*, 11 March 1884; rpt. as "Peck's Bad Play," New York *World*, 13 March 1884, p. 4. In this section I adapt and expand material from *Rhetorical Power*, chap. 4, copyright 1989 by Cornell University. Used by permission of the publisher, Cornell University Press.

27. Cf. Stephen Greenblatt, *Renaissance Self-Fashioning: From More to Shakespeare* (Chicago: University of Chicago Press, 1980), pp. 86–88, 119–20.

The titles of many 1884–85 newspaper stories testify to the cultural anxiety over what the New York *World* called "The Bad-Boy Boom."[28] Reports came in from all over the country. There was "The Louisville Bad Boy," who looks like an "angel" but "who respects persons and property least" and "who does all the wickedest and most sneaking things that can occur to a young imagination."[29] In Boston there were "Boys Out Shooting/ Fired by Dime Novel Emulation Two Boys Go a Roving with Rifles."[30] In Lowell there were "gangs of boy burglars" whose conduct and talk made it "evident that they were inspired by sentiment imbibed from yellow-covered literature."[31] The Detroit *Free Press* editorialized about "'The Bad Boy' of the Period" while the New York *World* reported on "Sad Juvenile Depravity/ The Astounding Record of One Week's Crimes and Plots/The Bad Boy as a Highwayman—Youthful Lawlessness in Every Quarter of the Land—The Effect of Dime Novel Literature."[32]

These news accounts illustrate the assumptions about the dangers of reading certain kinds of fiction that led to the banning of *Huckleberry Finn* by the Concord Free Public Library, an evaluative act of reading that I have elsewhere attempted to explain at some length.[33] *Huckleberry Finn* combines the bad-boy pranks of Aldrich's sketches with the examinations of conscience in Alcott's bildungsroman. And in the process the novel prefigures the negative part of its reception when it satirically thematizes the potent effects of fiction on impressionable young readers. Tom Sawyer's mind is directly affected by the romantic adventure stories he admires and then self-consciously imitates throughout the story. Though sometimes challenging his friend's expertise, Huck is often intimidated by Tom's superior knowledge of book-lore and usually falls in line behind his friend's outlandish schemes. Imitating the imitator, Huck is affected by books at second hand, as he comes to admire and repeat Tom's book-learned "style" in his own bad-boy escapades. At the end of the novel, Huck reproduces the fantasy of many an 1840s dime-novel reader when he determines to light out for the Western territories.

Alcott supposedly commented on *Huckleberry Finn*: "If Mr. Clemens cannot think of something better to tell our pure-minded lads and lasses, he

28. "The Bad-Boy Boom," New York *World*, 26 March 1884, p. 4.
29. New York *World*, 30 March 1884, p. 20.
30. Boston *Daily Globe*, 20 February 1885, p. 2.
31. New York *World*, 21 March 1884, p. 1.
32. Detroit *Free Press*, 30 March 1884, p. 4; New York *World*, 26 March 1884, p. 2.
33. See *Rhetorical Power*, chaps. 3 and 4.

had best stop writing for them."[34] Her hometown public library in Concord banned the novel from its shelves, and the library committee called it "trash of the veriest sort": "not elevating" in its plot, "coarse" in its humor, and "irreverent" in its style. One member added: "The whole book is of a class that is more profitable for the slums than it is for respectable people."[35]

Of course, many other readers disagreed with this verdict. Indeed, if fiction could be abused in this way for the harm it might cause, then it followed for some that fiction could also be used to achieve beneficial effects. Another resident of Concord and a family friend of the Alcotts, Franklin Sanborn, penned one of the most laudatory reviews of *Huckleberry Finn*: "I cannot subscribe," he wrote, "to the extreme censure passed upon this volume, which is no coarser than Mark Twain's books usually are, while it has a vein of deep morality beneath its exterior of falsehood and vice, that will redeem it in the eyes of mature persons. It is not adapted to Sunday-school libraries, and should perhaps be left unread by growing boys; but the mature in mind may read it, without distinction of age or sex, and without material harm."[36]

Sanborn's judgments are especially interesting because of the professional positions he held and the personal connections he had. He was the inspector for the Massachusetts State Board of Charities, which supervised the reform schools for juvenile delinquents. He also proposed and taught the nation's first Applied Social Science course at Cornell University. In April 1885, shortly before he wrote the *Huckleberry Finn* review, Sanborn took his Cornell students to visit the New York State Reformatory at Elmira. The superintendent of the facility was then Zebulon Brockway, who had moved from the Detroit House of Refuge and become the foremost authority on the reformatory techniques of managing older delinquents and first-time offenders.

In 1884 Brockway had established at Elmira an English Literature class as "an experiment in a more intensive use of literature for reformative effect."[37] Besides classic British drama and poetry, the curriculum soon included fiction by Goldsmith and Irving, Hawthorne and Howells, and even Hughes's *Tom Brown's School Days*. As the school secretary put it, litera-

34. Louisa May Alcott to Francis Hedges Butler, quoted in Thomas Beer, *The Mauve Decade: American Life at the End of the Nineteenth Century* (1926; rpt. New York: Vintage Books, 1961), p. 9.
35. "'Huckleberry Finn,'" St. Louis *Globe-Democrat*, 17 March 1885, p. 1.
36. "Our Boston Letter," Springfield *Daily Republican*, 27 April 1885, p. 2.
37. Brockway, *Fifty Years*, p. 273.

ture was studied "over and over and minds heretofore innocent of culture became saturated with the drinkable gold of the classics."[38] But the reformative effect intended by reading such books went beyond simply using good literature to teach love of culture and desirable morality. The results of the first examinations for the course showed signs "of mental confusion, of indifference, of ineffectual groping after an author's very palpable meaning, signs" which the instructors read as revealing "a likely material for mental discipline of the most valuable kind." Thus the school secretary concluded, "The only means of removing these difficulties seemed to lie in repeated doses of the same medicine."[39] For Brockway, the use of literature offered an added disciplinary bonus: the required reading for the course made it possible, he claimed, "to tell with considerable certainty at any moment what occupies the mind of any man," thus conveniently extending the reformatory's strategy of surveillance.[40]

In its second year, 1885, the course in literary study became mandatory, with examinations being used to determine the prisoner's grade-standing and progress towards release. Brockway later observed in his autobiography (dedicated, by the way, to Sanborn) that this educational training in literary taste was particularly enhanced by discussions in the practical morality classes. Visiting lecturers added to these classroom attempts to turn cultural enrichment into ethical improvement.[41]

One such visitor, as I have said, was Franklin Sanborn. While at the reformatory he noted the librarian's negative opinion of a certain controversial novel. Subsequently, Sanborn wrote to Brockway: "I have read 'Huckleberry Finn,' and I do not see any reason why it should not go into your Reference Library, at least, and form the subject of a debate in your Practical Morality Class."[42] Perhaps Sanborn's letter had something to do with the fact that another of the uplifting lecturers at Elmira was Mark Twain himself, who read from *Huckleberry Finn* during a visit in July 1886.[43]

38. F. Thornton Macauley, "Report of the Secretary of Schools," *Annual Report of the Board of Managers of the New York State Reformatory at Elmira, for the Year Ending September 30, 1885* (Elmira: Reformatory Press, 1885), p. 30.
39. Macauley, pp. 28–29.
40. Brockway, "Report of the General Superintendent," *Annual Report of the State Reformatory at Elmira, 1885*, pp. 12–13.
41. Brockway, *Fifty Years*, pp. 273–76.
42. *The Summary*, a weekly newspaper published by the Elmira Reformatory, quoted in the *Critic*, N. S. 3 (30 May 1885): 264.
43. *Mark Twain's Notebooks & Journals*, vol. 3, eds. Robert Pack Browning, Michael B. Frank, and Lin Salamo (Berkeley: University of California Press, 1979), p. 244.

4

At the end of Part Second of *Little Women*, Jo March marries Professor Bhaer and exchanges a "wilderness of books" for a "wilderness of boys," as she and her husband establish a home for male orphans.[44] It took Alcott seven years of interrupted writing to complete the fourth and final volume of the *Little Women* series, an 1886 book called *Jo's Boys, and How They Turned Out: A Sequel to "Little Men"*. During that period, she too was invited to local reformatories attempting to use fiction as one of many strategies for instilling self-discipline in adolescent and older inmates. In June 1879 Alcott and her father spoke to 400 young men at the Concord State Reformatory. She told a story from her earlier Civil War nursing experiences, and later described her success in affecting her listeners. First in her journal, using one of the tropes we have come to recognize, she wrote that by "watching the faces of the young men" near her, she could see that they "drank in every word," and she became so interested in watching these faces that she forgot herself and "talked away 'like a mother.' "[45] This maternal disciplining through fiction is typical of how Alcott represented the use of books in her domestic novels for adolescents. And her journals further demonstrate the confidence she shared with her community in the reformatory effectiveness of reading or listening to literature.

A year after Alcott's story-telling at the Concord State Reformatory, a young former inmate paid her a visit. She wrote in her journal that he "[c]ame to thank me for the good my little story did him, since it kept him straight and reminded him that it is never too late to mend." She concluded the entry, "Glad to have said a word to help the poor boy."[46] The next time Alcott represented the self-disciplining that can follow from hearing the right kind of story was when she reused this incident in one of the central chapters of *Jo's Boys*.

Dan, a neglected boy taken into the March home at Plumfield in *Little Men*, had become a young man by the time of *Jo's Boys*, still with "wayward impulses, strong passions, and . . . lawless nature."[47] During a

44. The first quoted phrase is from the initial volume of *Little Women*, p. 60, and the second is from Alcott, *Little Women, or Meg, Jo, Beth and Amy: Part Second* (Boston: Roberts, 1869), p. 347.

45. Alcott's journal, June 1879, quoted in Martha Saxton, *Louisa May: A Modern Biography of Louisa May Alcott* (New York: Avon Books, 1978), p. 390.

46. Alcott's journal, December 1880, quoted in Ednah D. Cheney, ed., *Louisa May Alcott: Her Life, Letters, and Journals* (Boston: Little, Brown, 1917), p. 340.

47. Louisa M. Alcott, *Jo's Boys, and How They Turned Out: A Sequel to "Little Men"*

return visit, he confesses to Jo that his "devilish temper" is more than he can manage, and Jo, who had a similar "bosom enemy" in *Little Women*, responds sympathetically and counsels her ex-ward to "guard your demon well, and don't let a moment's fury ruin all your life. . . . Take some books and read; that's an immense help; and books are always good company if you have the right sort" (127, 130). She gives him the Bible but also some German tales, which she uses to allegorize his search for "peace and self-control" (130).

Jo's counsel fails, however, for when Dan leaves Plumfield on his treck west he ends up killing a man in self-defense and is thrown into prison. The prison warden was "a rough man who had won the ill-will of all by unnecessary harshness" (213), and Dan, in humiliation and despair, soon resolves to attempt an escape. But before he can bring off his plan, the prisoners are visited during chapel by a "middle-aged woman in black, with a sympathetic face, eyes full of compassion" (216). She tells them a story and gives as its moral the hope that all was not lost if they would be patient, penitent, and submissive and learn to rule themselves. Like the ex-prisoner who visited Alcott, Dan is changed by the story he hears and resolves to wait out his sentence and "like the wiser man in the story, submit, bear the just punishment, [and] try to be better for it" (218).

Alcott also visited another reformatory while writing *Jo's Boys*. At the Women's Prison at Sherbourne, she read a story to the inmates and took time to talk with the resident physician about the health of the female prisoners. Perhaps such a juxtaposition of activities suggests a connection made between moral and physical reform in the prison's gentler methods of affectionate discipline, which Alcott's journal describes as indicating "patience, love and common sense and the belief in salvation for all."[48] Certainly the connection of the physical with the intellectual and moral development of reformatory inmates is clear in Brockway's Elmira institution. The year after he introduced literature courses into the curriculum, the superintendent proposed an experimental "Class in Physical Culture." The instructor, Hamilton D. Wey, reported that the object was to discover whether "physical culture as comprised in frequent baths, and massage, and daily calisthenics under the care of a competent instructor, would . . . result in at least a partial awakening and stimulation of dormant mental

---

(Boston: Roberts, 1886), p. 80. All further citations will be given by page number in my text.

48. Alcott's journal, October 1879, quoted in Saxton, p. 390.

power." The first class had some success, according to Wey, though the students' "advancement in school work was not steadily onward, but rather intermittently progressive. . . . For a time they would learn with comparative ease and appear to assimilate their mental food, when suddenly and without apparent cause . . . their minds would cease to work" and their "mental awakening" would stop for as long as several days.[49]

Wey later remarked that the foundation of his course was the "recognition of physical training as a factor in mental and moral growth," and he criticized earlier pedagogical theories for ignoring the laws of physiology and overlooking "the physical basis of brain work."[50] Institutional practices and scientific assumptions like Wey's constituted a significant part of the rhetorical context in which the physicality of metaphors for reading became literalized in advice manuals and education guides of the 1870s and 80s. Chapter 17 of *Jo's Boys* refers to several of these books, including an 1874 collection of essays edited by Anna Brackett, *The Education of American Girls.*[51] In a section of her essay called "Physical Education, or, the Culture of the Body," Brackett comments on the extreme difficulty in separating the "physical" from the "moral side of education" in considering the effects of a girl's active imagination (62). She then notes the availability of the "most dissipating, weakening, and insidious books that can possibly be imagined" and complains about "the immense demand which there is for these average novels." Brackett asks, "How stem this tide of insidious poison that is sapping the strength of body and mind? How, but by educating [girls'] taste till they shall not desire such trash." Such "trashy books" must be kept out of the house; when they are "not actually exciting and immoral in tone and sentiment, they are so vapid, . . . so devoid of any healthy vigor and life, that they are simply dissipating to the power of thought, and hence weakening to the will." Brackett does not condemn all novels, only "poisonous and weakening literature." She concludes: "as we are grateful to our parents for the care and simple regimen which preserved our physical health for us, we thank them also for the care which kept out of our way the mental food which they knew to be injurious, and for which they themselves

49. H. D. Wey, M. D., "Report of the Experimental or Class in Physical Culture," *Annual Report of the Board of Managers of the New York State Reformatory at Elmira, for the Year Ending September 30, 1886* (Elmira: Reformatory Press, 1887), pp. 59, 66–67.

50. Wey, "A Plea for Physical Training of Youthful Criminals," *Proceedings of the Annual Congress of the National Prison Association of the United States, Held at Boston, July 14–19, 1888* (Chicago: Knight & Leonard, 1888), pp. 185–87.

51. Anna C. Brackett, ed., *The Education of American Girls* (New York: G. P. Putnam's Sons, 1874). Further citations will be made in the main text.

had been too well educated to have any taste" (64–66). In a later section on "Mental Education, or, the Culture of the Intellect," Brackett advocates "plenty of good reading" for girls (77) but also includes this advice: "Exercise . . . must, in mind as well as body, be regular, and increase steadily in its demand. . . . Our first work must be to give such judicious exercise that the mind shall acquire a habit of exercise and an appetite for it, and not to spoil at the outset the mental digestion" (75).

Brackett's more figurative use of the metaphoric link between reading and the body is echoed later in the collection by Edna D. Cheney (soon to become Alcott's first biographer). In "A Mother's Thought," she employs the trope against arguments that young women are physically incapable of strenuous intellectual activity. She rejects the claim that "an idle brain insures a healthy body" and argues that "the brain, as the ruling organ of the body, requires a healthy, rich development; and this can only be secured by regular exercise and training, fully using but not overstraining its powers" (135). She adds later: "We must remember that the brain craves thought, as the stomach does food; and where it is not properly supplied it will feed on garbage. Where a Latin, geometry, or history lesson would be a healthy tonic, or nourishing food, the trashy, exciting story, the gossiping book of travels, the sentimental poem, or, still worse, the coarse humor or thin-veiled vice of the low romance, fills up the hour—and is at best but tea or slops, if not as dangerous as opium or whisky" (137).

Indeed, throughout Brackett's collection, this rhetoric of reading serves a dual purpose: it continues to figure the physical effects of reading fiction while it gets adapted to new arguments recognizing women's abilities and advocating their rights in higher education. Brackett gives the latter argument its final form when in her concluding essay she proposes the only jury she thinks capable of evaluating the sources of women's mental and physical health: Only when we have all the cases and statistics before us, she writes, "shall we be in a condition to attempt a rational solution of the question, what it is that makes our American girls sick. . . . But . . . we venture to claim that this is a woman's question—that the women themselves are the only persons capable of dealing with it" (388).

Alcott writes this empowering rhetoric into *Jo's Boys* when she gives a different turn to her gustatory metaphors for reading. In "Among the Maids," Jo advises one of her female college students concerned about what the doctors called her "inherited delicacy of constitution":

> "Don't worry, my dear; that active brain of yours was starving for good food. . . . It is all nonsense about girls not being able to study

as well as boys. . . . [W]e will prove that wise headwork is a better cure for that sort of delicacy than tonics, and novels on the sofa, where far too many of our girls go to wreck nowadays. They burn the candle at both ends; and when they break down they blame the books, and not the balls." (x)

5

In the 1870s and 80s, many college professors justified the academic study of modern languages and literatures by arguing that a philological approach to this subject matter offered as much exercise in "mental discipline" as the same study of the Greek and Latin classics.[52] Some argued, in fact, that courses in the modern languages offered more benefits in mental training than those offered by the classical curriculum. As one professor put it: "The sense of discrimination in regard to the meaning and force of words is sharpened. The literary taste is developed by contact with" the best of modern literature. "And above all, the reasoning, judging, and combining faculties are in constant exercise."[53] But it was not only advocates of the new university who used physical tropes for reading and study. Even the defenders of the old college did so: Noah Porter, president of Yale, put the negative spin on the metaphors for reading novels:

The spell-bound reader soon discovers . . . that this appetite, like that for confectionary and other sweets is the soonest cloyed, and if pampered too long it enfeebles the appetite for all other food. The reader of novels only, especially if he reads many, becomes very soon an intellectual voluptuary, with feeble judgment, a vague memory, and an incessant craving for some new excitement. . . . It now and then happens that a youth of seventeen becomes almost an intellectual idiot or an effeminate weakling by living exclusively upon the enfeebling swash or the poisoned stimulants that are sold so readily under the title of tales and novels.[54]

52. See Gerald Graff, *Professing Literature: An Institutional History* (Chicago: University of Chicago Press, 1987), chap. 4; and Michael Warner, "Professionalization and the Rewards of Literature, 1875–1900," *Criticism* 27 (Winter 1985): 1–28.
53. F. V. N. Painter, "A Modern Classical Course," *Transactions of the Modern Language Association of America* 1 (1884–85), p. 116.
54. Noah Porter, *Books and Reading: or, What Books Shall I Read and How Shall I Read Them*, 4th ed. (New York: Scribner, Armstrong, 1877), pp. 231–32; quoted in Catherine Sheldrick Ross, "Metaphors of Reading," *Journal of Library History* 22 (Spring 1987): 149. In this extremely useful article, Ross demonstrates how the trope of reading as eat-

This last quotation illustrates the complex way in which assumptions about gender traverse the cultural rhetoric of reading in the late nineteenth century. Here the debilitating effects of novels are themselves figured as feminine: not only are female book readers susceptible to injury but male novel readers are in danger of being feminized. In any case, by the 1880s, the physical tropes for mental activity were constantly employed within the gendered assumptions about the dangers and benefits of reading books.[55] Cultural arbiters of taste worried most about boys who might become criminals through imbibing too many sensational adventure tales or crime stories and about girls who either weakened their minds by consuming sentimental romances or overtaxed their brains with too much strenuous mental exercise in the study of books. At several cultural sites, feeding on fiction was carefully monitored so the use of books would not be abused. Many agreed with the editor I quoted at the beginning of this essay, who advised his female correspondent: "Patrons of fiction—the large majority of whom are women—waste their time and fritter away their intellectual force upon [worthless] productions. . . . Let them not think that they do themselves no harm by accustoming their brain to insipid food. Like the rest of the moral, intellectual and physical man, if the mind is not exercised it deteriorates, the deterioration becoming more and more apparent after each failure to supply proper aliment."[56] Thus, the condescending editor figuratively shakes his head in despair over the poor, hopeless women readers "who feed their brains with novels and their palates with confectionary."

---

ing influenced the policies of librarians as they followed the lead of other groups and began professionalizing their activities in the 1870s and 80s. She writes, "The real content of a book, its ideas or information, is thought of as a *thing* that can be swallowed. The relationship between the librarian who knows which books are healthful and the passive reader who is wheedled into swallowing resembles that existing between a doctor and a patient. As Charles A. Cutter put it [in an 1881 *Library Journal* editorial], the librarian has a new role that is not just a 'book-watchman' but a 'mental doctor for his town'" (p. 157).

55. I am not claiming that either metaphors of reading as eating or gendered assumptions about the dangers of reading fiction are unique to late nineteenth-century America. I am claiming, though, that these tropes and arguments interact and function differently than they had in the past because they inform and enable new social practices and new institutions using literature for various purposes—practices and institutions that I have been describing throughout this essay. For more on American attitudes toward female fiction reading in other periods, see Cathy N. Davidson, *Revolution and the Word: The Rise of the Novel in America* (New York: Oxford University Press, 1986); and Janice A. Radway, *Reading the Romance: Women, Patriarchy, and Popular Literature* (Chapel Hill: University of North Carolina Press, 1984).

56. "Young Women and Novels," p. 2.

Maternal Discourse and the Romance of
Self-Possession in Kate Chopin's *The Awakening*

Ivy Schweitzer

Mothers are the only goddesses in whom the whole world believes
—message in a Chinese fortune cookie

Only the subject who is both self-possessed and possesses access
to the library of the already read has the luxury of flirting with the
escape from identity—like the loss of Arachne's "head"—promised
by an aesthetics of the decentered (decapitated, really) body.
—Nancy Miller, "Arachnologies"[1]

Kate Chopin's *The Awakening* raises many genre questions about
the differences in a romance written by a woman, and, most specifically,
it raises the question of whether a mother may be the hero of romance.
Hester Prynne immediately comes to mind. There are certain superficial

This essay comes into being thanks to my women colleagues, especially Mary Childers,
Carla Freccero, and Marianne Hirsch, and to Tom Luxon, with whom I thought out my
ideas on, and share the amazing experience of, motherhood. Thanks also go to David
Leverenz and Don Pease for their astute readings of earlier drafts.
1. Nancy K. Miller, "Arachnologies: The Woman, the Text, and the Critic," in *The Poetics
of Gender*, ed. Nancy K. Miller (New York: Columbia University Press, 1986), p. 274.

similarities between Hawthorne's mid-nineteenth-century romance of Puritan New England and Chopin's story set in New Orleans and environs in the early 1890s. Both stories use a woman's awakening to sensuality, sexuality, autonomy, and adultery as a means to explore the romantic conflict of the self and society. One reader places Edna Pontellier alongside Hester Prynne, Huck Finn, and Ishmael as characters in "the classic tradition of American novels in which the hero or heroine . . . challenges less a particular institution than the entire organization of society" but recognizes Edna's difference in her refusal "to be reintegrated into the existing order."[2] I would like to consider the possibility that this difference, which I would also argue Hawthorne's text preserves to a lesser extent for Hester at the end of the tale ("Here had been her sin; here, her sorrow; and here was *yet* to be her penitence"), is the difference of maternity.

No reading of *The Scarlet Letter* can be accused of ignoring Hester's motherhood; nevertheless, her story is most frequently read as the archetypal American clash of individual and society. Recently, Sacvan Bercovitch summed up this broad approach when he commented, "Hawthorne's portrait of Hester is essentially a study of the lover as social rebel."[3] However, we only see her as such for a brief and, Hawthorne implies, misdirected moment in the forest. For most of the story Hester is inseparable from Pearl who is the sign of her sin and, more important, the "cause," so to speak, of her motherhood. Even when Hester returns alone to the community and "freely" resumes the letter, which has been interchangeable with Pearl, she takes on the mantle of a selflessness that seems quintessentially maternal, down to her collusion with her community's insistence on socialization, the point of which is, as Bercovitch remarks, "not to conform, but to consent."[4]

"This code of liberal heroics," he concludes, produces the form of subjectivity demanded by an American ideology of the self. It

> builds on the double sense of self-containment, as retaining and restraining the self. It teaches us to sustain certain ideals and to deny the immediate claims of their certainty upon us. It directs us to possess the self by being self-possessed—which is to say, to

2. Michael T. Gilmore, "Revolt Against Nature: The Problematic Modernism of *The Awakening*," in *New Essays on "The Awakening,"* ed. Wendy Martin (Cambridge: Cambridge University Press, 1988), pp. 62–63.
3. Sacvan Bercovitch, "The A-Politics of Ambiguity in *The Scarlet Letter*," *New Literary History* 19 (Spring 1988): 632.
4. Bercovitch, "The A-Politics of Ambiguity," p. 630.

hold the self intact by holding it in check. The novel urges a gradualism and consensus in the expectation that gradually—"when the world should have grown ripe for it"—consensus will yield proximate justice for the community, and for the individual the prospect of unadulterated love.[5]

The love referred to here, the consequence of consensus, is heterosexual not maternal love. Construed as the "individual" and as the "social rebel," Hester occupies the traditionally male-specific role of "lover," a role emptied of the maternity that both enables and determines her identity and social function. This maternity, in the form of Pearl, rescues her from complete lawlessness and prevents or preserves her from becoming another Anne Hutchinson—an antinomian, radical individualist, and origin, "the foundress of a religious sect." Hester's maternity, as Amy Lang points out, "prefigures her redemption, which, in turn, implies her ultimate containment as a figure of danger and dissent."[6] Although Bercovitch argues that through Hester Hawthorne champions a corporate consensual selfhood as opposed to an antinomian and (ironically) masculinist notion of the self, like most readers he reads Hester's story as if self-sacrifice, intersubjectivity, mutual dependence, even violation, were never part of her experience or the institution of motherhood.[7] When the only valued, sanctioned, and heroic form of American selfhood is self-possession, then seeing the maternal figure as a representation of a liberal, national individualism risks ignoring the crucial findings of feminist psychoanalytic theory where maternity becomes "the confrontation between the subject and the species—the point where the subject emerges as such."[8]

5. Bercovitch, "The A-Politics of Ambiguity," p. 630.
6. Amy Schrager Lang, *Prophetic Woman: Anne Hutchinson and the Problem of Dissent in the Literature of New England* (Berkeley: University of California Press, 1987), p. 173.
7. Bercovitch expands his reading of *The Scarlet Letter* and liberal ideology in a companion piece to the one cited above, "Hawthorne's A-Morality of Compromise," *Representations* 24 (Fall 1988): 1–27. Hester remains to the end "the dissenter as agent of socialization, a self-professed sinner self-transformed into a herald of progress" (23). The theme of motherhood and Hester's motherhood have been the specific concern of several recent essays. See, for example, Nina Baym, "Thwarted Nature: Nathaniel Hawthorne as Feminist," in *American Novelists Revisited: Essays in Feminist Criticism*, ed. Fritz Fleishman (Boston: G. K. Hall, 1982), pp. 58–77 and "Nathaniel Hawthorne and His Mother: A Biographical Speculation," *American Literature* 54 (1982): 1–27; and, with a different theoretical emphasis, Joanne Feit Diehl, "Re-Reading *The Letter*: Hawthorne, The Fetish, and the (Family) Romance," *New Literary History* 19 (Spring 1988): 655–74.
8. Mary Jacobus, *Reading Woman: Essays in Feminist Criticism* (New York: Columbia University Press, 1986), p. 145.

Although Edna Pontellier's "conflict between individual autonomy and social conformity" has been viewed from a gender-specific as well as universal perspective,[9] a similar decentering of her motherhood has taken place.[10] In one sense Edna begins where Hester left off, appearing thoroughly socialized when we meet her at the beginning of her quest: "At a very early period she had apprehended instinctively the dual life—that outward existence which conforms, the inward life which questions."[11] Though described as "the self-contained" type (*A* 18), she has not fully consented inwardly. Whereas Hester's quest is forced upon her—unmarried, she experiences both her sin and repentance through her motherhood—Edna

9. Wendy Martin, ed., "Introduction," *New Essays on "The Awakening"* (Cambridge: Cambridge University Press, 1988), p. 7.

10. Per Seyersted, the author of the only critical biography of Chopin, pointed out in 1969 the "remarkable feature of *The Awakening* that the protagonist thinks nothing of disregarding her traditional duties toward her husband and of challenging the sacred concept of matrimony which the heroines of Mmes. de Stael and Sand had been fighting . . . as if Edna's creator considers these aspects of woman's emancipation too elementary for further comment and wants to move on to the really fundamental—and more taboo—factor which her predecessors had shied away from: the children" (Per Seyersted, *Kate Chopin: A Critical Biography* [Baton Rouge: Louisiana State University Press, 1969], p. 145). Nevertheless, male critics often predicate the universal nature of Edna's experience, an assertion which leads to the condemnation of her final act; see Priscilla Allen's summary of critical positions in "Old Critics and New: The Treatment of Chopin's *The Awakening*," in *Authority of Experience: Essays in Feminist Criticism*, eds. Arlyn Diamond and Lee R. Edwards (Amherst: University of Massachusetts Press, 1977), pp. 224–38. Female readers more often focus on Edna's experience as a woman, but until recently, her motherhood was an ancillary, not central, fact. For example, Nina Baym comments: "The issue of self and society is certainly bigger than a 'woman's issue,' and Chopin's greatest contribution to the woman question—as it was called in her own day—may well be her use of a female protagonist to represent a universal human dilemma" ("Introduction," *The Awakening and Selected Stories* [New York: Modern Library, 1981], p. xxxiv). Cynthia Wolff goes so far as to say: "The importance of Chopin's work does not lie in its anticipation of 'the woman question' or of any other question; it derives from its ruthless fidelity to the disintegration of Edna's character. Edna, in turn, interests us not because she is a 'woman,' the implication being that her experience is principally important because it might stand for that of any other woman. Quite the contrary; she interests us because she is human—because she fails in ways which beckon seductively to all of us. Conrad might say that, woman or man, she is 'one of us'" ("Thanatos and Eros: Kate Chopin's *The Awakening*," *American Quarterly* 25 [October 1973]: 450). In Wolff's reading, Edna becomes a kind of failed Hester, a sermon against a narcissism which is never redeemed.

11. Kate Chopin, *The Awakening*, ed. Margo Culley (New York: Norton & Co., 1976), p. 15, hereafter cited in my text as *A*; secondary materials will be referred to in my notes as *Norton*.

drifts into her quest for selfhood, a quest which even the narrator encourages us to believe has universal, not merely gender-specific, implications: "Mrs. Pontellier was beginning to realize her position in the universe as a human being, and to recognize her relations as an individual to the world within and about her" (*A* 14–15). Edna, however, comes slowly and without much visible pressure—she is rarely burdened with her children's care or criticized by those around her—to feel oppressed and to see the source of that oppression in her role as mother and the very facts of motherhood.[12]

The Awakening, written by a woman who was herself a mother of six and a widow at thirty, raises the perennial American question of individualism in terms of maternity precisely in order to explore and explode its opposite, the ideology of self-possession as the pre-eminent mode of a masculine American subjectivity. Edna's difference, her refusal to be reintegrated into the bourgeois, patriarchal order, that is, her controversial suicide, is her way of rejecting that society's notion of selfhood conceived as self-possession and all that implies. Edna's search takes her to the very limits of the myths of individualism and power at the base of the bourgeois tradition. Readers disagree about whether her sensuous merging with the sea is a triumphant leap beyond those limits or a resigned defeat at the very verge. I would like to entertain Anne Goodwyn Jones's insight that "the novel does what Edna cannot,"[13] that it gives us a glimpse into a realm beyond the dualities in which its heroine is caught where the vision of a different kind of maternity holds out the possibility of recuperating womanhood, selfhood, and society.

Motherhood and individuality seem mutually exclusive; thus, Edna's struggle for autonomous selfhood entails a rejection of her responsibilities as mother, an interpretation the text itself advances. In her despondent vigil the night before her death, this vivid image comes into her mind: "The children appeared before her like antagonists who had overcome her; who had overpowered and sought to drag her into the soul's slavery for the rest of

---

12. The critique of motherhood as oppression and the application of political language to the domestic realm were familiar in nineteenth–century suffrage literature, but they appear in English as early as analyses by Mary Astell in the late seventeenth century and Mary Wollstonecraft in the late eighteenth century. Dorothy Dix, in her advice to women column in the New Orleans *Daily Picayune* dated October 29, 1899 (some months after the publication of Chopin's book) used the same language of oppression, tyranny, slavery, and freedom to describe women's domestic relationships especially with children and husbands: "Chief and foremost among these oppressors are children" (*Norton* 131–33).
13. *Tomorrow is Another Day: The Woman Writer in the South, 1859–1936* (Baton Rouge: Louisiana State University Press, 1981), p. 182.

her days. But she knew a way to elude them" (*A* 113). It is curious that the children loom so large in her final meditations, because they appear to make so little demand on her time and attention throughout the story. As the wife of a successful Creole financier, Edna has several servants, one of whom, the mute and dreamy quadroon nurse, follows her two boys around incessantly. For the last half of the story, the children are not even present, having been sent off to live with Edna's mother-in-law in the suburb of Iberville. Yet, in her mind, they have become the slavedrivers of her soul, seeking to possess it, just as the white slaveowners possessed the bodies of the quadroon's ancestors. For all of her adolescent self-containment and the apparent freedom of her adult and socially privileged position, Edna does not feel she possesses herself.[14]

At the same time, the text also recuperates motherhood by using birth as the metaphor for Edna's awakening. The chaotic beginning of her new "world" of sensations and impressions is hyperbolized as an annunciation of the birth of wisdom by the Holy Ghost (*A* 15), which foreshadows her own "virgin birth" at the end. Her final gesture of autonomy, her self-authorized death, is also figured in terms of birth: "How strange and awful it seemed to stand naked under the sky! how delicious! She felt like some new-born creature, opening its eyes in a familiar world that it had never known" (*A* 113). Here Edna's unfettered physical response to the sensuousness of the familiar world renovates it and regenerates herself. In images now conventional in women's literature, she gives birth to herself as a creature which has become its own mother. Note that the narrator does not specify the gender of this creature nor its humanity. Edna's final responses to the world are purely physical. Elsewhere in the story, Dr. Mandelet, an old family friend consulted by Edna's husband about her "morbid condition," finds "no repression in her glance or gesture. She reminded him of some beautiful, sleek animal waking up in the sun" (*A* 70), a description the narrator endorses for the emergence of Edna's sexual nature in her affair with Arobin (*A* 78). Edna as "new-born creature" has reversed the usual developmental process and the conventional plot structure by metaphorizing and integrating the mother function and by turning an ending into

14. Conventionally, motherhood should make young girls into mature women, into "self-possessed" adults. The dispossession of self which is often and more likely a consequence of the experience of motherhood is a taboo subject. One of the best autobiographical treatments of this sense of dispossession, and a woman's valiant efforts to construct some semblance of intersubjectivity, is Jane Lazarre's *The Mother Knot* (Boston: Beacon Press, 1976).

a beginning.[15] I will look more closely at this final scene, but I want to suggest at the outset that there are competing versions of motherhood at work in this text: the social and existential demands of motherhood which oppress Edna, and the metaphors of self-birth and the seductive, maternal sea which liberate her.

The utter difference between these two versions of motherhood is brought out in the violent juxtaposition of the final metaphor of self-engendering and Edna's account of her own children's births. In the penultimate scene, as she attends her friend Adèle's delivery, "Edna began to feel uneasy. She was seized with a vague dread. Her own like experiences seemed far away, unreal, and only half remembered. She recalled faintly an ecstasy of pain, the heavy odor of chloroform, a stupor which had deadened sensation, and an awakening to find a little new life to which she had given being, added to the great unnumbered multitude of souls that come and go" (A 109). Edna's passivity and her unthinking compliance in the deadening of her sensations stand in stark contrast to the vibrant woman hungry for sensual experience she becomes. Her awakening from this forced sleep brings vagueness, not the sharp, sometimes poignant, clarity of her subsequent awakenings around which the text is structured. Only oxymoron, the figure of self-contradiction, can describe her experience of giving birth. Her existential revulsion is clinched in her reaction to Adèle's labor: "With an inward agony, with a flaming, outspoken revolt against the ways of Nature, she witnessed the scene torture" (A 109).[16] From the mother's perspective, birth is a horrendous imposition, a scene not from a domestic, but from an overly explicit gothic romance. Adèle's justification of women's suffering, whispered to Edna as she leaves, "Think of the children, Edna. Oh think

15. For more on the way women writers of romance subvert the traditional, androcentric narrative plot, see Rachel Blau DuPlessis, *Writing Beyond the Ending: Narrative Strategies of Twentieth-Century Women Writers* (Bloomington: Indiana University Press, 1985) and Marianne Hirsch, *The Mother/Daughter Plot: Narrative, Psychoanalysis, Feminism* (Bloomington: Indiana University Press, 1989).

16. I quote Kenneth Eble's version of this gruesomely apt phrase in Kate Chopin, *The Awakening*, ed. Kenneth Eble (New York: Capricorn Books, 1964), p. 288. Seyersted prints it as "scene of torture" (*The Complete Works of Kate Chopin* [Baton Rouge: Louisiana State University Press, 1969], 2: 995), and Culley amends it by inserting an "[of]" between the two words, while Nina Baym prints it as "the scene's torture" (*The Awakening and Selected Stories*, p. 343). This confusion points to the need for an authoritative text of the book. I cite the version I am most familiar with and which seems to me to express Edna's violent emotions at the time.

of the children! Remember them!" (*A* 100), is precisely what Edna does as she evaluates her situation during the midnight vigil which follows.

But she has provided herself with pressing reasons not to think of her children, for she expects to find Robert, her beloved, waiting for her, and this fantasy of love acts as a deferral to decision and action. As she recalls Adèle's final words, we are told, "She meant to think of them; that determination had driven into her soul like a death wound—but not tonight. Tomorrow would be time to think of everything" (*A* 110). When she finds that Robert has left, forsaking their love as impossible because by society's standards she is not free, she realizes not the intractability of social convention but the ephemerality of romantic desire: "There was no human being whom she wanted near her except Robert; and she even realized that the day would come when he, too, and the thought of him would melt out of her existence, leaving her alone" (*A* 113). Despite their absence, the children, with their absolute rights and undeniable demands, come "like a death wound" between Edna and what she has come to conceive as her true desire, having her own way (*A* 110). Stripped, or so she thinks, of every fictitious social constraint and every desire, Edna imagines her struggle for autonomy and self-fulfillment in a world of traditional roles and values as a battle between a mother and her children.

The relationship of mother and child has long served in the political realm as an analogue for the existence of "natural" rights, but those generally accrue to males, not females.[17] Indeed, concerning her rights as an individual, Edna has no other models but male ones. *The Awakening* begins by commenting on the origin of Edna's reductive concern for her own rights with an ironic scene in which her husband is frustrated in the free exercise of his privileges. He has been seated in front of the main house of the exclusive Creole resort on Grande Isle attempting to read his newspaper, but is driven away by the "noise" of two birds hanging in cages on either side of the doorway. They "were the property of Madame Lebrun," the proprietress, "and they had the right to make all the noise they wished. Mr. Pontellier had the privilege of quitting their society when they ceased to be entertaining" (*A* 3). Chopin's language is very precise about the distinction between rights and privileges. The birds have rights only insofar

17. The most relevant text in this regard is Tom Paine's revolutionary pamphlet, "Common Sense," in which the failure of England, the mother country, to assume the responsibilities natural to a mother with respect to her child, the American colonies, is the justification for revolution.

as they are the property of someone whose rights of ownership extend to them and are to be respected. Chopin's joking metonymic depiction of birds with rights that supersede Mr. Pontellier's "privilege" of escape foreshadows her use of the image of birds throughout the story, but in this passage she lays out the rights and privileges that obtain between husband and wife in late nineteenth-century America. Mr. Pontellier, though a client and guest of Madame Lebrun, clearly has no rights in this situation; what privilege he has he owes to his status and position as a free and independent agent. But he does have rights vis-à-vis his wife, who is his property, as the birds are the property of Madame Lebrun.[18] By virtue of being owned by him, Edna derives specific kinds of rights—the privilege of a limited escape from irritation—of which he patronizingly reminds her a moment later. He leaves her in the company of Robert, who refuses to join him for billiards (and male bonding, by which Robert renounces his male privileges) at a neighboring hotel: " 'Well, send him about his business when he bores you, Edna,' instructed her husband as he prepared to leave" (*A* 5).

Edna's privileges derive, by way of marriage, from her husband. They are a parroting/parody of self-possession and do not extend to the more crucial disturbances of "society" from which she might want to escape. In this first scene she acts as his surrogate for the exercising of exclusive rights of possession he is too well bred to enforce. Legally, she is his possession, as the narrator makes clear in Léonce's first words (and the text's first human words) directed to her as she comes up from the beach with Robert: " 'You are burnt beyond recognition,' he added, looking at his wife as one looks at a valuable piece of personal property which has suffered some damage" (*A* 4). Thus, Edna's voice, that is, her subjectivity, is also derivative, as a closer look at the caged birds makes clear.

Like Hawthorne, Chopin places "on the threshold of our narrative" objects of significance—a parrot and a mockingbird suspended in cages on either side of the door. Although this door does not open from a prison, Edna's dawning awareness of the price of her privileged status in her husband's world makes it seem like one. The parrot repeats several phrases, "*Allez vous-en! Allez vous-en! Sapristi!* That's all right!" and can, in addition, "speak a little Spanish, and also a language which nobody under-

---

18. For a sketch of the "repressive legal condition" of women under the Napoleonic Code, which was still the basis of the laws governing the marriage contract in New Orleans at the time the tale was set, see Culley's note, "The Context of *The Awakening*" (*Norton* 118).

stood, unless it was the mocking-bird" (*A* 3). These languages, French ("Get away"), a Creole dialect ("For God's sake!"), English (an expression of permission or acceptance), and Spanish coexist alongside a language incomprehensible to everyone but, perhaps, the bird who mindlessly imitates it.

Readers have seen in these caged birds a symbol of Edna's domestic imprisonment, a reading re-enforced by a popular song of the time which recounted the unhappy marriage of a young woman to a rich older man with the refrain "She was only a bird in a gilded cage." [19] The doubling, however, here suggests a more complex significance. Each of the parrot's exclamations is repeated by the three major male characters, Robert, Edna's beloved; Alceé Arobin, Edna's lover; and her husband, respectively. These exclamations reproduce the speech of the men in the novel who are the models for (yet, ironically, repeat) the parrot's imitations. But coming from birds, they are nothing but sounds, their meaning assigned on the basis of a linguistic order entirely alien to the birds as birds. *We* hear a message about the danger of Edna's situation in the parrot's parody—"Get away, for God's sakes, that's all right," giving her permission to escape. In the first scene it is Léonce, her husband, who escapes their chatter, an escape Edna, like the mockingbird imitating the parrot's imitations, attempts throughout the story to replicate. The narrator, however, hints that Edna as well as the men around her are suspended and trapped in a parrot-like reproduction of discourse. She also hints at the existence of "an unknown language," a flood of voicing which grows louder and more insistent as Edna's story unfolds.

"Voicing" and "voices," the media of subjectivity, are recurrent motifs, intimately tied to Edna's dawning awareness of her rights not as property but as an individual. She had formerly conceived of these as simply the right to the privacy of her thoughts, a form of self-censorship that is a legacy of her apprehension of the "dual life": "She had all her life long been accustomed to harbor thoughts and emotions which never voiced themselves. They had never taken the form of struggles. They belonged to her and were her own, and she entertained the conviction that she had a right to them and that they concerned no one but herself" (*A* 47–48). Coming as she does from "sound old Presbyterian Kentucky stock" (*A* 66), enmeshed, as the narrative reveals, in the hypocrisy of weekday sins and

19. Dorothy Dix refers to this song by using its imagery in her column (cited above, note 7), "A Strike for Liberty": "No amount of gilding ever made a cage attractive to the poor wretch within" (*Norton* 132).

Sunday repentance—the disjunction of words and acts—Edna learns early not to give voice to her desires. Her inner world from childhood is filled with conventional infatuations and romantic fictions of love. Upon marriage to a man who adored her and with whom "she fancied there was a sympathy of thought and taste between them, in which fancy she was mistaken" (A 19), she renounces her inner world whose desires she considers fictitious and her inner self whose reactions she distrusts, for an outer world she considers "real." "As the devoted wife of a man who worshipped her, she felt she would take her place with a certain dignity in the world of reality, closing the portals forever behind her upon the realm of romance and dreams" (A 19). This is a description of female self-censorship and self-containment. As the gap narrows between her outer conformity and her inner rebellion, she begins not only to demand her rights as an individual and give voice to her thoughts and emotions, but to act upon them—as a romantic hero must, but a mother in this world cannot.

As Edna listens more attentively to the voices within her and compares them to the reality without, she discovers that her world provides her with only two options for her development, options which are gender-coded and extreme. She can resign herself to her "fate" as a woman, a position in this text always modified by the role of "mother," or she can demand her practical and existential freedom as an individual, a freedom to explore the range of her desires conventionally reserved for men. These mutually exclusive options anticipate, in a remarkable way, psychologist Carol Gilligan's recent findings about the gendered nature of moral development. Gilligan demonstrates that women's traditional "failure" to develop morally derives from their failure to achieve separate and autonomous selves. But this evaluation depends upon a male model of selfhood from which normative cultural standards for women sharply diverge. Instead of continuing to see women as morally underdeveloped, lacking in phallic power, or "deviant," Gilligan suggests that "the failure of women to fit existing models of human growth may point to a problem in the representation, a limitation in the conception of the human condition, an omission of certain truths about life."[20]

One of the important "truths" omitted in the conception of the human condition available to Edna is the fact of female desire. Female passionlessness was a staple feature of the Victorian cult of "true womanhood,"

20. Carol Gilligan, *In a Different Voice: Psychological Theory and Women's Development* (Cambridge: Harvard University Press, 1982), p. 2.

and is re-enforced in this text by the modification of "woman" by "mother."[21] Women of the class to which Edna belongs are defined by their repro-ductive capacity and social caretaking role. They are meant to discover their identity through intimate relationships of interconnection, rather than through independence, autonomy, and the self-definition of work. That is, their desire should not be directed towards themselves but always towards others, children, husbands, the romantic double. Even before the crucial series of Edna's awakenings, she does not fit the role prescribed for mid-dle class women. Wryly brushing aside Mr. Pontellier's vague sense that "his wife failed in her duty toward their children" (*A* 9), the narrator then declares, "In short, Mrs. Pontellier was not a mother-woman" (*A* 10). These women, she continues in a good-humored tone of mockery, "idolized their children, worshipped their husbands, and esteemed it a holy privilege to efface themselves as individuals and grow wings as ministering angels" (*A* 10). The privilege granted by their position is the privilege of self-erasure.

Edna's friend, Adèle Ratignolle, is, we are told, "delicious" as the "embodiment" of the "rôle": "There are no words to describe her save the old ones that have served so often to picture the bygone heroine of ro-mance and the fair lady of our dreams" (*A* 10). Like the open book she is compared to "which every one might read" (*A* 15), Adèle is a surface of cli-chés, easily accessible as the fulfillment of romantic "dreams" in which we all take refuge from "reality"—including, as this extraordinary text makes clear, the "reality" of motherhood. Motherhood, like the fictions of romance, is a discursive function of a certain ideology, here a bourgeois ideology which makes femininity and maternity inseparable, crucial to the mainte-nance of patriarchal society and laissez-faire capitalism, but incompatible with female desire, autonomy, or independent subjectivity.

From Edna's perspective, however, motherhood is the introduction to a double alienation, the traumatic separation from her children and the gap between the images of the role she is required to play and the reality of her *individual* experience. Whether or not she is directly involved in her chil-dren's care, the fact of her being a mother entails the sacrifice of her self, her desire, and her freedom to an imposed responsibility, social convention, stifling respectability, and domesticity. It is also hard, sometimes painful work for which there is no possibility of reparation and which is trivialized as

21. For the positive as well as negative aspects of this social construct, see Nancy F. Cott, "Passionlessness: An Interpretation of Victorian Sexual Ideology, 1790–1850," *Signs* 4 (1978): 219–36.

"natural," attributed to "instinct," or rendered invisible, and, in the case of Adèle, "charming." This split between the experience and image of motherhood is most clearly evident in the course of Adèle's "labor," in which she performs the physical labor of birthing a child and the cultural labor of maintaining the requisite image. Adèle shocks Edna, who has repressed the experience of her own children's births, by "relating to old Monsieur Farival the harrowing story of one of her *accouchements*, withholding no intimate detail" (*A* 11). This "freedom of expression" contrasts sharply with the "lofty chastity which in the Creole woman seems to be inborn and unmistakable" (*A* 11). The double labor women must perform to bridge the gulf between the image and the reality of motherhood is the sign of contradiction. Edna refuses to bridge that gulf, refuses, as she repudiates her marriage and all its implications, to be the bridge-builder, "pontellier," implied in her married name. In doing so, she finds a space of resistance within that contradiction.

The alternative to the "soul's slavery" of the "mother-woman" is clearly represented by Mademoiselle Reisz, "a disagreeable little woman, no longer young, who had quarreled with almost everyone, owing to a temper which was self-assertive and a disposition to trample upon the rights of others" (*A* 26). Anti-social, asexual, and non-maternal, Mademoiselle Reisz is an accomplished musician who, at the expense of intimacy and attachment, pursues a career and achieves the individuation and autonomy Gilligan defines as masculine. Her position outside of motherhood and community grants her certain privileges, that is, the masculine privilege to ignore or override the rights of others in the name of a higher, abstract end. Thus, her art, it is universally agreed, has the stamp of "abiding truth" (*A* 27).

In her pursuit of a selfhood which is not defined by the self-censorship and non-development of the "mother-woman," Edna is both drawn to Mademoiselle Reisz and repulsed by her, another sign of the contradiction which distinguishes her position. It is her music that awakens Edna to both her own repressed sensuality and her desire, which takes the rather predictable form of a romantic attachment to young Robert Lebrun. After the significant night of August 28th, on which she is so shaken by Mademoiselle Reisz's playing, finally masters the art of swimming during a midnight dip, lounges in a hammock with Robert at her side silently experiencing the moment "pregnant with the first-felt throbbings of desire" (*A* 31), and resists her husband's subsequent demands that she come to bed, Edna awakens and sends for Robert to accompany her to the *Chênière*. In "commanding his presence," she unconsciously exercises the same conjugal rights which her husband tried and failed for the first time in their marriage to exercise the previous night. Robert leaves for Mexico, and when Edna returns to New Orleans at the end of the summer, she begins more and more to act on her desires, embarking on a series of imitations of masculine strategies for autonomous identity.

At first, her rebellions seem trivial. She declines to chastise the cook for a meal not to her husband's liking, and he upbraids her with a patronizing comparison of her domestic and his commercial authority: "Suppose I didn't look after the clerks in my office, just let them run things their own way; they'd soon make a nice mess of me and my business" (*A* 52). But Edna is beyond being bought off with the notion of "separate spheres" and its paltry version of female domestic power. She refuses to keep her "reception day," does not return visits of influential society women, and begins "to do as she liked and feel as she liked" (*A* 57). She refuses to accompany her husband on a business trip which includes a visit home to attend her younger sister Janet's wedding. Janet, referred to by Mr. Pontellier as "something of a vixen" (*A* 66), is finally being socialized; Edna declines to attend this rite of passage. She tells her husband that "a wedding is one of the most lamentable spectacles on earth" (*A* 66). Having the privilege of no meaningful occupation, she takes up again her pastime of painting, spending what seems to Mr. Pontellier inordinate amounts of time in her atelier at the top of the house. "For a time she had the whole household enrolled in the service of art," just as ambitious men in capitalist patriarchies enlist their whole households in the service of their wealth and comfort (*A* 57).

With her husband gone, and her children safely installed in Iberville, Edna is completely free to explore the world of her desires. It looks, in many respects, like the world of the men around her, the only models for autonomy she has come to know as wife and mother. As if perceiving the opulence of the home she lives in for the first time, she embarks on a self-satisfied tour of inspection. Earlier, we learned that "Mr. Pontellier was very fond of walking about his house examining its various appointments and details," possessions "he greatly valued . . . chiefly because they were his" (*A* 50). Edna is not quite so appropriative, approaching the flowers in the garden "in a familiar spirit and ma[king] herself at home among them" (*A* 72). She begins choosing her own society and amusements. One day at the races, which earlier in the story she had attended with her father, a Kentucky horse breeder, she sits "between her two companions as one having authority to speak." Childhood memories of horses, stables, and "blue grass paddocks" excite her, but "She did not perceive that she was talking like her father as the sleek geldings ambled in review before them" (*A* 74). In the exercise and unrestrained display of her knowledge she is unconsciously masculine. Gambling for high stakes and winning, as her husband does at billiards and on the Stock Market, is intoxicating, but another forbidden male pleasure.

The masculine mask Edna has no choice but to don in her quest for selfhood also affects her relationship to work and to representation. Women of Edna's class labor but are denied work; they must depend for their comfort upon husbands and female servants. Yet every major and minor female character in the story practices an art, a fact that reflects the pervasive gender splitting which, in the middle classes, requires men to engage in trade and business and women to cultivate culture for private consumption. Mademoiselle Reisz, a musician and composer, represents one extreme possibility; she exemplifies the artist with "the brave soul. The soul that dares and defies" (*A* 63) conventionality, transgresses boundaries, and transcends gender in her pursuit of the purely beautiful and eternally truthful. Her opposite is Adèle Ratignolle, also an accomplished pianist who "was keeping up her music on account of the children, she said; because she and her husband both considered it a means of brightening the home and making it attractive" (*A* 25). These extremes are another contradiction in woman's position, as illustrated in the fourteen-year-old Farival twins, "always clad in the Virgin's colors, blue and white, having been dedicated to the Blessed Virgin at their baptism" (*A* 24), who are, nevertheless, learning the piano as part of their training as "mother-women." The tragic implication of such contradictions forms part of the allegorical background at Grande Isle (the inseparable lovers, the lady in black) and is continuously foreshadowed as we hear the twins obsessively practicing a duet from the romantic opera "Zampa," whose involved plot includes a lover's death in the sea. Edna refuses both of these alternatives and takes the masculine path, eventually turning her dabbling in paints into a lucrative profession.

It is, however, through work she loves to do that Edna glimpses the possibility of non-alienated labor and true gratification: "She had reached a stage when she seemed to be no longer feeling her way, working, when in the humor, with sureness and ease. And being devoid of ambition, and striving not toward accomplishment, she drew satisfaction from the work in itself" (*A* 73). It is appropriate, then, that she begins to sense the radical incongruity of the society's requisite maternal image and her experience of motherhood through her attempts at "realistic" visual representation. The first sketch we see her doing at Grande Isle and which "[s]he had long wished to try herself on" is Madame Ratignolle. "Never had that lady seemed a more tempting subject than at that moment, seated there like some sensuous Madonna, with the gleam of the fading day enriching her splendid color." At this early point in her artistic (also spiritual/sexual) development, her sketch is "a fair enough piece of work, and in many respects satisfying" (*A* 13), but because it bears no resemblance to its subject, she destroys it. Several months later, when she determines to begin "studying" with a local artist and dealer, she expresses her artistic aspirations to Adèle as her desire to be able "to paint your picture some day" (*A* 55).

Edna's desire to capture the romanticized maternal image places her in a masculine position by linking her to the masculine world of representation and power. By imagining Adèle as "some sensuous Madonna," she stereotypes, fetishizes, and silences her. The cultural myths of woman's threatening sexuality, which must be both sacrificed to and made safe by the necessities of reproduction, and also spiritualized as a venerated source of religious mystification—these myths are all actively at play in the idea of a virgin mother. She is at once saintly in her self-sacrifice and sensuous in her beauty, but American Victorian culture also popularized an erotics of maternal sacrifice and a spiritualization of feminine beauty. This excess and doubling have made the Madonna a popular subject for (male) artists. Edna, with the aid of the narrator, imagines a representation of Adèle as the epitome of contradiction: the female body at once pure and used, simultaneously marked and unmarked by male desire, accorded tremendous power in Catholic cultures like that of the Creoles, and effectively stripped of all power in the patriarchal world, the most exalted and idealized portrait of the social and religious institution of motherhood. It is a role impossible for any woman to embody. At the same time, Edna's image of Adèle is also her acknowledgment of the alluring sensuality of pregnant women—in the previous chapter we learn that Adèle is expecting her fourth child.

Yet, this full, excessive beauty cannot be captured. Edna's disappointment at her failure to produce a mimetically accurate image of her friend suggests her desire to get beyond the entangling roles which separate image and reality. I would like to suggest a context for understanding how Edna's striving for selfhood and her experience of motherhood are bound up in her practice of art. In her efforts to achieve autonomous selfhood, Edna imagines bringing together the two parts of her "dual life" by casting off her maternal responsibilities and living out her romantic dream —freedom, on the one hand, and merger with the beloved, on the other.

She strives for a unified, self-reliant, and coherent subjectivity, an interior coherence vouchsafed to the bourgeois subject, but denied to women. "The woman-subject," according to Julia Kristeva, because of her reproductive capacity is "more of a *filter* than anyone else—a thoroughfare, a threshold where 'nature' confronts 'culture.'"[22] Culturally, the mother is projected as the ultimate guarantee of symbolic coherence; what this fantasy reveals, however, is "that the maternal body is the place of a splitting, which, even though hypostatized by Christianity, nonetheless remains a constant factor of social reality" (*DL* 238). The maternal body, internally divided in the act of giving birth, represents the split subject, separate, different, and disunified, but pregnant with meaning.

Kristeva's provocative exploration of maternity offers a revision of the Freudian and Lacanian models of subjectivity by privileging the maternal presence in the pre-oedipal stage, rather than the paternal and oedipal, in the formation of the gendered and speaking subject. She argues for the existence of a hidden and "inexpressible" maternal discourse, traces of which come to light in certain fifteenth-century depictions of the Madonna. The maternal image acts as a "screen" upon which the unconscious of the (male) artist records "those clashes that occur between the biological and social programs of the species" (*DL* 242). Emerging from depictions of the mother's "body rejoicing" is a "jouissance" which is available, though "mute," to women through their experiences of giving birth. In her study of "Motherhood According to Giovanni Bellini," Kristeva distinguishes two attitudes towards the maternal body which prefigure opposed modes of representation in the West, the Madonnas of Leonardo da Vinci and those of Bellini. Leonardo paints the traditional objects of veneration, the idealized mother, protective of and one with the child, an emblem of unity, the maternal space figured and fetishized. Bellini's Madonnas, by contrast, are "iconographic," produced through the "predominance of luminous, chromatic differences beyond and despite corporeal representation." They seem to be "beyond figuration," retaining "the traces of a marginal experience, through and across which a maternal body might recognize its own, otherwise inexpressible in our culture" (*DL* 239).

Edna does not yet recognize her own marginal experience through which she might "hear meaning" (Kristeva puns on "jouissance" as "j'ouis sens," "I hear meaning"), but finally, I think, recognizes and responds to

22. *Desire in Language: A Semiotic Approach to Literature and Art*, trans. Leo S. Roudiez (New York: Columbia University Press, 1980), p. 238; hereafter cited in my text as *DL*.

something kindred in the seductive, maternal voice of the sea. She has repressed her own experience of giving birth, a process by which, Kristeva claims, woman can return to the body of her own mother (*see DL* 239), a reunion Edna achieves metaphorically when she swims into the gulf. Through art, however, she wants to "reproduce" Adèle's image as the symbol of unity, the guarantor of the subjective coherence she perceives and imitates in the masculine realm of work, property, and passion. Only when she witnesses the actual birth, the trauma of separation, does she glimpse the contradiction between the socially authorized image of motherhood and her discontinuous one which is unrepresentable. This internal division, revealed by her art, enables her to see that she is neither a failed mother-woman whose highest privilege is self-scarifice nor an imitation of a (male) individual who derives his privileges by sacrificing the rights of others. Yet having no model for an uncharted, alternative selfhood, she continues to follow the path of masculine, and as her late-night reading suggests, Emersonian (quintessentially American) self-reliance.

As her art work "grows in force and individuality" (*A* 79), Edna decides to move to a small cottage around the corner nicknamed "the Pigeon House." Freedom and independence unencumbered by responsibility have become crucial to her search for phallic subjectivity. But like the birds in their cages reflexively repeating what they have heard ("*Instinct* had prompted her to put away her husband's bounty in casting off her allegiance" [*A* 80; my emphasis]), and especially like the mockingbird who instinctively imitates an imitation, Edna will find this "house" a coop, a cage of her own devising. Newly awakened to her own desires, she is socially powerless in a system whose possessive individualism she can only reinscribe in her own small world. By selling her means of self-expression, she converts her unalienated labor into commodities. She even negotiates with a dealer for the sale of her Parisian sketches "in time for the holiday trade in December" (*A* 103), work she had not yet done and can only do if she accompanies her husband abroad on a trip he will finance. By becoming a producer, rather than remaining a re-producer, Edna enters more deeply into the system of exchange in which she was considered "goods" to be acquired and possessed.[23] Kristeva concludes, "Is not the object-oriented

23. For the definition of "goods" and a Marxist/feminist analysis of women as goods in a "homosexual" economy, see Luce Irigaray, "When the Goods Get Together," trans. Elaine Marks, in *New French Feminisms: An Anthology*, ed. Elaine Marks and Isabelle de Courtivron (New York: Schocken Books, 1981), pp. 99–110.

libido always masculine?" (*DL* 264). A different, "essentially feminine libidinal economy" of which unidealized maternity is an aspect and emblem Edna has yet to imagine.[24]

Free, now, to realize her infatuation with Robert, Edna acts out the pattern of the male hero of romance, defining herself as a self through her desire for the other. Formerly a woman defined as the object of male desire without desire of her own, now with the illusion of agency, she experiences an intoxicating sense of power. She becomes the aggressive lover wishing to possess the beloved completely, to "lose" herself, as she says, in a narcissistic merger which requires the possession of a self to lose. Her behavior towards Robert in the final portion of the story is characterized by a complete role reversal in which Edna is aggressive and Robert is passive. After their inconclusive and anti-climatic first reunion at Mademoiselle Reisz's, they meet accidentally at a small restaurant on the outskirts of the city. As she goads him about his selfishness in leaving her and pursuing his own career, Edna says: "I suppose this is what you would call unwomanly; but I have got into the habit of expressing myself" (*A* 104). When they return to her cottage, she declares herself, in words and acts, a free agent. Leaning over him, she asks if he is asleep and kisses him for the first time, completely inverting the gender roles of the Sleeping Beauty fairy tale to which the title of the novel makes ironic reference. She had enacted the female role of this fairy tale during their romantic stay on the *Chênière Caminada* during the summer, but even then she woke herself without any help. Now acting the part of the prince, Edna must rouse her beloved from his sleep of silence, convention, and inaction.

24. I am indebted to Jacobus, *Reading Woman*, p. 144 and especially the chapter entitled "*Dora* and the Pregnant Madonna," for an illuminating reading of Kristeva's sometimes opaque prose and for the clarity of her theoretical comments on motherhood. Leslie Rabine applies the notion of an alternative feminist economy to the writing of romance and the representation of women's experience of the very emblem of bourgeois, privatized selfhood—romantic love. Using terms similar to Kristeva's and Jacobus's, she differentiates "feminine historicity" from the traditional romantic "male quest for imaginary totality" which constitutes woman as object and therefore as "other" and so excludes her from romantic discourse and linear, goal-oriented development. Feminine historicity challenges the privileged myths of such discourse and of such developmental paths by rejecting the return to a unified totality or resolution of contradictions. Instead, it seeks to enter into history and the "network of differences," gaps, and lacks it discloses. Thus, Rabine writes, and here her sexual/historical analysis bears upon Chopin's dilemma, "Romantic love passion which seems to epitomize a private, self-enclosed relation, leads back into a network of social contradictions" (Leslie Rabine, *Reading the Romantic Heroine: Text, History and Ideology* [Ann Arbor: University of Michigan Press, 1985], pp. 12–13).

The commercial implications of Edna's freedom to act suggest her unwitting and devastating discovery about the nature of selfhood as defined by the dominant culture. In a passage that is usually cited as Edna's moment of freedom, she begins by sounding like a conventional mother as she scolds Robert for his "wild dream of [her] in some way becoming [his] wife," but finally speaks in her husband's voice:

> "You have been a very, very foolish boy, wasting your time dreaming of impossible things when you speak of Mr. Pontellier setting me free! I am no longer one of Mr. Pontellier's possessions to dispose of or not. I give myself where I choose. If he were to say, 'Here, Robert, take her and be happy; she is yours,' I should laugh at you both." (A 106–7)

The chastising, infantilizing maternal voice has become fully articulate with the legislating, commanding patriarchal voice, even at the moment of Edna's rejection of male power over her person and her self.

Without a chance for further explanation, Edna is called away to Adèle's bedside, where her illusion of romanticized maternity is finally shattered. In her shocking declaration to Robert, her free agency is contingent on her literal self-possession. She can speak for herself because she is self-sufficient. But she can only articulate terms of non-interference, the conditions of her freedom from male possession. She cannot imagine new terms for this transgressive relationship, or for her transgressive self. In her articulation, she has uncovered the ultimate logic behind the fiction of autonomous selfhood in an androcentric world: that "reality" is a system of exchange, that power is the ability to enter and trade on that market, and that freedom is only the freedom to own oneself and to give oneself where and to whom one chooses. She has experienced herself as property, with certain privileges of class and race, and the "romantic" rights accorded to mothers. When she expresses to Mademoiselle Reisz her resolve "never again to belong to another than herself" (A 80), she articulates not only her desire for autonomy in the very same male language of ownership, but also her freedom of romantic choice in the related terms of possession. But to conceive of the self as that which can be possessed, and thus given away, necessarily assumes the possibility of self-as-property, the same assumption that underlies slavery.[25] As a woman tied by biology, class, and

25. For a more detailed discussion of this dynamic, in which "the capitalist and the masochist [Freud's description of the nature of female heterosexual pleasure] are one and the same" (64), see Walter Benn Michaels, "The Phenomenology of Contract," Raritan 4 (1984): 47–66.

circumstances to the fate of being eternally reproductive, Edna struggles to disengage herself from this self-sacrificing repetition, to produce a self, herself a speaking "I." Her quest reveals the Althusserian nature of subjectivity: to be a subject is to be subjected to the fictions of independence, power, and free will.[26]

Subjectivity, then, is produced by discourse and reproduced by ideology. To possess one's self means authoring the socially sanctioned fictions of that self. Try as she may, Edna cannot make her stories work towards a narrative resolution; she cannot, that is, author a paternal or patriarchal story. When, for example, she attempts to lull her sons to sleep with a bedtime tale, the traditional province of the maternal, "Instead of soothing it excited them, and added to their wakefulness. She left them in heated argument, speculating about the conclusion of the tale which their mother promised to finish the following night" (A 44). At an elegant dinner party to which Mr. Pontellier has invited Dr. Mandelet so he can "observe" Edna professionally, all the guests are invited to tell stories. Mr. Pontellier recalled "his youth, when he hunted 'possum in the company of some friendly darky." The Colonel, Edna's father, "related a somber episode of those dark and bitter days" of the Civil War, in which "he acted a conspicuous part and always formed the central figure." The doctor, drawing on his professional confidences, "told the old, ever new and curious story of the waning of a woman's love, seeking strange new channels, only to return to its legitimate source after days of fierce unrest." Edna tells "of a woman who paddled away with her lover one night in a pirogue and never came back." Although "pure invention," according to the narrator, "every glowing word seemed real to those who listened." The men tell the male story of the American romance, solitary, heroic, aggressive, or didactic. Edna's is a tale of the merger of two souls "rapt in oblivious forgetfulness, drifting into the unknown," inconclusive and interminable, yet "real" (A 70).

Behind this tale is the story suppressed throughout Chopin's narrative which Edna cannot tell, what Marianne Hirsch calls "maternal discourse."[27] In the course of the novel Edna awakens to her feelings, which

26. For a sustained discussion of the subjected nature of bourgeois subjectivity, see Louis Althusser, "Ideology and the State," *Lenin and Philosophy and Other Essays*, trans. Ben Brewster (New York: Monthly Review Press, 1971), pp. 127–86.

27. For a discussion of the nature of "maternal discourse" and the role it plays, or does not play, in feminist theory and criticism, see Marianne Hirsch, *The Mother/Daughter Plot*, especially chapter five, "Feminist Discourse/Maternal Discourse: Speaking with Two Voices."

manifest themselves in an intense desire for another with whom she wants to drift away and lose herself, but who is absent for a good part of the story. This desire is, in Freudian culture, based on a lack which she endeavors throughout the story to fill with phallic objects and the exercise of phallic power. She desires to possess the beloved and merge with him in a pre-oedipal return to an undifferentiated satisfaction of needs—thus, the rhythm of the narrative recapitulates Edna's patterns of eating and sleeping. Psychoanalysis equates the penis and the child, assuming that what women lack, physically and culturally (that is, power and its symbol), can be replaced by a child. But Edna's behavior towards her children has been consistently inconsistent, her fondness "uneven, impulsive. . . . She would sometimes gather them passionately to her heart; she would sometimes forget them" (*A* 20). What she cannot face is that her "occasional intense longing" for them, and her more sustained desire for Robert (in many ways a child, her narcissistic double, and certainly an oedipalized son) are born of two traumatic separations, the birth of her children and the early death of her mother.

In fact, Edna's desire for merger with Robert pales next to her experiences with women—her intense bonding with Adèle that day on the beach looking out to the Gulf when she reveals her deepest self, or her strange fascination/repulsion with Mademoiselle Reisz. Adèle calls Edna a "child"; Mademoiselle Reisz calls her a "queen"; to imagine a self she must reconcile and integrate these two conflicting positions. That integration, healing the split between image and reality, subject and object, is precisely what her female experience, freed from "the great motherhood lie,"[28] could offer her. Yet, being a mother, woman, and subject reciprocal with objects; speaking a language capable of expressing difference not as lack but as otherness; having a community to support and encourage such a sense of selfhood—these are not possibilities in the world Edna inhabits.

That world dismisses as hysterical, petulant, inconsequential, and even psychotic women's expressions of pain, anger, fear, frustration, desire, and even power. This is especially clear in the crucial scene of Edna's attendance upon Adèle during her delivery. She has left Robert at the moment of her fantasied possession of him to fulfill her promise to come to Adèle "in her hour of trial." She finds the "romantic heroine" in a state of high agitation, upbraiding her husband and doctor in imperious tones, which under normal circumstances would be unacceptable, for what she

28. Jane Lazarre, *The Mother Knot*, p. 156.

perceives as their neglect of her: " 'This is too much!' she cried. 'Mandelet ought to be killed! Where is Alphonse? Is it possible I am to be abandoned like this—neglected by every one?' " (A 108). Not only has male appropriation of gynecology and obstetrics rendered her completely dependent upon a male presence for this biologically female function, but it also renders the women supporting her, Edna and Josephine, the nurse, invisible to her. She can only feel secure in professional male hands, and she demands this security vouchsafed to her as the reward for her compliance with the act of reproduction. She is in "transition," the stormiest phase of first-stage labor in which women "need strong emotional support and unfailing encouragement," yet Dr. Mandelet "paid no attention to Madame Ratignolle's upbraidings. He was accustomed to them at such times, and was too well convinced of her loyalty to doubt it" (A 108).[29]

As they leave "the scene torture," Mandelet, perceiving Edna's agitation, attempts to draw her out, in the manner of a friendly analyst. He assures her, "I know I would understand, and I tell you there are not many

29. The literature of birth and delivery describes "transition" as a stormy and taxing period at the end of the first stage of labor when the cervix is almost fully dilated. According to one childbirth educator, during this period "contractions follow each other relentlessly with hardly a pause between, and they tend to become arhythmic, with sharp peaks and sometimes with more than one to each contraction. The build up of energy with each may be so sudden and tumultuous that there is no time for slow breathing. . . . The very length of the contractions may demand every bit of concentration and determination you are able to summon, and you will need strong emotional support and unfailing encouragement. Your partner's attention must not waver for a minute and he should repeatedly communicate to you his confidence in you and his love. . . . You may suddenly feel that it is all too much, hard work and that you cannot go on and would like to go home and forget about having a baby. Or you may become irritable with everyone around you and hypercritical of the help your partner is giving. . . . You are also very likely to feel that you are not making any progress at all and have lost all sense of time" (Sheila Kitzinger, The Complete Book of Pregnancy and Childbirth [New York: Knopf, 1986], pp. 207–8). Although this maternal work seems familiar to us now, nineteenth-century doctors were not the only ones to dismiss the maternal experience and discourse of transition. Writing sardonically about the "liberated" seventies, Lazarre recounts how she behaved when her doctor "instructed" her on the futility of screaming: "I yelled with an intensity I am sure he discounted as a symptom of the psychosis often exhibited by women in transition. . . . But I had never been more sane," she concludes, juxtaposing expertise and experience (Lazarre, The Mother Knot, p. 29). Dr. Mandelet patronizes Adèle in this time of extreme disorientation and vulnerability, and Edna cannot even recognize what is happening; Josephine, though, has seen it all before. If I had not been myself preparing for childbirth when I revised this essay, I would not have recognized this crucial representation of maternal experience.

who would—not many, my dear," and promises, "We will talk of things you never dreamt of talking about before. It will do us both good" (*A* 110). Yet Edna cannot speak the unspeakable. When he asks if she is going abroad with her husband when he returns, she replies, "Perhaps—no, I am not going. I'm not going to be forced into doing things. I don't want to go abroad. I want to be let alone. Nobody has any right—except children, perhaps— and even then, it seems to me—or it did seem—" (*A* 109). She breaks off at the point of uttering the unutterable, that children have no rights over the lives and selves of mothers, and the doctor, "grasping her meaning intuitively," puts her dilemma in the only terms it can bear in his paternalistic understanding: "The trouble is . . . that youth is given up to illusions. It seems to be a provision of Nature; a decoy to secure mothers for the race. And Nature takes no account of moral consequences, of arbitrary conditions which we create, and which we feel obligated to maintain at any cost" (*A* 109–10). He is only able to make the conventional distinction between "natural" and culturally imposed conditions which are morally reprehensible or outmoded. A sympathetic understanding in the patriarchal world of the text cannot go beyond this limit. Though he offers to listen to Edna, he has already formulated her "trouble." He remains deaf to Adèle. Perhaps the only words in the text in which the mother speaks herself, without the distorting images of romance, are silenced.

The suppressed voice within Edna, which speaks at the moment of her awakening of Robert, becomes, at the moment of her death, one with the voice of the sea. It is "a loving but imperative entreaty" (*A* 14) which she has heard beckoning her throughout the book. The sea's offering, however, is not just a voice; this haunting description reappears as a refrain throughout the text:

> The voice of the sea is seductive; never ceasing, whispering, clamoring, murmuring, inviting the soul to wander for a spell in abysses of solitude; to lose itself in mazes of inward contemplation. The voice of the sea speaks to the soul.
> The touch of the sea is sensuous, enfolding the body in its soft, close embrace. (*A* 15)

In the entreaty of the sea, voice and touch are inseparable, the one leading the soul to solitude through a language without words, the other totally enveloping the body in a physical caress. The two images contradict each other, and though there is no transition between them, are clearly meant as complements of each other: the soul seeks and is drawn to romantic separateness, solipsism; the body desires the presence and feel of another. They constitute modes of communication and experience which the social world deems separable and unrelated in the model of selfhood based on self-possession.

For Edna, voice and touch are intimately connected in her experience of desire, the experience of difference and separation which constitutes her gendered self. When, for example, she longs for her loved ones, it is with a "hungry heart," wanting from her children "the sound of their voices and the touch of their cheeks" (A 94), remembering how with Robert "she . . . had heard his voice and touched his hand" (A 102). Even as she presides over her birthday dinner, a decadent display of opulence and her final parodic use of her husband's wealth, shimmering and self-contained, "the regal woman, the one who rules, who looks on, who stands alone," she still feels "the old ennui overtaking her . . . like an obsession . . . the acute longing which always summoned into her spiritual vision the presence of the beloved one, overpowering her at once with a sense of the unattainable" (A 88). The self-possession she experiences from the exercise of phallic power (ruling, looking on, standing alone) is finally unsatisfying. In her mimicry of male subjectivity, something of her female otherness remains unfulfilled, nagging, subversive. She does not seek to become a writer, but a painter, working in color, tone, and shape, and the art that most moves her is music, the form most resistant to semiosis. The only female writer in the book is a Miss Mayblunt who, on seeing the figure of Victor bedecked as the image of "Desire" at the climax of the dinner, renounces her medium of expression and exclaims, "Oh! to be able to paint in color rather than in words!" Even the writerly function which Kate Chopin as author performs is derogated; she reinscribes herself in her novel as "Chopin," the (male) composer whose preludes, played by Mademoiselle Reisz, enthrall Edna. Language is the province of the paternal and the patriarchy and comes into being as the result of the split between the self as experience and self as object. Only the mockingbird in the cage at the opening of the story, the wild bird domesticated, comprehends the male discourse the parrot mimics, and reproduces it, but with a difference—with wordless song.

Ultimately, Edna rejects the masculine autonomy achieved by Mademoiselle Reisz because it is disconnected from the body. The misanthropic, self-possessed little musician makes music which shakes her audience, but seems to leave her untouched. She is cold and sexless, even unnatural. With something of a voyeur's appetite for vicarious pleasure, she raves about Edna's physical beauty while envying her sensibility and vibrant responses to life. Unlike Edna, her relationship to the physical world is one of scorn and disdain. Although she summers at Grande Isle, she avoids water and never swims in the sea. She eschews the food provided for her, living instead on chocolates "for their sustaining quality . . . in small compass" (*A* 48), and wears a "batch of rusty black lace with a bunch of artificial violets pinned to the side of her hair" (*A* 26). Her eccentric "artistic" temperament is the height of romantic self-involvement which she fuels in Edna by mediating between her and the absent Robert through the letters he writes from Mexico. In a scene of unsurpassed self-indulgence on both women's parts, Edna sits in Mademoiselle Reisz's shabby attic room half-swooning over one of Robert's letters as Mademoiselle plays ravishing impromptus.

By contrast, Edna has awakened slowly over the course of the novel to her physical nature, her sensuality, and her right to enjoy them. The ultimate irony is that, along with all her other mimicry of masculine freedom, the satisfaction of her desire shatters her romantic illusions as she is forced to accept her sexual nature in her affair with Arobin. Experiencing passion separate from love, a split between the physical and emotional "natural" to men but "unnatural" and forbidden for women, she understands the rupture upon which her being has been founded. Still holding on to a dream of merger with Robert, in which passion and love might also merge, she is confronted with the stark reminder of that part of her physical nature she has tried to ignore in her flight to freedom—her motherhood. Her children are a responsibility she cannot evade. This shocking realization, coupled with the shattering of her romantic illusions, sends her back to the beach at Grande Isle where she will "elude" the tyranny of the children, that is, an overwhelming maternal responsibility which amounts, in her eyes, to a soul-killing self-sacrifice.

In the long night before her death, she recalls an argument she had with Adèle during the summer. She declared her "right" to her self and said "she would never sacrifice herself for her children, or for any one" (*A* 48). When Adèle protests vehemently, Edna explains, "I would give up the unessential; I would give up my money, I would give my life for my children; but I wouldn't give myself. I can't make it more clear; it's something which I am beginning to comprehend, which is revealing itself to me." When Adèle counters, alluding to the authority of scripture, that "a woman who would give up her life for her children could do no more than that—your Bible tells you so," Edna rejoins, "Oh, yes you could!" (*A* 48), thereby distinguishing life from self, mere existence from a sense of identity. In that midnight meditation Edna understands "now clearly what she had meant long ago . . ." (*A* 113). She gives up her life for her children precisely because she refuses to give up her "self." Instead, Edna willingly gives up a life in which selfhood is defined either in terms of self-possession or self-sacrifice.

Her merger with the sea is not the regression beyond childhood to infantile narcissism one Freudian reading calls it.[30] Rather, it is presented as a progression backwards through a series of memories to a sensuously maternal space, the space in which she can recapture her lost mother and her own "far away, unreal, and only half remembered" motherhood (*A* 108). Edna's quest has progressed through culturally determined feminine roles and an imitation of the phallic world of power and ends as Edna stands naked on the beach, in what appears to be her final imitation. Earlier, on hearing "a short, plaintive, minor strain" played by Madame Ratignolle which "Edna had entitled 'Solitude,' " she imagined the figure of a man, naked, standing on the seashore in an attitude of "hopeless resignation as he looked toward a distant bird winging its flight away from him" (*A* 26–27). But, answering the seductive voice of the sea, Edna is not hopelessly resigned, and the bird emblematizing this moment, though disabled with a broken wing, is at least free of its cage. They both enter the sea.

In seeking a form of subjectivity which is not merely solitary, but also reciprocal, not phallic, but maternal, Edna moves through the paternal and phallic-ruled social and linguistic network Jacques Lacan defines as the symbolic order, to what Kristeva calls the "semiotic," an "archaic language" of instinctual drives heard in the rhythms, melodies, and bodily movements of the mother and present at the earliest intimation of difference between mother and child. This semiotic space borders on, runs counter to, yet is inscribed within the symbolic order as unsettling disturbances "heard in the 'unconscious' of linguistic practice."[31] The semiotic is, here, imaged as the sea, whose voice Edna finally heeds and whose gulf or gap she enters. This transitional space indicated by the gerund formed by the progressive

30. Arguing from a strict and uncritical Freudian perspective, Wolff states that "with her final act Edna completes the regression, back beyond childhood into time eternal." Interestingly, although she would claim Edna's experiences as universally applicable (see note 5 above), she regards her attitudes towards maternity as crucial motivation for her death; that death, though, must be seen as part rebellion and part revenge: "If life cannot offer fulfillment of her dream of fusion, then the ecstasy of death is preferable to the relinquishing of that dream" (Wolff, "Thanatos and Eros," p. 450). Wolff's perceptive essay, which fails because it takes the novel's text and Freud's at their word, shows just how far feminist psychoanalytic theory has come.

31. Jacobus, *Reading Woman*, p. 149.

tense verb of the title, "the awakening," the space of difference between the binary opposites she cannot resolve, is familiar yet completely new, a return to the pre-oedipal, to that which has not been conscious. No longer drifting aimlessly or hanging suspended or sleeping, Edna "reached out with a long sweeping stroke" to meet the touch and reciprocate the embrace of the sea (*A* 113).

As she goes on, swimming back through her own childhood, "think-ing of the blue-grass meadow that she had traversed when a little child" es-caping the hypocritical words of her father's Sunday prayers, "believing that it had no beginning and no end," she rehearses her progress through the various stages of possession. She thinks first of "Léonce and the children. They were a part of her life. But they need not have thought they could pos-sess her, body and soul." She imagines Mademoiselle Reisz's contempt, for Edna rejects the isolation and bodilessness of the artist. Finally, she recalls the misunderstanding of the beloved she strove to possess whose final words could be the suicide note she declines to write: "Good-by— because, I love you" (*A* 114).

At the moment of her death and her release, an ending indistin-guishable from a beginning, she no longer sees images. She has escaped the figural, and in her recapturing of intense fragments of memory, the voices become the wordless sounds of progressively less human and less discursively bound objects:

> Edna heard her father's voice and her sister Margaret's. She heard the barking of an old dog that was chained to the sycamore tree. The spurs of the cavalry officer clanged as he walked across the porch. There was the hum of bees, and the musky odor of pinks filled the air. (*A* 114)

The very style of the novel's final sentences enacts the progression back-wards. The voice of the father, who had recommended to Mr. Pontellier, "Authority, coercion are what is needed. Put your foot down good and hard; the only way to manage a wife," and who "was perhaps unaware that he had coerced his own wife into her grave" (*A* 71)—this voice gives way to the voice of Margaret, Edna's cold and matronly sister and substitute mother, a woman who could not satisfy Edna's longing for the lost maternal body. These markers of gendered subjectivity's stages give way in turn to a sym-bolic, inhuman sound, the barking of an old dog, which, despite its age, is still threatening enough or still trying hard enough to escape, to require chaining—the revolt of the wild against domestication.

Near the end, even Edna's perceptual agency is shed. The sounds and smells that follow are not presented as Edna's memories, or even explicitly as objects of her senses, but as subjectless sounds. "The spurs of the cavalry officer clanged," as if we have entered, unmediated, the very world of the sounds, a metonymic space where perceiving subject and perceived object are fused. The regalia of masculinity and the accoutrements of romantic infatuation which so alienated Edna from herself and which she infused with meaning merely sound themselves.

Finally, in words of unlocalized and unspecified being, "There was" only the wordless musicless hum bees produce not with mouths, but with their wings and bodies, and the rich fragrance of pinks. Although Edna is drowning in water, the figures for her final consciousness are located in the air. Earlier, the narrator offered this metaphor for Edna's final gesture, "a bird with a broken wing . . . beating the air above, reeling, fluttering, circling disabled down, down to the water" (A 113), the remnants of Mademoiselle Reisz's mythology of the artist. Unlike the "narcotic" effect of purely sensual love or the heavy odor of chloroform which deadened Edna's sensations during childbirth, the sounds and smells of the final sentence check the downward mood and movement. At the same time, they work insistently against any suggestion of transcendence; bees and flowers are close to the earth, and the color pink, for the late nineteenth century, is gender-coded to signify the feminine. The closing allusions of Edna's death initiate an awakening which goes beyond the limits of her own powers of comprehension. The ending begins with the incipient or potential pollination of flower by bee, a fertilization across different species and outside the realm of the human, a fertilization which is at once impersonal, non-appropriative, and symbiotic, asexual yet extremely erotic, inevitable, and as ancient and vital as the world before words.

The New Historicist Return of the Repressed Context

Realism, Ideology, and the Novel in America (1886–1896): Changing Perspectives in the Work of Mark Twain, W. D. Howells, and Henry James

Robert Weimann

To approach the American novel at the end of the nineteenth and the beginning of the twentieth century is to be confronted with a bewildering variety of trends and achievements; even within the main stream of realism, the field is too vast for one paper to attempt to do more than chart some of the new developments formative of a more highly critical function of literature in late nineteenth-century American society. Moreover, the changing correlations between the novel and reality and the new departures in narrative form constitute a process which, emphatically, does not begin in 1886 and does not end in, say, 1917. To study its antecedents seems altogether impossible without taking into account the work of Herman Melville, or the earlier fiction of Mark Twain (whose *Huckleberry Finn* came out in 1884), and, of course, the European nineteenth-century realistic novel, especially in France, England and Russia. What is more, the literary history of these years, and especially of the novel, is significant precisely because the rise of a more critical type of realism coincides with, and is inductive to, that national process of cultural self-definition which, in the words of Alfred Kazin, "rests upon a tradition of enmity to the established order. . . . Modern American Literature was born in protest, born in rebellion, born out of the sense of indirection which was imposed upon the new generations out of the realization that the old formal culture—the 'New England Idea'—could no longer serve."[1] This, of course, involves a vast area of social, cultural, and ideological crises with which the emerging critical modes of realism in the novel are only partially identical, even though the rise and flowering of this realism is unthinkable without an element of "protest," "rebellion," and that "sense of indirection" inherent in the loss of previously valid criteria of cultural identity and social function.

But the crucial question is not, simply, that of the social content and literary meaning of this rebellion, but also the way it affects (and reflects) newly critical departures in the assimilation of reality in America. As against the dominant "ideology of national unity and enlightened progress,"[2] the realist writer of fiction feels a need, hardly shared by even the most enlightened sections of his middle-class audience, for reassessing the validity of some of the current liberal assumptions about culture and society and the way the novel was to participate in and inform the changing modes of interplay and communication between the two. In the earlier nineteenth century, such assumptions were normally shared by writers and readers alike; at that time, the novel (in its popular domestic as well as in its more sophisticated forms) assumed a more homogeneous audience prepared to affirm the use of cultural forms as a means of social control and moral education in terms of the imaginative refinement of the bourgeois ethic of work, conduct, and progress. But in the last two decades of the century, almost unnoticeably, such liberal assumptions about literature and society begin to refuse to inspire the more critically realistic essays in fiction, and some of the traditional conceptions of the role of the novel as a medium of consciousness and communication commence to show signs of strain.

These new departures in contemporary fiction appear to be related, in a profound if largely indirect way, to some of the basic social and eco-

1. Alfred Kazin, *On Native Grounds* (New York: Reynal and Hitchcock, 1942), p. 22.
2. Heinz Ickstadt, " Öffentliche Fiktion und bürgerliches Leben—der amerikanische Roman der Jahrhundertwende als kommunikatives System," *Amerikastudien—Theorie, Geschichte, interpretatorische Praxis* (Stuttgart: Sonderheft. Hg. v. Martin Christadler und Günther H. Lenz, 1977), p. 225. Cf. "The Novel and the People: Aspects of Democratic Fiction in late 19th Century American Literature," *Proceedings of a Symposium on American Literature*, ed. Marta Sienicka (Poznań: Wydan, Naukowe Universytetu im. Adama Mickiewicza, 1979), pp. 96, 102: where Heinz Ickstadt points to the availability of this ethical code for, initially, popular and serious fiction alike.

nomic changes in this period.[3] To suggest the nature of these changes it must suffice here to say that their forcefulness largely has to do with the fact that industrial capitalism in the USA thrived relatively late and then so rapidly that the formation of monopolies and a corporate mode of capitalism, following hard upon the heels of the industrializing process itself, caused a break-up of many of the traditional forms of social and political relationships in nineteenth-century American society. What is noteworthy in the present context is that these economic and political changes went hand in hand with various symptoms of crisis in the substance and function of the dominant cultural and political ideologies, including both the New England heritage of Emersonian idealism and the agrarian and Western traditions of the frontier with its elementary forms of democracy.

Whereas, the majority of the novelists in earlier nineteenth-century society were, despite critical reservations, still in a position to identify with most of the generally accepted positions in social morality and ideology in the eighties and nineties, the novelist in America, as soon as he opts for a position of realism, finds it increasingly difficult to consider himself as a spokesman of either the leading bourgeoisie or, indeed, the broader sections of middle-class society. The point that wants to be made is that the writer tends to repudiate hitherto largely unchallenged and broadly accepted norms of social ideology and sexual morality and that in doing so (and only in doing so) he is able to confront, to apprehend and comprehend the changing nature of society in America, with all the unfathomed contradictions that this involves. It is in this respect that (as my title suggests) the crisis in the traditional norms of ideology and the rise of a more highly critical type of realism can be viewed, genetically and functionally, as connected and, in a complex and largely unexplored way, as interconnected.

In this connection, the element of economic and social change must not, of course, be viewed in isolation from, or as unmediated by, contemporary developments in the fields of philosophy, religion, and natural science. The crisis in the validity and acceptability, for the writer, of given norms of ideology coincides with and is augmented by developments in the fields of the philosophy of positivism and determinism, evolutionary biology, and the physical sciences. It was precisely because many of these assump-

3. For a summary of the evidence on how "Die kapitalistische Zentralisation geht bei Euch mit Schritten von Siebenmeilenstiefeln" (Friedrich Engels to Sorge, 1. 29. 1886) see Jürgen Kuczynski, "Der anti-monopolistische Roman der Muckrakers in den USA," *Gestalten und Werke* (Berlin und Weimar: Aufbau-Verlag, 1971), 2: 202–10.

tions in ideology, science, and religion could no longer be taken for granted that a novelist like William Dean Howells welcomed a new type of realism "dispersing the conventional acceptations by which men live on easy terms with themselves, and obliging them to examine the grounds of their social and moral opinions."[4] Again, it was the realist writer of fiction who, finding "conventional acceptations" intolerable, proceeded to reject the "easy terms" of the ideological consensus and to recognize the need afresh "to examine the grounds" of hitherto received "social and moral opinions."

The resulting strains, uncertainties, and transitions in the literary consciousness can be traced wherever the socially accepted modes and functions in the communication of norms and ideals, and their relatedness to the realities of living in society, seem either no longer self-evident or deprived of their previous sanctions and justifications. Such a crisis in consciousness foreshadowed that greater rift between literature and American society which, one or two decades later, was to suffuse the most acute criticism and journalism of the period. By the time that Van Wyck Brooks wrote his *America's Coming of Age* (1913/14) many traditional ideas of the dominant culture appeared to him as "a world of ineffectual dreams and impotent ideals":

> Certainly ideals of this kind, in this way presented, in this way prepared for, cannot enrich life, because they are wanting in all the elements of personal contact. Wholly dreamlike and vaporous, they end by breeding nothing but cynicism and chagrin; and in becoming permanently catalogued in the mind as impracticable they lead to a belief in the essential unreality of ideas as well.[5]

Van Wyck Brooks was, in this connection, not primarily concerned with the state of literature, but by pointing to "the essential unreality" of the dominant ideas he left no doubt that the traditional correlations between American "life" and American "ideals," between the social reality and the literary consciousness, had entered a state of crisis. Now some of the most widely accepted ideas, together with their whole frame of ideological reference, appeared "undefined, unexamined, unapplied." In a situation like that, the

4. William Dean Howells, *Harper's Magazine* 112 (May 1906), p. 959; cited in H. Wayne Morgan, *American Writers in Rebellion: From Mark Twain to Dreiser* (New York: Hill and Wang, 1965), p. 62.
5. Van Wyck Brooks, *America's Coming of Age*, 2nd printing (New York: B. W. Huebsch, 1924), pp. 176, 23.

task of the realist writer of fiction was to redefine and re-examine them and to jettison, as "no longer genuine or adequate," those "catchwords over which the generality of our public men dilate":

> The recognized divisions of opinion, the recognized issues, the recognized causes in American society are extinct. And although Patriotism, Democracy, the Future, Liberty are still the undefined, unexamined, unapplied catchwords over which the generality of our public men dilate, enlarge themselves, and float (careful thought and intellectual contact still remaining on the level of engineering, finance, advertising, and trade)—while this remains true, every one feels that the issues represented by them are no longer genuine or adequate.[6]

When Brooks complained about there being "no community, no genial middle ground" between "transcendent theory ('high ideals')" on the one hand and "a simultaneous acceptance of catchpenny realities"[7] on the other, he did articulate at least part of the dilemma which the rising critical impulse in late nineteenth- and early twentieth-century realism had to cope with. What was involved was more than the awareness of a rift "between university ethics and business ethics"; what was at stake was even the possibility of facing the gap, in terms of communication and ideology, between education and reality, consciousness, and experience.

To explore this rift and to achieve a vision of its depth and meaning involved almost insuperable difficulties, and it led to over-simplifications from which even the most courageous critical minds in the muckraking movement were not exempt. As Irene Skotnicki has shown in her study of the work that went into *The Shame of the Cities*, Lincoln Steffens, in his investigation of seven major city administrations, assembled plenty of evidence according to which, as he himself stated, "Big business everywhere is the chief source of political corruption."[8] But Steffens, with all the wealth of evidence before him, utterly failed to perceive that the highly conspicuous increase in administrative corruption was in many ways related to the growth of a monopolizing economy and the formation of newly influential vested interests. For him, the changing pattern of American society, even

6. Brooks, pp. 166f.
7. Brooks, p. 7.
8. Quoted in Irene Skotnicki, "Zu einigen Aspekten der journalistischen Leistungen von Lincoln Steffens innerhalb der Bewegung der 'Muck-rakers,'" *Potsdamer Forschungen* Reihe A, Heft 36 (Potsdam: hg. von Heinz Wüstenhagen, 1979), 115.

at its most vulnerable point, was to be viewed in accordance with the assumptions of the liberal ideology which emphasized the political failure of the individual, not his social context, as the responsible agent of the decline of American democracy. The contradiction was between the revelation of the stark truth of administrative corruption in the cities and the inability, on the part of the literary investigator, to read his own evidence except in terms of the individualistic norms of the prevalent ideology. In the case of Lincoln Steffens, the contradiction was resolved years later when, in his *Autobiography*, he looked back at his muckraking days and remarked that then "I could hardly believe what I was seeing, and that I could not, in so short a time, change my mind to fit the new picture. I was not yet over my education . . . I needed time to adjust my imagination to the facts as they were, not more experience, but time."[9]

To adjust the imagination and to reassess its changing role in society was a task not less challenging for the novelist. This points to the significance of the connection, so crucial for the new realist's vision, between the crisis in the functions of moral control, ideological affirmation, and social synthesis and in the rise of a more highly searching and distancing perspective on society. In the so-called popular fiction of the time, the crisis in the traditional functions of the liberal imagination was brought to a head by commercializing forces which turned the novel into a marketable commodity whose exploitation and availability began to be rated higher than its presumed moral services and capacities for ideological instruction and integration. As Hans Holzhaider has shown in his study of *Amerikanische Konsumliteratur: 1865–1885* (1976), by 1880 the traditional moral functions, or what passed for them, were gradually superseded by more purely entertaining and sensational standards. But on a less marketable level, the more profound assimilation of reality (and, hence, the search for a new critical function of the novel in society) on the one hand, and the freely ranging communication with a wider public and the affirmation of the prevalent middle-class attitudes and responses to literature on the other, became, if not mutually exclusive, at least an increasingly problematical connection. The resulting adjustments in the novelistic consciousness and the changing modes and means of its communication were, of course, tentative and groping rather than radical. Still, in the last two decades of the nineteenth century these adjustments can, I think, be traced in the work of three of the

9. *The Autobiography of Lincoln Steffens* (New York: Harcourt, Brace and Company, 1931), p. 343.

most widely acknowledged novelists of the time who all, in their different ways, tend to move beyond the received modes and forms of the liberal transactions of literature and ideology. This move may be associated with significant new departures in the later work of Mark Twain, especially since *Puddn'head Wilson*. It can be traced in the New York period in the fiction of William Dean Howells, as well as, in the late eighties, in the novels of Henry James, and it is differently and more radically present in the subsequent work of Crane, Norris, London, and Dreiser. The critical element in the work of these highly diverse novelists, it is suggested, can be viewed in terms of the crisis in the traditional functions of a previously accepted body of ideas and assumptions, out of which crisis these writers grope for a newly critical assimilation of and communication with their society.

My following notes cannot, of course, attempt to survey this movement at large: they will confine themselves, deliberately, to three instances in the work of the three major novelists of the period where signs of crisis and transition, as never before in the history of the nineteenth-century American novel, become quite unmistakable. Unlike Crane, Dreiser, and Norris, this period in the work of Twain, Howells, and James is transitional in the fully historical sense of the word. These older novelists remain deeply indebted to some of the most traditional nineteenth-century standards in social ideology, novelistic communication, and moral control, but they begin to sense their precariousness and respond in their own creative ways. From the point of view of the twentieth century, they may well be claimed to anticipate some distinct elements in the crisis of both the liberal imagination and the traditional modes of narrative, and they at least in part reveal new perspectives on an increasingly problematical relationship between art and individuality and the coming to terms with the impersonal forces of society.

1

For that, the work and thought of the later Mark Twain is a case in point. Reared in an environment which was agrarian, provincial, secure, optimistic, and resonant with the belief in the unbounded possibilities of the individual (of which his own career seemed to offer so profuse a confirmation), Twain in his later years was so deeply and irretrievably disillusioned not only because his personal sense of misfortune, loss, and bereavement tended to corroborate the darkest springs of his humor, but also because the newer reality seemed to throw into doubt the very foundations to which he had clung in the face of growing doubt and skepticism. It was because he himself had his deepest roots in the pioneer tradition of spontaneous thought and practical action that he was singularly ill-equipped to adjust his highly personalized modes of consciousness to the new impersonal realities of economic centralization, political corruption, imperialist expansion and exploitation, and the changing social and cultural norms of a city-centered life. It was not simply that a great self-made writer like Mark Twain lacked the formal education that would have allowed him to systematize and stabilize his response to a rapidly changing environment. If this did play its part by rendering him at the mercy of clichés used to explain, in the most abstract of terms, his own and man's follies and shortcomings, it certainly was not the whole truth.

To understand the nature of this crisis, the depth and persistence of Mark Twain's despair must be taken as a symptom of the complete absence, for him, of any viable alternative to the prevalent norms of social morality. In his late philosophical sketches which Bernard De Voto has published in *Letters from the Earth*, under the subtitle "The Damned Human Race," Mark Twain almost helplessly, as it were, is thrown back again and again on either the cynical use or the rejection of current ideological concepts of morality. Considering man as greatly inferior to the "Higher Animals" for his greed, cruelty, robbery, and hypocrisy, he sums up his indictment by saying that man alone "is constitutionally afflicted with a Defect" which "is permanent in him, indestructible, ineradicable." And he continues:

> I find this Defect to be *the Moral Sense*. He is the only animal that has it. It is the secret of his degradation. It is the quality *which enables him to do wrong*. It has no other office. It is incapable of performing any other function. It could never have been intended to perform any other. . . .
>
> Since the Moral Sense has but the one office, the one capacity— to enable man to do wrong—it is plainly without value to him. It is as valueless to him as is disease. In fact, it manifestly *is* a disease.[10]

A few lines later, when he restates the "Moral Sense" as "the Primal Curse," he relates it to the distinctively human "presence of consciousness." At first sight, this appears to reflect nothing but incertitude, and the emphasis, with its repetitive and almost obsessive negation of ideological concepts such as "the Moral Sense," seems curiously removed from any understanding

10. Mark Twain, *Letters from the Earth*, ed. Bernard De Voto (New York: Perennial Library, 1974), p. 181.

of the social function of consciousness. Yet, when Mark Twain proceeds to speak of the inverted "office" of contemporary morality (in the sense that the Moral Sense enables man "to do wrong"), there is, perhaps, an implication that it is the debased social *function* of contemporary ideas and ideals, which, as he notes, "is the secret of degradation." "Function," here, is Mark Twain's word, and although the abstract quality of his indictment is only another indication of some desperate confusion of cause and effect, the idea is not altogether absent that it is the apologetic quality of this function which is unhelpful and even degrading. (Man, as he puts it in *The Mysterious Stranger*, "is not able to perceive that the Moral Sense degrades him to the bottom layer of animated beings and is a shameful possession."[11])

If, on a theoretical plane, Mark Twain's critique of the "function" of contemporary ideology cannot appear satisfying, his concern with the ideological corruption of the "Moral Sense" is in itself quite consistent. Not only does he use the same concept in a narrative like *The Mysterious Stranger*, but he also uses this concept in his more directly political writings to underscore his moral indignation. Take only such well-known pamphlets as *To the Person Sitting in Darkness* or *King Leopold's Soliloquy* which point to the contemporary background of that false consciousness by which a growing gulf between the moral postulates of the democratic heritage and the actual practice of politics at home and abroad was apologetically covered up. Referring to imperialist expansion and exploitation in Asia and Africa, particularly in China, the Philippines, and the Congo, Mark Twain coins a phrase which is absolutely sarcastic: "the Blessing-of-Civilization Trust."[12] Here his language is ironically revealing, not only because it is that of the "trust," but also because the underlying purpose is one of "accumulation." In the words of Mark Twain: "This world-girdling accumulation of trained morals, high principles, and justice." But the verbal irony suggests the same confused mixture of bewilderment and anger that can be traced in his rejection of the "Moral Sense." What the novelist is concerned with is the dichotomy between social morality and social practice, in the face of which words like "brotherhood," "love," and "happiness" assume an ironic ambivalence through the ideological quality of their received usage. In other words, the Moral Sense of contemporary civilized society is so permanently and ineradicably abused and is so manifestly "a disease" that it is disrupting rather than fulfilling the traditional function of consciousness.

11. In *The Portable Mark Twain*, ed. Bernard De Voto (New York: Viking, 1974), p. 181.
12. "To the Person Sitting in Darkness," in *Portable Mark Twain*, p. 599.

The underlying confusions between "civilization" and exploitation, between "high principles" and dirty practice, find their most consistent expression in *The Mysterious Stranger*. There, the sixth chapter opens with the image of "a great factory of some sort" where "men and women and little children were toiling in heat and dirt and a fog of dust." They were "clothed in rags" and, in the course of a fourteen-hour day, turned into abject poor slaves, because, as Twain says, the "Moral Sense" provided the factory owner with the necessary finer difference between what he thinks is right and what he thinks is wrong. What is reflected in the morality of the factory owner is, obviously, a good deal of the false consciousness of the ruling class. Here the author comes closest to a definition of the functions of contemporary ideology when he rejects the self-deceptions of mankind as a "colossal humbug": Satan, the hero, is quoted as saying that man's life is a permanent and uninterrupted mode of self-deceit. In a situation like that, "sanity and happiness are an impossible combination": the acquisition of knowledge and the act of recognition cannot but lead to unhappiness. The true function of consciousness, then, is a tragic one. In the words of Twain: "No sane man can be happy, for to him life is real and he sees what a fearful thing it is." [13]

To emphasize the element of tragedy (almost Nietzschean in its antithesis between consciousness and sanity, knowledge and happiness) is not of course to deny that, until the end, and throughout his recurring moods of despair, Mark Twain continued to assert and reassert a liberal version of Jeffersonian democracy and Enlightenment humanism.[14] And yet, his position is such that the resulting irony and ambivalence, of which his Satan is of course the supreme embodiment, had long since become a powerful impetus in his search for a more adequately critical representation of reality in the novel, especially in a masterpiece like *Puddn'head Wilson*, which appeared in 1894. This book is of special interest here, because it is Mark Twain's major novelistic achievement in the nineties and reflects that crucial phase in his career in which he attempts to adapt the tradition of West-

---

13. *The Mysterious Stranger*, p. 735.
14. Consider, for instance, Twain's concept of "democracy," as "the common voice of the people," which is defined by "each of you, for himself and on his own responsibility," so that society is viewed as nothing more than the sum of its parts, a conglomeration of individuals of which "each must for himself alone decide what is right and what is wrong." This is taken from that fragment of a book called "Glances of History" or "Outlines of History"; see *Letters from the Earth*, p. 98.

ern humor and frontier realism to a critical vision of the changing needs and contradictions of contemporary American society. The novel draws on that ideological reassessment of American society which, more than anything else, accounts for it being a kind of watershed in Mark Twain's literary biography.[15] If the book is, as F. R. Leavis has suggested, "Mark Twain's Neglected Classic,"[16] it is also, in the words of James M. Cox, a work which foreshadows "The End of Mark Twain's American Dream."[17]

The watershed quality of the novel may perhaps best be illuminated by a comparison with *A Connecticut Yankee in King Arthur's Court* (1889), where the emphasis is not only on the brutally absurd obsolescence of feudal institutions and the smart vulgarity of nineteenth-century Hartford, Conn., but on the assumption that a critique of overthrow of inhuman social institutions will, ultimately, help to reassert the original values of the American heritage, progress, reason, and individuality. But in *The Tragedy of Puddn'head Wilson* these values are utterly strained, and the whole book seems to be saying that, in the present world, they can no longer be taken for granted.

At the center of *Puddn'head Wilson*, there is a searching and consistently ironic reassessment of some of the narrative correlatives of the liberal ideology, especially of current assumptions of identity and individuality. The interchange of two babies, one the future white master, the other the future slave, establishes an almost parabolic framework within which the definition of personal identity is viewed as a function of its social context. The irony in such a definition of individuality is underlined when, on a different level, Mr. David Wilson on his arrival in Dawson's Landing comes to be misunderstood not through the absence but also through the forceful assertion of a witty and highly original personality. Wilson, after the initial display of his black-humored wit, is treated by the villagers as a "puddn'head," as a fool. For twenty years Wilson is not free to practice his profession and the villagers refuse to accept his sarcastic wittiness as the crucial mould of his personal identity, for the "first day's verdict made him a fool": "his

15. R. E. Spiller, *The Cycle in American Literature: An Essay in Historical Criticism* (New York: Macmillan, 1955). But see my comments in "Wandlungen und Krisen amerikanischer Literaturhistorie," *Literaturgeschichte und Mythology* (Frankfurt am Main: Suhrkamp, 1977), pp. 241–45.
16. R. F. Leavis, "Mark Twain's Neglected Classic," *Commentary* 21 (1956): 128–36.
17. "The End of Mark Twain's American Dream," *South Atlantic Quarterly* 58 (1959): 351–63.

deadly remark [that he wished he "owned half of that dog"] had ruined his chance."[18]

Wilson's unsuccessful attempt at establishing his truly legitimate identity corresponds to Roxy's successful but unlawful attempt at establishing an illegitimate identity for her slave-born son Charleston. Once Roxy has changed her master's son with her own, both their identities are radically confused: whereas the false Master Tom is treated like a gentleman only to end up a coward, snob, and gambler (and is finally sold "down the river"), the rightful heir, once he has acquired a negro's gait, speech, and bearing, will never again feel at ease in the white man's parlor.

In ironically blurring the profiles of his main characters, Mark Twain has, in the full sense of the word, written a novel without a hero. But while the hero's consciousness proves to be an altogether unreliable vehicle of meaning, the reader cannot validly refer himself to the represented standards of society's counter-perspective. What we have in the novel is a highly modern element of "indeterminacy"[19] which reflects the crisis of some of the norms and means of communication, social and aesthetic— a crisis which, while affecting the representation of characters and their relationships, at the same time begins to involve the nature of the reader's response. Not only are the citizens at Dawson's Landing mistaken about the true identity of both Wilson and the false Tom, but also their own level of consensus is ridiculously shallow and changeful. When Wilson "has resigned" from the position of puddn'head, one of the citizens remarks that that position "isn't vacant—we're elected."[20] At this point, the reader's response is shifting, and there is an element of insecurity in relating himself to the previously represented norms of social communication inside the novel.

Thus, the paradox about identity is social as well as personal, and the insecurity in the very foundations of the public sense of right and wrong, baseness and respectability, is at the heart of the novel at large. The relationship between social appearance and individual reality is gravely upset; social roles can be performed with the help of a persona whose true

18. Mark Twain, *Puddn'head Wilson*, ed. Malcolm Bradbury (Harmondsworth: Penguin Books, 1979), p. 59f.
19. Wolfgang Iser, *The Act of Reading: A Theory of Aesthetic Response* (Baltimore: The Johns Hopkins Univ. Press, 1978), p. 170–79. In an earlier study Wolfgang Iser had inquired into the historical background of "the observable increase of indeterminacy" in modern literature. Cf. *Aspects of Narrative*, Selected Papers of the English Institute, ed. J. Hillis Miller (New York: Columbia University Press, 1971), pp. 1–45.
20. *Puddn'head Wilson*, p. 224.

meaning can no longer be derived from any moral consensus or generally valid system of morality. At this point, Mark Twain breaks through the crippling circumstances of a half-accepted, half-rejected ideology in crisis and achieves the courage of his artistically vindicated convictions: in the world of Dawson's Landing, the "Moral Sense" is not a hallowed acquisition of either a social tradition or a traditional society, but rather a function of those contradictions which the story indicates without bothering to resolve.

When Puddn'head Wilson meets the white Master's and the white negro's children in the baby-wagon, he asks the question "How do you tell them apart, Roxy, when they haven't any clothes on?" This points to the cruel absurdity of racial discrimination among infants, but over and beyond that, it questions the nature and legitimacy of current social conceptions as superficial and exterior to the true identity and practice of human beings in society. If the whole issue of individuality and identity is, finally, a matter of fingerprints, the whole tradition of American individualism must be profoundly flawed. Mark Twain points beyond not only the hopes and illusions of the gilded age, but also the humor and realism of the frontier, and he anticipates some of the profoundly ironic parabolic forms of twentieth-century realism.

2

If Mark Twain is so significant because his life and work link two different periods in the social and literary history of the American people, William Dean Howells's fiction is no less remarkable in that, although with greater degrees of continuity, it spans the same era of transition. The Brahmins's "favorite child," Howells becomes the first great champion of the realist movement in America. In his Boston years, Howells found it possible largely to identify himself with middle-class optimism, the attitudes of self-confidence, and the belief in the progress of American culture and society. At that time, Howells, as Alfred Kazin notes, had "no reason to think of realism as other than simplicity, Americanism and truth."[21] Realism for him involved the sympathetic treatment of the individual experience and the social relationships of ordinary people: "the large, cheerful average of health and success and happy life."

But when Howells wrote these words in the editor's column of *Harper's New Monthly Magazine* of September 1886, he was about to engage

21. *On Native Grounds*, p. 14.

himself in that quiet intellectual revolution which was to transform Howells "from an optimistic believer that existing American institutions had produced a satisfactory way of life into a humble and agonized doubter."[22] Now his feeling was that "it is coming out all wrong in the end, unless it bases itself anew on real equality."[23] More than anything else it was the Haymarket trial which opened his eyes to the new contradictions which were changing the social and ideological climate in America. At that time, Howells came close to what Karl-Heinz Wirzberger called a "Bruch mit den Anschauungen seiner eigenen Klasse."[24] It is of course true that the revolutionary quality of his rebellion remained half-hearted and that, as George Bennett has shown, "Howells's education in socialism was not totally converted to artistic gain," so that in *Annie Kilburn* and even in *A Hazard of New Fortunes* the novel "seems to say more than it proves."[25] But despite such highly significant gaps between social consciousness and literary achievement, the new phase for Howells did involve an ideological upheaval of considerable magnitude. Howells, especially in his old age, may have remained "a monumental example of the antiquated nineteenth-century conscience," but it was a "conscience upon whom a new order of society had placed an intolerable burden."[26] In his most challenging response to the changing world around him, the novelist had to surrender, at least in part, his own "conventional acceptations" of what had become the apologetic functions of the dominant ideology: of all perspectives it was that of the agonized doubter which pointed the way to a critical dimension in his realism.

To trace this change in the novels themselves is to realize that it does not involve a straightforward line of development; in some areas of his fiction, notably in his sexual morality, Howells always remained a Victorian gentleman and never repudiated the conventional standards of his time and place. Even so, the change in question is remarkable enough, and in order to suggest at least some of its directions I propose to look at and compare two of his better known novels.

22. Everett Carter, *Howells and the Age of Realism* (Philadelphia: Lippincott, 1954), p. 171.
23. Quoted in George N. Bennett, *William Dean Howells: The Development of a Novelist* (Norman, Oklahoma: University of Oklahoma Press, 1959), p. 180.
24. Karl-Heinz Wirzberger, "The Simple, the Natural, the Honest. W. D. Howells als Kritiker und die Durchsetzung des Realismus in der amerikanischen Literatur des ausgehenden 19 Jahrhunderts," *Z A A* 9 (1961): 43.
25. *William Dean Howells*, pp. 176, 179.
26. *On Native Grounds*, p. 32.

The Rise of Silas Lapham, to begin with, can perhaps best be viewed as the culmination of the optimism by which a widely accepted ideology is directly brought to bear on the novelistic functions of cultural control, education, progress, and unity. There is a vision of unambiguous, ethical choices for the hero, since the forces and passions that inspire the thought and action of a given personality are, ultimately, to be found in the individual himself. For that, the career of Silas Lapham, American self-made man, can serve as a consistently illuminating example. There is a connection between his rise, in wealth and business, and the achievement of his moral integrity through financial bankruptcy. What we have is, in either case, "the traditional American belief in a self-sustained individuality and morality which is capable of rising to an occasion without any evident preparation or training."[27]

It is true, the novel reflects Howells's deepening concern with the social and economic changes that had overtaken and replaced the America of his youth, and he displays a growing awareness of the widening gulf between wealth and poverty. And yet, against a background of financial speculation and industrial competition, the bourgeois ethic of middle-class honesty, thrift, perseverance, and personal integrity is, in the teeth of financial speculation and ruin, triumphantly vindicated. By rejecting a most favorable but dishonest offer made by an anonymous group of buyers, Silas Lapham reasserts the standards of decency and fair play, thus vindicating the business ethic of the rising middle class.[28]

The book is written in a tradition of realism where the novelist is in a position throughout to draw on a frame of values which is shared and upheld by both his characters and the vast majority of his readers as the representatives of the class from which the author himself is descended. Since between the novelist's consciousness and that of his readers the mode of communication is so direct and lively, the literary transaction and, in particular, the reader's response hardly allow of any indeterminacy. If Silas Lapham is a bragging and swelling *nouveau riche*, incapable of concealing his "suspicion," "meanness," and "ferocity,"[29] Dryfoos comes to back up financially a literary journal, whose managing director is prepared

27. Leon Howard, *Literature and the American Tradition* (Garden City, New Jersey: Doubleday, 1960), p. 207.
28. William Dean Howells, *The Rise of Silas Lapham* (New York: Airmont Classic, 1968), p. 127.
29. Howells, *Silas Lapham*, p. 97, 50.

to do everything "to let the public know that it owes this thing to the liberal and enlightened spirit of one of the foremost capitalists of the country."[30] But the "liberal and enlightened spirit" explodes as soon as the capitalist begins to put pressure on the management to dismiss Lindau, the German-American revolutionary who radically repudiates the role of capital in both the journal and in society at large: "You *atfertise*, and the gounting room sees dat de etitorial-room toes'nt tink." Thus, the commercialized status of the journal reflects the state of the republic in the age of imperialism: "a republic dat is bought oap by monobolies, and ron by drusts and gompanies, and railroadts andt oilcompanies." It is true that, at the end, the millionaire is deeply affected by the loss of his son who is killed during a strike, but his "regeneration" remains "incomplete," and there is a "hopeless absurdity" in his "endeavour at atonement." This is so, when his last word on the nature of social relationships is "it was a dog eat dog, anyway." Still, the book closes on a note of reconciliation and renunciation which at least in part is challenged. At the same time, the ending of the novel attempts to reintegrate the novelistic vision of the world into the contemporary realities of middle-class existence. The crisis being over, the strike ended, the dead buried, the novelist is gathering together the threads of his fabulation pointing beyond the world of the novel as valid symbols, not of criticism, but of continuity. The final perspective of the book follows the pattern of the traditional nineteenth-century novel, where the function of realism is that of helping to come to terms with life as, for better or worse, it is lived in the present.

3

Mark Twain and W. D. Howells had responded politically, in their complete *Weltanschauung* as well as in their fiction, to the transition from the reconstruction period to a fully developed industrial form of monopoly capitalism in America. The same cannot quite be said of their exact contemporary, Henry James, whose predominantly literary reaction seems so much more removed from the primary planes of social and political reality that it can easily be underrated in its emphasis and significance. Whereas Twain and Howells established a number of interactive links between their own rebellion and the larger movements of their time (anti-imperialist and

30. William Dean Howells, *A Hazard of New Fortunes*, with an introduction by Tony Tanner (London: 1965). My quotations: pp. 287, 244, 254, 286, 446, 441, 411, 405.

populist in their direction, in Howells's case even a theoretical interest in socialism and social democracy), Henry James is so deeply, not to say passionately, preoccupied with the pursuit of his own craft of fiction that he has no other choice of desire than to cultivate his only art as a supremely sensitive receptacle of exquisite consciousness.

And yet, James, in the middle and late eighties, almost unnoticeably moves in the direction of a more highly critical type of realism, by which, in *The Bostonians*, the New England heritage of political reform and social progress is painfully and even satirically reassessed. At the same time, or very shortly after, in *The Princess Casamassima*, the prospects of bourgeois democracy are seriously made to confront the underground world of political anarchism and social revolution until, in *The Tragic Muse*, the traditional liberal conception of the role of art and the artist in society is critically revised and redefined from a point of view which, in more than one way, anticipates the dilemmas as well as the triumphs of the twentieth-century writer and the changing social function of fiction. Whatever James, in these books, did to the middle-class sensibility and ideology of his time, they were ill received and spitefully or, at best, indifferently reviewed. Having immeasurably transcended the horizon of the ideological expectations and liberal conventions of his audience, James, through his departure from the ideological assumptions of his middle-class readers, came to comprehend and assimilate the social trends and movements of his time with a realism unprecedented in his oeuvre so far.

Among these three books, *The Bostonians* (1886) is the more noteworthy in that its theme is steeped in American cultural and political history: the cause of women's emancipation, viewed in the specifically Bostonian context of a social reform movement which, on the one hand, is linked to the heroic past of Abolitionism and, on the other, to the more modern manifestations of the spiritual bankruptcy of the New England tradition. James had sensed its declining moral fervor and was perfectly aware of the changing social and economic context against which the traditional idealism of the reforming impulse had to be reexamined. Thus, in representing some of the defeats and illusions of the feminist movement of his day, James satirically challenges the most recent and, at the same time, the most hallowed ideologies of the contemporary causes of bourgeois reform and progress.

His heroine, Olive Chancellor, attempts to advance the reform movement by forming and maintaining a fervidly tense and unconsciously lesbian relationship with lovely Verena Tarrant, the great "feminine hope" of public assemblies. Her father, Selah Tarrant, a Spiritualistic humbug, and the suitor who is favored by her parents, Mr. Pardon ("reporter, interviewer, manager, agent"), represent what is perhaps the most scathing comment that James has made on the decaying phase of the democratic element in the ideological crisis of America's foremost liberal reform movement. The newspaperman ushers in the modern, the sensational, the irresponsible functions in the progress of the press as a commercialized mass-medium. Like Pardon, Selah Tarrant aspires to share in the most compromising forms of expression of contemporary ideology: "The newspapers were his world, the richest expression, in his eyes, of human life; and, for him, if a diviner day was to come upon earth, it would be brought about by copious advertisement in the daily prints." [31]

"The vision of that publicity" is shown as one of the debased views of progress which is both ingenuously rose-colored and sordid. James does not, as Mark Twain does, articulate the cynical element in the concept of "the moral sense"; but he does hint at the same degrading degree of incongruity between consciousness and reality when Tarrant is described as "a moralist without moral sense"—an extraordinary phrase which implies not only that he is "destitute of the perception of right and wrong" but also, and more generally, that this sort of morality has become emptied of both a socially acceptable and personally disinterested meaning: a morality without standards, serving very questionable, if not disreputable, functions.

If Tarrant and Pardon are minor and largely satirical characters, the critical re-evaluation of the changing functions of the New England tradition involves pathos as well as tragedy. At its most serious level, these are associated with Olive Chancellor, in whose character, as F. R. Leavis noted, the author "relates the conscience, the feminism, the culture, and the refinement" [32] of New England. But her unquestioned refinement is tainted with some inbred "morbidness" against which the unrelieved tenseness of her championship for "the new truths," "her immense sympathy for reform," and the parlor quality of her definition of "human progress" [33] are made to appear even more abstract and removed from the full human experience of naturally living a fulfilled life in society. Olive Chancellor is attached to Miss Birdseye who represents the problematical continuity between the heroic

---

31. Henry James, *The Bostonians* (Harmondsworth: Penguin Modern Classics, 1980), pp. 89, 96.
32. F. R. Leavis, *The Great Tradition: George Eliot, Henry James, Joseph Conrad* (Harmondsworth: Penguin, 1962), p. 153.
33. *The Bostonians*, pp. 11, 20, 30, 19; cf. below: pp. 31, 342f., 345f.

past of the abolitionist cause and the later movement of reform: "She was heroic, she was sublime, the whole moral history of Boston was reflected in her displaced spectacles." If, at the beginning of the novel, the Bostonian lady appears "deliciously provincial," and "one never pretended that she, poor dear, had the smallest sense of the real," towards the end her state of blindness is such that the actual realities as well as the future of the New England culture is ironically concealed from her closing eyes. On her deathbed she appears "as a battered, immemorial monument" of "the heroic age of New England life": what is left in her is a "desire to reconcile and harmonize," so that she, "with benignant perversity," deludes herself in her dying words about the future: "you mustn't think there's no progress because you don't see it right off; . . . everything has got started," or so she believes, when, in fact, everything in Olive Chancellor's campaign is threatened with collapse. At that moment, Olive herself, in her anguish, is much closer to the novel's vision of the future with her outcry: "I shall see nothing but shame and ruin!"

The debacle seems complete and there is no alternate perspective on the world of the novel. If anything, the authorial consciousness itself is deeply involved in the representation of the crisis of the foremost cultural tradition of nineteenth-century America. For was not James working on the decay of the very tradition that he continued to use within his own frame of reference as a novelist? The question points to the precariousness of the intellectual sources and resources of his own consciousness. In that respect, *The Bostonians* was an exercise in self-criticism which might well be compared with the divided perspective on bourgeois society in *The Princess Casamassima*. James may have known little and cared less about the aims and ways of the organized working-class movement of his time, but he did ask a number of highly startling questions through an imagination which, in his own words, was "the imagination of disaster" (letter to A. C. Benson, 1896). Since James himself confessed that he tended to "see life as ferocious and sinister." Lionel Trilling may have a point when, in *The Liberal Imagination*, he writes about *The Princess Casamassima* that the novel "has at its very center the assumption that Europe has reached the full of its ripeness and is passing over into rottenness, . . . that it may meet its end by violence and that this is not wholly unjust."[34]

There is no doubt that, with *The Bostonians* and *The Princess Casa-*

34. Lionel Trilling, *The Liberal Imagination: Essays in Literature and Society* (London: Mercury Books, 1961), p. 61.

massima, James had achieved a realism with a newly critical perspective on some of the foundations of contemporary bourgeois society. When James, early in 1888, wrote to William Dean Howells that his reputation as a novelist had been dreadfully injured by these two novels, at least part of the reason must be sought in the changing nature and social function of that criticism in fiction. James himself, as Edith Wharton recorded, genuinely suffered from a lifelong disappointment at his lack of popular recognition; but when we come to consider that, at the same time, commercialized publishing and cheap journalism began to achieve hitherto unprecedented dimensions, James' failure, at the height of his powers, to engage a contemporary middle-class audience reflected a crisis in literary communication not unlike the one that Thomas Hardy was to face a few years later when, after *Jude the Obscure* (1896), he gave up writing novels. Henry James, as is well known, after *The Tragic Muse* (1890) entertained similar plans, and he did, in fact, forsake the genre for a number of years when he turned to writing for the stage.

The crisis however, in which James found himself was not simply one induced by an unfortunate lack of public recognition. This factor, no doubt, must have had a powerfully unsettling effect on the author, but ultimately it was the larger constellation of social and ideological change which induced James to reconsider both the form and the function of the traditional type of novel that he was writing. It is, I think, not fortuitous that, even before *The Tragic Muse*, his vision of the relationship of art to politics involved a break with some of the most cherished illusions of the liberal imagination. In *The Princess Casamassima* there is, in connection with the perversion of the hero's illusion of the freedom of his will, the suggestion that, in the last resort, it is art which makes endurable the "bloody sell" of life. Whether or not Hyacinth is a Schopenhauerian hero,[35] James does begin to reassess, critically as well as sarcastically, the traditional relationship between art and society, between the function of the artist and the role of the politician. In *The Tragic Muse*, such reassessment leads him to a new and proud emphasis on the independence, the self-respect, and the uniqueness (if not the autonomy) of the role of the artist in society. The central figure in the novel, Nick Dormer, promising politician, begins to conceive of his future career as a liberal Member of Parliament as "talking a lot of rot" which "has nothing to do with the truth or the search for it: nothing to do with intelli-

35. Joseph J. Firebaugh, "A Schopenhauerian Novel: James's *The Princess Casamassima*," *Nineteenth Century Fiction* 23 (1958): 194f.

gence, or candor, or honor." In the context of the book such rejection of a well-prepared political career appears as a symptomatic break with the illusion that the late nineteenth-century liberal political ideology can in any respect serve as a valid vessel of a viable source of consciousness. Nick Dormer forsakes his politically influential fiancée: he rejects "the old false measure of success" and chooses to become an artist so as to be able to enjoy "the beauty of having been disinterested and independent; of having taken the world in the free, brave, personal way."[36]

The longing for a disinterested kind of independence, the preference for "the free, brave, personal way" must be read as symptomatic, not only of the changing position of the artist in bourgeois society, but also of the new foundations on which James sets out to redefine the function and the art of fiction. In that, he comes close to the Nietzschean position (as formulated by Thomas Mann) "that life can be justified only as an aesthetic phenomenon."[37] In this connection, the American novelist as well as the German philosopher respond to the late nineteenth-century crisis in ideology by sharing "the impulse to achieve a self-definition independent of one's national or class origins, the impulse to be free of the limitations imposed by a particular time and place."[38]

This involves vast consequences for the narrative form and communicative function of the novel—consequences which, in this context, can scarcely be hinted at. But perhaps it is not fortuitous that, beginning with *The Tragic Muse*, Henry James gradually begins to surrender some of the traditional forms of narrative representation and novelistic rhetoric. There is a connection, I suggest, between his hero's option for "the free, brave, personal way" and James's redefinition of the novel as a "direct, personal impression of life." In each case, it is the directness in the personal mode of relating oneself to reality that helps to leap over the crippling effects of the conventional "acceptations" and assumptions in the traditional ideology—what James calls the "ignorance," the "density," "the love of names and phrases, the love of hollow, idiotic words, of shutting the eyes tight and making a noise."[39] For the artist, the personal, direct impression is the "free" way and, be it noted, the "brave" way of apprehending and com-

36. Henry James, *The Tragic Muse* (Harmondsworth: Penguin Modern Classics, 1978), pp. 74f., 124f.

37. Stephen Donadio, *Nietzsche, Henry James and the Artistic Will* (New York: Columbia University Press, 1978), p. 61.

38. Donadio, p. 90.

39. *The Tragic Muse*, p. 75.

prehending the world—a way which, to an unprecedented degree, is independent of the distorting perspectives and the false consciousness in the dominant positions and presentations of contemporary ideology. As Van Wyck Brooks had put it, "ideals of this kind, in this way presented, in this way prepared for, cannot enrich life, because they are wanting in all the elements of personal contact."[40] Personal contact was just another form of obtaining "the personal, direct impression," through the direct rendering, in dialogue rather than authorial comment, of the business of living and feeling in society. Thus, the triumph and advance in the art of realism in the representation of consciousness, on the one hand, and the precariousness of the artist's isolation in society, on the other, were reciprocally related. James, much less than Howells and even Mark Twain, did not enjoy the benefits to be drawn from a broad social movement; he could not relate to a frame of reference in terms of which the idea and practice of democracy could be rejuvenated beyond the illusions and corruptions of liberalism. It was, surely, the price of his isolation from powerful forces in history that accounted for the "ambiguity" of his narrative technique which was to reach "a point where we almost feel that the author does not want the reader to get through to the hidden meaning."[41] James no doubt was the first of the great moderns to use narrative indeterminacy as almost a form of vengeance upon his audience. At the same time he turned back to webs of narrative about individuals who, with their highly cultivated and articulate sensibilities, realized themselves in an inordinate degree of consciousness and choice in the building up (or the destruction) of their relationships. Such novelistic images of highly cultivated individuals reflected and, at the same time, attempted to overcome the crisis in the function of the liberal ideology; for they resembled those "beautiful artifacts" which "were finally the only aspect of his high civilization which did not crumble when firmly grasped."[42]

40. Cf. note, 5.
41. Edmund Wilson, "The Ambiguity of Henry James," *The Triple Thinkers* (Harmondsworth: Penguin Books, 1962), p. 114.
42. Annette T. Rubinstein, "Henry James, American Novelist or: Isabel Archer, Emerson's Granddaughter," *Weapons of Criticism*, ed. Norman Rudich (Palo Alto CA: Rampart's Press, 1976), pp. 315f.

American Literature and the New Historicism:
The Example of Frederick Douglass

Gregory S. Jay

Rhetorics of History

Even seasoned observers of academic fashions may feel giddy notic-
ing the rise of something called the "New Historicism," especially as we
had just grown accustomed to pronouncements—whether celebratory or
derogatory—that there was no getting "beyond formalism." Like any label
for a movement in criticism, "New Historicism" serves more as an indicator
of associated tendencies than as the proper name for a specific or coherent school. Thus in accord with the accounts of Brook Thomas and David
Simpson, I will use "new historicism" in a quite general sense rather than
restrict it to the movement associated with Stephen Greenblatt (and consequently shall drop the capitalization of the phrase).[1] Thomas and Simpson agree that what makes this return to history "new" is the influence
of poststructuralism, which has undermined the premises of both the old

1. Brook Thomas, "The New Historicism and the Privileging of Literature," *Annals of
Scholarship* 4:4 (Summer 1987): 23–48; David Simpson, "Literary Criticism and the Return to 'History,'" *Critical Inquiry* 14:4 (Summer 1988): 721–47.

historicism and the aesthetic formalism which were two sides of a single theoretical coin.

As a professional sign, the phrase "new historicism" often signals a negative reaction to the legacies of New Criticism, structuralism, and deconstruction, each of which is perceived, rightly or wrongly, as insufficiently responsible to something called "history" (or "politics" or "society" or even "reality"). Alternatives offered by new historicism include a return to empirical scholarship, revivals of the critique of ideology, studies of how material conditions determine writing and publication, research on gender, race, and class in the production of literature, and inquiries into the structural affinities of representational and social systems.[2] At its best, new historicism reminds us of issues we have forgotten or repressed, expands the canon we study, and provides new methods for literary and cultural interpretation. At its worst, new historicism is the old historicism, or the old Marxism, or the old sociology of literature, or some confused mixture of these with current jargon and a bogus claim to the banner of political correctness.

As Judith Newton has shown, it is no accident that the revisionary return to history has paralleled the emergence of feminist, African-American, and postcolonial criticism.[3] Insofar as the old historicism centered the subject of development, teleology, and progress on the notion of the Spirit of Man, these critiques have decentered that historicism in demonstrating that the "Man" of History has usually been male, European, and middle or upper class. In various ways these movements have insisted on reading the intersection of the literary and the aesthetic with the historical and the political. Each in turn has been divided by its response to the poststructuralist revolt. The need to affirm the experience and identity of female, African-American, and non-European writers has, some argue, a priority over the philosophical deconstruction of identities and representations. Moreover the antifoundationalist character of poststructuralism is viewed as a disabling indulgence when it comes to the question of action. Meanwhile, mainstream critics increasingly turn to previously marginalized authors, such as Frederick Douglass, for examples that will illustrate the return of criticism to history and politics, since such a choice already implicitly questions the aesthetic, ideological, and institutional criteria that have

2. For an important warning against the conflation of Marxism and new historicism, however, see Carolyn Porter, "Are We Being Historical Yet?" *South Atlantic Quarterly* 87:4 (Fall 1988): 743–86.

3. Judith Newton, "History as Usual?: Feminism and the 'New Historicism,'" *Cultural Critique* 9 (Spring 1988): 87–122.

guided past literary scholarship. After a discussion of recent efforts to historicize criticism, then, I want to turn to the writings of Douglass, focusing principally on his *Narrative of the Life of Frederick Douglass, An American Slave, Written By Himself* (1845).[4] Specifically I shall explore a kind of rhetorical criticism that will situate the historical and political dimensions of Douglass's work without sacrificing the sense that current deconstructions of representation make any "return" to history or politics as grounded positivities an illusory goal at best.

Douglass's new status as a canonical figure originates not only in his race and class, and not simply in his position as an historical-political actor as well as writer, but also in the kinds of texts he produced and in the way they came into being. If the point of new historical criticism is not simply to describe the past, but to change it (and so the present and the future, too), then we are likely to focus on authors and texts that undertook similar missions. Feminist, African-American, and postcolonial studies practice a moral criticism insofar as their choice of authors and modes of commentary are informed by value judgments concerning what is "good" socially and politically rather than just aesthetically. The author of three autobiographies, a novella, and hundreds of speeches, Douglass worked in genres that challenge our theories of aesthetic form and literary reference. Their didactic and political intentions underscore their determination by extra-literary forces; this determination strengthens their claim to reference and thus underwrites critical commentaries that wish to use Douglass's work to link literature firmly to past and present political agendas (and thus sometimes tacitly to reject the "textualism" of poststructuralism).

However, Douglass's character as a *rhetorician*, both as a producer of public orations and as an author of private texts, proves an obstacle to any theory of his texts' referentiality, since Douglass so consistently relies on conventional artifices of representation to achieve his persuasive effects. I find this *aporia* (Paul de Man's term for undecidable impasses between statements and their forms of representation) to be an opportunity, rather than a catastrophe, for the "return to history." I would argue that historical understanding proceeds as an interpretive commentary on the specific character that this aporia between reference and representation takes *within* a particular work and *between* that work and the discourses and institutions that condition its production and reception. "Ideology" is but

4. Frederick Douglass, *The Narrative and Selected Writings*, ed. Michael Meyer (New York: Random House, 1984); hereafter cited parenthetically in my text.

a name for the bridging devices (or tropes) required to suspend such aporia and so enable communication, understanding, and action. (In this sense, there is no privileged critical position "outside" of ideology, but then again no particular ideology has the power to control every instance of expression in a given culture.) Thus, aporia is not the end of history, but the occasion for its (re)production.[5] This way of theorizing ideology draws on but complicates the "symbolic action" model for describing the text as a resolution of real social contradictions (a tradition running from Aristotle through Kenneth Burke, Northrop Frye, Lévi-Strauss, and Fredric Jameson).[6] The text's attempts to resolve its *own* contradictions may not be simply conflated with a symbolic resolution of some set of "external" social or material conditions. Nor can the internal contradictions and ideological suspension bridges of other discourses be simply described as homologous to those of a contemporary literary text. Rhetoric directs its work simultaneously, and sometimes incoherently, towards both what it conceives as "internal" formal or conceptual problems and what it represents to itself as the "external" conditions, forces, and persons it addresses.

In specific instances, then, the crossing of poststructuralism and deconstruction with the new historicism may result in the transformation and revival of rhetorical criticism. As such, rhetorical analysis needs to describe: (1) the set of discursive possibilities offered to the writer by the cultural archive; (2) the assumption within the text of a contemporary audience whose knowledge must both be used and resisted; (3) the projection within the text of a future audience constituted by its decipherment of the text; (4) the social and institutional sites of the text's production and reception; (5) the figurations of subjectivity offered or deployed by the text; (6) the effects of reflexivity inscribed in the text; (7) and the possible contradictions between the text's cognitive, performative, didactic, aesthetic, psychological, and economic projects. In reading Douglass's rhetoric, and in particular the relation between his self-representations and the political movements of his time, I hope to sketch a mode of commentary that attends equally to history's dictates and language's powers; in questioning his texts' referential status I mean to deepen and disseminate, rather than dissolve, the political agenda to which his work belongs. In this I will follow cur-

5. For an elaboration of this argument see my essay, "Paul de Man: The Subject of Literary History," *MLN* 103:5 (December 1988): 969–94.
6. For a recent endorsement and application of this model see Brook Thomas, *Cross-examinations of Law and Literature: Cooper, Hawthorne, Stowe, and Melville* (Cambridge: Cambridge University Press, 1987), pp. 6–7.

rent African-American theorists who view the representational character of "racial" identity as opening a site for progressive historical struggle, one to be preferred over the paralyzing (and false) choice between affirming a socially constructed identity and nihilistically rejecting any self-naming at all. "Rhetoric" will become my word for this site, as well as naming a kind of commentary that situates textuality materially in the social moment, historical stage, and ideological drama of its (rhetoric's, the text's, the commentary's) production.

New American Historicisms

The accounts by Thomas and Simpson make it unnecessary to rehearse here the rise of the new historicism. In sum, new historicism differs from the old historicism when (and if) it postulates theories of the historical which extend and correct the general critique of positivism, empiricism, chronology, causation, and representation proffered by structuralism and deconstruction. This general critique prevents us from assuming that we know what history is, where it takes place, who makes it, and whether history is ever distinct from the manner of its representations. At the same time, the study of representation is always in danger of lapsing back into a formalism that overlooks the social and institutional history of texts, as well as the power relations that inform all intellectual inquiry. Like the old historicism, the new historicism places the text among the events of its own time, reconstituting that context and deciphering the way in which history informs the practice of the text, and the way in which texts inform the practices of history. Unlike the old historicism, the new historicism disseminates the boundaries of what constitutes the text's "context," proliferating a seemingly infinite series of discursive, material, and institutional histories that overdetermine the text. New historicism claims to have a new idea of what history *is*, both in terms of what objects critics study and how self-conscious critics are about the way they study them. It questions the "privileging of literature" even as it extends textualist ontology into the being of historicity itself. And it rejects models of historical totality even as it seeks to describe the culture formed by the specific competing and interactive material and discursive forces of the disparate subcultures. The contexts new historicism produces for the text, and the way it reads the relation of texts and contexts, should avoid the prejudices and errors and naivete of the old historicism, especially its complacency about what properly belongs to history and its failure to question how its own agenda defines, retrospectively, the stories we authorize about the past.

216

The Americanist school of new historicism sees itself primarily as a revolution against what Carolyn Porter rightly called the "American ahistoricism" of such critics as F. O. Matthiessen, Richard Chase, R. W. B. Lewis, Leslie Fiedler, and Charles Feidelson.[7] Turning against the social progressivism of Parrington and away from the Marxism of the 1930s, this tradition of study applied the tenets of the New Criticism to the symbolism, language, and moral ambiguities of "classic American literature," a canon of works often consisting of the same familiar (white male) names: Hawthorne, Emerson, Thoreau, Melville, Whitman, Twain, James, and Eliot. These authors were usually portrayed as seeking aesthetic or psychological alternatives to life in society, an escapism still dominating the thematics of such brilliant books as Richard Poirier's *A World Elsewhere* and Leo Marx's *The Machine in the Garden*. In a pioneering study too often overlooked, H. Bruce Franklin traced the history of aestheticism and racism that produced this canon, including the textbooks and pedagogical attitudes supporting it.[8] Franklin's analysis of canon formation and his proposal that slave narratives be placed at the center of American literary history acutely forecast the concerns of subsequent work on African-American and women writers. Franklin's main example is Douglass's *Narrative*. Porter continued Franklin's argument by demonstrating that this critical tradition repeated, rather than analyzed, the alienation from society and economic life represented by these authors, and so these critics missed the real and powerful historical dimensions of such texts.

The attempt to combine new historicism with ideology critique can be sampled in the collection edited by Sacvan Bercovitch and Myra Jehlen, strangely entitled *Ideology and Classic American Literature*.[9] What seems odd here, of course, is the retention of the "classic" canon: while the editors may have intended this ironically, or as a deconstructive reinscription, the fact remains that the vast bulk of articles treat the same expected figures and perform no substantive displacement of the notion of the "classic" that the title somewhat opportunistically exploits. The singular exception

7. Carolyn Porter, *Seeing and Being: The Plight of the Participant Observer in Emerson, James, Adams, and Faulkner* (Middletown: Wesleyan University Press, 1981). For a critique of Porter's book see my "America The Scrivener: Economy and Literary History," *Diacritics* 14:1 (1984): 36–51.

8. H. Bruce Franklin, *The Victim as Criminal and Artist* (New York: Oxford University Press, 1978).

9. Sacvan Bercovitch and Myra Jehlen, eds., *Ideology and Classic American Literature* (Cambridge: Cambridge University Press, 1986).

is an excerpt from Houston Baker's *Blues, Ideology, and Afro-American Literature* which treats the economics of slavery in Douglass's *Narrative*.[10] Jehlen's introduction attempts to justify the use of "ideology" as a key term for the volume, and it proceeds through a rather awkward summary of the term's various definitions and uses, until one wonders what—beyond its connotations of proper political skepticism—the term's usefulness could be.

In his review of this and other volumes by what he calls the "New Americanists," Frederick Crews observes that Jehlen's recourse to "ideology" in the pejorative sense, while it usefully corrects the masking of political interests by aesthetic arguments, ultimately falls victim to its own binary logic.[11] The New Americanists debunk the ideological pretense that "great art must be decoupled from the struggle for social dominance." Aesthetic ideology "makes sense to them as a repressive strategy, a means of keeping the lid on divisive differences of interest such as those between slave masters and slaves, land clearers and those whose territory was thereby seized, and more recently between the purveyors of 'Americanness' criticism and the groups that find their traditions frozen out by that criticism" (74). Foucault and Crews notwithstanding, there remains a formidable dimension of truth in the repressive hypothesis, though not when it takes the form of a binary opposition between ideology and demystification. Poststructuralism begins, as it did for the Roland Barthes of *S/Z*, with the deconstruction of this opposition. Crews points out the contradiction involved when the methods used to debunk white male writers are cast aside in efforts to canonize and affirm formerly marginalized authors (though I sense I have more sympathy with this process than does Crews). In the latter cases, one should not lose sight of the interdependence of analytic and prescriptive historicism or of the fundamentally moral character of the premises for this kind of literary history. In other words, accusing others of having an ideology can become a way of avoiding the responsibility for justifying one's own. Jehlen does not respond to the displacement of "ideology" as a master term worked out by Derrida and other poststructuralists. The use of ideology as an umbrella term allows the editors to evade, rather than confront, the tough question of how to conceive the historicity of writing after we have deconstructed such notions as the "idea" and the "logos," or "matter," "economy," and even "sign."

10. Houston Baker, *Blues, Ideology, and Afro-American Literature* (Chicago: University of Chicago Press, 1984).
11. Frederick Crews, "Whose American Renaissance?" *New York Review of Books*, 27 October 1988, pp. 68–81.

In contrast, Walter Benn Michaels's collection of essays, *The Gold Standard and the Logic of Naturalism*, swings to the other extreme by contending that "ideology" is a name for a nonexistent phenomenon.[12] Michaels dissents from "the genteel/Progressive view of important works of art as in some sense transcending or opposing the market," a view he finds even in recent "oppositional criticism." Michaels condescendingly brushes aside such a description, or use, of literature for cultural criticism: "transforming the moral handwringing of the fifties and sixties first into the epistemological handwringing of the seventies and now into the political handwringing of the eighties does not seem to be much of an advance" (15, n.16). With some glee he attempts to show that works such as Charlotte Gilman's "The Yellow Wallpaper" epitomize, rather than demystify, the culture of marketplace consumption. Similarly, Michaels criticizes his own previous work on Dreiser (nonetheless reprinted as the volume's opening chapter) for trying to assess "Dreiser's attitude toward capitalism: it depended on imagining a Dreiser outside capitalism who could then be said to have attitudes toward it" (19).

Michaels's version of the new historicism will then pursue what Simpson calls an "analytic" description of cultural totalities as it eschews any prescriptive reading of history's itinerary or, even worse (in his opinion), any indulgence in the problems of ethical and moral judgment. Michaels defines his project in explaining why he chose the term "naturalism," rather than "realism," for the period in question:

> Insofar as naturalism has been continually (and plausibly) defined as a variant of realism, it has been caught up in endless theorizing about the nature and very possibility of realistic representation: do texts refer to social reality? if they do, do they merely reflect it or do they criticize it? and if they do not, do they try to escape it, or do they imagine utopian alternatives to it? Like the question of whether Dreiser liked or disliked capitalism, these questions seem to me to posit a space outside culture in order then to interrogate the relations between that space (here defined as literary) and the culture. But the spaces I have tried to explore are all very much within the culture, and so the project of interrogation makes no sense; the only relation literature as such has to culture as such is that it is part of it. (27)

12. Walter Benn Michaels, *The Gold Standard and the Logic of Naturalism: American Literature at the Turn of the Century* (Berkeley: University of California Press, 1987).

A number of fallacies are at work in this neo-pragmatist version of historicism. While Michaels rightly rejects a schema that makes "literature" the privileged "outside" to culture's nefarious determinations, he does so by ignoring how texts are constituted by a complex and often contradictory set of attitudes towards the heterogeneous archive which in turn constitutes the culture to which it belongs. It would be absurd to suggest that a text, or an author such as Dreiser, contained no contradictions, and Michaels's own keen readings everywhere show that they do. Michaels might respond that such contradictions nonetheless belong to the "culture," not to some space "outside" of it. Yet this transforms "culture," a priori, into an organic totality which is all "inside" and no "outside." Michaels must idealize the historical period's many events and discourses into the monolith of "the culture" in order to contain the question of opposition "within" it, and so tacitly to disable "oppositional criticism." His own criticism, then, in adopting a variant of antifoundational pragmatism, caricatures "culture" as a totality both organic *and* mechanical—since it automatically enforces its assumptions upon its subjects without their having the capacity to resist it. There is truly a sophistry in arguing that Dreiser (or the literary critic) cannot dislike or interrogate the culture he belongs to; this presupposes that the culture exists as a single attitude or belief, whereas cultures are uneven, changeable, and provisional associations of individuals, groups, artifacts, and institutions, any one of which may provide the basis for the evaluation or interrogation of the other. Michaels's dismissal of moral, epistemological, and political problematics as so much intellectual detritus ultimately produces a theoretical position that is profoundly conservative (or even reactionary).

Whereas Michaels's version of a poststructuralist new historicism provides no point for opposition and change, Russell Reising's neo-Marxist resistance to poststructuralism provides him with all too many. Reising resumes Carolyn Porter's argument and critiques the careers of major American literary theorists after WW II. Reising's "Conclusion: The Significance of Frederick Douglass" attempts to illustrate his thesis that "theorists of American literature have failed adequately to approach American texts in a specifically cultural and social context."[13] By placing Douglass "within the mainstream" of what Matthiessen called "the American Renaissance," Reising alters our sense of the literary canon and suggests a re-historicized reading of figures such as Emerson, Thoreau, Hawthorne, Melville, and

13. Russell Reising, *The Unusable Past: Theory and the Study of American Literature* (New York: Methuen, 1986), p. 17.

Stowe (269). But his analysis uses too many of the terms of traditional literary history—beginning with the dubious "American Renaissance"—and does not exactly spell out how to relate texts to their "material and historical context."

Rather than set aside the kind of hierarchical canon formation his book has criticized, Reising chooses to nominate Douglass "as a literary artist and thinker of the first rank" and to argue that his *Narrative* "anticipates" many of the themes of the period's major figures, including that most ahistorical theme of "an individual's relationship with his community" (257). Yet there is no single community in Douglass's world, neither of whites divided geographically and culturally nor of blacks whose disparate social formations exist only within prescribed limits. And when, if ever, Douglass becomes an "individual" is a major interpretive crux of his autobiographies, not a grounded term upon which a reading can be based. One should insist, on the contrary, on reading Douglass's and other antebellum texts by placing them within specific discursive histories. These would include the legacy of the eighteenth-century idea of Enlightenment rationality and legal personhood; the dialogue of that legacy with Romantic theories of genius and individuality; the corresponding rise of the moral psychology of sentiment and its emotional epistemology, which plays such a strong role in the literature of this period; the informing power of gender in the literary marketplace and its representations of social and moral realities; the formal conventions of slavery literature—pro and con—already popular in Douglass's time; and of course the relation of all these discourses to the rise of economic structures and social institutions that supported or were antithetical to them. Even a "Marxist" reading should never assume the isolate existence of "the individual" or "the community" in this period, but examine the crisis involved in the *invention* of both.

Poststructuralism and the African-American Text

How, then, might one proceed to conduct a reading of Douglass that might be both literary and historical, rhetorical and political? Whereas Reising largely dismisses poststructuralism, a new generation of African-American critics, including Houston Baker, Hazel Carby, and Henry Louis Gates, Jr., are adapting the critique of representation to their readings of black literature and criticism. According to Gates, "We urgently need to direct our attention to the nature of black figurative language, to the nature of black narrative forms, to the history and theory of Afro-American criticism, to the fundamental relation of form and content, and to the arbitrary relationships between the sign and the referent."[14] Gates builds upon the arguments of Baker, Peter Walker, and Robert Stepto to reject any naive or politically reductive view of black autobiographical works as straightforward accounts of life, and his example is again Douglass.[15] The strategic revisions that went into the successive versions of his autobiographies show, in Gates's words, that "Douglass was demonstrably concerned with the representation in written language of his public self, a self Douglass created, manipulated, and transformed, if ever so slightly, through the three fictive selves he posited in his three autobiographies" (103). One might add that the portrait is considerably complicated by the personae orchestrated in Douglass's hundreds of recorded speeches—oratorical performances that took many liberties with the facts and which alternately fashioned Douglass in the figure of the slave, the preacher, the criminal, the saint, the journalist, the worker, the revolutionary, the son, the father, and the prophet.

Other black critics, notably women, have expressed their disagreement with the work of Baker and Gates, citing Audre Lorde's maxim that "The master's tools will never dismantle the master's house."[16] As in the controversies between humanism and poststructuralism or feminism and poststructuralism, the anti-essentialism of deconstructive theories is seen as a threat to the imperative need for an affirmative politics of identity. Each side, however, is committed to the common task of rewriting the history of African-American literature and asserting its power to resist the master's dictates. Such recent innovations in African-American criticism can assist

14. Henry Louis Gates, Jr., *Figures in Black: Words, Signs, and the 'Racial' Self* (New York: Oxford University Press, 1987), p. 41.
15. See Robert B. Stepto, *From Behind the Veil: A Study of Afro-American Narrative* (Urbana: University of Illinois Press, 1979); and Peter Walker, *Moral Choices: Memory, Desire, and Imagination in Nineteenth-Century American Abolition* (Baton Rouge: Louisiana State University Press), 1978.
16. Joyce A. Joyce cites Lorde in her reply to the responses of Gates and Baker to her critique of their position. See Joyce, "The Black Canon: Reconstructing Black American Literary Criticism," *New Literary History* 18:2 (1987): 335–44, and " 'Who the Cap Fit': Unconsciousness and Unconscionableness in the Criticism of Houston A. Baker, Jr., and Henry Louis Gates, Jr.," *New Literary History* 18:2 (1987): 371–84; Houston Baker, "In Dubious Battle," *New Literary History* 18:2 (1987): 363–69; and Henry Louis Gates, Jr., " 'What's Love Got to Do with It?': Critical Theory, Integrity, and the Black Idiom," *New Literary History* 18:2 (1987): 345–62. For a commentary on this debate see Michael Awkward, "Race, Gender, and the Politics of Reading," *Black American Literature Forum* 22:1 (Spring 1988): 6–27.

222

in the radical rearrangement of historical and literary periods and their canonical contents; of ways of writing history and literary criticism; and of the very issues defined as constituting the essence of the American story. In the realm of literary theory, however, this rewriting should not proceed on the basis of outmoded stereotypes of black writing as realistic, mimetic, descriptive, documentary, referential, or somehow less literary and more political than white texts.

Though cautious about adopting the white man's critical theories, black feminist critics such as Hazel Carby are reopening the question of history and representation in their accounts of women in African-American writing. Carby cautions against the mimetic fallacy and any essentialist theory of black female experience or language. For Carby, "language is a terrain of power relations. This struggle within and over language reveals the nature of the structure of social relations and the hierarchy of power, not the nature of one particular group. The sign, then, is an arena of struggle and a construct between socially organized persons in the process of their interactions; the forms that signs take are conditioned by the social organization of the participants involved and also by the immediate conditions of their interaction." [17] Linguistic power, then, is more than a negative or disciplinary agency: it establishes and sustains a social group's life and character. Language is enabling, positing, and persuasive as well as oppressive. Carby's account does show the traces of a deterministic materialism in which signs are "conditioned by the social organization" while the conditioning of social organization by signs is passed over. Nonetheless, her argument marks a significant moment in African-American theoretical debate as well as in the general discussion of how to articulate the historical with the literary.

Baker and Gates share this view of language as a terrain of social struggle. In their work on Douglass, they stress the dialectic of subjection and empowerment inherent to the African-American's achievement of literacy in his master's tongue. (Thus they provide a sometimes explicit allegory justifying their own use of the Euro-American masters' theoretical tools.) For the slave the achievement of literacy is itself a political and even metaphysical revolution, as it defies the dominant culture's negative definition of her or his very human being. Slaves are defined by a lack of civilization, reason, and the capacity for articulate expression; the equa-

17. Hazel V. Carby, *Reconstructing Womanhood: The Emergence of the Afro-American Woman Novelist* (New York: Oxford University Press, 1987), pp. 16–17.

tion of logos, soul, and being works to exclude the black from the category "human." In his 1855 autobiography, *My Bondage and My Freedom*, Douglass recalls that "I was generally introduced as a *'chattel'*—a *'thing'*—a piece of southern *'property'*—the chairman assuring the audience that *it* could speak."[18] The inherent antagonism between black speaker and white language means that a distancing, a revision, or a troping of language will always be fundamental to the style of black discourse, a phenomenon Gates calls "signifyin' " (*Figures* 48–54).

In *The Journey Back*, Baker describes the complex fate which awaited those black Americans who first sought to articulate their experiences of slavery in the New World. Robbed of their native culture, they had lost their tongue, their means of self-definition and expression. Thrust into an alien land, they had to learn the language of the oppressors, which they then would have to turn to their own purposes. Of the slave, Baker writes that "he first had to seize the word. His being had to erupt from nothingness. Only by grasping the word could he engage in the speech acts that would ultimately define his selfhood."[19] He would have to parrot, then parody, then talk back to, his master's voice. For Baker and others, the *Narrative* of Frederick Douglass is the exemplary tale of this linguistic alienation; moreover, it foregrounds the achievement of literacy as the key to liberation. But Baker argues (36–37) that because Douglass must adopt the rhetoric of the dominant culture—especially its Christian morals and sentimental psychology—to define his experience, he inevitably misses the otherness of black life even as he represents it: "Had there been a separate, written black language available, Douglass might have fared better. . . . The nature of the autobiographer's situation seemed to force him to move to a public version of the self—one molded by the values of white America" (39). *The Journey Back* shows this estrangement not only increasing towards the *Narrative*'s close, but also overwhelming (and degrading) Douglass's subsequent autobiographical writings until he resembles none other than the Uncle Tomish Booker T. Washington, to whom Douglass has always been compared since the waning of his reputation in the 1870s and 1880s.

It is wrong, however, to establish the discussion on terms contrasting an "authentically lived experience" with its "mistranslation" or "betrayal

18. Frederick Douglass, *My Bondage and My Freedom*, ed. and with an introduction by William L. Andrews (Urbana: University of Illinois Press, 1987), p. 220.
19. Houston Baker, *The Journey Back: Issues in Black Literature and Criticism* (Chicago: University of Chicago Press, 1980), p. 31.

into language." The availability of a native language does not guarantee an unalienated speech or a mimetic transcription. Nor are such languages homogeneous in their cultural representations of lived experience. Since blacks had never lived as slaves in America before, they of course could have had no language for this life, no native "terms of order" for the experience. Had they been able to perpetuate their African languages and cultures they might have had a nonwhite rhetoric to figure their experience, but then they would not in that case have *had* the experience, for slavery meant precisely the cultural expropriation and transformation of a people. Douglass had no choice but to draw upon the cultural archive of white society and then transform his materials rhetorically. For example, Baker misleadingly characterizes Douglass's appendix on Christianity as trying to justify his status as a true Christian. Actually the appendix continues Douglass's assault on the institutional and political practice of Christianity in the United States, keeping strictly to the policy of Garrisonian abolitionism in its harsh critique of religion's role in the slave states. The "true" Christianity Douglass endorses is a *figure* for a morality quite other than that of the professedly "true" Christians of the United States, North and South. In adopting their rhetoric and their religion, he inserts an otherness into both, gives voice to the hypocrisies and flaws within them, and thus puts an alien discourse serviceably to work for the black experience.

In *Blues, Ideology, and Afro-American Literature*, Baker takes his concern with writing in a more avowedly poststructuralist direction, though this is combined with cultural anthropology and a strong dose of neo-Marxism as well. Here he calls the *Narrative*'s rhetoric a "palimpsest" in which a deeper level belies the figurations offered at the surface. "The tones of a Providentially oriented moral suasion," he argues, "eventually compete with the cadences of a secularly oriented economic voice."[20] Baker reads the "economic coding" in Douglass as a tale of the expropriation of "surplus value" in Marx's sense. He attributes this knowledge to Douglass himself who now turns out to be anything but an Uncle Tom or Booker T.: "Douglass heightens the import of this economic coding through implicit and ironic detailing of the determination of general cultural consciousness *by commerce*" (45). Douglass "has arrived at a fully commercial view of his situation" by the book's latter half, says Baker, and despite Douglass's idyllic representation of New England's commerce, Baker finds him slyly subverting this traffic by the very act of writing and selling his story: "The

20. Baker, *Blues, Ideology, and Afro-American Literature*, p. 43.

nineteenth-century slave in effect, *publicly* sells his voice in order to secure *private* ownership of his voice-person" (50; Baker's emphasis). As a salaried spokesman for Garrison's American Anti-Slavery Society, Douglass turns surplus value towards the cause of liberation.

Baker's new reading of Douglass leaves two important questions in its wake. First, is the representation of surplus value in Douglass's *Narrative* a sign of the author's knowledge or a trace of documentation, that is, a trace of the real which *we* make apparent by recourse to Marxist theory? Second, does the *Narrative* unfold progressively towards an "ultimate convergence" in this knowledge, or do the economic and moral codes operating in Douglass's rhetoric more often run at cross-purposes or into aporias that no narrative or history can totalize? A comparison to another autobiography of antebellum America, Thoreau's *Walden*, might be of use here, since the latter should be considered—historically as well as theoretically—as another escaped slave's narrative. The opening chapter on "Economy" skillfully deploys the diction of business metaphorically, thus undoing the denotational and alienating value system that money and its powers enforce. "But men labor under a mistake," Thoreau writes, when materialist objectivity and possessiveness rule their perceptions.[21] They undertake Herculean labors in order to acquire and maintain properties. It is in this context that Thoreau writes: "I sometimes wonder that we can be so frivolous, I may almost say, as to attend to the gross but somewhat foreign form of servitude called Negro Slavery, there are so many keen and subtle masters that enslave North and South. It is hard to have a Southern overseer; it is worse to have a Northern one; but worst of all when you are the slave-driver of yourself" (4). It is a point made earlier by Emerson in his "Lecture on the Times," and one feels compelled to point out the luxury of the observation for these two white men of privileged New England.[22] Yet the power of Thoreau's language to abstract extravagantly—to play and pun and generalize—allows his text to articulate a critique of capitalism in a way strikingly different from Douglass's text.

Like the Transcendentalists, Douglass will represent individual emancipation of the soul as the heart of the quest for freedom, relegating economic and political issues to the margins. The reliance of the *Narra-*

21. Henry David Thoreau, *Walden and Civil Disobedience*, Norton Critical Edition, ed. Owen Thomas (New York: Norton, 1966).
22. Ralph Waldo Emerson, "Lecture on the Times," *Works*, (Boston: Houghton, Mifflin and Company, 1883): Vol. 1, pp. 266–67.

tive on the rhetoric of religious and moral truth actually works to preclude a wider study of slavery's historical dimensions; Thoreau, by virtue of his style, ties slavery North and South to a myriad of economic, philosophical, social, scientific, and literary events in his age. As Douglass speaks of his experiences in the South, and in the Maryland shipyards and in Nantucket, his criticism of racial and working class conflicts always stresses the religious and the moral over the monetary, eliding or obscuring the essentially capitalist nature of the slave industry. When Douglass introduces the story of his "resistance" to the overseer Covey, he declares: "You have seen how a man was made a slave; you shall see how a slave was made a man" (75). I shall return later to this crucial chapter and its 1855 revision, but here the important point is the Transcendentalist cast of Douglass's "glorious resurrection" after the fight: "My long-crushed spirit rose, cowardice departed, bold defiance took its place, and I now resolved that, however long I might remain a slave in form, the day had passed forever when I could be a slave in fact" (81). It is difficult to see the difference between this declaration and Thoreau's insistence that the essence of slavery lies in the individual's failure to enact a radical program of self-conception or self-reliance. Douglass here portrays slavery as a psychological or moral "fact" and relegates its economy to mere "form." His identification of freedom with economic self-determination leads, as many have noted, to the complicity of his discourse with the laissez-faire capitalism that had produced slavery in the first place.[23]

Later in the book Douglass confronts the economics of slavery more directly when he hires his time out at the shipyard. The introduction of wage labor into the schema of slavery makes the expropriation of the value of the slave's labor easier to recognize, since it appears in the ready representation of coinage: "I was now getting . . . one dollar and fifty cents per day. I contracted for it; I earned it; it was paid to me; it was rightfully my own; yet, upon each returning Saturday night, I was compelled to deliver every cent of that money to Master Hugh" (104). Douglass calls this expropriation by "power" a kind of "piracy," but he does not expressly see any analogy

23. William Andrews argues that Douglass goes from being a chattel slave to being the political slave of Garrison and that only in the 1850s, with the writing of *My Bondage*, does Douglass liberate himself. See Andrews, "The 1850s: The First Afro-American Literary Renaissance," in Andrews, ed., *Literary Romanticism in America* (Baton Rouge: Louisiana State University Press, 1981), pp. 38–60; and *To Tell a Free Story: The First Century of Afro-American Autobiography, 1760–1865* (Urbana: University of Illinois Press, 1986), pp. 214–39.

between wage labor *per se* and the expropriation of the value of the slave's labor. It is in regard to this moment, I think, that Baker overstates his case for Douglass's knowledge. The partly feudal and relatively primitive character of southern slavery as a mode of production dictates that the subject it produces will perceive private property as a desired, if currently prohibited, goal. Slavery, as the alienation of the body itself, is especially likely to produce discourses that privilege the sanctity of private property, though this is generally true for the historical development of capitalist thought as it follows the increased production, distribution, and access to private property after the Renaissance. Since the overt design of the *Narrative* rests on the acquisition of freedom and the ownership of one's own body, Douglass's argument tends to merge quite neatly with the emergent social formation of American capitalism and its thinking about private property. Only from the standpoint of a different historical moment, or from within the subjectivity of a different class relation, will private property appear to be itself an alienating notion, as it is for Thoreau.

When Douglass arrives in New Bedford after his escape, he contrasts its "proofs of wealth" with the squalid conditions characteristic of the South, polemically reversing the common portraits offered by proslavery writers. In New Bedford, "Every man appeared to understand his work, and went at it with a sober, yet cheerful earnestness, which betokened the deep interest which he felt in what he was doing, as well as a sense of his own dignity as a man" (116). These pages could be compared to Thoreau's harsh description of economic labor at the outset of *Walden*, where the enslavement of the body towards material ends leads to "mean and sneaking lives" of corruption, "trying to get into business and trying to get out of debt, a very ancient slough, called by the Latins *aes alienum*, another's brass" (4). Thoreau's punning perception of the alienation inherent in labor under capitalism contrasts sharply with the teleology of freedom and manhood in Douglass. Situated historically, this difference may be thought of in terms of the unevenness of development separating white economics from black. Never having worked through to the stage of wage labor, Douglass cannot be expected to theorize the contradictions awaiting the worker at that next turn in the dialectic. Thoreau, however, from the standpoint of a laboring middle-class now being subordinated to mass industrial capitalism, and thus threatened with the loss of a purely private or individual control over production and market-value, is positioned to speak about a different phase in the history of political economy and its subjects.

This brief comparison of Douglass and Thoreau suggests, as I have argued, that the intersection of language and history should be read through a kind of *rhetorical* analysis which combines a poststructural critique of representation with a constant attention to the text's conditions of production. *Walden* and the *Narrative* were not texts produced by artists in tortured seclusion writing only for themselves or posterity. They were didactic, performative discourses designed to make a difference in their culture's public affairs. They worked, sometimes self-consciously and sometimes not, with the modes of representation informing the communities of their time.

Frederick Douglass: The Speech of the Historical Agent

In rhetorical terms, Douglass's *Narrative* must be situated in the literary histories of the sermon, the political stump-speech, the sentimental novel, the slave narrative, and the reform lecture among others. The often-discussed "realism" of Douglass's text is not simply mimetic but owes much to the required style and topoi of these genres. Often ghost-written by white abolitionists, pamphlets telling the tales of escaped slaves countered the "master's moonlight and magnolias portrait of slavery" with their own stock story, a "dramatic, sometimes starkly horrifying, and hard-hitting eyewitness account of human bondage from the vantage point of one of its victims."[24] Douglass drew on the devices of these stories for his public orations, which often lasted more than two spellbinding hours.

Douglass began speaking at abolitionist meetings in 1841, three years after his escape, and became literally an agent of Garrison's American Anti-Slavery Society. As a speaking subject, Douglass becomes the agency through which the literary and social ideologies of his time speak, and his autonomy is consistently undermined by his role as agent. Yet as Baker and Gates argue, Douglass's mastery of the master's tongue transforms him from the dictated subject of ideology into the agent of historical (and literary) change. Douglass's texts, then, are exemplary in that their subject is neither a predetermined automaton of the Symbolic nor a so-called autonomous self freely creating its world. The metaphor of agency suggests rather that the subject occupies a dynamic historical position in which he or she may at once be the medium for ideology's reproduction and the device for its undoing. For the Symbolic cannot reproduce itself without agents, and this dependence creates a supplementary relation of

24. William Loren Katz, ed., *Five Slave Narratives* (New York: Arno Press, 1968), pp. xviii–xix.

ideology to agency that opens up the space for a difference (though not for any imaginary liberation of "free will").

The first version of the *Narrative* was not published until 1845, some four years after he became an agent. It is tempting to see the *Narrative* as the polished public version of an address delivered many times during those years as Douglass repeated the heartfelt truth of his former life. In *My Bondage and My Freedom*, Douglass himself maintains that "during the first three or four months, my speeches were almost exclusively made up of narrations of my own personal experience as a slave" (360–61). Critics often repeat Douglass's story of how his white abolitionist friends Foster, Collins, and Garrison pressured him to stick to this simple narrative, avoid abstract pronouncements, and pepper his eloquence with "a *little* of the plantation manner of speech" (361–62). According to Douglass, writing after his bitter break with the Garrisonians in the early 1850s, the dramatic and largely empirical style of the book is partly a result of the censorship he suffered on the podium. As an escaped slave, his job was to witness his suffering objectively, not to assume the authority to speak *in principle* or as an *authority*, for this even his largely white abolitionist audience would not accept. "It did not entirely satisfy me to *narrate* wrongs; I felt like *denouncing* them" (361–62). Thus the predominance of "verisimilitude" over "abstract and reflective" knowledge in the *Narrative* of 1845 is not the result simply of its unified argument for a materialist epistemology, as Reising would have it. Rather it indicates the formal limitations of the slave narrative genre and its site of production.

Yet the matter is not quite this simple. John W. Blassingame argues that "Douglass exaggerated the restrictions placed on him during his first months," as "white abolitionists advised him *not* to give the details of his slave experience for fear that he might be recaptured. The private letters of white abolitionists and news accounts published between 1841 and 1845 furnish little evidence to support Douglass's assertion."[25] In fact from the start Douglass spoke on a wide range of general topics and denounced slavery, Christian hypocrisy, and northern racism.[26] Douglass's speeches, like the *Narrative* and his subsequent autobiographies, framed their illustrative episodes and examples with lengthy passages of exhortation, ridicule,

25. John W. Blassingame, ed., *The Frederick Douglass Papers, Series One: Speeches, Debates, and Interviews* (New Haven: Yale University Press, 1979), 1:xlviii.
26. See Waldo E. Martin, Jr., *The Mind of Frederick Douglass* (Chapel Hill: University of North Carolina Press, 1984), pp. 22–23.

and denunciation. While the reliability of these early newspaper transcripts is questionable, one finds in them little of the plantation speech and self-humbling Douglass purportedly adopted.

In October of 1841, the *Pennsylvania Freeman* published the first extant account of Douglass's rhetoric. In it he does begin with a confession of embarrassment, a resolution to tell of his bloody personal experience in slavery, and introduces his often-to-be-repeated story of how Thomas Auld quoted from the Bible as he whipped Douglass's lame cousin Henny. He concludes, however, by bluntly stating that "emancipation, my friends, is [the] cure for slavery and its evils. It alone will give to the south peace and quietness. It will blot out the insults we have borne, will heal the wounds we have endured, and are even now groaning under, will pacify the resentment which would kindle to a blaze were it not for your exertions, and, though it may never unite the many kindred and dear friends which slavery has torn asunder, it will be received with gratitude and a forgiving spirit."[27] What Douglass may have resented in retrospect was the relative generosity of this rhetoric, which spoke in the voice of a cautious abolitionism that hesitated to condemn its audience. Yet if the bitter sarcasm that would later characterize Douglass's best writing and speeches is absent in these lines, the seeds of its growth appear a bit later in the paragraph when Douglass turns to the topic of Northern racism: "The northern people think that if slavery were abolished, we would all come north. They may be more afraid of the free colored people and the runaway slaves going south. We would all seek our home and our friends, but, more than all, to escape from northern prejudice, would we go to the south. Prejudice against color is stronger north than south; it hangs around my neck like a heavy weight."[28]

Editorial accounts frequently mentioned the force of Douglass's sarcastic oratory, and the published speeches from the period 1841 to 1845 show Douglass fully in command of various rhetorical postures as he speaks on a wide range of issues. In the *Herald of Freedom* of 16 February 1844, editor Nathaniel P. Rogers reported that Douglass "began by a calm, deliberate and very simple narrative of his life," including numerous incidents later represented in the *Narrative*. Rogers found it "interesting all the while for its facts, but dullish in manner . . . though I discerned, at times, symptoms of a brewing storm." Douglass "closed his slave narrative, and gradually let out the outraged humanity that was laboring in him, in indignant and

27. *Papers* 1:4.
28. *Papers* 1:5.

terrible speech. It was not what you could describe as oratory or eloquence. It was sterner, darker, deeper than these. It was the volcanic outbreak of human nature long pent up in slavery and at last bursting its imprisonment. It was the storm of insurrection. . . . He was not up as a speaker—performing. He was an insurgent slave taking hold on the right of speech, and charging on his tyrants the bondage of his race." [29] Of course Douglass *was* "up as a speaker—performing." His skill lay in *impersonating* a *natural* eloquence, so as to link the antislavery cause to the eternal moral truths of the human heart (obscuring slavery's economic and political dimensions). This naturalization of his oratory would in effect make Douglass more palatable, as it effaced his capacity for cultural education and thus made him, as a black man, more a thing of nature than of culture.

On 6 May 1845, just prior to the publication of the *Narrative*, Douglass addressed the Twelfth Annual Convention of the American Anti-Slavery Society in New York City's Broadway Tabernacle. He previewed the contents of the book and gave the most complete account yet of his past. The second half of Douglass's speech, however, went on to discuss crucial issues involving the principles and strategies of the abolitionist movement and to mock the North for its connivance in the return of fugitive slaves:

> The people at the North say—"Why don't you rise? . . ." Who are these that are asking for manhood in the slave, and who say that he has it not, because he does not rise? The very men who are ready by the Constitution to bring the strength of the nation to put us down! You, the people of Massachusetts, of New England, of the whole Northern States, have sworn under God that we shall be slaves or die! And shall we three million be taunted with a want of the love of freedom, by the very men who stand upon us and say, submit, or be crushed? . . . You say to us, if you dare to carry out the principles of our fathers, we'll shoot you down. . . . Wherever I go, under the aegis of your liberty, there I'm a slave. If I go to Lexington or Bunker Hill, there I'm a slave, chained in perpetual servitude. I may go to your deepest valley, to your highest mountain, I'm still a slave, and the bloodhound may chase me down. (*Papers* 1.32–33)

It was the success, inventiveness, confidence, linguistic power, and complexity of his speeches that prompted doubts about Douglass's claim to being an ex-slave, a suspicion that finally motivated the writing of the

29. *Papers* 1:26–27.

Narrative in order to invent and establish the personal authenticity audiences required for a speaker who ranged so far into public issues usually restricted to educated white men. The often-praised "simplicity" of the *Narrative* and its concentration on "personal" experience are thus an intended result of a political and rhetorical decision, not the spontaneous outburst of an untutored soul or the product of an unmediated "realism."

The rhetorical genealogy behind the *Narrative* helps account for the variable quality of its style, which in fact often departs from the simple dramatic accounting of incidents and spirals into melodrama, sarcasm, ridicule, and denunciation—all characteristics widely found in Douglass's speeches and in the rhetorical genres from which he borrows. This occurs most frequently in the context of religious hypocrisy, which following Garrison, Douglass emphasized. "A great many times have we poor creatures been nearly perishing with hunger," he writes, "when food in abundance lay mouldering in the safe and smokehouse, and our pious mistress was aware of the fact; and yet that mistress and her husband would kneel every morning, and pray that God would bless them in basket and store!" (64). Whatever its calculated realism and horrifying detail, the fact remains that the *Narrative* is full of a metaphorical and hortatory rhetoric typical of its period and at variance with the claim for the text's simple verisimilitude. The constant use of Christian diction and imagery, as in the famous passage about how the fight with Mr. Covey signals Douglass's "resurrection" from slavery, is one example, as is the repeated characterization of Covey as a "snake." Despite Douglass's outbursts against the hypocrisy of Christianity his rhetoric everywhere utilizes the terms of his oppressors as he invokes the diction and imagery of Christianity. What de Man might call the aporia between denunciatory statement and figurative language here might be accounted for by the public nature of Douglass's project. His real audience was most often not fellow blacks, but curious whites, newspaper reporters, and the powers that be in Washington. He could not extend the implications of the hypocrisy of southern Christians to the North without endangering his cause, though in his speeches he sometimes crossed the line. Nor could he find a handle for his revolutionary purposes without engaging the moral epistemology of his audience, which was rooted in Christian texts and ethics. He appealed, quite frankly, to the transcendental character of Christian principles in a war against a very political and historical foe.[30]

30. In his book, *The Mind of Frederick Douglass*, Martin seems to take Douglass's rhetoric at face value. He describes Douglass as combining "Christian and natural rights elements" with "an instinctive belief in the inviolability of human freedom." Abolitionism "was

The religious and moral tropology of Douglass's rhetoric, then, creates a dynamic interchange between ahistorical principles and historical institutions and practices. His recourse to apparently transcendental concepts is reflected also in the sentimental rhetoric of the book, which has bothered many readers (as has, at least until very recently, the sentimental power of nineteenth-century women's fiction). Like Hawthorne in his discourse of "sympathy" in *The Scarlet Letter* or Stowe in her sublime rhetoric of maternal love in *Uncle Tom's Cabin*, Douglass manipulates eighteenth-century ideals of sentimental morality and nineteenth-century political romanticism in protesting the inhumanity of slavery. Michael Meyer's introduction to his edition of Douglass's *Narrative* cites as example the page and a half on Douglass's "poor old grandmother" whose years of faithful service to her master yield only ingratitude as she is turned out to die. Douglass depicts, in stock melodramatic terms, the "dim embers" of her "desolate" hearth and the crushing "gloom" as she faces the impending "grave" without her family's comfort: "She stands—she sits—she staggers —she falls—she groans—she dies—and there are none of her children or grandchildren present, to wipe from her wrinkled brow the cold sweat of death, or to place beneath the sod her fallen remains" (60–61).

Such scenes recall popular antislavery engravings of the antebellum period which similarly focused on slavery's violations of hearth, home, and family. Meyer denigrates the passage as overwritten, melodramatic, and heavy-handed, and significantly (and negatively) aligns it with the "sentimental romances" of the era.[31] Such an evaluation is based on an aesthetic and mimetic, rather than rhetorical, reading. Even the literal or referential sense of this story, so long and often used by Douglass, may be doubted. According to Dickson J. Preston, Douglass knew by 1849 that his grandmother had been taken from her "desolate hut" by Thomas Auld and given a place in the master's kitchen.[32] Though he called some of his remarks on Auld "unjust and unkind," Douglass reprinted the passage about his grand-

---

rational, or enlightened, as well as intuitive, or romantic. It exemplified the basically consistent Enlightenment and romantic notions of man's innate goodness" (20). My point is that Douglass's degree of adherence to these discourses cannot be separated from their rhetorical utility; I doubt that even Douglass was always in control of the difference. Douglass's *experience* certainly contradicted the thesis of "man's innate goodness" even as he appealed to that notion as an enabling *figure* for abolitionist persuasion. And his belief in freedom's "inviolability" was a thoroughly historical, rather than "intuitive," creation.
31. *Narrative*, ed. Meyer, pp. xviii–xix.
32. Dickson J. Preston, *Young Frederick Douglass: The Maryland Years* (Baltimore: Johns Hopkins University Press, 1980), pp. 229–30, n.10.

mother verbatim in the 1855 *My Bondage and My Freedom*, and included as an appendix an 1848 letter to Auld repeating the claim that his grandmother had been "turned out like an old horse to die in the woods" (*My Bondage* 427).

It is the semiotic and allegorical uses of such passages as *emblems* of slavery that we must examine. The calculated appeal of Douglass's passage is *not* to an historical fact or political position but to an emotional and moral verity—the sanctity of the family—thus aligning antislavery rebellion with the powerful conventions of domesticity. As in his ambivalent use of Christian ethics against Christian hypocrisy, here Douglass uses the family against slavery, scarcely suggesting that the paternalism and property relations at the heart of the slave system might also play a part in the construction of domestic relations. The connection between slavery and feminism, in fact, was at this moment being forged by various reform figures, including Douglass himself, making this aporia all the more puzzling and powerful.

The ahistorical and apolitical character of Douglass's rhetoric in the 1845 edition of the *Narrative* must be understood, moreover, within the context of the debate over the strategies of abolitionism in this period. This debate, between Garrisonians and radicals, played an important role in shaping some of the *Narrative*'s most important passages, as can be seen from changes Douglass made in later years when he turned against Garrison and advocated a political and military solution to the "slave question." The Garrisonian position which Douglass accepted in the 1840s (though evidently with some doubts) emphasized, in Waldo Martin's words, "the strategic value of moral suasion and the importance of altering public consciousness. He [Douglass] fully adopted the Garrisonian doctrine of immediate and unconditional emancipation of the slaves as a moral and Christian duty."[33] But this moral and voluntarist abolitionism stressed the dissolution of the North's ties to the slave states rather than any actively communal, public, or political assault on the institution of slavery. It denounced the Constitution as a "proslavery" document incapable of bringing about any change, and Garrison called on his followers to cease voting. The Garrisonian position of nonresistance did not call for a political intervention by the present government against the slave states and did not advocate the use of military force. In these principles radicalism and moderation were linked as white northerners were offered a chance to wash

33. Martin, *Mind*, p. 22.

their hands of an evil set apart from themselves. Above all, Garrisonianism urged *moral persuasion* as the essential tactic of the abolitionist cause. It would be through argument and example that slavery was overthrown.

Thus it was the function of escaped witnesses like Frederick Douglass to inspire *feelings* of horror, shame, and guilt rather than to urge overt political or military measures. The rhetoric of the *Narrative*, along with the reading lesson at Mrs. Auld's, suggests the validity of the Garrisonian position; the fight with Mr. Covey, however, belies that message and contains the seeds of Douglass's later break with Garrison, for he will come to believe that a real physical struggle against the slave powers—like his friend John Brown's—is the only real solution.[34] Eric Sundquist narrates this as a progressive change, embodied in the rebellious identification of Douglass with the revolt of Madison Washington recounted in Douglass's 1853 story "The Heroic Slave" and culminated by the identification of Douglass with the Founding Fathers throughout *My Bondage and My Freedom*.[35] While this is a plausible reading, it transforms a reiterated contradiction in Douglass's work into a gradual evolution, ignoring the recurrent citations of Washington and of the Revolutionary Fathers in Douglass's speeches since the early 1840s. The psychological cast of Sundquist's new historicism, like that of Peter Walker, pays rather too much unquestioned attention to Douglass's search for fathers and manhood and rather too little to the political conditions of his rhetoric. In contrast Martin finds that from early in the 1840s Douglass "deemphasized the Garrisonian doctrine of nonresistance. . . . Having been compelled to resort to violence in self-defense and to assess the viability of violence as a strategy for slave emancipation and black liberation, on a personal as well as ideological level, Douglass understood and personified resistance."[36] The conflict between the primacy of moral suasion and the necessity of violent resistance, then, belongs to the original structure of Douglass's rhetoric and informs the contradictory tropes, episodes, statements, and self-figurations of his works.

How does the reading lesson with Mrs. Auld construct its allegory of the text's rhetorical theory? When Mr. Auld forbids his wife to continue Frederick's education, he justifies the injunction by saying: "If you give a nigger

34. See Franklin, pp. 18–22.
35. Eric Sundquist, "Frederick Douglass: Literacy and Paternalism," *Raritan* 6:2 (1986): 108–24. See also Robert Stepto, "Storytelling in Early Afro-American Fiction: Frederick Douglass's 'The Heroic Slave,'" *Georgia Review* 36:2 (Summer 1982): 355–68.
36. Martin, *Mind*, p. 24.

an inch, he will take an ell. A nigger should know nothing but to obey his master—to do as he is told to do. Learning would *spoil* the best nigger in the world" (*Narrative* 49). What we might not hear here is something Douglass's contemporaries could scarcely ignore, which is what Mr. Auld does *not* say. He does not say, as public racist discourse of the period would dictate, that Mrs. Auld's efforts are futile because of Frederick's innate biological inferiority. In the privacy of this conversation, Mr. Auld does not bother to repeat the standard rhetoric, bolstered in the antebellum period by the growth of a "racial science" of Negro incapacity, childishness, or animality, as advocated by Dr. Samuel Cartwright and others.[37] Rather Auld speaks frankly in terms of power, and the not-so-subtle lesson Douglass overhears is the old truth that knowledge and power are interdependent. Literacy, the passage implies, is the route to freedom. The evaluative distinction between public and private discourse that grounds the truth claims of this lesson, however, cannot be stabilized or sustained by a text which everywhere depends on rhetorical conventions for its force of persuasion. While the *personal* and historical experiences of Frederick Douglass seem to operate as the guarantors of the text's validity, the rhetoric of the text abstracts him to fashion his truth as a *representative* figure. So James McCune Smith, in his introduction to *My Bondage and My Freedom*, will say that Douglass "is a Representative American man—a type of his countrymen" (xxv). Douglass achieves this typological status through his reliance on the transcendental rhetoric of Christianity and the allegorical devices of sentimental humanism, without which his story would remain merely the isolate experience of a single individual. Here also, as Baker argued, is the danger for Douglass, as the specificity of his black tale gets whitewashed in the effort to become the "Representative American man." A difference inheres, however, in that the problems of literacy and resistance are not the same for the black slave and the white abolitionist. While Douglass gives voice to Garrisonian pacifism, his text speaks of the black subject's necessity and right of revolt. In this specificity his message ceases to be universally representative, as the black man's freedom entails an actual struggle against the power of the white.

Having taught himself to read despite Auld's prohibition, Douglass finds in *The Columbian Orator* a published dialogue in which a thrice-

---

37. See, for a contrasting example, Harriet Wilson's 1859 novel *Our Nig: or, Sketches from the Life of a Free Black* (New York: Random House, 1983), where Mrs. Bellmont asserts that "people of color" are "incapable of elevation" (p. 30).

escaped slave debates his master, and "the conversation resulted in the voluntary emancipation of the slave on the part of the master" (*Narrative* 54). This lesson provides an allegory of the Garrisonian position: "The moral which I gained from the dialogue was the power of truth over the conscience of even a slaveholder" (55). A subsequent episode, however, flatly repudiates this moral. Beaten senseless by the slave-breaker Covey, Douglass flees back to Thomas Auld to argue his case. "My legs and feet were torn in sundry places with briers and thorns, and were also covered with blood," he recalls, his martyrdom a type of Christ's: "In this state I appeared before my master, humbly entreating him to interpose his authority for my protection." Auld's response was that Douglass probably "deserved it" and must go back to Covey (77–78). Auld will not sacrifice his investment. So much for the liberating powers of representation! This scene immediately precedes the climactic fight with Covey, a juxtaposition that implies Douglass's early dissent from Garrison's advocacy of nonresistance. Douglass carefully portrays his resistance as defensive and walks a very fine line here rhetorically. The episode is no simple recollection, but an allegory advocating slave revolt to blacks while signaling the requisite pacifism to whites. "He can only understand the deep satisfaction I experienced," writes Douglass, "who has himself repelled by force the bloody arm of slavery. . . . I did not hesitate to let it be known of me, that the white man who expected to succeed in whipping me, must also succeed in killing me" (83).

Douglass expands and revises this key chapter for *My Bondage*, and again Meyer finds it "less successful" and too didactic. Read allegorically, however, the revision reveals what the "directness" and "simplicity" of the *Narrative* obscured.[38] On his way back from Auld's to Covey's, Douglass meets up with another slave, Sandy Jenkins. Sandy convinces Douglass to carry a magical root which will supposedly protect him from any whipping by a white man. "The root," observes Baker, "does not work. The physical confrontation does." In the *Narrative* this signifies a "displacement of Christian metaphysics by African-American 'superstition'" and "the inefficacy of trusting solely to any form of extrasecular aid for relief (or release) from slavery."[39] In context the root's significance is even more specific, as

38. For a thorough discussion of how *My Bondage* revises the *Narrative*, see Andrews, *To Tell a Free Story*, pp. 214–39. Andrews argues that Douglass turns away from the paternalism and individualism of the *Narrative* to the affirmation of black heritage and community in *My Bondage*.
39. Baker, *Blues*, p. 47.

Frederick returns to find Covey on his way to Sunday meeting. The Sabbath puts off his whipping for only a day. Anti-sabbathism was another of Garrison's tenets, and here is equated, through the root, with superstition. The equation is made very clear in *My Bondage* when Douglass says, "I suspected, however, that the *Sabbath*, and not the *root*, was the real explanation of Covey's manner" (148; Douglass's emphasis). This incident accords with Douglass's entire polemic against relying on American Christianity for one's secular salvation. Yet it also implies that the doctrine of moral suasion might itself be a superstition, that the difference between the hypocrites and the Garrisonians, like the difference between Sandy and Mr. Covey, might be less than one imagined.

The revisions in *My Bondage* make these subversive twists more decipherable. Sandy is called a "genuine African." "Now all this talk about the root," Douglass recalls, "was, to me, very absurd and ridiculous" (239). The past tense allows Douglass both to flatter his audience's piety and to indicate a possible change in his disparaging attitude. "It was beneath one of my intelligence," he writes, "to countenance such dealings with the devil, as this power implied. But, with all my learning—it was really precious little—Sandy was more than a match for me. 'My book learning,' he said, 'had not kept Covey off me,' (a powerful argument just then), and he entreated me, with flashing eyes, to try this" (239). The primary scene of Douglass's "book learning" was his reading of the *Columbian Orator*. According to Sandy's criticism, Douglass's belief in the liberating power of the white man's language was a superstition. Only by holding on to a symbol of his African roots—to a different divination of his situation—can Douglass be saved. This in turn means that while the doctrine of moral persuasion may be a fit belief for white abolitionists, it is of no use to black slaves whose lives are otherwise rooted. If, as Peter Walker and Sundquist argue, Douglass's texts appear to express a desire to achieve the status of white manhood, this desire runs alongside a countermemory of genuine African roots, and thus of a difference that can be traced but not brought to light in the white man's language.

"My religious views on the subject of resisting my master," writes Douglass, "had suffered a serious shock. . . . I now forgot my *roots*, and remembered my pledge to *stand up in my own defense*" (*My Bondage* 242; Douglass's emphasis). The referent of "roots" can only be Douglass's "book learning," and beyond that his roots in Garrisonian abolitionism, and, deeper still, his roots in slavery's expropriation of the slave's cultural legacy and the consequent fettering of the slave's ability to fight (and speak) back.

Douglass's split racial genealogy, like his split allegiances to white abolitionism and black resistance, riddle his rhetoric with contradictions and
reversals, as forgetting one tangle of roots means recalling another. "I was
resolved to fight," he now writes, "as though we stood as equals before
the law. The very color of the man was forgotten" (242). This assertion
plays to the humanism of white abolitionism and comforts the audience as
it erases the different color of the speaker before them, who is thus up-
rooted from blackness. In another reading, however, for Douglass to forget
Covey's color means that he forgets the *significance* accorded to it by slave
discourse and the state apparatus that supports it. Or, he remembers its
roots in prejudice, power, and the arbitrariness of categories like "black"
and "white."

Douglass is "compelled to give blows, as well as to parry them,"
when Covey's cousin Hughes attempts to tie his hand (*My Bondage* 243).
When the battle ceases to be of two individuals and becomes a social act of
enforced bondage, the situation and strategy change: "I was still *defensive*
toward Covey, but *aggressive* toward Hughes," who receives a sickening
blow (243). To the refusal of fellow slave Bill to help Covey, Douglass now
adds a new scene as Caroline, a slave forcibly made into a "breeder" by
Covey, appears and ignores Covey's pleas for aid. "We were all in open
rebellion," recalls Douglass (245). The rhetoric he adds to the conclusion
gives primacy to force and power: "A man, without force, is without the
essential dignity of humanity. Human nature is so constituted, that it cannot
honor a helpless man, although it can *pity* him; and even this it cannot do
long, if the signs of power do not arise" (247; Douglass's emphasis). While
these revisions obviously reflect the kind of militant support of slave revolt
expressed in "The Heroic Slave," they operate as rewritings that elicit the
repressed in the *Narrative*, and in abolitionism, that concern the "signs of
power." "Humanity," "nature," and "man" are signs in a terrain of struggle
over properties: Douglass now asserts the rights of a black difference in
appropriating the force and meaning of these signs. In rereading his own
earlier version of the Covey fight, he remarks its events as "signs of power,"
an emblem scene in the history of abolitionism and of the discursive fight
that will culminate in the Civil War.

Ideologies of Rhetoric

Baker's *Blues, Ideology, and Afro-American Literature* proposes to
use the poststructuralist Marxism of Jameson, with its semiotic materialism

and its critique of the "ideology of form," to advance a new hermeneutic for African-American criticism and to thereby construct new terms for a history of the literatures produced in America. "The ideological orientation foregrounded for 'Afro-American literary history' under the prospect of the archaeology of knowledge," writes Baker, "is not a vulgar Marxism, or an idealistically polemical nationalism. . . . Rather than an ideological model yielding a new 'positivism,' what interests me is a form of thought that grounds Afro-American discourse in concrete, material situations. Where Afro-American narratives are concerned, the most suitably analytical model is not only an economic one, but also one based on a literary-critical frame of reference" (25). In accord with Baker, I have focused my reading of Douglass on the economy of his texts' rhetorical mode of production, convinced that in this case such a method best combines the insights of materialism and literary theory. An archaeology of Douglass's rhetoric displays its over-determination by the material conditions of his life, the legacies of African experience, the political circumstances of his speech and writing, the psychological character of his attitude toward symbols of authority, the literary devices of romanticism and sentimentalism, the philosophical diction of the Enlightenment, and the language of Christian humanism. While each of these institutions of representation contributes to the history of Douglass's texts, they do not together form a single "ideology" or narrate an epochal totality. To write Douglass's history within the confines of any one of them would be, as Baker notes, both an inevitable temptation and an interpretive limitation.

Rhetoric, as I have construed it, may name the process of struggle, adjustment, resolution, and disruption between these heterogeneous representational forces. For this case, rhetoric also becomes the means by which racial difference—marked by the hyphen in "Afro-" or "African-American"—receives its various determinations. (One might say that the strategic choice of the name "African-American" underscores this historical-differential character of a people's identity rather than calling it a timeless essence.) In this sense, rhetoric cannot be identified with "ideology." Ideology rather names those provisional moments when the economy of some set of these forces yields a balance, a surplus value, or breaks the conceptual bank. Within a text, for example Douglass's, an ideology of form such as "heroic individualism" may negotiate the contradictions between economic and psychological registers, covering over the collective character of economic contradictions and the social nature of subjectivity. While this mystification may borrow its tropes from previously articulated ideological forms within an available cultural archive, it may also generate possibilities of contradiction between the text and the archive. And here the difference of "race," as an always to be determined character rather than an essence, interrupts. Douglass's heroism both borrows the language of Christian humanism, placating his audience and whitewashing his story, *and* subverts that humanism insofar as its rhetorical construction depends upon maintaining the speculative difference between Euro-American civilized humanity and its barbarian "other."

Thus it would be erroneous to interpret Douglass's invocation of humanistic discourse as only ideological in the negative sense—that is as a maneuver that allows just a bit of rebellion before recovering power in the name of the hegemonic forces of control. The practice of that discourse, historically, by Douglass, reinscribes a difference that white hegemony cannot efface. As a speaking subject Douglass constantly trades on the shock value of his eloquent literacy, on the *irony* of his appearance and speech. Dialectically, one cannot *understand* Douglass without recognizing his humanity, and to recognize his humanity is to transform the history and category of the "human" as his era conceives it. This process unfolds even if, and as, Douglass the man mediates this effort through other desires that condition it—his desire to recover the authority and love of the father, his desire to accede to white society and power, his desire to be recognized as a "man" in the gendered sense. Recalling Baker and Gates on the black speaker's always-already alienated relation to white language, one can argue that the black subject makes a space for opposition within ideology by just opening his or her mouth. Even if the intention were to espouse the ideology, as it is with Douglass when he indulges the rhetorics of entrepreneurship, individualism, and sentiment, the mode of production and the subject's material life in history generate contrastive ironies that divide the totality of expression against itself. The force of the hyphenated difference marking "African-American" language cannot be contained by the ruses of ideology. Recalling the distinction formulated by David Simpson, one could argue that while an "analytic" historicism attends to the description of the various archival registers of representational forces and their material conditions of production, a "prescriptive" historicism will utilize the findings to reconstruct alternative narratives for social and literary history. In this latter aspect the interpretation of the African-American difference entails that the reader make a decision about the ends of criticism. Involved here will be an ethical as well as a hermeneutic circle, for the values that motivated the analysis find their end in the moral narratives that result, which in turn motivate other analyses that inevitably challenge their antecedents.

An important contribution of African-American studies, in this regard, is the way it mobilizes the difference of race in order to undo the limits of history, ideology, and rhetoric. The African-American experience of slavery and oppression dictates that we must factor material conditions into the history of ideas and literature; moral and ethical considerations likewise motivate the interpretive process, while also determining a different relation between the reading subject and the speaking subject than had once obtained under the sway of aesthetic humanism. The difference of race continually prompts a reminder of one's *own* particularity, one's own marginality, one's own construction by a limited rather than total history. As one deciphers the rhetorical-institutional history of race difference, a perception of ideology in its repressive mode gives way to a reading of ideologies in their representative functions, which include acts of affirmation, establishment, and progressive empowerment, even as these may require the troping translation from one ideological or social idiom into another (as Douglass translates terms from white discourse into the language of his own liberation). Once rhetoric becomes a method for analyzing the *process* by which history unfolds through the struggles *within* and *between* discourses, then the possibility of changing history (past, present, and future) through rhetoric becomes an understandable, practical, and responsible proposition.

"Ours by the Law of Nature": Romance and Independents on Mark Twain's River

Howard Horwitz

1. Independence Betrayed

Mark Twain nominated the steamboat pilot "the only unfettered and entirely independent being that lived in the earth." "His movements were entirely free; he consulted no one. . . . Indeed the law of the United States forbade him to listen to commands or suggestions" from anyone.[1] This legally sanctioned independence underwrites Twain's romance of piloting, the nature of which, I think, has been too narrowly conceived. The aesthetic values of Twain's romance are also clearly economic and professional, and as Henry Nash Smith has observed, Twain's discussion of piloting "bears . . . directly on [his] thinking about the problem of values." Yet critical discussion of "the *art* of piloting," in James Cox's phrase, has neglected the economics of piloting's aesthetic values.[2] These economics warrant exami-

---

1. Mark Twain, *Life on the Mississippi* (New York: Signet—NAL, 1961), pp. 93–94. Subsequent references to this edition will appear in the body of the essay.
2. Henry Nash Smith, *Mark Twain: The Development of a Writer* (1962; rpt. New York: Atheneum, 1972), p. 78; James Cox, *Mark Twain: The Fate of Humor* (Princeton: Princeton University Press, 1966), p. 114. The italics are Cox's; throughout, all italics are repro-

nation because Twain's romance of the pilot's independence figures the idealized security of property rights that a free market economy seemed at once to promise and occlude.

Economic and aesthetic values are densely interwoven on the Mississippi, but Mark Twain presents two accounts of their relation. On one hand, the pilot's artistry is meaningful because it delivers "a quarter of a million dollars' worth of steamboat and cargo" (57). Moreover, Twain imagines the cub's famous "lesson in water reading" (63), when Horace Bixby teaches him to read the river "just like A B C" (49), as economic mastery: "Now when I had mastered the language of this water," Twain writes, "I had made a valuable acquisition" (67) from which "I am to this day profiting" (125). The art of piloting consists here in its expertise in appropriating the Mississippi, and piloting is one episode in the river's "historical history" (15), the story of human attempts to "make it useful" (18). Piloting is thus conceptually allied to what was then called river "improvement": federally instituted in 1879 through the Mississippi River Commission, the goal of improvement was to "curb," "confine," and "tame that lawless stream" (172).

On the other hand, some resent attempts to engineer the river and make it useful. The "old-time" mate, Uncle Mumford, who doubts that the Commission's engineers can "tame [the Mississippi] down, and boss it around," is outraged that the Commission plans to "make navigation just simply perfect, and absolutely safe and profitable" (173–75). In this view, the river is "remarkable" (13) precisely because it resists human management. By its cutoffs and flooding the river "plays havoc with boundary lines and jurisdictions" (14), enabling a man to go to bed in one state and wake up in another. Island 74 epitomizes the sublime "physical history" (15) of the river: after a cutoff, this "freak of the river" belongs to neither Arkansas nor Mississippi, and so "has sorely perplexed the laws of men and made them a vanity and a jest" (208).

To those like Uncle Mumford who feel the muddy Mississippi, unlike clear and hard-bottomed European rivers, "ain't [the] kind of a river" (174) humans can manage, disinterested aesthetic appreciation of the river's sublime power and beauty seems more appropriate than the Commission's

---

duced from cited passages. Like Smith, Cox too has generally defined the aesthetics of piloting as a question of value, without probing the social significance of the term (see 118). For other discussions of piloting as art, specifically writing, see: Edgar Burde, "Mark Twain: The Writer as Pilot," *PMLA* 93 (October 1978): 878–92; and Edgar M. Branch, "Mark Twain: The Pilot and the Writer," *Mark Twain Journal* 23 (Fall 1985): 28–43.

instrumentalism. One "old gentleman" recommends "unbounded admiration" for "the primeval wildness and awful loneliness of nature and nature's God." "What grander river scenery can be conceived," the gentleman declares, than the "enchanting landscape" of the river's bluffs and valleys (332–33). Twain employs similar language to lament the effects of learning to pilot. When the cub Sam Clemens "had mastered the language" of the river, "I had made a valuable acquisition. But I had lost something, too" (67); "the romance and the beauty were all gone from the river. All the value any feature of it had for me now was the amount of usefulness it could furnish toward compassing the safe piloting of a steamboat" (68). Beauty, here, seems sacrificed to professional apprehension.

Henry Nash Smith and James Cox have shown how Twain's nostalgia for the "pretty pictures" passengers see on the river (67) depends on the "conventional aesthetic vocabulary" of the "sentimental tradition of art"; Twain discards such vocabulary, they argue, to achieve the true romance of piloting.[3] But Twain's exaltation of piloting partially retains the sentimental impulse that the professional aesthetics of piloting would seem to belie; his pilot, Bixby, claims to read not by means of professional techniques, but rather by instinctive communion with the unmanageable river. The pilot reads the river because he has "*the* shape of the river" "*in [his] head*," and by "instinct" "naturally *know*[s]" where to steer even when the surface of the water is the most deceptive or the night the most black (59, 66). Though the pilot's instinct is clearly a professional achievement, Bixby's description omits its qualities of work and appropriation. With the shape of the river naturally in his mind, the pilot seems not to use nature, but merely to attend to it. Twain here invites us to imagine independence as a communion with nature prior to and independent of institutional practice.

The romance of piloting, founded on an intimacy with nature, exemplifies the theme of independence from custom so prominent in Mark Twain's writings. Most famously, Huckleberry Finn's experience on the river seems to offer pilotlike, instinctive independence, with the potential for democratic insurgency. Feeling at times "mighty free and easy and comfortable on a raft," as it "float[s] wherever the current want[s] her to go,"[4] Huck learns to respect a slave as a friend and implements this feeling by risking damnation and determining to liberate Jim from incarceration on the

3. Smith, *Development of a Writer*, p. 79; Cox, *Fate of Humor*, p. 114.
4. *Adventures of Huckleberry Finn* (New York: Norton, 1977), pp. 96–97. Subsequent references to this edition will appear in the body of the essay.

Phelps's farm. The apparent invitation to such natural freedom in Twain's early works, as opposed to the pessimism of his later ones, very much underwrites their wide mythological appeal.

But the independence gained from association with the river is lost, many have protested, when the river is forsaken or accommodated to the market. When Huck leaves the river, he sacrifices his moral freedom—his concern for Jim—and follows Tom and Tom's "authorities," the adventure books that pattern the cruelly protracted freeing of, as Tom imagines it, not Jim, but Louis XVI, the disenfranchised Dauphin (or Dolphin). Similarly, in Part 2 of *Life on the Mississippi*, when postbellum government engineering "has knocked the romance out of piloting" (171) and the "intruding" railroad supplants steamboating (109), the heroic story of piloting gives way to unfocused lists of trade statistics. With these developments, Edgar Burde writes, the "individual talent" once exemplified by the pilot is "replaced by economic institutions as the chief source of authority." In such lapsarian accounts of the river books—which indeed encapsulate most assessments of Twain's entire career—critics argue that individual authority surrenders to institutional authority, just as Huck surrenders to Tom's "authorities."[5]

The lapsarian account assumes that the sublime river and its readers must be out of the market in order to be independent. This romantic assumption hypostatizes what is only one impulse in Twain's account of piloting; often, piloting is explicitly a form of economic mastery. This instrumentalist aesthetic, as we will see by way of an excursion into the river's history, was central to the nineteenth-century imagination; for appreciating the Mississippi's beauty and power was thoroughly compatible with a desire to profit by it. Twain's romance of the free and independent pilot, centerpiece of what he called his "standard work" on the river,[6] epitomizes at once the liberal premises central to the nineteenth-century imagination

5. Burde, "The Writer as Pilot," pp. 882, 884. See also: Van Wyck Brooks, *The Ordeal of Mark Twain* (1920; rpt. New York: Meridian, 1955), pp. 59, 140, 238. On Huck Finn's surrender to Tom's authorities, see Cox's chapter on the novel and Leo Marx's *The Machine in the Garden* (New York: Oxford University Press, 1964), pp. 319–41. Cox's book is the most eloquent and thorough diagnosis of Twain's career as a falling off from the moral achievement of Huck's declaring he will go to hell to free Jim.
6. *The Love Letters of Mark Twain*, ed. Dixon Wecter (New York: Harper, 1949), p. 166. For an extended discussion of the planning, research, and composition of Twain's "Mississippi book," but one which does not examine the historical bearing of the book and its aesthetics, see: Horst Kruse, *Mark Twain and "Life on the Mississippi"* (Amherst: The University of Massachusetts Press, 1981).

and a contradiction in those premises. Twain's vision both exemplifies and attempts to resolve the tension in the liberal conception of independence. The independence necessary to domesticate the sublime is no transcendental condition, but rather a freedom of property rights, a function of market relations. Because Twain, like many of his contemporaries, idealized the freedom of property rights as an absolute freedom, and because absolute freedom is, of course, unattainable, he aestheticized piloting as "entirely free" and the pilot's work as instinct. Both points are inaccurate, but Twain exaggerates aesthetic authority in order to justify and insure social authority. He tries to secure the absolute proprietorship he desires by imagining the pilot as a king, and feudal authority as the perfection of market independence.

2. "Ours by the Law of Nature"

The fact that Mark Twain calls learning to pilot "mastering" the language of the river and a valuable acquisition suggests that piloting interpretation is an appropriation of nature. Twain had long conceived of piloting in this way. In 1866, he wrote his mother and sister that "verily, all is vanity and little worth—save piloting." Twain's literary career was not yet established, and his future projects were still uncertain;[7] hence, his invocation of a former career of conspicuous authority is understandable. If this letter's bathos prefigures Twain's later pessimism, in which vanity seems the essence of all motivation, here piloting signifies the possibility of valuable human endeavor. Twain's sense that the river is the site and occasion of value leads him "to suspect" the "lurid eloquence" of the old gentleman's encomium to the river's sublimity (332). And sure enough, the gentleman is a tour guide whose admiring appreciations are his wares.

A skill for conveying commerce on the river, piloting exemplifies the appropriative transaction with nature that defined economic activity until the end of the nineteenth century. This tradition dates at least from Aristotle, for whom economy entails the "management" or "use of the resources" that "Nature intends and provides" for man. To justify private property in a world God has given "to mankind in common," Locke revised Aristotle's notion of economy as stewardship of nature and so formulated the definition of

7. Later in the letter he confesses that "I do not know what to write" (*Mark Twain's Letters*, Vol. I, ed. Albert Bigelow Paine [New York: Harper, 1917], p. 101: letter of 20 Jan. 1866).

property underwriting the liberal tradition. Because divinely bestowed upon all men, the earth belongs to no particular man. But God "hath also given [man] reason [by which] to make use of it," and when man applies his reason, in the form of labor, to a thing in its "natural state," he removes it "out of the hands of nature," "excludes the common right of other men," and "appropriate[s] it to himself." Labor "put[s] the difference of value on everything," which untreated has none. Thus for Locke property is created in a two-step process of differentiation. First, nature is given to mankind; then, individuals appropriate parts of nature from nature and other persons. Economics textbooks published during Twain's days on the river echo Locke's two-step creation of property and value, affirming that no "recognized possession and value attach to" nature's "gifts" until they have been "appropriated."[8]

Plainly within the liberal tradition, Mark Twain does not think appropriating the river transgresses nature. He recounts how LaSalle wooed the Indians with gifts, then raised a "confiscation cross" to take "possession of the whole country for the [French] king . . . while the priest piously consecrated the robbery with a hymn." Twain disdains LaSalle's pious robbery not because the French appropriated "the mighty river" from nature or God, but because they "stole" it from its true "owners," the Indians (22). The river's status undergoes no transition from inviolate nature to property, because it seems preordained to be made "ready for business" (23).

Twain's point is even more radical. Even to notice the river means already to understand its potential value. Because de Soto "was not hunting for a river," when he "found" the Mississippi, "he did not value it or even take any particular notice of it" (18). In this formulation, when de Soto has no interest in the river, not only does he fail to remark its majesty, he hardly perceives it. The "mere mysteriousness" of the river's course and size "ought to have fired curiosity." But "apparently nobody happened to want such a river, nobody needed it . . . ; so, for a century and a half the Mississippi remained out of the market and undisturbed" (18). The mystery, resistance, and "awful solitude" (21) of the river were remarked and admired by Europeans only after they had recognized its economic potential. The Mississippi is referred to as "the mighty river" (22) only once there was a dispute about who owned it, which race or which nation.

8. *The Politics of Aristotle*, trans. and ed. Ernest Barker (New York: Oxford University Press, 1958), pp. 18–19; John Locke, *Two Treatises on Government* (New York: Hafner, 1973), pp. 133–35, 141; Rev. John Bascom, *Political Economy: Designed as a Textbook for Colleges* (Andover: W. F. Draper, 1859), pp. 24–26, 30.

This liberal aesthetic, as recounted by Twain, somewhat reduces the two-step dynamic of Locke's fable of property. Whether or not the Indians regarded the river as property, La Salle and de Soto admired the river as incipient property. This vision of nature informed the request for federal funds by the 1881 Mississippi Improvement Convention, which pronounced the river "prepared by the Creator for the use of the people." More familiarly, and humorously, Howells's Silas Lapham defends his controversial advertising practice—using rocks and hillsides as billboards—by declaring that "I never saw anything so very sacred about a big rock, along a river or in a pasture, that it wouldn't do to put mineral paint on it in three colours." Nature "is made for any man that knows how to use it."[9]

This liberal impulse was baldly expressed when Spain closed the Mississippi to trade in 1802. Recent American settlers protested on grounds that they had improved the river and its surrounding lands: "The Mississippi is ours by the law of nature; it belongs to us . . . by the labor which we have bestowed on those spots which before our arrival were desert and barren." In so affirming the Lockean principle that "the law man was under was rather for appropriating," the settlers' protest rather crudely reduces Locke's two-step notion of the creation of property, virtually eradicating any difference between labor and nature. Labor here not only establishes proprietary rights, but also constitutes the law of nature itself; and nature is essentially the application of human effort. Later histories of the river and petitions for federal aid for river improvement proudly invoked the settlers' protest.[10] And its liberal impulse to appropriate was deemed not just a right, but an aesthetic principle.

Timothy Flint, popular novelist and author of travelogues and natural histories, articulates an exemplary appreciation of the river's sublimity. In *Recollections of the Last Ten Years in the Valley of the Mississippi* (1826), Flint likens the "entirely novel" and "fresh scene" of the river to "the springtime of existence," relieving one's ordinary sense of "sickness and

9. *Official Report of the Proceedings of the Mississippi River Improvement Convention* (St. Louis: Great Western Printing Co., 1881), p. 77; William Dean Howells, *The Rise of Silas Lapham* (New York: Norton, 1982), pp. 13–14.

10. François de Barbé-Marbois, *The History of Louisiana*, trans. anon. (Philadelphia: Carey & Lea, 1830), p. 215; Locke, *Two Treatises*, p. 138. For two subsequent invocations of the settlers' protest, see: Emerson Gould, *Fifty Years on the Mississippi: Gould's History of River Navigation* (St. Louis: Nixon-James Printing Co., 1889), p. 288; and Alex D. Anderson, *The Mississippi and Its Forty-four Navigable Tributaries* (Washington: Government Printing Office, 1890), p. 7.

sorrow."[11] Ironically, this primordial spring is populated with tombstones, the "imperishable traces" of generations that have perished by the river's power. Therefore, "no thinking mind can contemplate this mighty and re-sistless wave . . . without a feeling of sublimity." The correlative to nature's sublimity is progress. As an acolyte and "earnest lover of nature," Flint finds man's "magic" "transformation" and "improvement" of nature no less sublime than the river's threat to human generation, a transformation as unparalleled in history as the river is unique in nature.[12] Flint celebrates the aesthetics of a Jeffersonian political economy of improvement. In contrast to the "dishonest arts" of the speculator, with his "barbarous," "zigzag," "ugly farms," the backwoodsman, working the family plot, creates free-holding farms of "beautiful simplicity," "surveyed in exact squares." Flint's aesthetic logic, in which beauty and sublime power inspire regulated and regulating art, is reproduced in abbreviated form in Samuel Cumings's *The Western Pilot*, a river guide first published in 1822 and regularly updated. The islands on the Mississippi and Ohio rivers, Cumings writes, "are of ex-quisite beauty, covered with trees of the most delicate foliage, and afford the most lovely situations for a retired residence."[13]

Conceiving of the river's sublimity as a gift to commerce and do-mesticity, Americans acclaimed its capacity to "add vastly to the wealth of the nation." "The great valley of the Mississippi," explains an 1843 Senate report, is "destined to afford, in the most lavish abundance, nearly every-thing that human wants can ask." Here, the valley's greatness results from its capacity to oblige human desire and to inspire "the natural progress" of American civilization, "destined" to surpass "the historical wonder of Egypt."[14]

But the river's natural state impeded natural progress. Turbulent cur-rents eroded the soft riparian soil, obstructing and threatening trade. "Like the old woman's house floor," Cumings reminded pilots, the riverbed must be swept clean. Men lacked the technology for this household mainte-

11. Timothy Flint, *Recollections of the Last Ten Years in the Valley of the Mississippi*, ed. C. Hartley Gratten (New York: Knopf, 1932), pp. 87–88.

12. Flint, *The History and Geography of the Mississippi Valley* (Cincinnati: Flint and Lin-coln, 1832), pp. x, 87, 130.

13. *Recollections of the Last Ten Years*, pp. 171, 180, 194; Samuel Cumings, *The Western Pilot* (Cincinnati: George Conclin, 1847), p. 7.

14. Charles Ellet, Jr., *The Mississippi and Ohio Rivers* (Philadelphia: Lippincott, 1853), p. 223; "Report of the Committee on Commerce," by Mr. Barnett, *Senate Documents*, 27th Cong., 3rd Session, 9 Feb. 1843, pp. 1–2.

nance, but in language that reminds us of Foucault's analysis of the modern disciplinary society, the authors of an 1823 report to the House of Representatives hope that "the Mississippi will one day be confined, by stable limits, to its bed," with "the empire of its caprices" "mastered by artificial embankments."[15]

In the meantime, the steamboat was the most effective means of mastering the river's caprices. An old (and probably unironic) story recounts an elderly slave's response upon seeing a steamboat for the first time. Though like many people skeptical about the newly invented vehicle, he was awed by its ease of movement. "By golly," he shouted, waving his cap, "the Mississippi's got her Massa now." Americans saw in the steamboat a "sublime power and self-moving majesty" to match the river's own; it seemed to achieve a century's progress in five years, matching the "art of printing" in its benefits.[16]

However remarkable, the steamboat alone could not achieve sublime mastery. Various techniques of river improvement were available—clearing obstructions, constructing levees, evening channel depths. Debate about which to employ weighed financial rather than technical questions. Before the war, little federal money funded improvement, and this money was devoted mostly to clearing obstructions. Levees were constructed and maintained by individual proprietors of the river front. This state of affairs had both practical and theoretical causes. Practically, landowners could little afford appeals to Congress; whereas navigation interests (boatowners and merchants) had capital to invest in the fight against taxing their profits. As a matter of principle, however, nearly everyone resisted the idea that the federal government should fund improvement. Clearing obstructions perhaps deserved tax appropriations because the river was, after all, public property; but appropriating funds for levee construction and upkeep seemed "a reclamation project for the benefit of private property." Not until 1852 did an engineer, Charles Ellet, Jr., advocate levees as necessary to any comprehensive program of river improvement.[17] Such a sensible rec-

15. Cumings, The Western Pilot, p. 3; "Report of the Board of Engineers on the Ohio and Mississippi Rivers," House Executive Documents, 17th Cong., 2nd Session, 22 Jan. 1823, pp. 19–20.

16. Archer B. Hulbert, The Paths of Inland Commerce (New Haven: Yale University Press, 1920), p. 176; Morgan Neville, in Western Souvenir (1829), pp. 106–07, quoted in Henry Nash Smith, Virgin Land: The American West as Symbol and Myth (Cambridge: Harvard University Press, 1950), p. 157.

17. Arthur DeWitt Frank, The Development of the Federal Program of Flood Control on

ommendation was so long in coming more because of *laissez-faire* anxiety about government intervention in private affairs than because of limitations in scientific understanding.

The war ravaged the private levee system; uncontrolled flooding reduced 1870 land values to one-fourth of their 1860 levels.[18] Individuals could not finance renovation, but the federal subsidization now undeniably necessary would no less deniably subsidize private citizens. Rhetorical intensification allayed (as well as signaled) nervousness about government intervention in private affairs. The river grew in geographical and commercial size: in 1874, one Congressman likened its improvement to "conquer[ing] the Mediterranean"; another proclaimed the river to be "worth all the canals in the world," an estimate that ups the ante from antebellum days when the river's commerce was said merely to equal the trade of Europe.[19]

As the river grew rhetorically, its character was transformed. Proponents of federal funding effectively elided the fact of government intervention by imagining a virtual merger between nature's desires and actions and those of men. "Nature seems to have been mindful of the wants of the interior," declares one Congressman. But, remarks another, obstructions "neutralize" the river's "free and unrestricted commerce"; thus the valley itself, "the richest and oldest portion of our nation, is robbed of one-half or more" of its commerce.[20] This logic completes the abridgement of Locke's two-step justification of property: commerce and the desire for commerce belong not to man but to nature itself—to the interior, the valley, or the river. Whereas Americans once sought to master the river's caprices, they now want to fulfill them; more exactly, the river no longer has caprices but productive desires. With partisan interests attributed to nature (and thereby no longer partisan), nature itself (rather than any person or interest group) becomes the beneficiary of labor, which now seems not just a Lockean

---

the Mississippi River (New York: Columbia University Press, 1930), p. 77. On ideas about distributing the burdens of maintenance, see Chapter 1 of Frank's study, which was extremely helpful in describing issues behind debates and as a guide to research sources. Ellet made his recommendation in *Senate Executive Documents*, 32nd Cong., 1st Session, No. 49, 1852, which appeared in expanded form in 1853 as *The Mississippi and Ohio Rivers* (see note #14 above).

18. Frank, *Federal Program of Flood Control*, p. 31.

19. *Congressional Record*, 43rd Cong., 1st Session, 21 April 1874, p. 3242; *Appendix to the Congressional Record*, 43rd Cong., 1st Session, 4 June 1874, p. 411.

20. *Congressional Record*, 43rd Cong., 1st Session, 4 June 1874, p. 4569; *Appendix to the Congressional Record*, 43rd Cong., 1st Session, 4 June 1874, p. 410.

right but a moral imperative. Mankind seems to have been given nature to protect it from itself, and government intervention is justified because improvement helps nature gratify its desires.

With improvement no longer regulating nature, but rather liberating and fulfilling it, river policy transcends partisan interest and becomes the test of human sublimity. In 1877, President Hayes called improving the river "a matter of transcendent importance," and improvement becomes "the grandest of human enterprises," man's most "sublime undertaking."[21] The debaters' hyperbole registers their discomfort at allocating funds for private reclamation. At this point, as part of partisan hyperbole by which philosophical liberals justify intervention in the private sphere, we even begin to encounter classically transcendentalist rhetoric about obeying nature's laws. Man masters nature only by apprehending the "obscure" laws that rivers "obey just as much as the planets in their orbits." Proper improvement, Rep. Barbour Lewis of Tennessee declares, "is only carrying out the system of nature; it is following the law of the great Mississippi River exhibited by itself."[22]

These arguments climaxed on 21 June 1879 with a speech by James Garfield, then a House leader from Ohio. Responding to a joke rehearsing the Mississippi's resistance to human management, Garfield insisted that this "most gigantic of natural features of our continent, far transcending the glory of the ancient Nile," must be brought under "permanent" "management."[23] It is the duty of the governing to "devise a wise and comprehensive system" for "perfecting this great natural and material bond of national union." Garfield's speech about permanently and systematically perfecting nature was received with cries of "Vote! Vote!," and a week later

21. Rutherford B. Hayes, "Annual Report to Congress" (1877), *A Compilation of the Messages and Papers of the Presidents, 1789-1897*, ed. James D. Richardson, Vol. 7 (Washington: Published by the Authority of Congress, 1897), p. 619; *Congressional Record*, 43rd Cong., 1st Session, 21 April 1874, p. 3242.

22. *Congressional Record*, 43rd Cong., 1st Session, 6 June 1874, p. 4658; *Appendix to the Congressional Record*, 43rd Cong., 1st Session, 4 June 1874, p. 413.

23. Here is the primitivist joke, which was received with laughter: "It was said . . . by a great and eminent politician of Mississippi . . . that there were some things which were subject to the laws of science; that there were some things which could be controlled by man's ingenuity and man's devices; but that the Mississippi was not one of those things. He said that God Almighty, when he made [it] and bade its great floods flow from the mountains to the sea, said, 'Let her rip; there is no law to govern it'" (*Congressional Record*, 46th Cong., 1st Session, 21 June 1879, p. 2283).

the Mississippi River Commission was established, its charge to devise "a system of observations" to perfect nature and thus "promote and facilitate commerce."[24]

3. Miraculous Readers; Absolute Owners

Five decades of debate over the Mississippi conceptually transformed nature's sublimity: as the need for federally funded improvement increased, what once resisted human desire became an emblem of human desire and value, and, as such, a transcendent power, admired through systematic regulation. Although critics of Twain have opposed the pilot's art to engineering, piloting and engineering were two episodes in the continual appropriation of the sublime river. The river's very sublimity made it a theater for the pilot's "marvelous precision" (56); he "mastered its shape" (69). But the interpretive power of Mark Twain's pilot, the source of his independence, radicalizes the premises of postbellum appropriative appreciation of the river, thus dramatizing the economic fantasy potential in the liberal vision of independence.

The extreme character of Mark Twain's declaration of the pilot's independence is clear when read in its entire context: the pilot

> was the only unfettered and entirely independent human being that lived in the earth. Kings are but the hampered servants of parlia-

24. *Congressional Record*, 46th Cong., 1st Session, 21 June 1879, pp. 2283–84; "Report of the Mississippi River Commission," *House Executive Documents*, 46th Cong., 3rd Session, No. 95, p. 4; *The Statutes at Large of the United States of America*, Vol. 21, 28 June 1879, p. 38.
Seeking "a system of observations" to underpin what the "Preliminary Report of the Mississippi River Commission" called a "comprehensive system of control" (*House Executive Documents*, 46th Cong., 2nd Session, No. 58, p. 6), the nineteenth-century determination to control nature clearly evokes Foucault's thesis in *Discipline and Punish* about surveillance and regulation in the carceral society (trans. Alan Sheridan [New York: Vintage-Random, 1979]), from which various critics have evolved theses about the realist novel and other literary production as projects in social control and containment. But the rhetoric of improvement legislation departs from most formulations of the carceral thesis insofar as its goal is perfection, not simply control. That is, its management was enablement, "improvement," not merely constraint; or rather the constraint is itself a form of enablement. This logic is actually closer to that of Foucault's work after *Discipline and Punish*, like *The History of Sexuality*, Vol. 1 (trans. Robert Hurley [New York: Random—Vintage, 1980]), or "The Subject and Power" (*Critical Inquiry* 8 [Summer 1982]: 777–95), which usefully revise the earlier carceral thesis.

ment and people . . . ; no clergyman is a free man and may speak the whole truth . . . ; writers of all kinds are manacled servants of the public. . . . In truth every man and woman and child has a master, and worries and frets in servitude; but in the day I write of, the Mississippi pilot had *none*. (93–94)

Twain was fond of this notion of the independent pilot in a world of slavery. He once wrote Will Bowen, a boyhood friend who preceded him into piloting, "that *all* men—kings & serfs alike—are *slaves* to other men & to circumstances—save, alone, the pilot." Pilots are, therefore, "the only real, independent & genuine gentlemen in the world."[25]

But Mark Twain greatly exaggerates the pilot's independence and monarchial power. In his 1889 history of Mississippi navigation, Emerson Gould, himself a former pilot, disputes Twain's claim that the pilot was "entirely free," forbidden by law "to listen to commands or suggestions" from others (94). No such law existed, says Gould; the pilot harkened to the captain, who determined the steamboat's destination and oversaw its course.[26] Twain's characterization of the pilot's reading, for which his river book is most famous, is no less an exaltation.

In Twain's romance, piloting is an instinctive and natural interpretive capacity. Instinct becomes an issue when Bixby admonishes his inattentive cub to learn the A-B-C of the river. The cub memorizes the names of numerous points along the river; but cataloging alone does not reveal the river's shape, for its surface features are protean and even illusory. Shapes along the bank change as the boat moves; lines, fringes, or ripples on the water can signify reefs, bluff reefs, branches or logs, or nothing at all, mere wind reefs. Conversely, treacherous obstructions can lurk below smooth water. Nighttime is worse, for then remembered points will be either invisible or misleading, as straight lines on shore appear curved and curved ones straight.

The semiotics of the river, then, amount to a critique of empiricism. Because the river's physical features do not in themselves reveal "the *shape* of the river," Bixby insists, "you only learn *the* shape of the river," "the shape that's *in your head*, and never mind the one that's before your eyes" (58–59). In Bixby's anti-empiricist advice, piloting safeguards against

25. *Mark Twain's Letters to Will Bowen: "My Oldest and Dearest Friend,"* intro. Theodore Hornberger (Austin: The University of Texas Press, 1941), pp. 13–14: San Francisco, 25 Aug. 1866.
26. Gould, *Fifty Years on the Mississippi*, pp. 489–90.

perception, converting untrustworthy visual data into knowledge by inverting the ordinary visual process. The pilot masters the form before his eyes by willfully ignoring it. In Bixby's account, piloting is an epistemological romance, apprehending the real only by bypassing visible phenomena.

But if visible features provide no reliable clues to the river's shape, how does that shape ever become available? Instinct succeeds where empiricism fails. After encountering a "wind reef" that looks "exactly like a bluff reef," the cub moans, "How am I ever going to tell them apart?" "I can't tell you," Bixby replies. "It is an instinct. By and by you will just naturally *know* one from the other, but you never will be able to explain why or how you know them apart" (66). It does not matter that empirical procedures cannot with any certainty ascertain the shape of the river, because after sufficient training—"by and by"—one naturally and inexplicably "just knows" its shape. Bixby's formulation implies that one must never learn the shape: the knowledge is natural, untransmissible, even unlearned, although admittedly a product of laborious training (lasting two to four years).

Bixby's advice dispels anxiety about knowledge[27] by simplifying Locke's declaration of the compatibility of nature and labor. Bixby's simplification is less obvious but even more radical than the 1802 settlers' equation of nature with labor. In piloting, labor disappears in natural instinct; piloting is so natural that it is not labor. Piloting thus exchanges the "exquisite misery of uncertainty" (77) for the authority of effortless knowledge: "how easily and comfortably the pilot's memory does its work," "how placidly effortless is its way" (87). This ease is why piloting is a "wonderful science . . . and very worthy of [the reader's] attention" (93). The pilot's instinct is worthy because it relieves anguish about the true shape of nature and about the expenditure of labor necessary to discover it. Piloting interpretation is work that is not work, mastery that is ease, power that is effortless.

This assuagement is the real basis of the romance of piloting. Although instinct, the pilot's professional art, is acquired through a lengthy and difficult apprenticeship, its quality as labor is erased. The pilot's memory works "*unconsciously*," noting bearings and depth changes "without

27. Cox argues that the main objective of Mark Twain's romance of piloting is to assuage skepticism, which had been the aesthetic of *Roughing It* (*Fate of Humor*, 126). Forrest G. Robinson has more radically argued that "the river displaces depression" and a sense of sin "by emptying the mind of all content" (*In Bad Faith: The Dynamics of Deception in Mark Twain's America* [Cambridge: Harvard University Press, 1986], p. 204). My argument concerns the positive content supplanting what these critics identify as evacuated.

requiring any assistance from *him* in the matter" (87). Twain's need to elimi-
nate individual labor and agency from the art of piloting—a principle he
often applied to any writing or art[28]—leads him to omit mentioning the
work of loading and unloading cargo when docked. He glorifies the divine
authority and leisure of the pilot, when in fact the pilot had to supervise
loading.

There are obvious reasons why reading the river must be as auto-
matic as possible. But this exigency does not require that piloting be effortless. Twain's aestheticization achieves the romance of piloting by disguising the fact of labor. When he early on discovers that he must sacrifice
sleep and a warm bed to steer the boat at night, the cub begins "to fear
that piloting was not quite so romantic as I had imagined it was"; rather it is
"very real and worklike" (47). The cub's romanticization of piloting dissolves
in the reality of work. The whole point of laboriously learning instinct is to
forget having to labor. When he has acquired instinctive reading skill, then
the pilot can perform his job, a former pilot wrote, "without realizing that he
is making any mental effort."[29] With the labor of reading indescribable and
invisible, purportedly nonexistent, piloting seems not an act of interpretation, but rather a moment of aesthetic, nearly erotic, intimacy: the "face of
the water . . . became a wonderful book—a book that was a dead language
to the uneducated passenger, but which told its mind to me without reserve,
delivering its most cherished secrets as clearly as if it uttered them with a
voice" (66–67). When the labor of reading disappears, the water confides
in the pilot, and his knowledge enjoys the immediacy of the spoken word
which Plato in the *Phaedrus* charged the written word lacks.

This erotic aestheticization of piloting intensifies (or perhaps constitutes) the gratification provided by its economic rewards. Twain figures
instinct's placid storage of information as a laying-up of treasure that is
apparently exempt from Jesus' caveat about the transience of earthly rewards: "how *unconsciously* [instinct] lays up its vast stores . . . and never
loses or mislays a single valuable package" (87). The utter security Twain
associates with this instinctive knowledge inspired from the outset Twain
as well as the cub. Albert Bigelow Paine tells us that Twain, like the cub,

28. See: "What Paul Bourget Thinks of Us," *How to Tell a Story and Other Stories, The
Writings of Mark Twain*, Hillcrest Edition, Vol. 22 (New York: Harper, 1906), pp. 145–46;
and "Down the Rhone," *Europe and Elsewhere, The Writings of Mark Twain*, Definitive
Edition, Vol. 29, ed. Albert Bigelow Paine (New York: Gabriel Well, 1923), pp. 143–45.
29. George Byron Merrick, *Old Times on the Upper Mississippi: The Recollections of a
Steamboat Pilot from 1854 to 1863* (Cleveland: Arthur H. Clark Co., 1909), p. 93.

was prompted to explore the Amazon by reading "an account of the riches of the newly explored [upper] regions" of the river. Unable to sail south, the cub "must contrive a new career," and he enters "upon the small enterprise of 'learning' the Mississippi" (45), where he discovers more familiar riches. For, once a licensed pilot with a regular berth, Sam Clemens bragged to his brother, Orion, in 1859: "I can get a reputation . . . [and] can 'bank' in the neighborhood of $100 a month. . . . Bless me! . . . what vast respect Prosperity commands!" Still, this wealth is not measured just monetarily. A trick Clemens played on those pilots "who used to tell me, patronizingly, that I could never learn the river" illustrates both the respect he sought from piloting and the integral relation between that respect and the art of piloting. When paying dues to the Pilots' Association, Clemens made sure "to let the d——d rascals get a glimpse of a hundred dollar bill peeping out from amongst notes of smaller dimensions, whose face I do not exhibit."[30] The respect due prosperity is not merely a sham exploiting the inability of others to read the shape of Clemens' money roll. Twain's ruse exemplifies the art of piloting, of being expert in what visible evidence disguises.

Twain's exaltation of piloting skill is especially revealing because it is a fabrication. Another former pilot disputed Twain's characterization of the pilot's unconscious steering techniques.

> While the pilot was running a bend "out of his head" in darkness that might be felt, there were always well-known landmarks to be seen —shapes of bluffs so indistinct as to seem but parts of the universal blackness. But these indistinct outlines were enough to confirm the judgment of the man at the wheel in the course he was steering.[31]

It seems that Twain "elevated matters of professional skill to the level of the miraculous," as Louis C. Hunter writes in his standard history of western steamboating. Hunter points out that most pilots were familiar with only a limited portion of the river system and that while navigating their limited sections, pilots liberally referred to various river guides, called navigators. Earlier I referred to the most popular of these guides, Samuel Cumings's *The Western Navigator*, first published in 1822 and regularly updated through the 1850s. Besides consulting these navigators, pilots also referred to newspaper reports of river conditions and routinely shared information with other pilots.[32]

30. Paine, ed., *Mark Twain's Letters*, Vol. 1, pp. 33, 43–44.
31. Merrick, *Old Times on the Upper Mississippi*, p. 88.
32. Louis C. Hunter, *Steamboats on the Western Rivers: An Economic and Technologi-

Neither self-contained oracles of command nor miraculous readers of nature, pilots belonged to a professional network and operated empirically with the aid of books, charts, newspapers, and colleagues. Mark Twain's undoubted familiarity with this fact helps explain why he valued the Pilots' Association as "perhaps the compactest, the completest, and the strongest commercial organization ever formed among men" (99). Edgar Burde (following Van Wyck Brooks) considers the Pilots' Association the death of heroic reading and the compromise of the self because the pilot's innate and individual talent is now subordinated to institutional authority.[33] But to Twain, the association is "a beautiful system—beautiful," he wrote Will Bowen,[34] precisely because it consolidates the pilot's independence and power.

Since it organized informal cooperation among pilots into an efficient network of communication, and thus streamlined communication between water and pilot, the Association insured individual control over property, thereby enabling Twain to imagine the pilot an absolute monarch, or even super-regal authority—"here was the novelty of a king without a keeper" (94). "A cramped treasury overmasters" a monarchy, but not "the old business of piloting."[35] Twain's hyperbole here transmutes institutional power into a freedom from all economic constraint, a strategy that both idealizes the freedom offered by a market economy and reprises the idealization of freedom risked in the liberal vision.

The essayist W. S. Lilly expressed the characteristic view that the "essential condition" of freedom was unconditional control over property. Liberty is "the power of doing what one likes with one's own"; "property is nothing else than liberty realized."[36] As we have seen, this *laissez-faire* notion of liberty structured debates over funding river improvement. This precept was at issue, too, in debates about the Steamboat Act of 1852, which regulated owner maintenance and for the first time required formal licensing of pilots. Pilots and boatowners opposed such regulation as "an unjustifiable violation of human liberty." One senator conceded that regulation might reduce accidents and save lives, but nevertheless insisted: "Consider the value of a man's life compared with his happiness and his

---

cal History (New York: Octagon, 1949), pp. 242, 245–46. Hunter's book was extremely helpful as a descriptive history and guide to research materials.

33. Burde, "Writer as Pilot," pp. 881–84.

34. *Letters to Will Bowen*, p. 13.

35. *Letters to Will Bowen*, p. 14.

36. W. S. Lilly, "The Shibboleth of Liberty," *The Forum* 10 (Jan. 1891), pp. 509–11.

liberty, with the freedom and happiness of our race." "Life is transient and evanescent, but liberty and equal rights, I hope, will endure as long as man shall endure. . . . Can a man's property be his own, when you take it out of his own control . . . ?"[37] Regulation, then, threatens ownership; and since the self seems hardly distinguishable from its property, when control of property is constrained, so is the self.

The understanding here—that life is an aspect of one's property—revises as it inherits the Lockean tradition. For Locke, transaction with nature axiomatically expresses the integrity of the self. Each person owns himself, owns an "unquestionable" and exclusive "property in his own person." It is this sense of self as a divinely granted principle of self-possession that makes "the labour of his body and the work of his hands . . . properly his." Thus, when one "hath mixed his labour with" nature, he has "joined to it something that is his own, and thereby makes it his property." In the ideal, then, property is the pure expression, or vessel, of self. The argument against steamboat regulation focuses on Locke's declaration that in "a state of perfect freedom" man is "master of himself," able to act "without asking leave or depending on the will of any other man."[38] Hence, government intervention undermines freedom of life on the market.

Just as both the 1802 settlers and Bixby elide what Locke understood to be the original disparity between man and nature, this argument also reduces the metaphysical dynamic that is the signal achievement of Locke's account of the relation between the self and its property. It conflates or even reverses Locke's ontology of property. Locke's self owns its property because it owns itself; as a principle of ownership, the self is identified by and realized through its property. Lockean selfhood is a double relation, at once source and function of its alienable attributes. But then a tension

37. William M. Gouge, "Report on the Steamboat Act," *House Executive Documents*, 34th Cong., 1st Session, No. 10, 6 Nov. 1855, p. 423; *The Congressional Globe*, 32nd Cong., 1st Session, pt. III, 28 Aug. 1852, p. 2427. Although he recounts his brother Henry's death in a steamboat explosion, Twain never hints at the frequency of accidents. Many occurred, the result of pilot incompetence and owner negligence.

38. Locke, *Two Treatises on Government*, pp. 122, 134, 210. On the points introduced here, see C. B. Macpherson, *The Political Theory of Possessive Individualism* (New York: Oxford University Press, 1962), pp. 197–201, 229–38, 255–62; see, for example: Locke's notion of individualism "asserts an individuality that can only fully be realized in accumulating property" (255). For a related discussion of the Lockean self as an "identification" with its material properties and expressions, see Andrzej Rapaczynski, *Nature and Politics: Liberalism in the Philosophies of Hobbes, Locke, and Rousseau* (Ithaca: Cornell University Press, 1987), pp. 195–207.

exists between the self's inalienable authority over and identification with its material properties and expression, because self is at once distinct from and commensurate with its property or contingent attributes.[39]

Those who argued against the Steamboat Act acknowledged the imbrication of self with the property it putatively generates and attempted to resolve the ontological difficulty by paradoxically absolutizing both terms of the problematic equation. It is *because* freedom and personhood are known only through property that persons must have complete authority over it. Rather than property being guaranteed by the self, the self is authorized by unregulated control of property. Where Locke's notion of the free self served to describe and justify the workings of the market, opponents of regulation believe the free market itself generates independence.

The antebellum Mississippi steamboating industry seemed to embody the perfection of the liberal vision of the self. While eastern steamboating already tended toward corporate fleet lines, capitalization of western steamboating was private and local, often individually run. With the river considered national property, its use was free. This free passage encouraged private ownership, because capital was needed only for the transport vehicle and its maintenance, and not for the right-of-way costs, the roadbed maintenance, nor the terminal facilities demanded by railroad operation. Moreover, the irregularity of the river made the fixed schedules of eastern fleets impractical, thereby also encouraging small-scale ownership. The "tramp steamboat," locally operated, able to await cargoes or high water, and available to go wherever cargoes awaited, "had a great advantage over packets tied to a scheduled run." Thus, the river's capriciousness seemed to necessitate a pure form of small-scale free enterprise. This conjunction between nature's intractability and *laissez-faire* independence is emphatically expressed when, during his 1882 visit to the river, Twain glimpses Island #74, the one remarkably left by flooding as no longer part of Alabama or Mississippi. The absence of government jurisdiction ensures absolute freedom of ownership: "the owner is monarch of all he sees."[40]

39. For a fuller discussion of this dynamic in the Lockean account of property, and of the way it informed and was addressed in debates about Homesteading and turn-of-the-century debates about the nature of property, see Howard Horwitz, "*O Pioneers!* and the Paradox of Property: Cather's Aesthetics of Divestment," *Prospects: An Annual of American Cultural Studies* 13, ed. Jack Salzman (New York: Cambridge University Press, 1988), pp. 61–93.

40. George Rogers Taylor, *The Transportation Revolution: 1815–60* (New York: Rinehart, 1951), pp. 69–70; Albert Fishlow, *American Railroads and the Transformation of*

Enacting the premises of those opposed to the Steamboat Act for interfering with individual action, Mark Twain's romance of piloting is a romance of property rights: a radical idealization of *laissez-faire* ownership underwrites the pilot's unconstrained self; the pilot's interpretive prowess is a metaphor for unconstrained ownership. This is why Twain unequivocally applauds the Pilots' Association as the climax of the pilot's power and independence. The Association secures high wages and transfers licensing authority from the government to the pilots themselves; by standardizing the dissemination of river information, it improves water-reading, reduces accidents, safeguards property and life, and thereby obviates calls for government regulation. Pilots read best when they are free from outside authority and supervision.

4. Intruding on Romance

It is the romance of property rights that postbellum federal river improvement destroys. The epistemological romance of water-reading is not demolished by the River Commission's efforts, but rather changes occupations, transferring power from the pilot to the engineer, whose elaborate charts and lamps, levees, and local channel improvement enable one to "run in a fog now. . . . with a confidence unknown in the old days" (171). The army engineers read the river, the pilot reads their maps.

According to the revolutionary study of the river on which the Mississippi River Commission based its efforts, the engineer divines the shape of the bed below the opaque water. The study's authors, A. A. Humphreys and H. L. Abbott, note that the bed cannot be inferred from the appearance of the surface. So like pilots, engineers disregard the river's visible features. Measuring the volume of discharge and the velocity of the current at all widths and depths, they collect "fact upon fact, until the assemblage of all reveal[s] . . . the true conditions of the river." By this account, engineering observation is no simple empirical act. Engineers do not just measure; any assistant, like the depth-caller on a steamboat, can do that. Like the pilot, the engineer manipulates and assembles diverse data to envision the unseen bed and "the laws governing the flow of water in natural channels."

---

the Ante-Bellum Economy (Cambridge: Harvard University Press, 1965), p. 156; Hunter, Steamboats on the Western River, pp. 307, 567; Mark Twain's Notebooks and Journals, Vol. 2, 1877–1883, eds. Frederick Anderson, et. al. (Berkeley: University of California Press, 1975), p. 532.

Deducing hidden laws and the hidden channel from data that in themselves do not represent them, the engineer's empiricism, like the pilot's, is an anti-empiricist communion with natural law.[41]

Twain doubts the engineers' claim to control the river permanently by discovering its eternal laws, but he nonetheless admires their heroic enterprise.

> The military engineers of the Commission have taken upon their shoulders the job of making the Mississippi over again—a job transcended in size by only the original job of creating it. . . . the West Point engineers have not their superiors anywhere; they know all that can be known of their abstruse science. (172–73)

Their abstruse science god-like in its ambit, the engineers are the new experts in the mysteries of the river. Engineers are the latest avatars of pilots, having no superior anywhere.[42]

Twain is skeptical not about the heroic character of the Commission's project, but rather about its claims to perfect nature systematically. As we have seen, the rhetoric of perfection is what propelled the 1879 River Commission Act through Congress. Twain attacks the various "theories" of improvement (175) designed to accomplish this ideal, a theory being an *a priori* method for entirely and permanently mastering the river—damming, creating lakes, building levees, reinforcing the channel, or any fixed combination of these. Twain considers each theory a "contagious" "disease" (176), incapacitating by its very prescription men's ability to determine appropriate action. For Twain, a typical theory is analagous to "Sir Walter Scott disease" (266), whose "debilitating influence" prevents the South from understanding the truth of its social practices (237). The South's "imitation castles" merely copy the surface forms of chivalry without any sense that the surface, however obliquely, represents beliefs or practice (238). The South's productions lack the conception of dimension so crucial to reading the river. Twain's Southerners are unaware that romantic values arise in exploring and exploiting the disparity between surface and

41. A. A. Humphreys and H. L. Abbott, *Report upon the Physics and Hydraulics of the Mississippi* (Philadelphia: Lippincott, 1861), pp. 18–20, 28–29.
42. Even Uncle Mumford respects the scope of the Commission's intent: ". . . they are going to take this whole Mississippi, and twist it around and make it run several miles *upstream*. Well, you've got to admire men that deal in ideas of that size and can tote them around without crutches" (174).

substance. Mistaking surface for substance, form for value, the radical formalisms of theory and of Southern imitations of chivalry afflict their victims with a prefabricated system of perception.

Despite his suspicion of theory and of the goal of perfection, Twain retains his enthusiasm for the benefits of improvement; "if Congress would make a sufficient appropriation, a colossal benefit would result" (176). Even the less forgiving Mumford is eager to hedge his bets on the river's prospects: "the safe way, where a man can afford it, is to *copper* the operation, and at the same time buy enough property in Vicksburg to square up in case [the engineers] win" (174–75). But local benefits, Twain knows, do not add up to mastery or perfection, and even today we periodically see reports of flooding and cutoffs on the evening news.[43] After the Civil War, railway development permitted trade to circumvent the river's vagaries. It was the transition to the "intruding" railroad (109), more specifically to the corporate trend the railroad typified and accelerated, that truly destroyed Twain's romance of independence.

Whereas epistemological heroics have merely changed occupations, the organization of post-war production and trade frustrated Twain's ideal of the independent self. The railroad's sheer scale necessitated incorporation, and western steamboating, too, soon became a corporate enterprise.[44] It is hard to believe that you are independent and without superior when you are employed not by a local boatowner but by a large, distant office and take orders from a local manager who answers to a district manager, etc. The chain of command, once direct, is now oblique; responsibility, once centered, now dispersed. The fate of the steamboat barkeeper dramatizes this historical development which undermined, Twain thought, personal "dignity" (172). "In the old times, the barkeeper owned the bar himself . . . 'and was the toniest aristocrat on the boat.' " Now "the bars are rented and owned by one firm," which furnishes the liquor and salaries the barkeep. Individual enterprise gives way to franchised marketing. Post-war farmers along the river, who "don't know anything but cotton," are the corollary to the franchised barkeeper. They have no interest in the legendary self-sufficiency of the farmer, and so the barkeep makes most of his money selling them fruits and vegetables at a steep mark-up, 45¢ on a 5¢ outlay

43. Historical placards along the newly designed New Orleans riverfront area inform tourists of the river's continued erratic behavior, proudly citing Twain and Uncle Mumford's remarks about the river's untamable lawlessness.

44. Hunter, *Steamboats on the Western Rivers*, pp. 566–67.

(211–12). These farmers are more properly merchants and consumers than farmers.

The intruder railroad, then, intrudes mainly upon the romance of autonomy that Twain located in small-scale enterprise. Steamboating itself, Twain observes early on, once "intruded" on the keelboating industry, attracting commerce until "keelboating died a permanent death" (24). Twain is content with this intrusion because the economic organization of the two industries is the same and accommodates the same sense of self. But railroad economies of scale shatter the illusion of autonomy, which may be one reason Twain omits the fact that the steamboat industry's glory days already exhibited signs of decline. He mentions as an afterthought in Chapter XV that "the new railroad stretching up . . . to Northern railway centers, began to divert the passenger travel from the steamers" (109). Only a semi-colon separates this statement from the announcement of the war's annihilation of steamboating, and the two events seem contemporaneous. In fact, however, throughout the 1850s the steamboat industry weakened and was often depressed, due largely to the growth of the railroad, which by 1860 was the supreme transport service in the valley. During this decade, not only was the railroad's expansion utterly visible, but railroad companies began purchasing steamboat lines to provide connecting service among train lines.[45] Nevertheless, Twain forgets steamboating's difficulties and insists that its glory days perished, as it were, with the firing upon Fort Sumter. In fact only the mythological independent self, a notion already an exercise in nostalgia in the 1850s, died with the war.

5. It All Belongs to Me: *Huck Finn*
and the Feudal Fantasy

Not just nostalgia, Twain's romance is an exercise in historical fantasy, its aesthetic values deriving from an idealized vision of free enterprise and *laissez-faire* property rights. The pilot, I've argued, did not enjoy the independence Twain ascribes to him; nor could he have, for *laissez-faire* can never amount to the ontological independence Twain claims for the

45. Hunter, *Steamboats on the Western Rivers*, pp. 519, 585; Fishlow, *American Railroads*, p. 56; Taylor, *The Transportation Revolution*, p. 102; Hunter, *Steamboats on the Western Rivers*, pp. 488, 502. For a differently nuanced account of the health of steamboating during the 1850s, see: Erik Haites and James Mak, "The Decline of Steamboating in Antebellum Waters," *Explorations in Economic History* 11 (Fall 1973): 25–36.

pilot. Freedom always requires institutional sanction: legal protection, or the insurance of a Pilots' Association, or of the insurance underwriters of the vessels, whose leverage the Association exploited to gain power. So Twain's romance denies the labor of piloting, because when labor is visible, the self's involvement with institutions is all too evident, and its independence, the inalienability of its right to property, too obviously contingent.

As may already be evident, Twain suspends dependence and contingency by formulating his general desire for independence in the language of feudal power. To ensure that the pilot is no mere laborer or wage-earner, Twain imagines him a king, indeed "a king without a keeper, an absolute monarch" (94) who was never, unlike actual kings, "overmastered by a cramped treasury," the only person not a "manacled servant" (93). The Pilots' Association institutionalized and transcended monarchial power. It possessed, Twain wrote Will Bowen, "more than regal power," "for no king ever wielded so absolute a sway over a subject & domain as did that old Association."[46]

The language of slavery and feudal power had long figured in political disputes on the Mississippi. When the Spanish closed the river's mouth to trade in 1802, American settlers forecast that inaction would "make us vassals to the merciless Spaniards." "Shall we be their bondmen as the children of Israel were to the Egyptians? Shall one part of the United States be slaves, while the other is free?"[47] This outcry envisions free property relations supplanting a system of slavery. But recall that in Twain's discussion of piloting "*all* men . . . are *slaves* to other men & circumstances—save, alone, the pilot."[48] For Twain, slavery is not superseded by a free market, but persists, with pilots as master-kings, putting "all their wishes in the form of commands" (94), mastering others as they master the river. Here is independence as primary narcissism. Twain's account of piloting is not a critique of capitalism as the transformation of feudal service into service to capital. In his ahistorical vision, slavery transcends all social and economic forms, and gratification springs from enslaving rather than serving. Acknowledging that the pilot is a salaried worker would shatter Mark Twain's fantasy of power. Hence his aestheticization denies the eco-

46. *Letters to Will Bowen*, p. 13.
47. Quoted in Frederic Austin Ogg, *The Opening of the Mississippi: A Struggle for Supremacy in the American Interior* (New York: MacMillan, 1904), pp. 435, 437.
48. *Letters to Will Bowen*, p. 13.

nomic in order to guarantee economic rewards for the self he is trying to protect. Aestheticized autonomy is protected by a feudalism where only the enslaving aesthete/pilot is spared enslavement.

Adventures of Huckleberry Finn addresses perhaps more directly the same basic problem—the general security of property rights in the self —and it thus clarifies why Mark Twain must feel more kingly than a king to feel independent. Twain formulates the journey downriver in *Huck Finn*, widely celebrated as a quest for freedom, in the same monarchial terms, and with the same idealization of ownership, that inform *Life on the Mississippi*. When Huck arrives on Jackson's Island, he feels "ruther comfortable and satisfied" (34) essentially because "I was boss of it; it all belonged to me" (36). Such unqualified possession constitutes Huck's definition of kingship during his debate with Jim regarding King Sollermun's wisdom: kings "can have just as much as they want; everything belongs to them" (64). Owning everything, a king can have all he wants; like pilots, he need only formulate his desires as commands to gratify them. Feeling absolute proprietorship is essential to why "you feel mighty free and easy and comfortable on a raft" (96). Traveling at night, naked, the world ashore asleep, "we'd have that whole river all to ourselves for the longest time" (97).

Despite the ironic criticism directed at the King and Duke and at southern society's captivity by chivalry, the runaways conceive freedom as the consummation of monarchy. Twain imagines freedom in language contravening many of his actual political commitments because he senses that free market property rights only precariously secure the self in the way reductions of Locke imagined they could. The contingency of property, and hence of the self that realizes itself through property, is poignantly expressed after Huck and Jim meet on Jackson's Island. Jim explains that he ran away from Miss Watson because he was to be sold for $800; as property, a slave is, obviously, insecure, deprived of (in Locke's phrase) his "property in his own person." Jim then describes his various failed speculations, recounts the "signs" that predict his future wealth, and forswears lending any "mo' money' dout I see the security." He suddenly realizes he is no longer Miss Watson's property: "Yes—en I's rich now, come to look at it. I owns mysef, en I's wuth eight hund'd dollars. I wisht I had de money, I wouldn't want no mo'" (42).

Of course, when Jim owns himself he is no longer worth $800 and is far from rich. Laurence Holland has demonstrated the historical irony of this novel that goes about "setting a free nigger free" (227) two decades after the Emancipation Proclamation. Miss Watson's will frees Jim "to stand job-less and alone"; this freedom in-name-only exposes "the failure of [Twain's] world to flush [emancipation] out with the family, the opportunities, and the community which would give it meaning."[49] But Jim's exclamation signifies more than a historical failure of will. It exemplifies the liberal principle that one must sell one's labor to survive. Freedom to own property is the free-dom to turn yourself into property. Jim's joy elucidates to us, though not to him, the notion that to be free necessitates in a real sense becoming partially like a slave.

Historians have noted certain abolitionists' sense of the similarity be-tween market and slave economies. Harriet Beecher Stowe, for example, in essays like "A Family Talk on Reconstruction," felt that the market sys-tem was not so much the antidote to slavery as slavery was the epitome of the market. The term "free labor," as Walter Benn Michaels has observed, seemed dangerously like "shorthand for a free market in labor."[50] Although slaves' alienation from their property in their own persons is a legal fact, while that of free laborers is only a matter of institutional practice, what Stowe called "the condition of service" is common to both economic sys-tems.[51] Southern defenders of slavery as a fairer form of exploitation than capitalism adduced the same assessment of free labor. "Property in man" is the goal of all men, writes George Fitzhugh, a leading southern apologist. But in selling themselves, free laborers have less property in themselves

49. Laurence B. Holland, "A 'Raft of Trouble': Word and Deed in *Huckleberry Finn*," *Glyph* 5 (1979), p. 80.

50. Walter Benn Michaels, "Romance and Real Estate," *The Gold Standard and the Logic of Naturalism: American Literature at the Turn of the Century* (Berkeley: Univer-sity of California Press, 1987), p. 111. Michaels's essay is a powerful interrogation of the problematic ideal of the Lockean fable of property, what Macpherson calls "full pro-prietorship of [one's] own person" (*Theory of Possessive Individualism*, p. 231). In *The Antislavery Appeal: American Abolitionism after 1830* (Baltimore: The Johns Hopkins University Press, 1976), Ronald G. Walters describes the ways in which abolitionists both recognized and effaced a free labor market's apparent attenuation of the "self-ownership" they advocated and sought (p. 122; see generally pp. 111–23).

51. Harriet Beecher Stowe, "A Family Talk on Reconstruction," in *The Chimney Corner* (Boston: Ticknor and Fields, 1868), p. 68. For a full discussion of Stowe's complex atti-tude toward slavery as a form of free labor, see: Gillian Brown, "Getting in the Kitchen with Dinah: Domestic Politics in *Uncle Tom's Cabin*," *American Quarterly* 36 (Fall 1984): 503–23; and Brown's chapter on "Sentimental Possession" in *Domestic Individualism: Nineteenth-Century American Fictions of Self*, forthcoming from University of California Press. I am grateful to her for discussing with me the issues in this section of the essay.

and thus "less liberty than slaves"; they "are worse paid and provided for, and have no valuable rights"; free laborers are "miscalled freemen." [52]

Despite the isomorphism between the service of slavery and that of wage labor, the property rights of slaves and freemen, of course, differed vastly. Yet in Stowe's nervousness about and Fitzhugh's pleasure in the structural similarity, we see a possible result of inverting the etiology of the Lockean self and of identifying the self wholly in terms of its property. As C. B. Macpherson's analysis of Locke's "possessive individualism" suggests,[53] the problem is intrinsic to Locke's conception. If the self is a principle of ownership, expressed and realized in its property, then one's identity may come to be equated with the materials that represent it. Ideally, one is the inalienable master of oneself, and thus of one's labor and material property; but if identity is available only in terms of material property, which by definition is exchangeable, self and self-mastery are redefined—and hence revealed to be contingent—in every transaction. Opponents of regulation typically sensed how viewing identity as proprietary, and therefore imbricated with the alienable properties that express it, undermines an ideal self-mastery. To compensate, they radicalized Locke's notion of the market self in two ways that seem incompatible, but in fact tacitly support each other. Twain and his compatriots simultaneously defined the self utterly in terms of its property, yet insisted on its transcendence of material goods and convention. In this way one's rights to oneself may seem inalienable though realized through property. Without this idealization, the self's identification with and through its property may feel like subjection to a political order, or, in historically specific terms, like slavery.

The initial conflation of self with its property is analogous to the one Twain ascribes to the South, which confuses the architectural features of chivalry with its substance. Take away the imitation castles, and chivalry disappears; take away property, and the self doesn't exactly disappear, but, perhaps worse, becomes little else than the site of enslavement as labor. Twain and his compatriots mistake form for substance in idealizing the inde-

52. George Fitzhugh, *Cannibals All!, or, Slaves Without Masters*, ed. C. Vann Woodward (Cambridge: Harvard University Press, 1960), pp. 20, 32, 221. On the southern claim that, in Fitzhugh's words, "capital exercises a more perfect compulsion over free laborers than human masters over slaves" (32), and that slavery reduces the alienation of labor by functionally extending the family, see Eugene D. Genovese, *The World the Slaveholders Made* (1969; New York: Vintage–Random House, 1971), pp. 151–235.
53. Macpherson, *Theory of Possessive Individualism*, pp. 194–203, 255–62.

pendence offered by free-market property rights as an absolute autonomy, pre-social in its independence of the consent of others, finally atemporal in its transcendence of change, an ontological condition rather than a political fact or disposition of power.[54]

The historical and class specificity of this vision of freedom is illustrated by comparison with that of freed slaves or the "new negro," for whom freedom could *only* be a temporal and political achievement. Twain's pilot, typically, could not afford to imagine freedom as something that moves or results from political proclamations. But for Booker T. Washington, W. E. B. DuBois, and Frances W. Harper, for example, freedom "came" with the Union army and the Freedman's Bureau. It is a "possession," Washington writes, like a garment to "try on." The concreteness, and hence contingency, of freedom is evident when a male protagonist of Harper's *Iola Leroy* ponders the Union army's advance: "Freedom was almost in his grasp. . . . All the ties which bound him to his home were as ropes of sand, now that freedom had come so near."[55] Freedom, here, is not an absolute condition, but a transformative phenomenon to be grasped, breaking former bonds upon arrival. In these authors' works, freedom is explicitly realized through property, which verifies the otherwise mere abstraction of freedom by substantiating it.

If this conditional notion of freedom is the condition of black emancipation and what DuBois called "self-realization,"[56] Twain registers what many (whites) felt were its limits. The rhetoric of independence, initially employed to justify the market system, later came to imagine the market as the very source of independence, and hence absolutized independence in order to protect it from market contingencies. Since property has value and is property only by virtue of its exchangeability, the inalienability of property necessary to this idealization is precisely its fantastic element. No one can own in this way.

Unless, of course, you are king and own everything and everybody. If so, your material property is inalienable because exchange is superflu-

---

54. Richard Bridgman has recently argued that one of the dominant psychological and thematic principles of organization (or lack of organization) in Twain's travel writings was Twain's anxiety about change. See: *Traveling in Mark Twain* (Berkeley: University of California Press, 1987).

55. Booker T. Washington, *Up From Slavery* (New York: Penguin, 1986), pp. 22, 24; Frances W. Harper, *Iola Leroy; or, Shadows Uplifted* (Boston: Beacon, 1987), p. 35. On freedom as something that "comes," see also: Washington, *Up From Slavery*, p. 23; and W. E. B. DuBois, *The Souls of Black Folk* (New York: Signet—NAL, 1969), p. 47.

56. DuBois, *The Souls of Black Folk*, p. 49.

ous or negligible, and your property in yourself is secure because you need never labor nor compromise. Hence, it is thematically appropriate that Tom sees Jim's incarceration as an opportunity to rewrite the escape and restoration of the wronged Dolphin, the "natural son of Louis XIV" (204). Mark Twain's response to the hazards of market life is unique. He does not yearn for an agrarian, pre-market world of self-sufficient domestic production; nor does he espouse the southern claim that by extending the family slavery reduces the alienation of free labor; nor does he oppose slavery as either the subversion of market freedom or the institutionalization of capitalism's worst features. Instead, Twain invokes absolute monarchy as the perfection of free market property rights for the one independent master. "To become independent," Fitzhugh writes, " is to be able to make other people support you, without being obliged to labor for *them*."[57] Fitzhugh intends this statement as a critique of the free labor system; Twain would view it as what freemen implicitly want from property rights, but what only enslaving others can achieve.

The hyperbole of Twain's language suggests the impossibility, and hence urgency, of his fantasy. How could pilots be more kingly than kings? If kings "sit in chains" (93), do pilots sit tethered only by rope? The pilot's freedom, like that of any freeperson, is a freedom of contract. But because any contract amounts for Twain to manacled service, no one can enjoy the kind of freedom he and many other Americans labored in service to. If a historical and conceptual fantasy, Twain's labor-eliding romance of piloting interpretation and independence is a sensible strategy for repairing the contradiction in the liberal vision of independence and self. The more-than-regal independence Twain imagines for the pilot is impossible, and can obtain only outside social relations, in intimacy with the map of one's instinct.

57. Fitzhugh, *Cannibals All!*, p. 18.

Cataloging the Creatures of the Deep:
"Billy Budd, Sailor" and the Rise of Sociology

Susan Mizruchi

The task of interpreting American literary realism has always involved coming to terms with a poetics of sight.[1] Recently, critics have begun
to specify the problem of realist seeing as part of the larger historical problem of subjectivity and agency in the late nineteenth century—how was
individual (or collective) consciousness and action conceived in the era of
realism's emergence?

New Historicists who reassess the claims of historical reality upon
literary works are drawn to American realism, and their analyses have led
to new understandings of the realist subject. In place of the sobering recog-
nitions or heightened political consciousnesses found in an earlier era of
realist criticism, the subject in New Historicism is unconsciously positioned

For helpful suggestions at various stages of this essay, I would like to thank Jon Klancher,
Donald Pease, Alfred Young, William Vance, and Nancy Bentley.
1. See, among others, Alfred Kazin, *On Native Ground* (New York: Anchor, 1942); Lionel
Trilling, *The Liberal Imagination* (New York: Viking, 1950); Warner Berthoff, *The Ferment
of Realism* (New York: Free Press, 1965); Harold Kolb, *The Illusion of Life* (Charlottes-
ville: University of Virginia Press, 1969); and Edwin Cady, *The Light of Common Day*
(Bloomington: Indiana University Press, 1971).

within structures of social control. As a social observer, he is contained by his perceptions, just as he is contained by the manifold authoritative eyes that supervise his every move. Realist literature functions overall as a site for the management and assuagement of potentially critical energies, with realist authors its unwitting agents. What unites virtually all New Historicist interpretations of American realism is a ritual denial of critical viewpoint.[2] Literary authors and their texts are caught within a uniform net of subjectivity, for human understanding and desire are limited to the beliefs and activities generated by a capitalist system.

This essay reconsiders these issues by exploring the ideological underpinnings of late nineteenth-century arguments that homogenize and limit subjectivity and agency. My claim is that recent characterizations of realist subjectivity have similarities to a late nineteenth-century American sociological tradition: to study the rise of that tradition, and the challenges to it, is to locate an important historical context for our own critical discussions.[3] The problem of individual and collective consciousness and agency

2. See, for example, Walter Benn Michaels, *The Gold Standard and the Logic of Naturalism* (Berkeley: University of California Press, 1987); and Philip Fisher, "Democratic Social Space: Whitman, Melville, and the Promise of Transparency," *Representations* 24 (Fall 1988): 60–101.

3. The respective pragmatist and functionalist emphases of new historicism and sociology converge in a late nineteenth-century tradition which sees all human activity as interdependent, a flux "uninterrupted by intrinsic divisions and discrete boundaries." Social and cultural phenomena, individual and collective action, are viewed as functions and roles in vast social systems, and subjective understanding is held to be largely homogeneous, that is, uniformly conditioned by the logic of the social system. One way in which they differ is that new historicists, like pragmatist predecessors William James and John Dewey, deny the analyst an Archimedean standpoint, while sociologists insist upon analytical objectivity. In practice, however, new historicism's hopelessly conditioned interpreter and sociology's expert observer occupy the same hermeneutical stance: neutral analysts whose neutrality depends upon their strategic disregard for their own interpretive positions. For more on this pragmatist-functionalist tradition see Thomas Haskell, *The Emergence of Professional Social Science* (Urbana: University of Illinois Press, 1977), pp. 10–12 and passim, Morton White, *Social Thought in America* (Boston: Beacon Press, 1957), and Richard Rorty, *The Consequences of Pragmatism* (Minneapolis: University of Minnesota Press, 1982), especially chapters eight, nine, and eleven. For a useful critique of the neutraility claims of Karl Mannheim's Sociology of Knowledge, see Theodor Adorno, *Prisms*, trans. by Samuel and Shierry Weber (Cambridge: MIT Press, 1986), pp. 37–49. Sociologists have long recognized the significance of Pragmatism to sociology. The place to begin an exploration of these issues is Emile Durkheims's newly published lectures (1913–14), *Pragmatism and Sociology*, trans. J. C. Whitehouse, ed. John Allcock (Cambridge: Cambridge University Press, 1983). Also see: Stefan Collini, *Liberalism*

in the late nineteenth century was highly contested, a source of cultural tension and debate that engaged literary authors and sociologists alike. Those who dramatized and discussed the act of seeing and the more abstract issues of subjectivity and agency were impelled in part by anxiety as to whether the variety of possible subject positions could be kept within certain boundaries. The actual expansion of potential subject positions in this period of extreme demographic change—which included a rise in internal immigrants (hobos, unemployed workers, and also formerly excluded groups seeking entrance into the free labor force) as well as external immigrants (foreign-born Americans)—informs literary realist and social scientific views of subjectivity. I show how sociologists responded to increasing social heterogeneity and dislocation with arguments that emphasized the ultimate uniformity and limitedness of all social understanding; the regulatory powers of social models or types; and the elusiveness of causal explanation. The ideology of indeterminacy posited a vacuum in social knowledge that was to be filled by the expert empirical strategies of the professional sociologist. This essay considers Herman Melville's story, "Billy Budd, Sailor: An Inside Narrative" (written from 1886–1891), as a work of realism which theorizes the problem of social sight and visibility that so concerned sociologists in this era. By dramatizing its characters' variable access to sight, and variable control over social visibility and invisibility, the story reveals that any view of subjectivity is a political choice rather than a natural fact. And through the perspective of its narrator, the story elaborates the potential for a critical viewpoint "inside" the system.

It has been suggested that nothing so invests a culture with interest in a given phenomenon as the experience of disconnection from it.[4] It might be added that nothing so invests a culture with interest in a given phenomenon as the conviction that it can no longer be limited and controlled. These points both apply to the late nineteenth-century preoccupation with "sight." A culture of vigilance, which features the obsessive production of methodologies and theories about observation and visibility, is one which both doubts human capacities to see and doubts whether access to such powers can be kept within prevailing social boundaries.

---

and Sociology (Cambridge: Cambridge University Press, 1979). I have explored these issues further in an unpublished paper, "Americanist New Historicism at the Turn of the Century: The Critic as Social Scientist," presented at MLA Special Session, 1988.

4. See Erich Hobsbawm and Terence Ranger, The Invention of Tradition (Cambridge: Cambridge University Press, 1983); and Richard Terdiman, "Deconstructing Memory," Diacritics (Winter 1985): 13–36.

"Billy Budd" confronts the sorts of pressures upon sight that were culture-wide in this period. Aboard the story's fog-bound ship, the ability to control what is seen, and by whom, is a sign as well as a source of power. The sailors' dogwatch, the most common rite of the ship society, and the first level of a highly formalized hierarchy of sight, is strictly supervised by the officers. At the next level, John Claggart, the master-at-arms, otherwise known as the "chief of police,"[5] operates surreptitiously, his surveillance procedures invisible to all, including the Captain. Captain Vere has the greatest stake in controlling perceptions, and he is at once the character most troubled by the complications of seeing aboard the *Bellipotent* and the primary agent of obscurity. Vere acts in a variety of ways to limit the sight and understanding of his crew: consciously (Vere, "so contrived it that [his steward] should not catch sight of the prone one," 477); unconsciously ("Vere advanced to meet him, thus unconsciously intercepting his view," 478); and finally as a matter of "policy," (engineering, "the maintenance of secrecy, the confining of all knowledge" aboard ship, 480). All the concerns over watching and being watched in the story derive from a prevailing fear of social disorder. Set on the nervous British seas of the late eighteenth century, in the wake of the mutinies at Nore and Spithead and their historical shadows, British Jacobinism and revolutionary France, the story is a test case for the problem of authority and agency. But it is anxieties over social order—the anxieties of Melville's late nineteenth-century America—that finally seem most fully present in its characters and scenes.[6]

From 1866 to 1885, the year before he began writing "Billy Budd," Melville worked as a custom-house inspector for the port of New York. His correspondence from this nineteen-year period yields few direct impressions of his daily activities as an inspector, and his biographers devote little attention to his occupation, regarding it as a degrading interruption of his literary vocation, an unfortunate excursion into the fallen world of political spoils and trade economy.[7]

---

5. "Billy Budd, Sailor: An Inside Narrative," in *Great Short Works of Herman Melville*, ed. Warner Berthoff (New York: Harper and Row, 1969), p. 448. All subsequent references to this edition will be included parenthetically in the text.

6. The story's narration is an historical pastiche drawn by an inhabitant of late-nineteenth-century America. See the numerous allusions that range throughout the nineteenth century in *Billy Budd, Sailor*, ed. Harrison Hayford and Merton Sealts (Chicago: University of Chicago Press, 1962). This edition also reviews the story's complicated writing and editing history.

7. Michael Rogin departs from this critical consensus by introducing his chapter on "Billy

Apart from any record of his impressions, what might Melville have witnessed as an inspector for the New York custom-house in this era? By 1884, the average number of steamer ships entering the port of New York was forty a week; the job of the customs inspector was to examine the baggage of passengers, native and immigrant, assess the truth of their customs declarations, and collect duties on imported goods. "Inspectors, through long practice, become involuntary disciples of Lavater, and such expert citizens of human nature that they almost intuitively detect attempted fraud."[8] Among the passengers inspected, the immigrants were invariably "a motley crowd . . . representative of twenty-four different nationalities." By "1883 the number of immigrants recorded was 405,352 . . . immigrants being poorer now than formerly, only $9360 were collected in duties."[9] The work of the custom-house inspector was an exercise in vigilance, which involved "watching, exposure, and fatigue." And the custom-house itself was "the most scientifically organized and economically administered of American national institutions."[10] It is essential to an' understanding of "Billy Budd," that for nineteen years prior to its writing, Melville had first-hand knowledge of a social institution which was based on empirical and categorical expertise and was dedicated to the enrichment of the national government.[11]

Budd" with an allusion to Melville's custom-house experience. But his account is slanted to accord with a portrait of Melville as faded aristocrat, entirely identified with Vere in his defense of state authority, and intent on preserving the dignity of his inheritance against the encroachment of an "alien world: alien in its attack both on duty, and on the familial bases of political power" (*Subversive Genealogy: The Politics and Art of Herman Melville* [New York: Knopf, 1983], pp. 288–94). It is telling that Rogin omits any mention of what Melville was *actually doing* during his long tenure at the custom-house. As my reading suggests, "Billy Budd" is far from an endorsement of state authority and inherited privilege as against the threat of alien influences. Melville's manuscript revisions render increasingly questionable Vere's actions. [See Hayford and Sealts's edition, pp. 34–39, 175–83]. Moreover, the story testifies to Melville's deep engagement with the growing diversity of American society and the variety of responses to it, a fascination for cultural difference that is evident throughout his career, from the early anthropological investigations of *Typee*, to the anatomy of forms—philological, religious, philosophical, biological —in *Moby-Dick*. For another view of Melville in the custom-house, see Stanton Garner's "Surviving the Gilded Age: Herman Melville in the Customs Service," *Essays in Arts and Sciences* xv (June 1986), pp. 1–13.

8. "The New York Custom-House," R. Wheatly, *Harpers Magazine* LXIX (June 1884): 47.

9. "The New York Custom-House," 49–51.

10. "The New York Custom-House," 53, 61.

11. By indicating the significance of this late nineteenth-century historical and biographical context, I do not mean to argue that Melville set out in "Billy Budd" to write an allegory of contemporary American social change. But Melville knew the impact of the present

1

Late nineteenth-century America experienced social change on a scale and with a rapidity that was unprecedented in American history. The final eclipse of a fading feudal order with slavery's formal end (1865), the decline of religious belief, the rapid technological and industrial development and economic growth, and the extreme social stratification and labor instability that accompanied them, launched America into an unchecked absorption of industrial capitalism.[12] Among these changes was the dramatic increase in social heterogeneity brought about by immigration from southern and eastern Europe.[13] The immigrant influx reactivated a dormant Nativist movement whose rhetoric aligned ethnic and racial mixing with social anarchy. "There is no such thing as an American anarchist," declared one journalist in 1888. But immigration actually served to externalize an already existing class conflict. As John Higham has suggested, the simultaneous reaction against immigration by capital and labor in the 1880s reflected the growing chasm between them: while capitalists saw the immigrant as an agent of anarchy, laborers saw the immigrant as one means to their oppression.[14]

---

on any historical narrative, a preoccupation which had informed another story published nearly forty years before. In "Benito Cereno" (1854), an eighteenth-century slave narrative written in an era split by controversy over slavery, as well as in "Billy Budd," an eighteenth-century narrative about social disorder written in an era rife with class and racial conflict, Melville was obliged to "hold the Present at its worth without being inappreciative of the Past" ("BB" 441). Thus, Melville selected an historical-fictional setting for its strong affinities to his present, a distant yet compatible ship society which offered a realm for contemplating freely the exigencies of the late nineteenth century. For Melville, to reconstruct the past was to confront his own era in its full historicity, not as something personal which one "experiences," but as part of previous, and perhaps, future eras. In his recent overview of "Billy Budd" criticism, Robert Milder cites Melville's "response to contemporary social and political developments" as "among the most promising [avenues] for future investigation." The story, he suggests, illuminates "how social thought is a function of history," revealing "the consciousness of a late-nineteenth-century writer brooding on experience through the ideological cul-de-sacs of his age" (*Critical Essays on Melville's "Billy Budd,"* ed. Robert Milder [New York: G. K. Hall, 1989], pp. 14–15).

12. See, among others, Perry Miller, *American Thought: Civil War to World War I* (New York: Holt, Rinehart, and Winston, 1954); Karl Marx, *America and the Civil War* in *The Karl Marx Library,* ed. Saul K. Padover (New York: McGraw Hill, 1972), 2: 1–77; Robert Wiebe, *The Search for Order* (New York: Hill and Wang, 1967); Herbert Gutman, *Work, Culture, and Society* (New York: Vintage, 1977); Jackson Lears, *No Place of Grace* (New York: Pantheon, 1981); John Higham, *Strangers in the Land* (New York: Atheneum, 1966).

13. See Higham, pp. 110, 159.

14. Higham, pp. 85, 50. For more on capital-labor conflict and radical activism in this era,

The rise of external immigration also heightened awareness of what I have called the phenomenon of internal immigration. A prominent feature of late nineteenth-century American society was the rising visibility of panhandlers, hobos, and other populations of the homeless and the unemployed. These marginal figures who haunt the pages of literary realism (in Theodore Dreiser's "Captain" sequence from *Sister Carrie*, for example) attest to society's inability to assimilate all of its members. Their existence bespeaks the extreme inequities and human costs of a late nineteenth-century industrial capitalist system—fears which were displaced onto the figure of the foreign immigrant.[15]

Social scientists of the era devoted themselves to immigrant causes, and while there was a certain optimism in their zealous activity on behalf of the immigrant, the tenor of their attention suggests anxiety. A random sample of papers from the American Social Science Association between the years 1870 and 1890 includes essays on "Pauperism in New York City," (1873); "The Negro Exodus from the Gulf States," (by Frederick Douglass); "The Emigration of Colored Citizens from the Southern States," (1880); "Immigration and Nervous Diseases" and "Immigration and Crime," (1889).[16] An organization whose motto was *Ne Quid Nimis* ("Everything in Moderation") could not have confronted the waves of foreign immigration with complete confidence.

Advocates of the new discipline of sociology which developed from the broader field of social science took a more optimistic view of social heterogeneity. American society, argued F. H. Giddings and Albion Small, was capable of converting any variety of difference into one homogeneous American type. Herbert Spencer concurred, predicting in an 1882 visit to America that the American melting pot would produce "a better man than the world had yet seen."[17] The ideological dimensions of their arguments

---

see Bruce Nelson's study of Chicago anarchism, *Beyond the Martyrs: A Social History of Chicago's Anarchists, 1870–1900* (New Brunswick: Rutgers University Press, 1988), especially Part III, pp. 175–242.

15. See Carlos Schwantes's study of vagabonds and other social marginals in this era, *Coxey's Army* (Lincoln: Nebraska University Press, 1985), and Leah Hannah Fedler, *Unemployment Relief in Periods of Depression: A Study of Measures Adopted in Certain American Cities, 1857 through 1922* (New York: Russel Sage Foundation, 1936). Edward Saveth, in *American Historians and European Immigrants 1875–1925* (New York: Columbia University Press, 1948), analyzes the means by which one prominent intellectual group displaced threats of internal turmoil onto foreign immigrants.

16. *Journal of Social Science* (Boston: Damrell and Upham) numbers 3–27.

17. Quoted in Allan Nevins, *America Through British Eyes* (New York: 1948), p. 355.

are fairly obvious. What social scientists like Frank Sanborn had feared—
the decreased power of human understanding and action in an increasingly complex and elusive social world—sociologists learned to exploit. According to the logic of sociology, the assimilation of people from a variety
of backgrounds to the American way depended upon the severe circum-
scription and levelling of all social consciousness and agency. Sociological
assertions about the uniformity of subject positions, their repeated suggestions that every citizen (whether native born or naturalized) held the same
aspirations, did not deny extremes of inequality; rather, they separated desire and agency from outcome.[18] This wholesale containment of subjective
understanding became the basis for professional legitimacy. The sociologist claimed superior capacities of consciousness and action in a world
which supposedly privileged neither, a disparity consistent with laissez-faire
ideology. Laissez faire, as formulated by political economists earlier in the
century, had never precluded state intervention. Rather, it portrayed the
economic system as one that would run best without external regulation,
an assumption which greatly influenced social policy through the turn of
the century and later. Thus, in the face of widespread poverty and unemployment, government representatives of this era insisted that "economic
laws [were] a part of the machinery of the universe as much as the laws of
gravitation"; but to protect corporate business interests, they were willing to
intervene.[19]

The political climate which sustained sociological arguments for the
uniformity of subjectivity and for the absorptive powers of the American
melting pot found its key formulation in work by F. H. Giddings and E. A.
Ross on the uses of social types. Giddings described four major American
character types which he located in specific historical figures: "the forceful

18. For more on the ideology of success in this era, see my chapter on Dreiser's *An American Tragedy* in *The Power of Historical Knowledge: Narrating the Past in Hawthorne,
James, and Dreiser* (Princeton: Princeton University Press, 1988), pp. 242–94.
19. Quoted in Schwantes, p. 15. See the following works by historians on the late nine-
teenth century: Philip S. Foner, *History of the Labor Movement in the United States*
(New York: International Publishers, 1964), vol. 3; William Appleman Williams, *The Con-
tours of American History* (New York: World, 1961); Thomas C. Cochran and William
Miller, *The Age of Enterprise* (New York: Harper Torchbook, 1961); James Weinstein,
The Corporate Ideal in the Liberal State: 1900–1918 (Boston: Beacon Press, 1968); and
Alfred B. Chandler, Jr., *The Visible Hand: The Managerial Revolution in American Busi-
ness* (Cambridge: Harvard University Press, 1977). Also see William Graham Sumner,
What Social Classes Owe to Each Other (New York: Harper and Brothers, 1883), for a
famous presentation of laissez-faire ideology.

type," exemplified by Daniel Boone; "the convivial type," emblematized by the white plantation owners of the slave South; "the austere type," found among the New England Puritans; and "the rationally conscientious type," represented by Ralph Waldo Emerson and William Ellery Channing.[20] Giddings then applied his typology to New York City tenement dwellers, classifying "forty-six families . . . as forceful . . . one hundred and seventy-five . . . as convivial" and so on.[21]

E. A. Ross was quite explicit about the utility of type categories for purposes of social control. A diversified American society, too disparate to rely on spontaneous social obedience, he argued, had to devise new means for ordering itself. In his system, social conformity was achieved through models, "patterns and types [such as the ideal "mother," "priest," "soldier"] which society induces its members to adopt as their guide." Based on the principle of internal self-regulation, what he called "bind-[ing] from within," Ross's model left the individual "with the illusion of self-direction even at the very moment he martyrizes himself for the ideal we have seduously impressed upon him." At its most effective, social control is invisible. "The fact of control," Ross concludes, "is in good sooth, no gospel to be preached abroad . . . the wise sociologist . . . will not tell the street Arab, or the Elmira inmate how he is managed."[22]

A comparison of the major methodological concerns of late nineteenth-century sociologists with writings by the earliest practitioners in America pinpoints the ideological dimensions of these concerns. George Fitzhugh and Henry Hughes, the first authors in America to use the term "sociology" in their book titles, were basically rational apologists for slavery. They described sociology as a profession whose knowledge and practice could remedy modern society and, so, as a profession which had no place in the clear stable settings of the slave South. In *Uncle Tom's Cabin* (1852), Harriet Beecher Stowe also invokes rational empiricism in her confrontation with slavery. Like sociologists and literary realists of a later generation, Stowe and Fitzhugh are anxious about social difference, as exemplified by internal as well as external immigrants. Both view the black slave

20. "The American People," *The International Quarterly* 7, 2 (June 1903): 233–34.

21. *Readings in Descriptive and Historical Sociology* (New York: Macmillan, 1906), pp. 235–36.

22. *Social Control* (New York: Macmillan, 1901), pp. 244, 441. Though not collected as a volume until 1901, Ross' essays on social control appeared throughout the 1890s in *The American Journal of Sociology*. See Herman and Julia Schwendinger, *The Sociologists of the Chair* (New York: Basic Books, 1974), p. 203.

as a type of internal immigrant, but where Fitzhugh effaces difference by making blacks the emblems of social conditioning, model human sacrifices to the necessities of the system, Stowe exaggerates difference by portraying blacks as so immune to socialization that they must be deported at her novel's end.

2

George Fitzhugh's *Sociology for the South*, published in Richmond, Virginia in 1854, defines sociology as a modern science without relevance to the Edenic world of the slave South. Fitzhugh's title, in effect, is an empty signifier, for "sociology" represents liberal curative strategies that have no meaning under the "happy . . . conditions" of southern slavery. Sociology is a collection of remedies cooked up by "authors and schemers, such as Owen, Louis Blanc, and Fourier," to treat "the diseases [of] free society." A paternalistic slave society is harmonic because it is the only existing form of social organization that recognizes man's true nature as social. "Man," writes Fitzhugh, "is born a member of society, and does not form society." There is no such thing as "consent," for man is "born [society's] slave, and ha[s] no rights to cede."[23] For Fitzhugh, the negro slave is the model social being for a fully articulated social system. Within a slaveocracy, the negro as internal immigrant is entirely contained.

It would be premature to dismiss outright Fitzhugh's almost parodic denials of the conflicts of a southern slave system, without also recognizing that the book is a classic antebellum argument for a certain form of social organization.[24] Fitzhugh's slave society is a fading ideal type, a conflict-free caste system that has no application to the modern world. In defining his southern system *against* sociology, Fitzhugh is the first to identify sociology as a modern science, a discipline that emerges to articulate an ideology essential to capitalist development. It is critical that, among other things, later sociological writings express greater ambivalence toward the category of the individual. Where Fitzhugh simply annihilates it, by characterizing the

23. "Sociology for the South," in Harvey Wish, ed. *Antebellum* (New York: Capricorn, 1960), pp. 45, 58. Also see, Henry Hughes, *Treatise on Sociology* (New York: Lippincot, 1854).
24. Fitzhugh himself admitted that he had exaggerated his claims for southern "peace and fraternity." "I assure you, Sir," he wrote to George Holmes, a professor at the University of Virginia, "I see great evils in Slavery, but in a controversial work I ought not to admit them." Quoted in Wish, p. 20.

individual as a product of social conditions, later sociologists retain some notion of individual choice in recognition that the category of the individual, however embattled, is essential to capitalist ideology.

Fitzhugh's book helps to codify social and intellectual developments already well underway in this period. The institutional origins of American sociology lie in the 1865 founding of the American Social Science Association, whose roots can be traced to the creation in 1851 of a Board of Aliens Commission by the State of Massachusetts. The charge of this board was "to superintend the execution of all laws in relation to the introduction of aliens in the Commonwealth." The genesis of American sociology—from this Board of Aliens Commission, to the American Social Science Association, and on to the 1905 founding of the American Sociological Society (now known as the American Sociological Association)—reveals that, from its beginnings, the goal of American sociology was to mediate social diversity. The "science" of society may be said to have developed in response to the threat of social difference.[25]

Fitzhugh ends his book with an attack upon methods of human classification that become standardized by sociologists in the late nineteenth century. "We abhor the doctrine of 'The Types of Mankind,' " he writes, "first, because it is at war with scripture, which teaches us that the whole human race is descended from a common parentage; and secondly, because it encourages and incites brutal masters to treat negroes, not as weak, ignorant, and dependent brethren, but as wicked beasts without the pale of humanity" (A 95). Types are a derogatory method of human cataloging that have no place in an organic feudal order. In reality, however, the very rational social engineering methods that Fitzhugh supposedly despises reflect his own purpose: the containment of racial difference. Fitzhugh's social model is an assimilationist one, under which blacks are familiarized and controlled.

It is significant that the first move of Harriet Beecher Stowe in the

---

25. *Board of State Charities of Massachusetts: Third Annual Report* (1867), p. xxi. For more on the "origins" of American sociology see, L. L. and Jessie Bernard, *Origins of American Sociology* (New York: Thomas Crowell, 1943); Floyd House, *The Development of Sociology* (New York: McGraw Hill, 1936); Schwendinger, *The Sociologists of the Chair*; Thomas Haskell, *The Emergence of Professional Social Science*; and essays by Henrika Kuklick, "Restructuring the Past: Toward an Appreciation of the Social Context of Social Science," *The Sociological Quarterly* 21 (Winter 1980): 5–21; and "The Organization of Social Science in the United States," *American Quarterly* 28 (1976): 124–41.

preface to *Uncle Tom's Cabin* is to restore the category of black difference that Fitzhugh erases. Far from an invisible figure socialized into an ideal posture of self-sacrifice, the black in Stowe is "an exotic race," of "a character so essentially unlike the hardened dominant Anglo-Saxon race, as for many years to have won from it only misunderstanding and contempt."[26]

A pivotal example of literature's power to affect society, the novel, like the sociological theories being developed in this era, combines racist ideology with a commitment to empirical social description. Within its delineation of the various slave regions and slave economies, it offers a catalog of different forms of social organization, including: the Christian humanitarianism of the Shelby's; the utopian idyll of the Quakers; the laissez-faire realm of Augustine St. Claire (where social roles are chaotically mobile and bear no fixed relationship to the caste system of the larger society); and the autocratic regime of Simon Legree (where all power is centralized in a single arbitrary authority). Part moralism and part social realism, Stowe's narrative combines emotional harangue with minute empirical detail.

Stowe's realism is laced with racial determinism, and her view of human character holds strictly to innate biological attributes. It is a deterministic model which applies equally to whites and blacks: Simon Legree, who has followed the brutal dictates of an inherently evil nature despite his mother's "unwearied love, and patient prayers" (*UTC* 528), is its most dramatic example. Stowe's biologism also supports a caste system of superior light-skinned and inferior dark-skinned blacks, the latter of whom are the particular objects of a containing Christianity. Atheistic and educable mulattoes, like George Harris, exemplify miscegenation, but foretell a black pride and agency that is not so easily assimilable.

Stowe's racial politics are fundamentally confused: on the one hand, she seems convinced of the need for black difference; on the other hand, she locates the highest potential of blacks in those who are most white. In keeping with this, in the novel's closing prophecy, blacks are freed, educated, empowered, and then deported. These contradictions are manifest in Stowe's characterization of her mulatto protagonist, George Harris, who is given his own voice in a closing letter. Aggressively embracing difference, Harris wishes himself shades darker, calls for a separate black nation, and denounces directly the effacing powers of the American melting pot. "But, you will tell me, our race have equal rights to mingle in the American re-

26. *Uncle Tom's Cabin* (New York: Pocket Books, 1963), p. xix. All subsequent references are to the Penguin edition, (New York: 1981), and will appear parenthetically in the text.

public as the Irishman, the German, the Swede," he proclaims, "Granted they have. . . . But, then, *I do not want it*" (*UTC* 610). The contradictions between Harris's light-skinned superiorities, which alone have enabled his radical message, and his separatist views mirror the larger contradictions of the novel.

In Stowe's world, only the mulatto can articulate the value of black difference so essential to any genuinely radical idea of black identity. Stowe's dilemma anticipates the conflicting social programs of Booker T. Washington and W. E. B. DuBois. Washington's quiescent black enacts the syndrome of the internal immigrant in literal terms, by washing away his difference (the novel abounds in cleaning rituals), while DuBois's ironic "final solution" to the problem of the color line—make blacks disappear through mass extermination—presages his own far from ironic emigration to Ghana.[27] Despite its closing prophecy of black deportation, *Uncle Tom's Cabin* leaves an opening for late nineteenth-century parallels between blacks and immigrants, in testifying that "the first desire of the emancipated slave, generally, is education" (*UTC* 456).[28] Moreover, the resemblances between Stowe's slave and Melville's sailor protagonists (Uncle Tom and Billy Budd) suggest the continuities between slave consciousness and lower-class-consciousness in America. The submission and self-sacrifice enacted by Uncle Tom and Billy Budd are always one step ahead of the authorities and demonstrate their internalization of the tyrannical requirements of their societies.[29]

Slavery did not vanish miraculously from the American consciousness with its formal end in 1865. The institution, and the debates over social

27. See Washington's, *Up From Slavery* in *Three Negro Classics* (New York: Avon, 1965), especially chapter three, "The Struggle for an Education"; and DuBois's parable, "A Mild Suggestion," in *DuBois' Writings*, ed. Nathan Huggins (New York: Library of America, 1986), pp. 1138–41.

28. As Henry James's reformist zealot, Miss Birdseye, observes in *The Bostonians* (1886): "When causes were embodied in foreigners (what else were the Africans?), they were certainly more appealing" (Harmondsworth: Penguin English Library, 1985), p. 56.

29. For some suggestive psychological and political analysis of slave consciousness among America's lower class in historical perspective see, *The Hidden Injuries of Class* by Richard Sennett and Jonathan Cobb (New York: Vintage, 1972). In a chapter called "Freedom," the authors ask, "What does it mean to be unfree, in a class society?" To be "unfree," has two meanings. The simpler meaning is that "men cannot do what they want." The more complicated meaning "involves the idea of compulsion [where] the responsibility of self-validation . . . channels consciousness into the path of sacrifice and betrayal" (220). It is the latter form that is especially relevant to "Billy Budd."

and racial difference that it engendered, persisted in the circumstances— social, economic, and psychological—of blacks in the imaginations of later realist writers, and in the writings of sociologists. In the late nineteenth century, the question of how to assimilate over three million freed blacks into society coincided with the question of how to assimilate increasing numbers of foreign immigrants, whose presence served both to mirror and suppress the circumstances of various internal immigrants. The end of slavery and the rise of immigration pointed to the larger question of what binds a modern society rapidly losing its grip on traditional sources of social order: what keeps such diverse human populations in line? The fact that the first examples of sociology in America were last gasp defenses of slavery reveals how sociology arose out of the vacuum created by a declining slaveocracy and the accompanying anxieties about maintaining social order and mediating social difference.

3

In his 1874 book, *The Study of Sociology*, Herbert Spencer offers a classic formulation of an emerging sociological ideology. Through the image of a "single meal [where one] may take in bread made from Russian wheat, beef from Scotland, potatoes from the midland countries, sugar from Maurithuis, salt from Cheshire, pepper from Jamaica," he captures "the incalculable complexity under which each individual, and a fortiori each society develops, lives, and decays."[30] Spencer's image for the concealed and far-ranging links among and within societies embodies a typical experience of modernization, which the sociologist both expresses and exaggerates.

In conceiving the role of the professional sociologist, American founders like F. H. Giddings and Albion Small drew upon Spencer's notion of underlying causes to portray the sociologist as a deep and coordinated seer who could grasp fundamental social realities in their interrelations. The sociologist's aim was to see objectively and systematically, so as to supercede the narrow prejudices of the average social observer. They derided simple "empiricism," and distinguished their discipline of sociology from the field of social science by their commitment to "critical methodology" over "humanitarian sentiment."[31] In an increasingly mystifying and interdependent society, the sociologist, as holistic weaver, could unite "the

30. Herbert Spencer, *The Study of Sociology* (New York: Appleton, 1874), p. 14.
31. Albion Small quoted in Haskell, p. 203.

fragmentary knowledge of social relations" possessed by "the millions."[32] Like their European contemporaries, the authors of classic sociological works—Max Weber and Georg Simmel in Germany and Emile Durkheim in France—these American sociologists asserted the importance of a "value-free" social science.[33]

The rise of professionalization in the late nineteenth century was in part the means by which a social elite could revitalize and ensure its hegemony in the modern age.[34] The need to be "scientific," to establish some empirical authority for their profession, haunted even ministers of this era. As the Reverend Henry Ward Beecher wrote in 1872, "a science of management" was essential knowledge for every minister, and he suggested that the works of Spencer be added to the clerical curriculum.[35] For many social groups, the clamour for scientific credentials became a key means of combatting threats against their social status.

In his book on the rise of the medical profession, Paul Starr traces changing attitudes toward authority and science, from the Jacksonian to the Progressive eras. The common sense ethic of the Jacksonian period (what we have described as an excessive faith in empirical realities), which

32. Albion Small, "The Era of Sociology," *American Journal of Sociology* 1 (July 1895): 3, 6, 8. Also see, F. H. Giddings, "The Relation of Sociology to Other Scientific Studies," *Journal of Social Science* 32 (November 1894): 144–50.

33. Weber was less convinced of the possibility of a "neutral" social science than has usually been assumed. Indeed, his method of ideal types was an attempt to develop a system of categories which could account for the subjective factor. Weber's "objective" set of ideal concepts were designed to sustain some reflexive recognition of their cultural specificity. See *From Max Weber*, ed. H. H. Gerth and C. Wright Mills (Glenco: Free Press, 1946), "Introduction," "Politics as a Vocation," and "Science as a Vocation." Also see, "The Methodology of the Social Sciences," in *Weber: Selections in Translation*, ed. W. G. Runciman (Cambridge: Cambridge University Press, 1978). As one of the "princes of reason," a key articulator of a social scientific defense for corporate liberalism, Durkheim serves for Herman and Julia Schwendinger as an important European analog to the rise of American social science. See *Sociologists of the Chair*, pp. 70–71; 254–60; 261–66. Durkheim's work, *The Division of Labor in Society* (Glencoe: Free Press, 1947), written from 1883 to 1893, is especially pertinent to my arguments in this essay. Georg Simmel had the most direct influence on American sociology. Albion Small was already translating his essays for the *American Journal of Sociology* in the 1890s. See, *Georg Simmel: On Individuality and Social Forms*, ed. Donald Levine (Chicago: University of Chicago Press, 1971), "Introduction."

34. See, for example, Laurence Veysey, *The Emergence of the American University* (Chicago: Chicago University Press, 1965), p. 265.

35. Beecher, quoted in Haskell, p. 83.

tended to view scientific knowledge as widely accessible, gave way to a positivistic elitism, which portrayed scientific knowledge as highly abstruse and beyond the comprehension of the majority. "The less one could believe one's own eyes," writes Starr, "and the new world of science continually prompted that feeling—the more receptive one became to seeing the world through the eyes of those who claimed specialized, technical knowledge, validated by communities of their peers."[36]

As these studies show, professionals had a stake in promoting anxiety about the complexity of social life. And more than any other professional, the sociologist based his claim for expertise on his special capacities of sight. Just as illness, among physicians, is "good for business," so is indeterminacy for sociologists. Herbert Spencer's famous parable of the warped iron plate articulates the sociologist's relationship to this indeterminacy. In the form of an imaginary dialogue between a social reformer and a neutral observer who together contemplate a warped iron plate, the parable not only posits the ineffectiveness of all social observation and action, but also fills the vacuum with the acute empirical powers of the sociological expert. "How shall we flatten it? Obviously, you reply, by hitting down on the part that is prominent." But the attempt to flatten the plate by striking the prominent part only produces another warp. "A pretty bungle we have made of it. Instead of curing the original defect, we have produced a second. Had we asked an artisan practiced in 'planishing' . . . he would have taught us how to give variously directed and specially adjusted blows with a hammer elsewhere: so attacking the evil not by direct but by indirect actions."[37]

Spencer's parable has been rightly understood as a sociological endorsement of non-intervention and laissez-faire capitalism. But it also represents a claim for social dominance founded on professional expertise. Like the practiced planisher, the sociologist knows how to penetrate surfaces to apprehend the invisible patterns of causality that escape ordinary observation.[38]

36. Paul Starr, *The Social Transformation of American Medicine* (New York: Basic Books, 1982), pp. 19, 140.
37. *The Study of Sociology*, pp. 245–46.
38. A strong recent interpretation of "Billy Budd" to which I am indebted, Barbara Johnson's "Melville's Fist: The Execution of Billy Budd," [*The Critical Difference* (Baltimore: Johns Hopkins University Press, 1980), pp. 79–109], shows surprising affinities to Spencer's sociology. Despite obvious differences between his fundamentally unified world of evolutionary interdependence and her decentered world of perpetually deferred meanings, their formulations of historical agency are remarkably compatible. Johnson views

The politics of indeterminacy that inheres in Spencer's sociology is dramatized in "Billy Budd." In its themes, characterizations, and narrative structure, the story reproduces and criticizes the rationalization of social life that absorbed sociologists of the period. The story's world, like the society confronted by these sociologists, is rigorously ordered yet menacingly heterogeneous and represents responses similar to these sociological ones: characters who articulate the visual parameters of a fog-bound world and attempt to supercede it both through claims for exceptional understanding and through the application of classificatory schemes. In their insistence on scientific neutrality, the sociologists we have examined precluded questions about the political implications of their ideas. They failed to consider that their uncertainties, and the methods they devised to counteract them, emerged and functioned within specific socio-political realms. "Billy Budd" addresses many of the issues that are implied but subsumed within the inductive procedures of these sociologists: the exploitation of innocence; professionalization and the social inequalities it under-

---

the story as an allegory of reading, which dramatizes through Billy and Claggart the opposition between acceptance and irony that has split decades of criticism on the story. Vere is the historical reader who "interrogates both past and future for interpretive guidance," and places the story's events within the complicated context of naval mutinies and contemporary martial law (100). At the same time, however, Vere himself continually collapses ambiguity into polarity, to convert a difference within ("Vere as divided between understanding father and military authority") into a difference between ("Billy and Claggart"), which is mirrored by the historical displacement of internal revolution in France with the war between France and England (105–6). Johnson concludes that the story enacts "the twisted relations between knowing and doing: speaking and killing; reading and judging; which make political understanding and action so problematic . . . [and] prevents us from ever knowing whether what we hit coincides with what we understand" (108–9). The critical point of Johnson's reading involves the question of history. Though Vere is no doubt uniquely attached to history, and though there are significant parallels between his embattled authority and that of the eighteenth-century French monarchy, a full elaboration of the story's historical concerns would need to account for a greater range of contexts and to analyze the ways in which historical knowledge is exploited both within the story and without. To understand the particular uses to which history is put requires specifying the political consequences of any view of history. Johnson's conclusion, that hitting ("doing," "killing," "judging") should be avoided because the outcome of any historical action is unpredictable, recalls Spencer's warped iron plate passage. Johnson's reading reveals in its own right the sort of uneven conception of agency that informs laissez-faire ideology: as an agent who knows just how to "hit" the warped plate of textuality, Johnson's critic claims a special ability to navigate the story's pervading indeterminacies. Like Vere, the critic assumes an authoritative form of action, while others are confined to a universal framework of uncertainty and inaction.

writes; the controlling aims of social typologies and the forces that resist them. The story, we might say, offers a political perspective on a contemporary enterprise which vigorously denied self-reflection, however much it prized expert social observation.

4

The opening image of the black sailor at Liverpool, who fades like a superimposed movie still into "the Handsome Sailor," "the welkin-eyed Billy Budd," establishes the dramatic historical exchange enacted in the story.[39] As a shade from the past at least twice removed, a haunting reminder of the double casualties of the eighteenth-century slave trade, the black sailor registers the continuities between black slavery and free white labor.[40]

> In Liverpool, now half a century ago, I saw under the shadow of the great dingy street-wall of Prince's Dock (an obstruction long since removed) a common sailor so intensely black that he must needs have been a native African of the unadulterate blood of Ham—a symmetric figure much above the average height. . . . In jovial sallies left and right, his white teeth flashing into view, he rollicked along, the center of a company of his shipmates. These were made up of such an assortment of tribes and complexions as would have well fitted them

39. In the original manuscript of the story (Houghton Library, Harvard University), the handsome sailor was identified as "the *white* handsome sailor," (my emphasis) but Melville crossed out "white." Apparently, Melville feared that the two figures were so blurred readers would assume that Billy was black, and he felt the need to emphasize that Billy was indeed white. In the end he seems to have decided he was being heavy-handed. Another emendation on the same page (Harper and Row edition, p. 430) registers a similar concern and outcome: Melville's crossing out of the word "innate" from the phrase, "natural innate regality." Here too, Melville's stress on "inherence" apparently seemed, on second thought, too great. In this same vein, it is worth noting that among Melville's papers is a letter from Havelock Ellis, dated July 1890, in which Ellis asks Melville: "to what races you trace yourself back on father's and on mother's side, and what (if any) *recent strains of foreign blood* you lay claim to?" Ellis requests the information, he says, for a book he is writing on "the ancestry of distinguished English and American poets and imaginative writers, with reference to the question of race."

40. As Marcus Rediker points out in his fascinating study *Between the Devil and the Deep Blue Sea* (Cambridge: Cambridge University Press, 1988), Eighteenth-century "Liverpool profited . . . handsomely from the sailor's labor that carried commodities to the coast of Guinea to be exchanged for human cargoes." The slave trade proved equally deadly to white sailors and black captives. See pp. 43–47.

to be marched up by Anarcharsis Cloots before the bar of the first French Assembly as Representative of the Human Race. At each spontaneous tribute rendered by the wayfarers to this black pagod of a fellow—the tribute of a pause and stare, and less frequently, an exclamation, the motley retinue showed that they took that sort of pride in the evoker of it which the Assyrian priests doubtless showed for their grand sculptured Bull when the faithful prostrated themselves. (430)

With its themes of "representativeness," "purity of type," and "sacrifice," the passage introduces the story's major concerns. The black sailor is an ideal type, set amidst a startling "assortment of tribes and complexions." Like this African cynosure, Billy Budd will be a model for the working class. The sailor's first sighting, "under the shadow of the great dingy street-wall," prefigures Billy's "shadow[y]" entrance into the king's service as a victim of impressment, as well as his mysterious origins (323; 329–30). Both details suggest the lingering traces of a slave system: the tyrannical rule of capital over labor and birth as the utilitarian product of breeding.

But the passage places its greatest emphasis on the figure's purity of type. His blackness is singularly "intense," his blood "unadulterate," his body, "symmetric," his teeth genuinely "white": to be a pure type, the passage implies, is to be an anomaly. The sailor creates a hiatus, a disruption in conventional routines. Far from a model to live by, a force in the maintenance of social conformity and order, this type interrupts social regularity. Threatening rather than comforting, his superlative qualities appear uncontrollable, which seems to be the point of the sacrificial image which closes the passage. Sacrifice is a ritual about control, a way of "dealing" with the gods that symbolically captures efforts to defuse or placate forces beyond human powers. This passage, however, is not about controlling gods, but about controlling human beings. Moreover, what is really being sacrificed here is a concept—the concept of typological purity. This fading, recollected image of the black sailor represents the receding potential for typological stability in a modern society organized along the lines of "the division of labor."[41] In "Billy Budd," despite all the biological evidence to the contrary,

41. Durkheim's phrase is used to distinguish modern from primitive societies. Where primitive societies cohere by means of a common conscience which is reinforced by repressive and coercive strategies, specialized modern society coheres through the division of labor, and what he calls "an occupational morality for each profession." See *Emile Durkheim on Morality and Society*, ed. Robert Bellah (Chicago: University of Chicago Press, 1973), p. 111.

the purest white can be black because he has assumed the slave position in the American class system. The fact that the ideal specimen of Anglo Saxon purity has a crucial defect is further evidence for the instability of a new social classification system.[42]

The story's society features a proliferation of type categories as well as characters who resist classification altogether. Characters continually name one another—even more than is usual in Melville's works—which suggests a prevailing uncertainty about human identity. The fact that characters' names fluctuate and the accuracy of given labels is contemplated and questioned also contributes to the sense of indeterminacy. By extension, to have authority is to establish control over the act of naming. Captain Vere assumes the power to name things, to label and to interpret, as crucial to his rule. But Vere's systematic typing efforts are quite distinct from the sailors' naming. When members of the crew name each other— "Board-Her-In-The-Smoke" for Dansker or "Jemmy Legs" for Claggart— the names are both responsive and indeterminate. That is, the crew names in response to a characteristic of the individual, but the names do not clarify or codify any particular form of behavior so much as they obscure it. When a character is typed, however, he is set on an expected and predictable course of behavior. In contrast to the sailors' nicknames, which are insiders' jokes, familiar mainly to the sea commonalty, types are immediately recognizable and universal; they serve to emblazon and predetermine character. And they are binding precisely because they are affixed by an authority.

For Captain Vere, just as for E. A. Ross, social types are a means of establishing social regularity. They are also the aesthetic analog to the brutal underpinnings of his ship's regime. Thus it is appropriate that his famous testimony to the power of social forms appears at the close of the execution chapter where he has realized the martyred destiny of his authorized type. "With mankind," he says, "forms, measured forms are everything; and this is the importance couched in the story of Orpheus with his lyre spellbinding the wild denizens of the wood" (404). Captain Vere's belief in

42. In his essay "The Ideology of Modernism," Georg Lukacs discusses the special instability of social type categories in modern literature. Lukacs draws a distinction between realist literature which preserves concrete type categories and modernist allegory which banishes them. My view of the use of types in realism, however, is that it pictures both a fixity of types (featuring a concrete and coherent typicality) as well as an allegorical destabilization of types (replacing concrete typicality with abstract particularity). The latter allegorical form is part of what I am designating the portrayal of the political manipulation of types in "Billy Budd." *Marxism and Human Liberation* (New York: Delta, 1973), pp. 277–307.

social regularity is explicitly aestheticized. Both successful social orders and successful art are "spellbinding," they function to absorb and contain the wild elements in human nature. Rulers and artists subdue through mystification, by imposing an authority so all-encompassing and mesmerizing that it can be wholly internalized. Vere's authority is osmotic: so subtle and surreptitious that it makes deliberate effects appear inevitable.

Though we are told throughout the story of the common sailors' instinctive innocence, as it turns out, this innocence is carefully engineered by the ships' officers precisely because the sailors are so savvy. "Like villagers," the narrator remarks at one point, the sailors "take microscopic note of every outward movement or non-movement" (491). From the cautious removal of his interview with Claggart to closed quarters, to the "unostentatious vigilance" that supervises Claggart's burial (492), consistent and elaborate care must be taken to circumscribe their sight. Indeed, Vere's strategies recall "the policy . . . in the capital founded by Peter the Barbarian" (480).

Vere's power is based on a strategy of heightening and manipulating others' uncertainties while denying his own. As the sole source of coherence and comprehension aboard ship, as one who can exploit the powers of sight, Vere is able to label as he wills and to preclude challenges to his categories. At the same time, Vere makes his own forms appear neutral and disinterested; his power is founded on the impression that he is assisting in the elaboration of complex metaphysical realities, rather than imposing his own subjective judgments. Vere's ideology of neutrality is consistent with his exceptional "unobtrusiveness." "Any landsman," the narrator remarks, "observing this gentleman not conspicuous by his stature and wearing no pronounced insignia . . . might have taken him for the King's guest, a civilian aboard the King's ship" (445).

Vere's ideal, "forms, measured forms," expresses his allegiance to an older era of class stability and resistance to new ideas, especially those from "across the Channel." Yet that same ideal also signifies another intellectual plane for his sympathies—the conservative philosophy of an empirical social science and the cataloging language of social-functional types that accompanies it. Vere's anxieties and methods are akin to those of a new social scientific generation for whom irrational terror of a world seeming to elude traditional forms of belief combined with a commitment to empirical detail.[43]

43. In light of their shared anxiety about social control, and their shared interest in an empirical ethic that might counter it, it is not surprising that nearly all of the first sociologists

Vere's transitions from a state of uncontrollable anxiety about social chaos to a method of rational and systematic typecasting are evident in the collection of scenes that follow Claggart's accusation against Billy. Claggart's testimony throws Vere into a state of "perplexity, which proceeded less from aught touching the man informed against [Billy], than from consideration how best to act in regard to the informer" (474). Vere may be seen at this point as the aristocrat, threatened by the unreadable aspect of Claggart.

Claggart is described as a man on the move. He is the quintessential outsider, an emblem of social mobility, likened to "the uncataloged creatures of the deep." All details of character confirm this alien status. His complexion is "*singularly* contrasting with the red or deeply bronzed visages of the sailors." Some "sea gossips" speculate that he is a "chevalier"; others, a convict. We are told that "nothing was known of [Claggart's] former life," but despite this effort of self-erasure, "there lurked a bit of accent in his speech suggesting that possibly he was not such by birth, but through naturalization in early childhood." Claggart is the immigrant on his way up: "upon his entrance into the navy . . . assigned to the least honorable section of a man-of-war's crew, embracing the drudgery, he did not long remain there"; his "superior capacity . . . ingratiating deference to superiors . . . [and] austere patriotism" combine to ensure his rise (448–49). Yet it is precisely the intensity of his commitment to assimilate that marks his difference. Every note of his demeanor conveys exaggeration and struggle; every gesture is *acquired* rather than *native*. Not surprisingly, it is the "naturalness" of Billy's virtue that most incites Claggart's envy and antipathy.

Billy, in contrast to Claggart, conveys spontaneity and ease, and

---

experienced a crisis of religious faith. William Graham Sumner's story is representative. Trained as an Episcopal minister, he was drawn away by his first, inspired reading of Spencer, which led to a professorship in social science at Yale. In Perry Miller's words, Sumner "put his religious beliefs in a drawer and turned the lock . . . upon unlocking it, he found the drawer empty" [*American Thought: Civil War to World War II* (New York: Holt, Rinehart, and Winston, 1954), xxvi]. The lives of other sociologists reveal similar transitions from religious origins to empiricism: Giddings was a minister's son; Lester Ward, a minister's grandson; Emile Durkheim, a rabbi's son; Max Weber was caught between his father's secularism and his mother's Protestant faith; and Herbert Spencer was educated by a clergyman uncle. Likewise, every significant American realist author struggled against a religious legacy, among them: Herman Melville's legendary "quarrel" with the Calvinist God of his fathers; Stephen Crane's rebellion against his Calvinist minister father; Henry James's Swedenborgian inheritance; and Theodore Dreiser's turn from Catholicism to Spencerianism.

among all the story's characters, he is the most readily typed. The ideal "primitive man," he is Rousseau's savage, Caspar Hauser, and Adam all in one. The ease of typing Billy is not lost on Vere who casts Billy as martyr —"fated boy"—following his blow to Claggart. Billy is pastoral: at one with nature, his characterization implies an eternal order of upper and lower classes. Claggart is history: his characterization implies indeterminate, uncontrollable forces, among these the threat of ambitious immigrants moving into the mercurial middle classes. Claggart disrupts Vere's "settled convictions," described as a "dike against those invading waters of novel opinion, social, political, and otherwise" (446).

Despite their differences, however, there are significant affinities between Billy and Claggart. Billy is an immigrant too (though, as a victim of impressment, an unwilling one, closer to a slave than to the aggressively mobile Claggart), and he is at times also alien and mystifying to authorities. The first lieutenant, for example, misconceives Billy's farewell salute to *The-Rights-of-Man* as a "sly slur at impressment" (435). Likewise, where Claggart's speech is accented, Billy suffers at times from a common immigrant handicap, the inability to speak at all, which parallels his illiteracy, his inability to read the signs of his experience. Billy and Claggart suggest a distinction between internal and external immigrants; where Billy has wholly internalized the requirements of the social order, Claggart maintains a distance from those requirements, which he exploits for his own ends. Where Billy is acquiescent and easily typed, Claggart is threatening and foils it. This brings us to the gravest danger posed by Claggart's character—that far from being uniquely alien, he pinpoints the condition of alienation that is endemic to the rational world of the *Bellipotent*. Only Claggart and Vere are apprised of the radical separation between being and understanding in the story's world: "One person excepted [i.e., Vere], the master-at-arms was perhaps the only man in the ship intellectually capable of adequately appreciating the moral phenomenon presented in Billy Budd" (459). Vere cannot fully exploit the tools of alienation until their human emblem, who also recognizes their uses, is dead.

With Claggart out of the way, Vere is free to implement his rational-functionalist methods. First, Vere types Billy's blow as "the Divine judgment on Ananais," thus setting the event within a providential order of retribution —"an eye for an eye, a tooth for a tooth." Then he moves to the objective language of martial law and classifies Billy's deed as a "capital crime" to be dealt with categorically by the legal sanctions designed for such offenses at sea. Vere's unstable blend of fatalism and empiricism reveals the inseparability of objectifying language and the chaotic social world it seeks to regulate. Vere not only speaks the language of types, but in classical social scientific form at Billy's trial, he collapses intention claims into the necessities of the system. He stresses the jurors' functional obligations, rejecting any agency that is not predetermined by the system. As social functionaries, the jurors are mere witnesses to the system: "however pitilessly that law may operate . . . we nevertheless adhere to it and administer it." And convinced empiricist that he is, Vere looks to empirical details for solace. "To steady us a bit," he says at one point, "let us recur to the facts" (487).

Vere emphasizes social interdependence, uniformity of consciousness, and typicality, all rhetorical forms of containment which point toward and help to effect the ultimate display of his power—Billy's hanging. This is not to deny Vere's own tortured sense of indeterminacy, but to suggest that in addition to the fog that blinds all of society's members, there are mysteries strategically implemented by social authorities. Vere's uses of indeterminacy are most pronounced at the trial scene, where he coerces defendant and jurors into his own viewpoint by magnifying their uncertainties. At one point, for example, Vere interrupts the court's deliberations to note their "troubled hesitancy" (485), prescribing the court's irresolve in order to impose his own judgment. The court is not so much without its own opinions as incapable of voicing a view contrary to the captain's (488). The marine soldier's request to hear witnesses who might shed "lateral" light on the proceedings suggests the court's allowance of only a single authoritative point of view (484). Vere's is the model liberal-functionalist position: the claim for free speech within a dominant discourse which ensures that any counter-arguments will remain ineffectual.

Vere is not simply denying obscurity; he is actively promoting it, for his authority rests on the perceived chasm between his own expertise, the uncertainty of his officers, and the ignorance of the ordinary sailors. Like the sociologists we have discussed, Vere circumscribes sight—both rhetorically and literally. Through gestures as well as argument at the trial, in his "closeted interview" with Billy, in his manipulations of the crew before, during, and after the climactic cabin scene, Vere imposes a uniform subjectivity upon the ship's company. Each member of the ship inhabits a particular level of sight within the ship's social structure, which also exists within a dominant network of sight. Vere's role is to manage that network in the manner of the professional sociologist, to coordinate the various parts of a vast specialized society into a limited unity of consciousness. At the same time, Vere's typological system enacts an imperialistic notion of social selves which implies that knowing another involves shaping that other in accordance with one's own political necessities. This brings us to the character in the story who resists Vere's homogenizing tactics of familiarization and classification, Claggart.

In the cabin scene, at the moment of his direct accusation of Billy, all are transfixed by the spectacle of Claggart's eyes. Claggart's centrality here evokes the scene of his private testimony to Vere, which leaves Vere more anxious about the informer than the potential mutineer. In both instances, Claggart is the repressed catalyst. Even the story's title seems a displacement of its own action: it foregrounds the stillpoint of its character triangle and suppresses its real agent. The same is true of the story's double deaths. While Claggart's death is concealed, and his body never displayed, Billy's death is a spectacle, and his body, hanging from the yardarm-end, is the visual emblem of Captain Vere's authority.

What makes Claggart unpresentable is the fact that he is unrepresentable. As he approaches Billy in the cabin, the description moves into the past progressive tense: Claggart's eyes, "those lights of human intelligence, losing human expression were gelidly protruding like the alien eyes of certain uncatalogued creatures of the deep. The first mesmeristic glance was one of serpent fascination; the last was as the paralyzing lurch of the torpedo fish" (476). Heaping simile upon metaphor upon simile, the sentences struggle to type a figure who seems fundamentally immune to typing. The crucial phrase, "uncatalogued creatures of the deep," stamps Claggart as the unknowable outsider. When authorized as an epistemological truth, indeterminacy facilitates strategy-making and incites linguistic and political "play" or manipulation. When it appears in a person or in a collection of persons it thwarts artful or dictatorial controls.

Moreover, the phrase establishes an opposition between "creatures" who are not cataloged and human beings who presumably are. The image of creature populations beneath the sea who resist cataloging is meaningful by analogy, that is, in contrast to human populations on land who can be statistically known. To be known, as this passage defines it, is to be cataloged: captured by available categories for keeping track of human beings. Such concerns for population assessment and control can be traced to the earliest formal efforts to count population in the first American Census of 1790.[44] But it was not until the late nineteenth century that such categorical thinking was codified and institutionalized.[45]

44. Theodore Porter, *The Rise of Statistical Thinking 1820–1900* (Princeton: Princeton University Press, 1986), p. 37.
45. As Theodore Porter observes, statistical method "was seen as especially valuable for uncovering causal relationships where the individual events are either concealed from

In part the interest in the analysis of population developed from tallies of the Civil War dead. Categorical thinking about human beings was also a response to the pressures of mass immigration. The threat of mercurial hordes of creatures beneath the sea in "Billy Budd" figures the threat of mercurial hordes of immigrants riding the seas en route to Melville's America. Like Claggart, these immigrants were seen as alien agents, potential catalysts of plots to effect social disorder.

Claggart's story resembles a type of fantasy about immigration that captivated Americans in the 1880s, especially those of Vere's class: on their own, aristocrat and commonalty, represented by Vere and Billy, exist in Edenic harmony; the arrival of the alien serpent introduces social chaos. As John Higham observes, following the Haymarket bombing of 1886, (after which six immigrants were executed for the supposed incitement of violence), "the dread of imported anarchy haunted the American consciousness. No nativist image prevailed more widely than that of the immigrant as a lawless creature given over to violence and disorder."[46] The critical word here is "creature," which echoes the description of Claggart, as well as much of the newspaper rhetoric of the time, rhetoric which cast immigrants as "venemous reptiles," "the scum and offal of Europe," "snakes," and "inhuman rubbish."[47] As "creatures," they are faceless and swarming; they may be seen but not discerned. And this is precisely the effect of Clag-

---

view, or are highly variable." Statistics became the sphere of liberals who favored a limited definition of government action at the same time that they advocated intervention to defend selected interests (*The Rise of Statistical Thinking*, pp. 3, 17). Francis A. Walker contemplates, "Some Results of the Census," in the *Journal of Social Science* 5 (1874): 71–97, and L. L. and Jessie Bernard describe how sociologists interested in shaping human behavior "into conformity with the best standards and patterns of social organization that they knew . . . developed as methods to this end various types of analysis and measurement" [*Origins of Sociology*, p. 843]. See also the section entitled, "Early Conception and Promotion of Statistics in the United States," pp. 783–96. For another literary analysis of these issues from a different perspective, see Mark Seltzer's insightful essay, "Statistical Persons," *Diacritics* 17 (Fall 1987): 82–98.

46. Higham, p. 55.

47. All of these quotations from *Public Opinion* between 1886 and 1887, are cited in Higham, p. 55. Herbert Gutman also notes how "class and ethnic fears and biases combined together to worry elite observers about the diverse worlds below them and to distort gravely their perceptions of these worlds." Gutman quotes John L. Hart, a professor of English at the College of New Jersey, describing "the brute-like" immigrants, who oblige the "more intelligent classes . . . to guard them with police and standing armies, and to cover the land with prisons [and] cages . . ." *In the School-Room* (1879), see Gutman, *Culture, Work, and Society*, pp. 72–73.

gart: in a society where manipulating indeterminacy is a key to social order and power, Claggart, by being the more unobtrusive, challenges Vere's hegemony.

The most involved speculations on the powers of indeterminacy in "Billy Budd" center upon a discussion of Claggart's "nature":

> 'Natural Depravity: a depravity according to nature,' a definition which, though savoring of Calvinism, by no means involves Calvin's dogma as to total mankind. Evidently, its intent makes it applicable to individuals. Not many are the examples of this depravity which the gallows and the jails supply. . . . It folds itself in the mantle of respectability. It has certain negative virtues serving as silent auxiliaries. It never allows wine to get within its guard. It is not going too far to say that it is without vice or small sins. There is a phenomenal pride in it that excludes them. It is never mercenary or avaricious. In short, the depravity here meant partakes of nothing sordid or sensual. (457)

This passage describes a type that is immune to social description. Characterized by invisible nouns and adjectives—"negative virtues," "silent auxiliaries," "without vice," neither "sordid nor sensual"—existing only in negation, depravity can neither be confronted nor challenged. Like the fantasy of the immigrant, it is exceptional (not applicable to "total mankind,") but imperceptible. Indeed, its immunity to the vices and vulnerabilities habitually associated with human beings suggests that this depraved type is not human at all. It escapes classification by customary categories and thus eludes ordinary forms of social control ("the gallows and the jails").

The character type of natural depravity poses difficulties of interpretation like those of insanity. The surgeon ponders, "To draw the exact line of demarcation [between sanity and insanity] few will undertake, though for a fee becoming considerate some professional experts will" (479). Here, as in so many instances, indeterminacy is strategically manipulated. Since insanity poses a problem of detection, it is open to exploitation by "experts." Through such speculations, the story moves beyond anxieties about social indeterminacy to consider these assumptions within a political dynamic, as strategies of identifiable agents.

Claggart's invisibility stands not so much to oppose or criticize Vere's rule as to bleed it. The methodical siphon to Vere's authority, Claggart represents an unassailable opposition that threatens to absorb all the energies of his order. Naturally rather than consciously antagonistic, the element of inevitability in Claggart's portrayal pertains to a specific political reality. He threatens Vere's order precisely because he is completely identified with it. The alien outsider, he occupies the lowest rank among the ship's officers—the brute force behind Vere's authority. And, paradoxically, as the brutal fact of Vere's power, the invisible Claggart renders visible what Vere would prefer to conceal. He reminds Vere that his power rests upon an external force which he can neither identify nor control. But Claggart's role as the ship's "chief of police," also suggests the self-policing propensities of the immigrant, who internalizes social anxiety toward his threatening difference and guards himself as well as others accordingly. Claggart's character points to the double-function of the immigrant in American society as an unpredictable catalyst between capital and labor: on the one hand, reinforcing the status quo as a cheap work force in desperate pursuit of assimilation; on the other hand, representing all the qualities of the other that threaten social stability. In a single encounter, Vere's perceptions of Claggart can range from a sense of his "tact in his function," to a sense of his "patriotic zeal . . . supersensible and strained" (472).

As the "serpent," for whom "the Creator alone is responsible" (460), Claggart's character raises a subject that has long absorbed critics of "Billy Budd," its retelling of the Edenic myth. In the words of Milton Stern, the story is "a reworking of the Adam-Christ story, playing prelapsarian Adam and the Christ on a man-of-war and demonstrating the inevitability of the Fall and the necessity of Crucifixion."[48] It is appropriate that Stern finds not one but two general typologies in the story, a sign, as I have suggested, that the story destabilizes type categories, and also that it teaches as well as represents the activity of typing. The Edenic myth held a particular fascination for Americans in the late nineteenth century; the tale of the "fall" into technology was told and retold by classic and popular writers, social scientists, and even scientists. Henry James, for example, writing of Hawthorne, proclaimed the replacement of America's great provincial romancer by the great American novelist of institutional expansion and international intrigue, and he did so precisely in terms of a new national consciousness which had "eaten of the tree of knowledge."[49]

My reading of the story in the context of contemporary social science complements and extends traditional emphases on the story's biblical

48. *The Fine Hammered Steel of Herman Melville* (Urbana: University of Illinois Press, 1968), p. 211.
49. *Hawthorne*, 1879 (New York: Collier, 1966), p. 125.

dimensions. Both the biblical analogy which casts Billy as a prelapsarian Adam, and the sociological analogy which casts him as an innocent manipulated by a professional elite, view innocence as a deadly liability. By dramatizing the experiences of innocence in modern society, the story reveals the ideological continuities between certain views of providence and certain views of technology. Descriptions of late nineteenth-century industrialization tend invariably to give way to nostalgia for a prior more integrated social Eden.[50] Any narrative of the fall is a narrative of loss: to represent the end of innocence is to be barred from its timeless space as an inhabitant of history.

All of these fatalistic plots suppress a critical historical dimension of the opposition between innocence and knowledge which is dramatized in "Billy Budd": that the plot has very specific political and class contours. Billy's deathblow to Claggart is as self-regulatory as his blessing of Captain Vere just prior to his execution; for Claggart alone has the power to activate Billy's potentially subversive energies. As a Satanic/politically disruptive force, Claggart incites Billy to riot; he can effect the fall into knowledge that would destabilize Vere's Providential/paternal power over Billy. By killing Claggart, Billy kills the potential for opposition in himself and ensures his own containment by Vere's Edenic order.

The story thus historicizes and politicizes the Edenic myth casting Adam as the agent of his own containment, an Adam, in other words, who resists Satan and history. Since the classic Fall is also a fall into language or plotting, we might say that Billy, in striking Claggart dead, disables the story.[51] Vere's strategies leading to Billy's death effect a draining of the very possibility for story. From the cabin scene on, details are left increasingly to the reader's imagination: from Vere's solitary ruminations which "everyone must determine for himself by such light as this narrative may afford" (480), to Vere's and Billy's "closeted" interview (489). At the same time, however,

---

50. Even Thomas Haskell in his careful and incisive study, *The Emergence of Professional Social Science*, mutes the political aspects of the rise of professionalism in favor of a narrative which emphasizes the inevitable, and even universal struggle between "man" and technology. Thus, theories of "the end of American innocence" are presented as objective, rather than as ideological. See also, Henry May, *The End of American Innocence* (Chicago: Quadrangle, 1964); R. Jackson Wilson, *In Quest of Community* (New York: Wiley, 1963); and Richard Hofstader, *Social Darwinism in American Thought* (New York: Braziller, 1955). For an important counter-perspective see, David F. Noble, *America By Design* (New York: Oxford, 1977).

51. See "Melville's Fist," p. 87.

the narrative continues to oppose the rapidity of Vere's plot. The narrator announces: "Of a series of incidents within a brief term rapidly following each other the adequate narration must take up a term less brief, especially if explanation and comment here and there seem requisite to the better understanding of such incidents" (490). The opposition formerly between Vere and Claggart is transferred to Vere and the narrator, who finally kills him off with a canon blow from the *Athee*, a profane vessel designed, it seems, to deny Vere's neat biblical categories.

The story's narrator is the observer apprised of the limits of observation, who watches the clash of submissive force (Billy) and unconscious agency (Claggart) through the spectacle of Vere's power. In contrast to Vere, who merely uses history to his own ends, and Billy and Claggart, who represent, respectively, a mythical immunity to history and an untheorized absorption in it, the narrator is a theorist of history who understands the uses of sight and visibility. His object is to resist generic confines while at the same time acknowledging the inevitability of defined positions.

To avoid types in a world where eluding definition is a source of power—in this necessity lies the key link between the story's characters and narrative consciousness. In a description of "the Great Mutiny," which "national pride along with views of policy would fain shade . . . off into the historical background" (440), the narrator contemplates the inseparability of history and politics, and notes as well the crucial agency of narration in this respect. There is no such thing as "historical background," he suggests, for history exists in all social forms. The only way to manage history, therefore, is to domesticate it: "such events cannot be ignored, but there is a considerate way of historically treating them. If a well-constituted individual refrains from blazing aught amiss or calamitous in his family, a nation in the like circumstance may without reproach be equally discreet" (440). Likened to a member of the family, the historian is familiarized and contained. His discretion results neither from moral nor ethical convictions but from typological coercion. The narrator is caught in a trap of definitions: to write critical history is to risk being typed as either alien or insane. On the other hand, he possesses "inside" knowledge which contradicts the more benign version of the story's events such as that contained in the "authorized" naval chronicle. The narrator must avoid being labelled while relaying his version: tell a critical tale without being stamped by that telling. His aim is thus the *conscious* exploitation of invisibility, an aim which is best pursued, as he says, "by indirection."

Despite this elusive purpose, "Billy Budd"'s narrative is not about the invisible powers of omniscient narration. By announcing his own vulnerability to labels, and by struggling elaborately to avoid them, the narrator opposes the conventions of realist fiction. The narrative can be seen as a critique of realism that incorporates its terms and explodes them. As a reflection upon the political sources and ramifications of character-typing, the story's narrative *studies* rather than *exemplifies* it. Thus, the narrator observes at one point that Billy is somewhat reminiscent of Hercules, but adds that this "was subtly modified by another and pervasive quality" (436). Or he compares Billy to Adam, but in such equivocal terms as to undo the comparison: "Billy *in many respects* was little more than *a sort of* upright barbarian, *much such perhaps* as Adam *presumably might have been*" (438, my emphasis).[52]

Marked by qualification, evasion, inversion, and digression, the form of the narrative can be seen as a critique of the story's politics of indeterminacy and the exaggerated social controls that it enables. In contrast to Captain Vere's crisp functionalist categories, the narrator insists on the plot's ragged edges. Where Vere wages war against his uncertainties and acts with almost hysterical assurance to suppress them, the narrator makes uncertainty the basis of his aesthetic method. His narrative is a monument to indecision, a shrine to inconclusiveness; he accepts and builds upon what Vere flees. Throughout the story, the narrator criticizes military and generic requirements at the same time that his digressive and fragmentary narrative formally counters them. In a passage which, significantly, follows a discussion of the historian's constraints, he proclaims: "In this matter of writing, resolve as one may to keep to the main road, some bypaths have an enticement not to be withstood. I am going to err into such a bypath . . . at the least, we can promise ourselves that pleasure which is wickedly said to be in sinning, for a literary sin the divergence will be" (441). This seemingly disingenous apology for literary waywardness is in fact a powerful testimony to the critical potential of literary form. The narrator has

---

52. My point here raises the much considered question of Melville's modernity. As Charles Feidelson [*Symbolism in American Literature* (Chicago: University of Chicago Press, 1953)], for example, has suggested, American novelists, and Melville perhaps most of all, are generically closer to twentieth-century modernist writers than to nineteenth-century realists. In my view, the significant task is not to clarify the story's precise generic affinities, but to elaborate the ways in which it destabilizes generic norms. Thus "Billy Budd," as I argue above in discussing Lukacs, invokes the concrete typologies of realist fiction, as well as the abstract typologies of modernist allegory, in the name of its overall investigation of the political uses of such categories.

found a way out of the anxious limits of history writing by labelling his own enterprise fiction. Precisely because his task is taken so seriously, the historian is overwhelmed with considerations which require careful omissions and suppressions. The comparative lack of concern over fiction makes it a potential source of historical truth. Where history writing produces an inner censor who abridges detail, the presumed triviality of fiction writing allows for impulsive embellishments.[53]

The designation of the narrative as "inside" sets it in opposition to the objective forms of social (and aesthetic) theory which it also represents. The story's narrator is a mediator among various systems of knowledge, all of which claim an impartial, categorical understanding of society. Repeatedly, the narrator exposes man-made boundaries in their efforts to parade as natural facts. The elegiac images which close the chapter on Billy's execution are a case in point. "And now it was full day. The fleece of low-lying vapour had vanished, licked up by the sun that late had so glorified it. And the circumambient air in the clearness of its serenity was like smooth white marble in the polished block not yet removed from the marble-dealer's yard" (501). With the sun reduced from its former glory to the figure of a greedy pet and the air collected in the image of blank marble, the passage defuses and contains the horror of Billy's execution. Glory is shrunken to greed, and air commodified to marble—marketplace metaphors which foreshadow Billy's final self-image as a "pendant pearl" dangling "from the yardarm-end" (504).

The tone of inevitability in this passage is not ascribed to nature but to the specific human actions of the executioner, the marble-dealer, and the writer, each of them boundary makers (disciplinary, capitalist, and literary). Most resonant here, however, and distinct from the narrator's habitually sardonic tone, is the conviction of the writer's complicity with these other agents of civilization. Billy's execution is effected by a dependence on forms which are the very tools of writing. The passage affirms the connections between lyricism and barbarism, between monuments of civilization and the savage impulses they deny but underwrite. In the act of criticizing

53. Theodor Adorno, in *Aesthetic Theory*, offers an important model for my effort to understand how the story presents aesthetic form, as both *of* the world, while capable of a conscious and critical grasp of its workings: "Art undergoes qualitative change when it attacks its traditional foundations. Thus art becomes a qualitatively different entity by virtue of its opposition, at the level of artistic form, to the existing world and also by virtue of its readiness to aid and shape that world" (trans. C. Lenhardt [London: Routledge & Kegan Paul, 1984], p. 4).

the brutalities of social forms, the narrator locates the sources of his own narration. The storytelling process reveals the inseparability of social and literary effect. What the social disciplinarian sacrifices to confirm his power, the writer sacrifices for coherent aesthetic form.

The question of narrative method in "Billy Budd" brings us full circle in our discussion. In answer to sociologists who posit the uniformity and interdependence of subjects as a way of foreclosing difference and potential opposition, the story's "inside narrative" offers a method of conscious difference. In answer to New Historicists who claim that no subject possesses the terms for criticizing a society from within, the narrator exemplifies the possibility of internal critique. The narrator can be seen as akin to the feminist critic who views womens' alienation as both internal and external. In feminist method, the subject is self-conditioned according to external conditions, but a recognition of this fact can lead to alternative conditions.[54]

By positing such a dynamic within "Billy Budd," I am claiming a more general interactive understanding of literary works in history. To view literature as actively commenting on its own social conditioning, as actively shaping its culture in conscious as well as unconscious ways, we recover a crucial and salutary dimension of the historicity of the text. "Billy Budd" thus stands as a critique of developing sociological ideologies. For the story's narrator, the most reflexive of all Melville's authorial personae, writing will always lack the symmetry of pure form and this lack is a sign of its deeper complicity with "certain uncatalogued creatures of the deep."

54. See Catherine MacKinnon, "Feminism, Marxism, Method, and the State: An Agenda for Theory," *The Signs Reader*, ed. Elizabeth Abel and Emily Abel (Chicago: University of Chicago Press, 1983), especially pp. 247–56.

Violence, Revolution, and the Cost of Freedom: John Brown and W. E. B. DuBois

William E. Cain

John Brown and his raid are an epitome, a popular summary of the history of the United States between the Missouri Compromise and the Gettysburg celebration. Not a child has been born in the country since his death to whom John Brown does not symbolize the thing that happened to the heart and brain of the American people between 1820 and 1865. He is as big as a myth, and the story of him is an immortal legend—perhaps the only one in our history.——John Jay Chapman[1]

John Brown was right.—W. E. B. DuBois[2]

W. E. B. DuBois once referred to his biographical study of John Brown as his "favorite" among all the books he had produced, and, in his

1. John Jay Chapman, "Doctor Howe," in *Learning and Other Essays* (New York: Moffat, Yard, and Co., 1910), pp. 89–145, at p. 131.

2. W. E. B. DuBois, *John Brown* (1909; rev. ed. 1962; Millwood: Kraus-Thomson, 1973), p. 338. Future page references to this book will be given parenthetically in the text.

autobiography, he termed it "one of the best written" of them.[3] But literary critics and historians have apparently not shared DuBois's esteem for the book and have never paid it much attention. Indeed, no sooner was it published in the fall of 1909 than it began to fade from view amid the build-up and extensive advertising for the mammoth study of Brown by Oswald Garrison Villard, the grandson of William Lloyd Garrison and owner of *The Nation*. This rival volume received enthusiastic acclaim when it appeared in October 1910, and it effectively eliminated DuBois's book as competition. Between 1909 and 1916, DuBois's biography sold fewer than seven hundred copies, and it garnered only a small number of notices and reviews.

To later commentators on DuBois's career, the book on Brown has hardly seemed to count at all. Francis L. Broderick, in his 1959 biography, dismisses it as "more a part of DuBois's propaganda than his scholarship," and Elliott Rudwick, in a 1960 biography, does not even mention it.[4] Nor does the book enjoy high standing among scholars expert in John Brown and pre-Civil War studies. Stephen B. Oates, in a recent assessment, concedes that DuBois's biography provides a "scathing indictment of slavery and an impassioned defense of Brown as a revolutionary symbol," but he stresses that it exhibits "a cheerful disregard for scholarly accuracy" and hence excludes it from the roster of "serious" inquiries into its subject.[5]

Both Manning Marable and Arnold Rampersad have appraised the Brown biography more favorably. Marable has commended its "artistry" and "powerful political interpretation" of Brown's life; and Rampersad has keenly drawn attention to the influence of Hippolyte Taine on DuBois's conception of historical work and traced the implications of Brown's unyielding dedication to justice (and courageous acceptance of the need for sacrifice) for DuBois's sense of his own political vocation.[6] But the book is, I think, still

3. Herbert Aptheker, *Annotated Bibliography of the Published Writings of W. E. B. DuBois* (Millwood: Kraus-Thomson, 1973), p. 553. See also *The Autobiography of W. E. B. DuBois* (1968; New York: International Publishers, 1982), p. 259.
4. Francis L. Broderick, *W. E. B. DuBois: Negro Leader in a Time of Crisis* (Stanford: Stanford Univ. Press, 1959), p. 82, and Elliott Rudwick, *W. E. B. DuBois: Voice of the Black Protest Movement* (1960; rev. ed., Urbana: Univ. of Illinois Press, 1982).
5. Stephen B. Oates, "John Brown and His Judges," in *Our Fiery Trial: Abraham Lincoln, John Brown, and the Civil War Era* (Amherst: Univ. of Massachusetts Press, 1979), pp. 22–42, at p. 23.
6. Manning Marable, *W. E. B. DuBois: Black Radical Democrat* (Boston: G. K. Hall, 1986), p. 66, and Arnold Rampersad, *The Art and Imagination of W. E. B. DuBois* (Cambridge: Harvard Univ. Press, 1976), pp. 110–15.

richer and more significant than either Marable or Rampersad have suggested. Its writing and publication occurred at a crucial juncture in DuBois's
life, while he was contesting the formidable authority of Booker T. Washington, laboring mightily in the Niagara movement (1905–1909), and helping
to found the NAACP—and as he was also preparing to take the momentous step of exchanging his academic position at Atlanta University (where
he had taught since 1897) for a full-time post in the fledgling NAACP office
in New York.

In choosing to write about John Brown, DuBois entered a fervent debate and controversy. Brown was a resounding symbol, if for very different
reasons, to people in both the North and the South. To deal with him meant
undertaking the immensely challenging task of rightly gauging his significance and, furthermore, coming to terms with the violence and murderous
revolt that he unleashed. Less a biographer than an interpreter of charged
symbols, DuBois probes the nature of effective protest, the imperative of
revolution and the tragic appeal of violence, and, above all perhaps, the
basis in black experience for the heroism that the white crusader Brown
displayed. In *John Brown*, DuBois meditates upon his subject and reinter-
prets it so that it symbolizes black rather than white achievement. The study
of John Brown becomes, in DuBois's hands, an inquiry into the souls of
blacks and a rich, if also disquieting, celebration of the revolutionary action
that brave black people defined.

1

Like the bloody uprising in San Domingo and the insurrection of
messianic Nat Turner, whose name stood as "a symbol of wild retribution,"
John Brown's action at Harper's Ferry in 1859 quickly acquired extraordinary symbolic power.[7] To abolitionists in the North, John Jay Chapman
observed, Brown "was the living embodiment" of "the idea of atonement,
of vicarious suffering, a man who had sacrificed his life for the cause of
freedom and justice."[8] To those in the South, however, Brown embodied
the perversion of high ideals and the desecration of God's word. During the
Civil War period and afterwards, many southerners exasperatingly judged

---

7. Thomas Wentworth Higginson, *Black Rebellion: A Selection from Travellers and Outlaws* (1888; rpt. New York: Arno, 1969), p. 326.
8. Chapman, p. 133.

that no one seemed able to grasp the real nature of the crimes he had committed and sought to inspire. Robert Penn Warren intimated just this point in 1929 when he stated that "John Brown was a cipher, a symbol" in arguments that had "little concern one way or another with what sort of fellow he really was."[9]

Brown himself, it is clear, perceived and heightened the symbolism of his abolitionist campaign, treasonous revolt, trial, and execution. During the fateful span of his life in the 1850s, he recreated himself several times, changing from a man who had failed at various business enterprises to an avenging angel brandishing God's flaming sword against the apostate slavemongers of the Kansas territory, and then to a militant prophet-warrior launching an inter-racial incursion directly into the South, and, finally, to a devout soul suffering at the gallows with Christ-like valor. By his final years, Brown had in fact come frequently to situate himself in symbolic scenes, fashioning the legacy that Chapman, Warren, and so many others have either approved or disputed. This was particularly the case during his final meetings in Boston in the spring of 1859. Visiting George Henry Stearns, one of the Northerners who funded him, Brown presented Stearns with a pearl-handled Bowie knife he had seized from a pro-slavery foe at the battle of Black Jack when waging war in the Kansas and Missouri territories. Brown reflected that the two of them would probably "never meet again in this world"; the knife was a "token of his gratitude" and would, Brown hoped, possess in the future for Stearns some "little historic value."[10] Even more fatalistically, Brown called on the abolitionist Judge Russell and his wife and was especially attentive to their baby daughter whom he held balanced on his palms, saying to her, "Now when you are a young lady and I am hanged, you can say that you stood on the hand of Old Brown."[11]

Brown's earlier life contains many similar moments, equally resonant in their symbolism, though perhaps less deliberately crafted. In 1837, for example, Brown and his father attended a meeting to commemorate Elijah Lovejoy, an anti-slavery editor murdered by a pro-slavery mob from

9. Robert Penn Warren, *John Brown: The Making of a Martyr* (New York: Payson and Clarke, 1929), p. 432.
10. Cited in Jeffrey Rossbach, *Ambivalent Conspirators: John Brown, the Secret Six, and a Theory of Slave Violence* (Philadelphia: Univ. of Pennsylvania Press, 1982), pp. 204–5.
11. Cited in Stephen B. Oates, *To Purge this Land with Blood: A Biography of John Brown* (1970; rpt. New York: Harper and Row, 1972), p. 272.

Missouri. According to eyewitnesses, Brown listened to the denunciations of the pro-slavery forces and then, as the meeting ended, "suddenly stood up, raised his right hand, and vowed that here, before God, in this church, in the presence of these witnesses, he would consecrate his life to the destruction of slavery."[12] Two decades later, during a meeting in Boston with Senator Charles Sumner, Brown asked to see the coat that Sumner had worn when he had been brutally beaten by Preston Brooks on the Senate floor. Sumner handed Brown the blood-stiffened coat, and Brown examined it carefully; he "said nothing," but "his lips compressed and his eyes shone like polished steel."[13]

Responses to Brown and to the Harper's Ferry incident testify that North and South alike viewed Brown as both the inevitable by-product of perilous social and political conditions and the symbolic incarnation of sectional motives, grievances, and purposes. Largely because he wished to protect the Republican party from the fallout of the raid, Abraham Lincoln tried to paint Brown as an aberrant leader of a "peculiar" mission whose absurdity even the slaves—who had failed to rally to his banner at Harper's Ferry—"plainly" recognized.[14] But Lincoln was in the minority. William Lloyd Garrison, setting aside his non-resistant principles, concluded that Brown renewed the "spirit of '76" and made men realize the revolutionary rightness of taking arms against oppressors. For Garrison, Brown's climactic violent action signalled "progress, and a positive moral growth"; the campaign against slavery had reached a stage in which "carnal weapons" no longer functioned to uphold despotism but, rather, spurred the cause of Negro freedom and subverted southern tyranny.[15] On the other side of the issue, Stephen Douglas argued that Brown nightmarishly painted the consequences of all that the abolitionist Republicans had said and done. "I have no hesitation," Douglas declared,

> in expressing my firm and deliberate conviction that the Harper's Ferry crime was the natural, logical, inevitable result of the doctrines and teachings of the Republican party, as explained and enforced

12. See Oates, pp. 41–42.

13. Cited in David Herbert Donald, *Charles Sumner and the Coming of the Civil War* (1960; rpt. Chicago: Univ. of Chicago Press, 1981), p. 350.

14. Abraham Lincoln, "Cooper Union Address," cited in Richard Warch and Jonathan Fanton, eds., *John Brown* (Englewood Cliffs: Prentice Hall, 1973), p. 133.

15. William Lloyd Garrison, "Speech on John Brown," cited in Warch and Fanton, p. 109.

in their platform, their partisan presses, their pamphlets and books, and especially in the speeches of their leaders in and out of Congress.[16]

Douglas's language shows the conspiratorial vision of the slavery crisis that both North and South held in their polarized ways and that Brown so dramatically enlarged. Southerners were certain that Brown's action signalled the next stroke of the abolitionist enemy—violent assault against the people, property, and institutions of the South. Northerners, in turn, while mostly rejecting (and in unmistakable terms) what Brown had tried to engineer at Harper's Ferry, claimed that murder and insurrection were the punishments that the South was beginning to bring upon itself because of its persistent immorality. By clinging tenaciously to slavery, the South seemed to the North to be dedicated to a future of armed struggle and, eventually, civil war.

By the 1850s, as David Brion Davis has pointed out, such "conspiratorial imagery had become a formalized staple in the political rhetoric of both North and South, appropriated by eminent statesmen and journalists as well as by fanatics." Even more tellingly, Davis adds that "the idea of conspiracy was a symbolic means of accounting for the subtle truth that abolitionists and southern secessionists often played mutually supporting roles and seemed to be staging a premeditated performance to a bewildered and powerless audience."[17] To many in the North, the South's wicked plotmaking had grown steadily evident throughout the 1850s, as the Compromise of 1850, the Fugitive Slave Law, the Kansas-Nebraska bill, the Dred Scott decision, and efforts to revive the slave-trade succeeded one another. To southerners, these facts bore witness to the wisdom of the federal government and further solidified the South's determination to protect itself against increasingly irrational, virulent abolitionist tampering with hallowed rights and institutions. The eventual revelation that Northern intellectuals and members of the "secret six," including Theodore Parker and

16. Stephen Douglas, "Remarks to the U. S. Senate," cited in Warch and Fanton, p. 131.
17. David Brion Davis, *The Slave Power Conspiracy and the Paranoid Style* (1969; rpt. Baton Rouge: Louisiana State Univ. Press, 1982), pp. 7, 23. See also Oates, *Purge this Land*, pp. 234–37; C. Vann Woodward, "John Brown's Private War," 1952, in *The Burden of Southern History* (rev. ed. New York: New American Library, 1968), pp. 40–57; and Merton L. Dillon, *The Abolitionists: The Growth of a Dissenting Minority* (1974; rpt. New York: Norton, 1979), pp. 102, 150, 152, 161.

Thomas Wentworth Higginson, had backed Brown's insurrectionist scheme shocked but did not surprise the South.[18] It merely exposed publicly what the South already believed to be true about the North and it allowed southerners to justify their defense of a way of life most of them knew to be discredited with still more repressive measures against blacks and moderate whites.

Brown caused abolitionist rhetoric to flame higher than ever before. His attack on Harper's Ferry, imprisonment, trial, and execution led eloquent northerners to spurn the rule of "law" and to urge slaves, aided and abetted by whites, to rebel against—and, if necessary, to kill—their masters. Celebrating Brown as "a transcendentalist above all, a man of ideas and principles," Henry David Thoreau averred that "the question is not about the weapon, but the spirit in which you use it."[19] Wendell Phillips fiercely resolved that "it is honorable" to "break bad laws, and such lawbreaking History loves and God blesses!" "The lesson of the hour is insurrection," he proclaimed.[20] To Theodore Parker, several principles could now be clearly seen as "a part of the Public Knowledge of all enlightened men":

1. A man, held against his will as a slave, has a natural right to kill every one who seeks to prevent his enjoyment of liberty.

2. It may be a natural duty of the slave to develop this natural right in a practical manner, and actually kill all those who seek to prevent his enjoyment of liberty.

3. The freeman has a natural right to help the slaves recover their liberty, and in that enterprise to do for them all which they have a right to do for themselves.

4. It may be a natural duty for the freeman to help the slaves to the enjoyment of their liberty, and, as a means to that end to aid them in killing all such as oppose their natural freedom.[21]

If a man possessed "power" and "opportunity," he would be obliged to act upon these principles, as John Brown had done. "It would not sur-

18. See George M. Fredrickson, *The Inner Civil War: Northern Intellectuals and the Crisis of the Union* (1965; rpt. New York: Harper and Row, 1968), and Rossbach, *Ambivalent Conspirators*.

19. Henry David Thoreau, cited in James Redpath, *Echoes of Harper's Ferry* (Boston: Thayer and Eldridge, 1860), pp. 21, 28.

20. Wendell Phillips, cited in Redpath, pp. 58, 43.

21. Theodore Parker, cited in Redpath, pp. 74–75.

prise me," Parker stated, "if there were other and well-planned attempts in other States to do what Captain Brown heroically, if not successfully, tried in Virginia. Nine out ten may fail—the tenth will succeed."[22]

As these citations show, northerners and southerners themselves grasped the exorbitantly dramatic, deathly nature of the slavery crisis as it climaxed in the 1850s.[23] Doubtless this helps to account for the frequency of allusions during the period to the death-ridden tragedies of Shakespeare and—part of the same literary and cultural constellation—to violent deeds in epic literature and the Bible. This web of reference is extremely full and intricate in Brown's case, as one would expect for a heroic figure cloaked in myth, legend, and violent adventure. In his 1909 book, DuBois makes a version of this point about theatricalized violence overseen (and possibly sanctified) by God when he says that "to [Brown] the world was a mighty drama. God was an actor in the play and so was John Brown" (46).[24] DuBois's insight into the literary and religious contexts within which Brown lived, and according to which he was interpreted, rightly accents the symbolic dimension of the slavery crisis of the 1850s. It was a period when persons saw themselves as historical agents who performed destined roles and who naturally turned to fatefully momentous events and hugely significant characters in classic texts in order better to enrich and emblazon their conduct.

Brown may, in fact, occasionally strike us today as curiously akin to Shakespeare's Coriolanus, the unremittingly dedicated soldier who banished his banishers. This is especially so when one reads the transcript of Brown's memorable "conversation" with Governor Wise and others on the day he was captured. "I think you are fanatical," a bystander told Brown. To which Brown replied, "And I think you are fanatical."[25] Brown's black supporters, at the time of his death and afterwards, sometimes intriguingly invoked *Hamlet* when referring to their tragic white hero as a means of cele-

22. Parker, cited in Redpath, p. 80.
23. See, for example, Elijah Avey, *The Capture and Execution of John Brown: A Tale of Martyrdom* (1906; rpt. Chicago: Afro-Am Press, 1969), pp. 15–44.
24. For suggestive accounts of the theatricality of violence in ante-bellum literature and political life, see two essays by Eric J. Sundquist: "Suspense and Tautology in *Benito Cereno*," in *Glyph* 8: *Johns Hopkins Textual Studies* (Baltimore: Johns Hopkins Univ. Press, 1981), pp. 103–26, and "Slavery, Revolution, and the American Renaissance," in *The American Renaissance Reconsidered*, ed. Walter Benn Michaels and Donald E. Pease (Baltimore: Johns Hopkins Univ. Press, 1985), pp. 1–33.
25. Cited in Warch and Fanton, p. 78.

brating his bravery and rebutting charges that he was insane. The former slave and pastor of the Joy Street Baptist Church in Boston, Reverend J. S. Martin, noted at a service on the evening of Brown's execution that if Brown "was mad," as many had said, "his madness not only had a great deal of 'method' in it, but a great deal of philosophy and religion." [26] Nearly five decades later, Reverdy C. Ransom, another Boston pastor, somewhat differently said at the observance of John Brown Day at Harper's Ferry that "like the ghost of Hamlet's father, the spirit of John Brown beckons us to arise and seek the recovery of our rights, which our enemy, 'with the witchcraft of his wit, with traitorous gifts,' has sought forever to destroy." [27] Informed everywhere by murder and betrayal, *Hamlet* foregrounded the retributive violence that Thoreau, Phillips, and Parker had avidly described and recommended.

During the 1850s and in subsequent decades, Brown's allies and defenders symbolically linked him to Moses, Joshua, Hercules, John the Baptist, Spartacus, Peter the Hermit, Ignatius Loyola, Cromwell, William of Orange, the fathers of the American Revolution, Ethan Allen, Coleridge's ancient mariner, Toussaint L'Ouverture, Denmark Vesey, and Nat Turner. Frederick Douglass proposed Socrates and Jesus, and the eminent black historian, George Washington Williams, suggested Galileo, Copernicus, and Newton.[28] For black as well as white abolitionists, Brown served to connect their cause to scripture and to the American Revolution. As Charles H. Langston remarked, Brown's "actions were in perfect harmony with, and resulted from the teaching of the Bible, of our Revolutionary fathers and of every true and faithful anti-slavery man in this country and the world." [29] A black member of Brown's band, Osborne P. Anderson, sketched a similarly grand lineage, notably international in scope, when he professed that "there is an unbroken chain of sentiment and purpose from Moses of the Jews to John Brown of America; from Kossuth, and the liberators of France and Italy, to the untutored Gabriel, and the Denmark Veseys, Nat Turners and Madison Washingtons of the Southern American States." [30] By the late

26. Cited in Benjamin Quarles, ed., *Blacks on John Brown* (Urbana: Univ. of Illinois Press, 1972), p. 29. See *Hamlet* II. ii. 206–7.
27. Cited in Quarles, p. 83. See *Hamlet* I. v. 43.
28. Quarles, pp. 57, 73. See also Quarles, *Allies for Freedom: Blacks and John Brown* (New York: Oxford University Press, 1974).
29. Cited in Quarles, *Blacks on John Brown*, p. 12.
30. Osborne P. Anderson, *A Voice from Harper's Ferry: A Narrative of Events* (1861; rpt. Freeport: Books for Libraries Press, 1972), p. 2.

1850s and even more after his assault at Harper's Ferry, Brown "represented revolution itself."[31]

Samson is, however, likely the most compelling prototype for the violent Brown, for he dwells, arrogantly and destructively, in the sacred Old Testament text that Brown deeply absorbed and trusted. Brown seems to have sewn the Old Testament into his tough moral fiber; in an autobiographical letter to Henry Stearns (15 July 1857), he characterized himself as a "firm believer in the Bible," a book with which he had become "very familiar" and of which he "possessed a most unusual memory of its contents."[32] A man whom Brown employed in 1820 recalled that "Brown seemed always to have a text of Scripture at his tongue's end that would exactly apply to his argument and strengthen his position and I never knew a man who could at all times quote a verse of the Bible with as much force and as applicable as he could."[33] Samson's errors, ferocious career, and suicidal last act undertaken to purge the land with blood—all these fit Brown well; and he himself regularly invoked the example of Samson to confirm his identity and monumentalize it for others.

In a letter to Franklin Sanborn (24 February 1858)—one that DuBois cites at the end of his chapter on Brown's "great plan"—Brown states that "I expect nothing but to 'endure hardness'; but I expect to effect a mighty conquest, even though it be like the last victory of Samson."[34] Writing a month after Brown's capture, Frederick Douglass also invoked Samson as the figure whose labors Brown had imitated:

> His daring deeds may cost him his life, but priceless as is the value of that life, the blow he has struck, will, in the end, prove to be worth its mighty cost. Like Samson, he has laid his hands upon the pillars of this great national temple of cruelty and blood, and when he falls, that temple will speedily crumble to its final doom, burying its denizens in its ruins.[35]

Once captured, Brown welcomed his death, knowing both the dramatic possibilities that its preparations would offer and how fatefully divisive

31. Louis Filler, *The Crusade against Slavery, 1830–1860* (1960; rpt. New York: Harper and Row, 1963), p. 242.
32. Cited in Louis Ruchames, ed., *John Brown: The Making of a Revolutionary* (1959; rpt. New York: Grosset and Dunlap, 1969), p. 47.
33. Cited in Ruchames, p. 175.
34. Cited in Warch and Fanton, p. 38.
35. Philip Foner, ed., *The Life and Writings of Frederick Douglass*, (1950; rpt. New York: International Publishers, 1975), 2: 460.

would be its implications for the North and South. As he stated in a letter (23 November 1859),

> I think I feel as happy as Paul did when he lay in prison. He knew if they killed him it would greatly advance the cause of Christ; that was the reason he rejoiced so. On that same ground "I do rejoice, yea, and will rejoice." Let them hang me; I forgive them, and may God forgive them, for they know not what they do.[36]

Some of Brown's northern supporters pondered an attempt to rescue Brown before he was to be hanged, yet they chose finally to do nothing —not only because the chances for success were non-existent, but also because they recognized the explosive forces that Brown's execution would serviceably trigger. As James Redpath, one of Brown's most fervent disciples, affirmed after Brown had been caught: "living he acted bravely, dying, he will teach us courage. A Samson in his life; he will be a Samson in his death."[37]

Brown's most notable reference to himself as Samson occurs in a 15 November 1859 letter where he writes of his disappointment at the failure of the Harper's Ferry mission:

> I have been a good deal disappointed as it regards myself in not keeping up to my own plans; but I now feel entirely reconciled to that even: for Gods plan, was Infinitely better; no doubt; or I should have kept to my own. Had Samson kept to his determination of not telling Delilah wherein his great strength lay; he would probably have never overturned the house. I did not tell Delilah; but I was induced to act very contrary to my better judgment; & I have lost my two noble boys; & other friends, if not my two eyes.[38]

Brown claimed that his sympathy for the men he had taken hostage, and his concern for their families, led him to linger at the arsenal rather than to flee with his comrades and the weapons they had seized.[39] This departure from his own plan, however, meant simply that God had different designs for him. Like Samson, he had erred terribly; but, as Brown's own allusion forecasts, his error would enable him, like the later triumphant

36. Cited in Ruchames, p. 154. See also Brown's last speech to the court, 2 November 1859, cited in Ruchames, p. 134.
37. Cited in Oates, p. 317. See also Rossbach, *Ambivalent Conspirators*, pp. 232–35.
38. Cited in Ruchames, p. 144.
39. See Brown's letter of 1 November 1859, cited in Ruchames, p. 137.

Samson, to complete the work that God had truly intended him to perform. He would overturn the house of God's enemies, killing himself and them in a ghastly holocaust.

Interestingly, Brown's southern foes sought to appropriate the Samson story for their own ends, employing it to rally the pro-slavery cause and prophesy the havoc that would ensue if the North, impelled by Brown's example, took control of the federal government. In a January 1860 speech to the Senate, Robert Toombs thundered:

> Never permit this Federal government to pass into the hands of the Black Republican party. It has already declared war against you and your institutions. It every day commits acts of war against you: it has already compelled you to arm for your defence. . . . Defend yourselves! The enemy is at your door, wait not to meet him at your hearthstone; meet him at the doorsill, and drive him from the Temple of Liberty, or pull down its pillars and involve him in a common ruin.[40]

However much Toombs may have kindled southern passions, he failed in his effort to establish that the South, not the abolitionist North, could effectively play a Samson-like role. But his words, like Brown's, do intersect provocatively with innumerable references, in the speeches and writings of both northerners and southerners, to the perils of a "house divided against itself" and to the certainty of catastrophic violence if such self-division should persist. As Brown was led to the scaffold on the morning of his execution, he passed this note to one of the guards: "I John Brown am now quite certain that the crimes of this guilty land: will never be purged away; but with Blood. I had as I now think: vainly flattered myself that without very much bloodshed; it might be done."[41] Brown knew that his death would speed the spiral of violence: the North would inevitably see violence as the only answer to southern tyranny, and the South would in turn arm itself to repel its foes.

Brown thus ascertained his death as a stroke of providential irony that ensured the ultimate victory of divine justice. By executing him, the South was damning itself, writing its own epitaph, bringing the awful day of reckoning closer. For us, of course, even more than for Brown, the ironies of his raid on Harper's Ferry and its aftermath resonate with meaning. The

40. Cited in Oswald Garrison Villard, *John Brown, 1800–1859: A Biography Fifty Years After* (1910; rpt. New York: Knopf, 1943), pp. 565–66.
41. Cited in Ruchames, p. 167.

key officers in the U. S. cavalry troop that captured Brown were Robert E. Lee and J. E. B. Stuart; in loyally regaining control of the arsenal, they were serving on behalf of the federal government that they soon would steadfastly oppose.[42] A similar reversal appears in the conduct of Henry A. Wise, who, as governor of Virginia, condemned Brown's treasonous actions and yet who emulated them in April 1861 by organizing a conspiracy to commandeer the Harper's Ferry arsenal. As war drew near, Wise advised his southern neighbors to prepare against invasion, telling them to take "a lesson from John Brown" by readying their spears and lances.[43] But the most striking twist of all, the one that almost unbelievably confirms the tragic dimensions of Brown's career, is the angry presence, at the scene of the execution, of John Wilkes Booth. At the time a member of a Richmond rifle company, Booth would later act as the assassin of Lincoln and would thereby aid in Lincoln's sublime restaging and heightening of Brown's redemptive role.[44]

2

As a historical figure and symbol, as Samson-like warrior and redeemer of a nation, John Brown was complex, controversial, and dangerous when DuBois focused attention upon him in the early 1900s. Blacks had long cherished Brown as a hero rivalled only by Lincoln; he was a white man who had so totally identified with the enslaved Negroes that he showed no taint of prejudice and gladly surrendered his life in a desperate attempt to liberate them. But to white southerners—who had their own martyrs— Brown had usurped the rule of law and had sought to spark a murderous slave revolt. Turn-of-the-century southerners interpreted Brown's raid, we should recall, when virulent "Negrophobia" was at its height.[45] By the 1900s, Negroes lived in the land, and fearfully inhabited the white mind, as a "degenerate" race that whites controlled through disenfranchisement, segregation, and lynching. Brown's actions had always seemed horrifying, and they appeared even more vividly so to southerners fixated upon visions of black savagery, violence, murder, and rape.

42. Cited in Villard, p. 450.
43. Cited in Villard, pp. 465–66.
44. Cited in Villard, p. 555.
45. See George M. Fredrickson, *The Black Image in the White Mind: The Debate on Afro-American Character and Destiny, 1817–1914* (New York: Harper and Row, 1971), pp. 256–82.

To whites in the North meanwhile, and especially to liberal whites concerned about race relations, John Brown was a glorious, if disconcerting, kind of hero. He was primarily remembered not for his campaigns in Kansas and Missouri and later plans for insurrection in the South, but, rather, for the plain-spoken Christian dignity he had manifested during his imprisonment and trial. One could not overlook or deny his sins, it was said, yet one finally had to acknowledge his transfiguration; as Oswald Garrison Villard concluded in his biography, "in Virginia, John Brown atoned for Pottawatomie by the nobility of his philosophy and his sublime devotion to principle, even to the gallows. . . . It was the weapon of the spirit by which he finally conquered."[46] His example was powerfully inspirational—it impelled men and women to undertake the work of reform—but it was an example one could safely invoke. Nearly all agreed that Brown had finally realized his abominable errors and had chastened and sanctified his spirit during the last days of life.

DuBois researched and wrote his biography during the early years of the twentieth century, but, as Herbert Aptheker has said, "the tremendous symbol of John Brown" figures in work he did throughout his career.[47] DuBois had first studied Brown while doing research at Harvard under Albert Bushnell Hart and Edward Channing, and his 1909 book consolidates ideas about (and insights into) Brown that he had considered carefully and to which he would frequently return. In August 1906, three years before the book appeared, DuBois had addressed the meeting of the Niagara Movement that convened at Harper's Ferry and that pinnacled with a bare-footed "pilgrimage at dawn" to "the scene of Brown's martyrdom."[48] He took as his subject Brown's pertinence for the twentieth-century fight against racism. Blacks, said DuBois, had been deprived of the ballot, denied education, and cruelly burdened and abused by discrimination and segregation. "Against this," he affirmed,

> the Niagara movement eternally protests. We will not be satisfied to take one jot or tittle less than our full manhood rights. We claim for ourselves every single right that belongs to a freeborn American, political, civil and social; and until we get these rights we will never cease to protest and assail the ears of America. The battle we wage is not for ourselves alone but for all true Americans. It is a fight for

46. Villard, *John Brown*, pp. 586, 588.
47. Aptheker, pp. 91–92.
48. W. E. B. DuBois, *Autobiography*, p. 249.

ideals, lest this, our common fatherland, false to its founding, become in truth the land of the thief and the home of the Slave—a byword and a hissing among the nations for its sounding pretensions and pitiful accomplishment.[49]

DuBois's oratory echoed the rhythms of many similar speeches delivered by black and white abolitionists, speeches such as Douglass's 1852 address on "the meaning of July Fourth for the Negro," which blasted America for betraying its revolutionary ideals and warned of the mockery and contempt that this corrupted nation was deservedly casting upon itself.[50] DuBois obviously means to tie his own language for the Niagara Movement to the abolitionist cause, so that it can capitalize upon the moral rhetoric and behavior that the earlier movement had mobilized. His approach in the speech is a risky one, however, for it underscores the "battle" that the men and women of the Niagara movement, assembled in the South, must dynamically wage. Though DuBois means this term metaphorically, it inevitably carries with it associations of literal battles that were launched by rebellious slaves and white comrades and that shed the blood of southerners.

DuBois tries to forestall these violent possibilities. He declares that he and his followers should strive to complete (and surpass) the mission of the abolitionists by modelling themselves upon a saintly John Brown:

> We do not believe in violence, neither in the despised violence of the raid nor the lauded violence of the soldier, nor the barbarous violence of the mob, but we do believe in John Brown, in that incarnate spirit of justice, that hatred of a lie, that willingness to sacrifice money, reputation, and life itself on the altar of right. And here on the scene of John Brown's martyrdom we reconsecrate ourselves, our honor, our property to the final emancipation of the race which John Brown died to make free.[51]

Brown could not be a Samson, a suicidal berserker, for DuBois. That was a powerful but problematic image, pervasive in Brown's and others' writings of the 1850s and 1860s, and DuBois tried to resist it. Brown was,

49. W. E. B. DuBois, "The Niagara Movement: Address to the Country," 1906, in *Pamphlets and Leaflets* by *W. E. B. DuBois*, ed. Herbert Aptheker (White Plains: Kraus-Thomson, 1986), pp. 63–65, at p. 63.
50. See Foner, *Life and Writings of Frederick Douglass*, 2: 181–204.
51. W. E. B. DuBois, "Niagara Movement," p. 64.

instead, a second Christ, a connection that DuBois soon explained in a short piece he wrote for *The Horizon*—the Niagara Movement's magazine —in December 1909:

> This is Christmas time and the time of John Brown. On the second of this month he was crucified, on the 8th he was buried and on the 25th, fifty years later let him rise from the dead in every Negro-American home. Jesus came not to bring peace but a sword. So did John Brown. Jesus Christ gave his life as a sacrifice for the lowly. So did John Brown.[52]

But if Brown is like the crucified Christ, he is, revealingly, like the Christ who wields a sword, the Christ whom DuBois strangely says came *not* to bring peace. DuBois rejects violence yet incorporates it in his language of struggle and protest. Violence is recognized and contemplated: it exists as a real, beckoning option. It must, however, also be fended off, postponed, because of the suicide that it would guarantee for blacks who might fondly seize upon it. DuBois intends his own "battle" to be social, moral, and political: it will involve the self-defining challenges of endless self-sacrifice and fidelity to the cleansing ethic of steady, dignified, honorable work. Like Christ and John Brown, the true hero and exceptional man must suffer for the lowly, forging his identity through exhausting labor on their behalf.

3

DuBois's *John Brown* draws together his reflections on a formidable subject, though the book does suffer by comparison to the painstakingly detailed biographies by Villard and, more recently, by Stephen B. Oates. In writing his book, DuBois seems not to have done fresh archival work, relying heavily upon previously published sources, such as the two-volume *Life and Letters of John Brown*, edited by Franklin Sanborn (1885). When Villard critiqued DuBois's study, in an anonymous review in *The Nation*, he emphasized the mistakes in it and suggested that DuBois had failed to be properly skeptical toward his materials. Villard's review spawned a bitter exchange of letters between DuBois, Villard, and Paul Elmer More, who

52. W. E. B. DuBois, "John Brown and Christmas," *The Horizon: A Journal of the Color Line*, 5 (December 1909): 1; rpt. *Selections from the Horizon*, ed. Herbert Aptheker (White Plains: Kraus-Thomson, 1985), p. 85.

edited *The Nation* and who refused to print a letter from DuBois that sought to answer Villard's review.[53]

DuBois probably was hasty in gathering and inspecting sources, as Villard charged. And this will dismay readers familiar with the massive amount of original research that DuBois undertook for his Harvard dissertation on the slave trade (1896) and for the Atlanta University studies (1897–1915). Sometimes, too, DuBois appears not to have fully digested what Brown said about himself and others said about him, over-relying upon quotation and thereby lessening the impact of his argument. DuBois includes, for example, a seven-page quotation from Frederick Douglass that recounts an eventful meeting with Brown (102–09) and a four-page letter from Brown's eldest son (127–31). A few of the chapters, notably one that deals with Brown's plans for attacking slavery in the South, consist almost entirely of unexamined quotations.

Especially disappointing is the absence of commentary on certain key quotations. When Brown spoke to the court for the last time, he stated that he "never did intend murder, or treason, or the destruction of property, or to excite or incite slaves to rebellion, or to make insurrection"; and, as he concluded, he stressed this point a second time: "I never had any design against the life of any person, nor any disposition to commit treason, or excite slaves to rebel, or make any general insurrection" (quoted by DuBois, pp. 361, 362). One wonders how DuBois responded to these words of self-refashioning that portray Brown's mission as the opposite of what it indubitably was. In this instance as in others, DuBois neglects to query Brown's own representation of himself and allows Brown to occupy center-stage uncontested by critical judgment.

This verdict holds true as well for DuBois's sketchy account of Brown's violent forays in Kansas and Missouri and of the massacre of a group of pro-slavery men at Pottawatomie Creek. DuBois views this episode—which Villard, Robert Penn Warren, and Oates have treated very severely—as simply bearing painful witness to the "cost of freedom" (144). But here and elsewhere DuBois's silence reveals, I believe, his powerfully ambivalent feelings about Brown and his sympathy for the violent lessons that Thoreau, Parker, and other abolitionists had drawn from Brown's actions. DuBois was an angry but not a violent man. Yet, as his earlier writings on Brown intimate, he was allured by the murderous path that Brown

53. See *The Correspondence of W. E. B. DuBois*, ed. Herbert Aptheker (Amherst: Univ. of Massachusetts Press, 1973), 1: 154–64.

chose to pursue in Kansas and Missouri and was fascinated by the revolutionary combat that the abolitionist warrior aimed to wage in Virginia. After all, DuBois had seen vicious race riots explode throughout the South—including the terrifying Atlanta riot of September 1906—and he felt the appeal, if not the wisdom, of fighting against the Southern racists with whom Booker T. Washington and his minions had humiliatingly desired to reach an accommodation. In his *Autobiography*, he mentions that he could never conceive of killing a human being. "But," he adds, when the Atlanta riot broke out in 1906,

> I rushed back from Alabama to Atlanta where my wife and six-year old child were living. A mob had raged for days killing Negroes. I bought a Winchester double-barreled shotgun and two dozen rounds of shells filled with buckshot. If a white mob had stepped on the campus where I lived I would without hesitation have sprayed their guts over the grass.[54]

DuBois's respectful attention to Brown's battles and insurrectionist schemes, and his silently forgiving response to them, connect as well with his firm belief that the assault on Harper's Ferry could indeed have succeeded. It was not far-fetched, DuBois says, and it failed only because some of Brown's men, acting as a rear-guard, unaccountably delayed in transporting weapons and supplies to a local schoolhouse where, it was hoped, mutinous slaves and their white comrades would band together to fill out Brown's ranks. Scholars have not shared DuBois's belief in the feasibility of Brown's plan, but DuBois emphasized this point even more boldly in articles he wrote later in his life. He even termed the plan "a masterpiece," based on sound guerrilla tactics, that "could have worked."[55]

Whatever its scholarly flaws and oddly disconcerting (if highly suggestive) silences, *John Brown* remains a superb meditation on Afro-American cultural and political history and an impassioned rendering of Brown's mixed legacy—was he warrior or saint?—for the freedom struggles of the

---

54. W. E. B. DuBois, *Autobiography*, p. 286.
55. W. E. B. DuBois, "John Brown Liveth!," *West African Pilot*, 10 November 1951, 2; rpt. *Writings by W. E. B. DuBois in Periodicals Edited by Others*, ed. Herbert Aptheker (Millwood: Kraus-Thomson, 1982), 4: 168–69. See also "The Crucifixion of John Brown," *New Times* (Moscow) December 1959, 26–29; rpt. *Writings by W. E. B. DuBois in Periodicals Edited by Others*, pp. 302–6. See also "John Brown: God's Angry Man," *Freedom*, February 1951; rpt. *Newspaper Columns by W. E. B. DuBois, 1945–1961*, ed. Herbert Aptheker (White Plains: Kraus-Thomson, 1986), 2: 1108–9.

twentieth century. Only in a marginal way is *John Brown* "about" a white man. DuBois revitalizingly interprets Brown as a symbol of *black* achievement and aspiration—so much so that his book can quite reasonably be termed a study of the souls of black folk. In his preface, DuBois states that he intends to examine the facts of Brown's life "from a different point of view," adding that "the view-point adopted in this book is that of the little known but vastly important inner development of the Negro American" (7). DuBois's emphasis is startling, even shocking, for it judges Brown to matter for what he reveals about the development of blacks, not whites. For DuBois, Brown merits rapt notice because he lived on close terms with blacks, and, more than any other white American, has "come nearest to touching the real souls of black folk" (8). Through Brown—the man who stood with blacks "on a plane of perfect equality" (99; see also 247)—we can learn essential truths about black experiences, values, accomplishments. He enables us to peer into the often veiled soul of a maligned and abused people and to glimpse signs of black violence, vengeance, and determined, prolonged struggle.

The opening of DuBois's first chapter takes exactly this turn:

The mystic spell of Africa is and ever was over all America. It has guided her hardest work, inspired her finest literature, and sung her sweetest songs. Her greatest destiny—unsensed and despised though it be—is to give back to the first of continents the gifts which Africa of old gave to America's fathers' fathers.

Of all inspiration which America owes to Africa, however, the greatest by far is the score of heroic men whom the sorrows of these dark children called to unselfish devotion and heroic self-realization: Benezet, Garrison, and Harriet Stowe; Sumner, Douglass, and Lincoln—these and others, but above all, John Brown. (7)

Not only does DuBois assign Brown an extraordinarily lofty status—excelling even Lincoln's—but he also strikingly Africanizes American history, depicting Africa as the source for the best achievements of America and the land to which America's gifts will eventually return. America's heroes, black as well as white, exist because of the sorrowful lives of the "dark children" of Africa. The enslaved people themselves issued the call to selfless service and inaugurated the crusade that freed them.

Everywhere in his book, DuBois radically accents the strength and resistance of blacks: they fought against their masters, did whatever they could to counter brutality and mistreatment, and exemplified forms of courage from which white abolitionists learned and took inspiration. DuBois recognizes the extent of the repression that blacks faced and the dense network of law and custom that functioned to maintain the vicious status quo. But he misses no opportunity to highlight slave revolts and efforts by blacks on a small and large scale to flee to the North. "The flaming fury of their mad attempts at vengeance," says DuBois of rebellious slaves in Jamaica, Haiti, and South Carolina, "echoes all down the blood-swept path of slavery" (79). The "great black mass of Southern slaves were cowed," he observes, "but they were not conquered" (81).

> In Louisiana and Tennessee and twice in Virginia they raised the night cry of revolt, and once slew fifty Virginians, holding the state for weeks at bay there in those same Alleghanies which John Brown loved and listened to. On the ships of the sea they rebelled and murdered; to Florida they fled and turned like beasts on their pursuers till whole armies dislodged them and did them to death in the everglades; and again and again over them and through them surged and quivered a vast unrest which only the eternal vigilance of the masters kept down. Yet the fear of that great bound beast was ever there—a nameless, haunting dread that never left the South and never ceased, but ever nerved the remorseless cruelty of the master's arm. (81–82)

DuBois's imagery of the bloody black "beast" capitalizes upon the fearful rendering of impending cataclysm in the book of Revelation. Even more, it deliberately ratifies the fears of black violence that were common among the southern whites of DuBois's own day and that were given a grotesque, lurid form in Thomas Dixon's staggeringly racist best-sellers, *The Leopard's Spots* (1902) and *The Clansman* (1905). DuBois's tactic here is daring and dangerous; he emphasizes the slaughters committed by his oppressed people. Whites in the pre-Civil War period, DuBois suggests, had transformed men into animals or, more ominously, into beasts capable of terrible devastation. The "one thing" that saved the South from the horrors of Haiti, DuBois contends, was the "escape of the fugitives," the men and women who bravely chose to flee to the North and joined with free blacks there to form "the great black phalanx that worked and schemed and paid and finally fought for the freedom of black men in America" (82). Once in the North, the escaped slaves told of the slaveholders' crimes, and, as the case of Frederick Douglass attests, authenticated the potential for greatness that slavery punishingly denied. "Indeed," speculates DuBois about

John Brown, "it is not unlikely that the first black folk to gain his aid and sympathies and direct his thoughts to what afterward became his life-work, were the fugitive slaves from the South" (83). DuBois cites no evidence for this possibility, but it accords with the momentum of his argument: blacks showed the way to whites, directed the thoughts of white men such as Brown, and supplied the energizing motive for white abolitionism.

To understand the battle for liberation that seared America in the middle of the nineteenth century, DuBois maintains that we must hearken to the movement of the black masses, the stirring "below" that generated and vitalized the prominent leaders:

> A great unrest was on the land. It was not merely moral leadership from above—it was the push of physical and mental pain from beneath;—not simply the cry of the Abolitionist but the upstretching of the slave. The vision of the damned was stirring the western world and stirring black men as well as white. Something was forcing the issue—call it what you will, the Spirit of God or the spell of Africa. It came like some great grinding ground swell,—vast, indefinite, immeasurable but mighty, like the dark low whispering of some infinite disembodied voice—a riddle of the Sphinx. It tore men's souls and wrecked their faith. (121)

The apocalyptic specter that haunted the western world, DuBois counsels, reflected the painfully hard work that the enslaved performed on their own behalf: this is where the originating impulse for revolt and rebellion dwells. DuBois is intent upon reorienting his reader's sense of political struggle, which is made fundamentally by the masses, not by the exalted heroes (see also 134). In the process, DuBois redefines the history of abolitionism as the story of arduous black initiative, of blacks fighting for their freedom and stirring whites to help them. Although this book is obviously about John Brown, in one sense it concentrates on Brown in order to dramatize the black forces—the spell of Africa and the animations of the black masses—that worked through him.

DuBois's reading of the events of Brown's life falters only once, when he engages the failure of Douglass and other blacks to participate in the raid on Harper's Ferry. DuBois handles this matter unsteadily (see 109–10, 270, 344–46), perhaps because he believes that blacks erred militarily and morally when they refused to join Brown's ranks in significant numbers. The historical record attests that some blacks were part of the mission, but most rejected it as desperate and unworkable. Douglass himself reports in his autobiography that he feared Brown's action would commit the South even more absolutely to slavery: it would script a bloody spectacle that the South would use to organize its power all the more vindictively. Brown urged Douglass to accompany him, and "in parting," relates Douglass, "he put his arms around me in a manner more than friendly, and said: 'Come with me, Douglass; I will defend you with my life. I want you for a special purpose. When I strike, the bees will begin to swarm, and I shall want you to help hive them.' "[56] But Douglass was unconvinced.

DuBois sympathizes with Douglass's decision to reject Brown's offer, but he seems not to have agreed with it. Men fear the path that Brown followed and readily furnish sensible, prudent reasons for shunning it, but, claims DuBois, today we clearly see that "John Brown was right" (338).

> "Slavery is wrong," he said,—"kill it." Destroy it—uproot it, stem, blossom, and branch; give it no quarter, exterminate it and do it now. Was he wrong? No. The forcible staying of human uplift by barriers of law, and might, and tradition is the most wicked thing on earth. It is wrong, eternally wrong. It is wrong, by whatever name it is called, or in whatever guise it lurks, and whenever it appears. But it is especially heinous, black, and cruel when it masquerades in the robes of law and justice and patriotism. So was American slavery clothed in 1859, and it had to die by revolution, not by milder means. (340–41)

Brown's attack, then, was a failure, but his Samson-like behavior prophesied the violence on a grand scale that had inevitably to come if slavery were at last to die. Here, as often in his book, DuBois presents his ardent version of the American and Afro-American past and announces the fate that lies in store for white America at the beginning of the twentieth century. Slavery demanded revolution and so does the racism that permeates America in the early 1900s. The question is simply, what are the weapons with which this revolutionary warfare will be prosecuted? To keep blacks in check will require massive repression and violence, and such a policy is doomed to be counter-productive. By feverishly keeping down blacks, white Americans will only galvanize movements toward black self-assertion and resistance and kindle blacks' desire for violent measures to end their oppression.

Like many turn-of-the-century commentators, DuBois does mention

56. Frederick Douglass, *Life and Times of Frederick Douglass* (1892; rpt. New York: Macmillan, 1979), p. 320.

Brown's Christ-like virtues and crucifixion for the cause of freedom (e.g., 338), and he also unfolds the lesson of self-sacrificing idealism that Brown's career illustrates (356–57, 370). But DuBois's central message, etched in descriptions of violence, insists that "the price of repression is greater than the cost of liberty" (17; see also 76, 140). The price is not only the loss of talent and skill among subjugated people denied opportunities for advancement, but it is also the price paid by the dominant group: racial prejudice and hatred diminish America as a whole (17). Some might argue, DuBois observes, that changes in America's treatment of its black population will prove too costly in money, blood, and national identity to implement. But DuBois replies that the cost we must pay now will be far less than the cost that further repression will exact. Eventually, DuBois believes, the forces of freedom will prevail; if America balks at freedom now and deprives blacks of their rights, then it will be obliged to intensify its repressive actions— and will thus arouse blacks to an even higher pitch of opposition. When the South failed to free its slaves, he added, it ensured that revolutionary violence, beginning with Brown's raid and ending with the Civil War, would erupt devastatingly. It therefore ignorantly, self-destructively obliged itself to pay a price infinitely greater than would have been "the cost of liberty."

As he closes his book, DuBois reaffirms his basic message:

> This, then, is the truth: the cost of liberty is less than the price of repression, even though that cost be blood. Freedom of development and equality of opportunity is the demand of Darwinism and this calls for the abolition of hard and fast lines between races, just as it called for the breaking down of barriers between classes. Only in this way can the best in humanity be discovered and conserved, and only thus can mankind live in peace and progress. The present attempt to force all whites above all darker peoples is a sure method of human degeneration. The cost of liberty is thus a decreasing cost, while the cost of repression ever tends to increase to the danger point of war and revolution. Revolution is not a test of capacity; it is always a loss and a lowering of ideals. (395)

In this unsettled, complicated passage, DuBois warns America of the revolution certain to scar it if it persists in its barbarism by fostering racism at home and hellishly sustaining imperialism abroad. He uses Darwin against the social Darwinists by claiming that evolution tends toward progress and a better life for all. Darwin would never advise us, DuBois professes, that we should batter down the darker races of the world and, artificially and wrongheadedly, impose the primacy of the white race upon the evolutionary cycle. As DuBois notes earlier, "the present hegemony of the white races" threatens "by means of brute force a survival of some of the worse stocks of mankind. It attempts to people the best parts of the earth and put in absolute authority over the rest, not usually (and indeed not mainly) the culture of Europe but its greed and degradation" (379–80).

While DuBois's effort to subvert turn-of-the-century social Darwinism is convincing up to a point, it is, finally, somewhat strained. By turning a sociological weapon of the racists against them, DuBois surely did surprise many readers: he was demonstrating to them that Darwinian arguments could be employed for progressive as well as reactionary purposes. But DuBois's reliance on Darwinian notions of good and bad stocks of people and the evolutionary growth of the best types, and his worried concern about degeneration and decay—all these mistakenly locate him on the oppressors' terrain: he is giving credibility to their terms. DuBois's tactic is clever, yet it leads him into ungainly racialist categories of his own as he protests against the inveterate bad stocks of white people who gain sway over blacks in America and Africa.

Why is this closing section of *John Brown* skewed? Why the sudden, ultimately unpersuasive surfacing of Darwinian themes? I suspect that DuBois went astray, looking for and awkwardly handling "survival of the fittest" language, because he recognized on some level and, furthermore, wished to avoid the powerful logic of his book—a logic that propelled him toward an acknowledgment and, indeed, an acceptance of violence as the inevitable final stage of social and political protest. DuBois proposes that revolution "is always a loss and a lowering of ideals." Yet this is not the truth of John Brown as DuBois himself earlier defined it. DuBois declared that John Brown "was right": American slavery "had to die by revolution, not by milder means" (341). Writing in an era ravaged by Negrophobia, DuBois fastens himself to Brown's example and justifies the violent course that this white warrior followed. "The carnival of crime and rapine" Brown produced in Kansas "was a disgrace to civilization but it was the cost of freedom, and it was less than the price of repression" (140). But even as DuBois instructs us to see the revolutionary rightness of what Brown did in Kansas and Virginia, he also wants to stamp such vengeful conduct as wrong—and always wrong—because revolution undercuts ideals and prevents us from realizing them.

DuBois probably sensed this contradiction at the heart of his book. In 1962, for a new edition of *John Brown*, he inserted a passage directly after the paragraph about revolution I have quoted.

But if [this revolution] is a true revolution it repays all losses and results in the uplift of the human race. One could wish that John Brown
could see today the results of the great revolution in Russia; that he
could see the new world of Socialism and Communism expanding
until it already comprises the majority of mankind; until it has conquered the problem of poverty, made vast inroads on the problem
of ignorance and even begun to put to flight the problem of avoid-
able disease. It has abolished unemployment and is approaching
the great day when all men will do for the world what they are best
suited to do and will receive in return from the world not all that they
want but everything that each man needs. (395–96)

By 1962 a staunch Communist party member, DuBois here corrects
his own earlier judgment by affirming that revolution *can* embody the best
ideals of mankind and compensate for any costs incurred while prosecuting
it. In part DuBois is manifestly striving to celebrate the glorious revolutions
in the Soviet Union and China; at the height of the Cold War, he boldly contends that revolution is not a bad word and presses home that revolutions
do not always profane humanity. Yet DuBois is not simply bringing his book
into ideological line with his Communist positions of the 1950s and 1960s,
for his words are in basic accord with the tendency and drive of the book he
researched and wrote in the early 1900s. "The great mass" of oppressed
people in America, DuBois affirms in his 1909 text,

is becoming daily more thoroughly organized, more deeply self-
critical, more conscious of its power . . . . And as it grows it is sensing
more and more the vantage-ground which it holds as a defender
of the right of the freedom of human development for black men in
the midst of a centre of modern culture. It sees its brothers in yellow, black and brown held physically at arms' length from civilization
lest they become civilized and less liable to conquest and exploitation. It sees the world-wide effort to build an aristocracy of races
and nations on a foundation of darker, half-enslaved and tributary
peoples. It knows that the last great battle of the West is to vindi-
cate the right of any man of any nation, race, or color to share in the
world's goods and thoughts and efforts to the extent of his effort and
ability. (389–90)

If the brutal practices of racist America at the turn of the century
demand the rebirth of abolitionism; if the South in particular shows itself
deeply embedded in bigotry; and if the mass of mankind is steadily growing

in its power; then terrible, terrifying, but necessary battle and war lie ahead. "Persistence in racial distinction spells disaster sooner or later," DuBois prophesies. Men and women will therefore be forced one day to choose— as Frederick Douglass was forced to choose when the "dear old man" John Brown urged him to hive the bees soon to be set swarming in the South. This choice—one that DuBois both approvingly articulates and unevenly strives to countervail in his book—will be a choice between words and violent deeds, reform and revolution, peaceful conduct and the death-dealing strategies that John Brown adopted. As Brown declared to the court, in words that DuBois quotes to conclude his book, "This question is still to be settled—this Negro question, I mean. The end of that is not yet" (403). The most disturbing feature of *John Brown*, and the most provocative, alarmed tribute one can pay to it, is to say that DuBois passionately evokes and labors to resist the inescapably violent settlement of the Negro question.

Contributors

William E. Cain is Professor of English and Director of American Studies at Welles-ley College. His books include *The Crisis in Criticism* and *F. O. Matthiessen and the Politics of Criticism*. He is currently at work on a book about W. E. B. DuBois and will be contributing the section on American literary criticism, 1900–40, for the *New Cambridge History of American Literature*.

Wai-chee Dimock is author of *Empire for Liberty: Melville and the Poetics of Individualism*. She teaches at Brandeis University and is now working on a book tentatively entitled *Equality, Economy, Symmetry: American Literature and Social Organization*.

Howard Horwitz teaches in the Department of English and Comparative Literature at the University of Utah. The essay included in this issue is adapted from part of *By the Law of Nature: Form and Value in Nineteenth-Century America*.

Gregory S. Jay is Professor of English and Coordinator of the Graduate Program in Modern Studies at the University of Wisconsin–Milwaukee. He has edited two volumes on "Modern American Critics" for the *Dictionary of Literary Biography*. His essay on Douglass forms part of a chapter in his *America the Scrivener: Deconstruction and the Subject of Literary History*.

Steven Mailloux teaches in the English Department at the University of California at Irvine. He is coeditor, with Sanford Levinson, of *Interpreting Law and Literature: A Hermeneutic Reader* and the author of *Interpretive Conventions: The Reader in the Study of American Fiction* and *Rhetorical Power*.

John McWilliams is author of *Political Justice in a Republic: Fenimore Cooper's America, Hawthorne, Melville and the American Character*, and *The American Epic*. He is Julian Abernethy Professor of American Literature at Middlebury College.

Susan Mizruchi, author of *The Power of Historical Knowledge: Narrating the Past in Hawthorne, James, and Dreiser*, is Associate Professor of English and American Studies at Boston University. Her essay in this issue is from a new book entitled *The Culture of Vigilance: Social Types in Literature and Sociology, 1891–1925*.

Donald E. Pease is author of two books: *Visionary Compacts: American Renaissance Writings in Cultural Contexts* and *Deterrence Pacts: Formation of the Canon in the Cold War Era*. He is also editor of *American Renaissance Reconsidered* and *New Critical Essays on* The Rise of Silas Lapham. He presently holds the Ted and Helen Geisel Third Century Professorship in the Humanities at Dartmouth.

Ivy Schweitzer teaches American Literature and Women's Studies at Dartmouth College, and is the author of *The Work of Self-Representation*, a study of lyric, gender, and the construction of subjectivity in seventeenth-century New England.

Priscilla Wald is Assistant Professor of English at Columbia University. Her forthcoming book, *Constituting Americans: National Narrative and Cultural Identity in Modern United States Literature*, is scheduled for publication in the *New Americanists* series at Duke.

Michael Warner teaches in the English Department at Rutgers University. The essay in this volume is part of a book called *The Letters of the Republic: Publication and the Public Sphere in Eighteenth-Century America*.

Robert Weimann is Professor of Literature at the Akademie der Künste der Deutschen Demokratischen Republik. He is author of *Structure and Society in Literary History* and *Shakespeare and the Popular Tradition in the Theater*. He has also written extensively on American literature and literary theory.

Index

340

Poirier, Richard, 73, 216
Political economy, 34, 83–99, 250. *See also* Economics
Politics, 19, 32–33, 38–68, 52. *See also* Cultural/political barrier
Porte, Joel, 73
Porter, Carolyn, 216, 219
Porter, Noah, 156
Porter, Theodore, 296n.45–46
Poststructuralism: African-American literature and, 220–21; Baker and, 224; ideology/demystification opposition and, 217; New Historicism and, 210–11, 214; Reising and, 219
Pottawatomie Creek massacre, 321, 328
Poverty, 92–93, 98–99
The Power of Blackness (Levin), 14, 72
Prescott, William H., 82
Preston, Dickson J., 233
Primitive societies, 290n.41
The Princess Casamassima (H. James), 205, 207–8
Printing, 32–33, 38–68
Professionalism, 286, 287, 300n.50
Progressives, 7, 25
Prosperity, 94–95
Psychological: analysis, 126n.32; authorship, 116; modernity, 74
Puritan clergy, 67, 68
Puritans, 64, 105, 280

Rabine, Leslie, 176n.24
Racial difference, 240, 241, 242, 280–81, 283–84
Racism, 135, 230, 283, 318–19, 326–27
Railroads, 261, 264, 265
Rampersad, Arnold, 306, 307
Ransom, Reverdy C., 313
Reading, 38–68, 117, 144, 146, 155
Realism, 189–210: *Billy Budd* and, 302; Foucault and, 254n.28; naturalism and, 218; New Historicism and, 272–73; religion and, 293n.43; social types in, 291n.42
"Reality in America" (Trilling), 6, 9, 26
Rediker, Marcus, 289n.40
Redpath, James, 315
Reformatories, 137, 138–40
Reising, Russell, 24–25, 219, 229

Religion, 39, 108, 292–93n.43. *See also* Christianity
Republican party, 309, 316
Republicanism, 33, 63–68
Revolutionary War, 20, 23
Revolutions, 326, 327, 328–29
Rhetoric, 213, 214, 240, 242
Ricardo, David, 85–87, 88–89
The Rise of Silas Lapham (Howells), 203–4, 249
River pilots, 36, 242–71
Robinson Crusoe (Defoe), 145, 146
Robinson, Forrest G., 256n.27
Rogers, Nathaniel P., 230
Rogin, Michael Paul, 103n.6, 109n.12, 275–76n.7
Romance genre: American Studies and, 30–31; Chase on, 24, 25; desublimation of, 33–35, 36, 69–157; Melville and, 34; New Americanists and, 35–36; rationale for, 71–82; student movement and, 26, 27
Romantic love, 165, 176n.24, 186
Romantic theory, 220, 233n.30
Ross, Catherine Sheldrick, 156–57n.54
Ross, E. A., 279, 280
Rudwick, Elliott, 306
Russell, Thomas B., 308
Ryder, Annie H., 133

Samson (Biblical character), 314, 315–16
Sanborn, Franklin, 150, 151, 279, 314, 320
Satan, 116, 198
Say, Jean Baptiste, 87
Scarcity, 85–87
Schlesinger, Arthur, 25
Schlossman, Steven L., 137n.6
Scott, Walter, 74, 81, 82
"Secret six," 310–11
Seditious libel, 53, 54, 56–57, 58
Self-authorization, 114, 120, 123, 132
Self-discipline, 34, 143, 152–53
Self-dispossession, 163n.14
Self, Emersonian, 91–92, 97, 98–99
Self, imperial, 27–28
Self-possession: in *The Awakening,* 34–35, 158–86; free labor and, 268n.50; in *Life on the Mississippi,* 36; Locke

Library of Congress Cataloging-in-Publication Data
Revisionary interventions into the Americanist canon /
Donald E. Pease, editor.
p.   cm. (New Americanist)
"Text of this book originally published without the
present preface or index as Vol. 17, No. 1 of
boundary 2"—T.p. verso.
Includes index.
ISBN 0-8223-1478-9 (cloth). — ISBN 0-8223-1493-2
(pbk.)
1. American literature—19th century—History and
criticism—Theory, etc.   2. Literature and society—
United States—History—19th century.   3. Literature
and history—United States.   4. Canon (Literature)
5. Historicism.   I. Pease, Donald E.
PS201.R46   1994
813'.309—dc20   93-49688 CIP